THE WORLD WIDE WEB

THE WORLD WIDE WEB

A MASS COMMUNICATION PERSPECTIVE

Barbara K. Kaye
Valdosta State University

Norman J. Medoff
Northern Arizona University

Mayfield Publishing Company
Mountain View, California
London • Toronto

Library of Congress Cataloging-in-Publication Data

Kaye, Barbara K.
   The World Wide Web : a mass communication perspective / Barbara K.
Kaye, Norman J. Medoff.
     p. cm.
   Includes index.
   ISBN 0-7674-0030-5
   1. World Wide Web (Information retrieval system) 2. World Wide
Web (Information retrieval system)—Social aspects. I. Medoff,
Norman J. II. Title.
TK5105.888.K393   1998
004.67'8—dc21   98-30904
                                     CIP

Manufactured in the United States of America
10   9   8   7   6   5   4   3   2   1

Mayfield Publishing Company
1280 Villa Street
Mountain View, CA 94041

Sponsoring editor, Holly J. Allen; production editor, Julianna Scott Fein; manuscript editor, Pam Suwinsky; art manager, Jean Mailander; text designer, Joan Greenfield; cover designer, Laurie Anderson; art editor, Amy Folden; illustrator, Judith Ogus; manufacturing manager, Randy Hurst. The text was set in 10.5/13 Minion by Thompson Type and printed on acid-free 45# Highland Plus by Malloy Lithographing, Inc.

Acknowledgments and copyrights continue at the back of the book on pages 395–396, which constitute an extension of the copyright page.

 Printed on acid-free, recycled paper.

PREFACE

Just like other working people, professors often congregate in the hallway or around the water cooler to chat or commiserate. Some time ago, a typical conversation was going on, and the phrase, "It's just like herding cats," was overheard. The professor was probably referring to getting his students to pay attention during a lecture, or perhaps getting the upper administration to pay attention to his academic needs. But the phrase also seemed appropriate for the task of writing a book about the World Wide Web.

There are numerous concerns and issues surrounding the Web. Many people are concerned that users will become addicted to the medium, others are concerned that children may access unregulated adult content, and still others fear that personal information will fall into the hands of unscrupulous Web operators. Additionally, the Web has many different types of users and different uses. For example, some users want to be entertained, shoppers use the Internet for commerce, students turn to the Web for academic purposes, and graphic designers and computer experts show off their talents by creating interactive, appealing, and eye-catching sites. Integrating the various aspects of the Web into a singular focus was a challenging task. Moreover, with the ever-changing and improving Internet technology, the tremendous number of new Web sites, and the number of sites changing their content and locations, writing this book and keeping it up-to-date was a daunting task.

GOALS AND APPROACH

The goal of this textbook is to help mass communication students become familiar with the Web. As future communication professionals, mass communication students need to understand how the Internet works in general and how specifically it works for mass communication professionals in particular. The Web has quickly become an essential communications tool for professionals working in advertising, public relations, visual communication, broadcasting, and journalism. Our goal is to describe the Web as a tool that can be used for many different aspects of applied mass communication.

v

While much of this book is devoted to using the Web as a communications tool, a significant portion encourages students to employ a critical eye toward the impact of the Web on society. When dramatic technological changes occur, numerous important questions arise about the impact those changes will have on society. Ethical, legal, and social issues should be viewed as at least as important as whiz-bang technology.

Some chapters in the book deal with practical issues. Chapter 2 covers the critical evaluation of Web sources. Chapters 3–7 cover the specific professional applications of the Web, including radio, television, news, marketing/public relations, and advertising.

Conceptual topics, including social, theoretical, and legal and ethical issues, are covered in Chapters 9–11. Chapter 12 is devoted to future directions of the Web and the career opportunities that have become available as a result of the Web, and using the Web to find jobs in many fields.

FEATURES

Sample computer screens are featured throughout the book and used as examples of various aspects and applications of the Web. At the end of each chapter, Web addresses encourage students to investigate the Web through hands-on experience. Bold-faced terms throughout the text of the book are listed in the glossary, to help students understand the new Web terminology and jargon.

ACKNOWLEDGMENTS

While we have been trying to herd these cats, we have relied upon the help and support of numerous colleagues. Several rounds of reviews have been extremely helpful in making sure that our information was current, understandable, and appropriate for the needs of the growing number of university-level courses across the country. These reviewers include Susan B. Barnes, Fordham University; Cynthia Bascom, Butler University; Ann M. Brill, University of Missouri; Lori Collins-Jarvis, University of Southern California; Carla E. Gesell, University of Tennessee at Martin; George Albert Gladney, University of Wyoming; Rustin Greene, James Madison University; Lynne S. Gross, California State University at Fullerton; Joe Hall, University of Central Florida; Tim Hudson, University of Oklahoma; Steve Masiclat, Syracuse University; Dan Morris, Boise State University; Nancy Reist, San Francisco State University; and Samuel J. Sauls, University of North Texas.

Students at our respective universities have been both supportive and invaluable. Our very special thanks go to Rey G. Rosales and Moira Tokatyan whose dedication helped make this book a reality. We also thank Mark W. Anderson, Charles Kingsley, Zaigui Wang, Doyle Rockwell, Angela Wood, and Dave Folsom. We thank our colleagues Jerry Hostetler, Joe Foote, Mike Starr, and the faculty in the Department of Radio/Television at Southern Illinois University at Carbondale, as well as the faculty and staff at the School of Communication at Northern Arizona University.

We appreciate the support of the team at Mayfield Publishing Company—Julianna Scott Fein, Jean Mailander, Amy Folden, Marty Granahan, Randy Hurst, and Pam Suwinsky. Special thanks go to our sponsoring editor, Holly Allen, who has been with us on the project from the very beginning.

Finally, we gratefully acknowledge the special support (and patience!) provided by family members James B. McOmber and Natalie, Sarah, and Lynn Medoff.

Barbara Kaye, Ph.D.
Valdosta, Georgia

Norman J. Medoff, Ph.D.
Flagstaff, Arizona

CONTENTS

"I think I'm having a stroke." Those were the desperate words sent through the Internet by a minister in Scotland, moments before he suffered a life-threatening seizure. The minister was participating in an online genealogy forum when he became ill. Sensing he only had a few moments of consciousness left, he managed to type, "Helo, . . . have broblemd,,,thhimk I am wayin g stroke." The minister was somehow able to add his telephone number to the end of the message.

A forum participant in Boston sensed trouble when he saw the erratically spelled message. He immediately contacted an overseas telephone operator who located the minister's home address. Within minutes an ambulance was at the minister's home in a small town near the coast of the North Sea. Doctors claim the minister may have died had help not arrived in time.

The minister thanked his Internet rescuer on the telephone the day after the incident. The rescuer downplayed his involvement claiming that he is not a hero, but a "citizen who was able to help out."

("Minister Living Alone," 1996)

INTRODUCTION TO THE INTERNET AND THE WORLD WIDE WEB

1

THE INTERNET

The Internet is a brilliantly structured worldwide computer network. Its global nature facilitates communication among people of all nationalities from every country on the planet. It is a two-way communication system in which everyone is a potential message receiver and a potential message provider. With the Internet, people no longer have to wait until 6:00 P.M. to hear the evening news, or lament over missing an early broadcast of NPR's *Morning Edition,* because these programs are available on the Internet all day and are accessible at the audience's convenience, not the broadcaster's program schedule. Moreover, the Internet transforms an audience from mere receivers into information providers. Anyone with minimal skills and access to a computer network can post information on the Internet. Unlike traditional mass media providers, individuals who produce messages on the Internet do not need licenses or government permission, nor do they need to follow strict content guidelines, and, most important, they do not have to be millionaires.

The Internet is clearly changing the way people receive and transmit information. Everything from personal news to national news makes its way to intended receivers via this network of interconnected computers. The Internet lets us peek into strangers' lives by viewing their personal homepages with photographs of their dogs and children and descriptions of their favorite foods and movies. If this does not pique one's interest, well then, move to a corporate marketing site to find out about the latest products and prices, or click on a television network page and read about beloved stars or about an upcoming episode of a favorite television show. If this is not serious enough, access a national network news site for the latest in-depth coverage, and while there, check out the full text of the President's latest speech. Whether one is seeking a recipe, an airline schedule, the Jimmy Smits fan club, Toyota cars, up-to-the-minute local weather reports, major league baseball scores, Jimmy Hoffa disappearance theories, did O. J. really do it discussions, real estate listings in towns thousands of miles away, or a popular artist's latest CD, the point is, it is all there. All the information one could possibly absorb in a lifetime is available to everyone on the Internet. And better yet, it is convenient, easy to use, and in many cases free.

The Internet is changing media use patterns and the lifestyles of millions of people who have grown to rely on it as a source of entertainment, information, and communication. People are discovering this interactive medium, and with it new ways to access information and to communicate with others. The Internet is becoming increasingly important in the lives of many people around the world.

What Is the Internet?

The **Internet** can be defined as a huge network that consists of approximately 45,000 interconnected sub-networks worldwide with no single owner (Pavlik, 1996). The

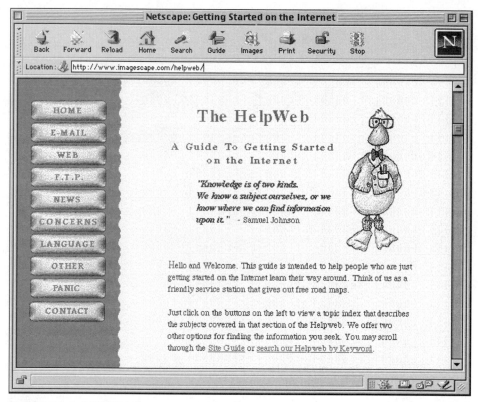

FIGURE 1.1 A KWOM Communications, Inc. Page

Internet is comprised of various text-only resources and the **World Wide Web,** which presents information in text, graphic, video, and audio formats. In addition to the World Wide Web, other Internet resources and applications include Gopher, WAIS, e-mail, listservs, Usenet Newsgroups, and chat forums.

WORLD WIDE WEB The Web is the most eclectic Internet application. The Web consists of a myriad of sites supplied by entities too numerous to count that are connected by a vast labyrinth of thousands and thousands of computers. While the other resources, such as Gopher, display information in a text-only format, the World Wide Web uses a combination of text, graphics, audio, and video presentations. With new easy-to-use point-and-click Web browsers, users can effortlessly travel from Web site to Web site. It is this burgeoning Internet resource that has captured the attention of millions. The Web is also having a great impact on traditional mass media, and thus it is the focus of this book.

GOPHER An early Internet tool, **Gopher** is a text-only menu-based interface for accessing Internet documents. Gopher was developed at the University of Minnesota, whose mascot is the "Golden Gopher," hence the Internet name "Gopher." Gopher organizes information in files for text-only retrieval.

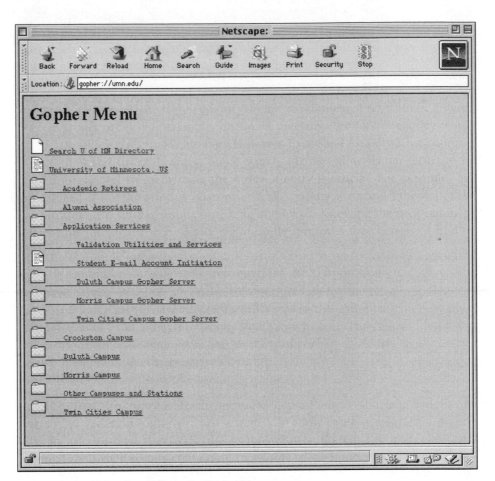

FIGURE 1.2 University of Minnesota Gopher Menu

WIDE AREA INFORMATION SERVICE   This text-only index of Internet databases acts as a search instrument. **Wide Area Information Service (WAIS)** is a system that looks for documents that contain key words entered by users and then returns a list of documents rated on how closely they match the search criteria. New easy-to-use World Wide Web search tools have diminished the use of WAIS.

ELECTRONIC MAIL   **Electronic mail (e-mail)** was developed in the early days of the Internet and is currently its most popular and widely used application. Individuals communicate with each other simply by writing messages on their computers and then electronically sending them to recipients' computers. E-mail is similar to a paper letter except the e-mail letter is electronically addressed and transmitted instead of being put into an envelope and mailed via the U.S. Postal Service.

Pioneer Consulting estimates that slightly more than 400 million people across the globe have access to e-mail. Further, it claims that 2.7 trillion e-mail messages were sent worldwide in 1997, and by the year 2000, it is forecast that a whopping 6.9 trillion messages will be transmitted around the world annually ("No Need to Phone," 1998; The Internet Index, 1997b).

LISTSERVS **Listservs** are similar to e-mail in that a message is sent to an electronic mailbox for later retrieval. However, e-mail messages are addressed to individual recipients, whereas listserv messages are addressed to the listserv's address and are forwarded only to subscribers' electronic mailboxes. Individuals must subscribe before any listserv messages are sent to their e-mail boxes. Many listservs are open to anyone who wants to subscribe; others are only available to a select group of individuals who are given permission to subscribe. Most listservs are topic-specific and aimed at individuals with common interests, such as gardening, computers, dog breeding, movies, and so on. Many clubs, organizations, special interest groups, and classes use listservs as a means of communicating among members.

USENET NEWSGROUPS A conferencing bulletin board system that has been in existence since the early 1980s, **Usenet Newsgroups** act as a discussion and information exchange forum for specific topics. Unlike listservs, participants do not have to subscribe, and messages are not delivered to individual electronic mailboxes. Rather, messages are archived for users to find and access at their convenience. A Usenet Newsgroup can be thought of as a bulletin board on which flyers are posted and left hanging there for people to come by, sift through, and read. On the other hand, using a listserv is similar to walking around a neighborhood putting flyers in everyone's mailboxes. As of mid-1997 there were about 20,000 Usenet Newsgroups with over 100,000 messages posted each day (Peters & Sikorski, 1997).

CHAT FORUMS Chat forums set themselves off from listservs and Usenet newsgroups by allowing participants to exchange live, real-time messages. In other words, chatters carry on "conversations" as they would on the telephone, but instead of *talking* and responding, participants *type* in messages to which others immediately respond. **Internet Relay Chat (IRC)** software must be installed to access a chat forum, and many types of IRC can be downloaded free of charge. Individuals interested in chatting can choose from among different chat channels such as news.net and other venues. The exciting part about chat forums is that one can carry on real-time, immediate-response conversations with people from around the world. Chat forums are catching on in such a big way that by the year 2000 it is estimated that chats will generate an excess of 7.9 billion hours of online use (Cleland, 1996).

MUDS, MOOS, AND MUSHES   MUDs (Multi-User Domain or Multi-User Dungeons), **MOOs** (Multi-User Domain—Object Oriented) and **MUSHes** (Multi-User Shared Hallucination) are very popular interactions and online games where participants are involved in fantasy adventures that they help create. MOOs and MUSHes are variants of MUDs and serve as text adventure games and chat rooms for exploring specific topics.

Some MUDs are socially oriented and encourage participants to gather and discuss topics, crack jokes, and engage in general bantering. Other MUDs involve role playing adventure games and solving puzzles using special MUD commands and lingo. The interactions usually take place in fictitious worlds, and in time periods ranging from prehistoric days to futuristic planets. Participants choose an identity for themselves. Players may opt to be elves, animals, monsters, or just human beings, playing themselves or personae of their choosing.

MUDs have a strong psychological appeal. Players are drawn to the intrigue and creativity needed to make their way around a virtual world that is never the same from one session to the next. MUDs can be very simple or complex. Some can consist of hundreds of rooms, or scenes involving hundreds of characters and objects (Pavlik, 1996).

MUDs can be accessed from many Web sites that compile links to the various adventure games. Just by entering the term "MUD" or "MOO" or "MUSH" on any search engine will yield a long list of links to these sites.

PROFILE OF WEB USERS AND WEB SITES

The Web's diversity and abundance of content are astounding and limitless. In July 1995, there were an estimated four million documents available on the Web; three months later this number had grown to eight and a half million pages, representing a 112 percent gain (Maudlin, 1995). One year later, the Web was estimated to contain between 16 million and 50 million pages of information; by 1998 the number of pages topped 150 million, and it is still growing (Caruso, 1996; Croal & Stone, 1996; Liberatore, 1998). By the year 2000 the number of online documents is expected to reach a mind-boggling 800 million.

Estimates of the number of people who use the Internet widely vary. Recent data of online users in the United States range from a low of 5.8 million ("O'Reilly Survey Sets," 1995) to 51 million users (26 percent of the U.S. population) ("About One in Four Adults," 1996; GVU's Seventh WWW User Survey, 1997). Other studies, whose estimates are not quite so divergent, report between 26.4 million and 37 million Internet users (American Internet User Survey, 1997; CommerceNet & Neilsen Research, 1995; Hoffman, Kalsbeek, & Novak, 1996a; McGarvey, 1996; MIDS, 1995; Taylor, 1997). An additional nine million users have tried the Internet but have not used it for at least one year (American Internet User Survey, 1997).

Before any medium can be considered a mass medium, a **critical mass** of adopters must be reached. Generally, critical mass is achieved when about 16 percent of the population has adopted an innovation (Markus, 1990), although, in the case of mass media 50 million users seems to be the milestone (Neufeld, 1997; "Why Internet Advertising," 1997). The rate of radio adoption crawled along for thirty-eight years before hitting the magic 50 million users, but television only took thirteen years and cable ten years to achieve this goal. Internet adoption is racing along at a pace that guarantees 50 million regular users by 2002, only eight years after its emergence as a consumer medium (Neufeld, 1997; "Why Internet Advertising," 1997).

The number of Web users who surf the Net for more than ten hours a week has increased from 29 percent in 1995 to just over one-half by mid-1997. Users tend to spend about 13.6 hours a week cruising the sites ("What's Your Daily Dose," 1997). Almost one-half of users visit at least one Web site daily, and six out of ten users access their e-mail everyday (American Internet User Survey, 1997).

Although previous claims stated that early users of the Internet tended to be white males with high socioeconomic status, more recent studies suggest a demographic shift as the Internet becomes more mainstream (Hoffman, Kalsbeek, & Novak, 1996b). Although male users still dominate the Web, women's share of use has increased to between 31 and 40 percent, and women users tend to be slightly younger (31.9 years) than their male counterparts (33.4 years). The average income ($58,000) of those who connect to the Internet remains high, but has fallen slightly as more students go online. Almost one-third of Web or Net users hold computer-related jobs and one-quarter are employed in education (American Internet User Survey, 1997; GVU's Seventh WWW User Survey, 1997).

COMMUNICATION MODELS AND THE WORLD WIDE WEB

Traditional mass media follow a "one-to-many" model of communication. In other words, one source speaks at one time to many people who comprise a homogeneous mass audience. When Peter Jennings delivers the news, or the *New York Times* prints an article, they are each one voice sending messages to a mass audience. Mass communication vehicles include broadcast, cable, satellite television, radio, print media, books, magazines, and theatrical films. Messages sent from these media are designed to appeal to and reach a mass audience. Everyone who is tuned to a particular radio station will hear the same commercial, and moviegoers see the same version of a film. Generally, the mass media communicate with the public as a mass audience rather than as individual human beings.

The one-to-many mass communication model differs from the interpersonal (one-to-one) model of communication that occurs when one person talks to another. When two people are conversing, they generally take turns speaking and listening, and thus they receive immediate feedback through either a verbal response or body language. By interpreting feedback and by knowing the recipient, individuals can tailor their conversations to one another's feelings, beliefs, or attitudes. Interpersonal communication is just one means of one-to-one communication; other means include telephone calls, e-mail, letters, and videoconferences. One-to-one communication gives people flexibility when personalizing messages, but clearly is not very efficient when trying to reach large groups.

The marriage of computing systems and the Internet has given rise to a hybrid model of communication. A "many-to-one" model is a cross between mass broadcasting and interpersonal communication. With mainframe computers, local and wide area networks, and other database systems, large amounts of information are entered by many different sources and are stored until retrieved by individuals who select only the information they want or need. Most computer systems allow people to pick and choose the information they are interested in and ignore the rest.

The Internet's easy-to-use interface moves it into the many-to-one mode of communication. But is it? Many argue that it is a new mass medium that delivers mass messages to a mass audience of Web users, and thus follows the traditional one-to-many model of communication. For example, each Web user who visits the *CNNInteractive* Web page has access to the same information as everyone else, regardless of their personal beliefs, attitudes, or opinions. The news is not tailored for each person.

On the other hand, new Internet technologies are being developed that allow individuals to select information based on personal preferences. In this way, the Internet is not a mass medium at all, but a new interactive medium. On the *PointCast* Web site, users fill out a personal profile form and select which news they are most interested in, and then the site selects, organizes, and delivers a personalized version of the news. On the *TV Guide Online* site, users enter the types of programs they are most interested in and the cities in which they live, and *TV Guide* compiles and e-mails them personal television viewing schedules. Web sites will soon deliver advertising messages based on individual demographics. If a young woman is surfing the Net using her home computer and comes to a site where Toyota has purchased advertising space, she may see an ad targeted to her age and gender group that shows a different model of car than a fifty-year-old man will see when he accesses the same Web site from his home computer. Also, using Internet technology, individuals can interpersonally communicate and interact via e-mail and Internet telephone and with audio and video message displays.

The Internet crosses the boundaries that have traditionally delineated the three modes of communication: mass (one-to-many), interpersonal (one-to-one), and computing (many-to-one). By virtue of its nature, the Internet allows for all three types of communication, with a fourth communication mode, many-to-many, emerging. On the Internet everyone can be a producer or a receiver, individuals can receive and send personal or mass messages, and information can be provided by many and accessed by many as a mass audience or stored for individuals to select and retrieve. The Internet is a vehicle for interpersonal communication and interactivity, mass-delivered messages, and information storage, processing, and retrieval. It is a true communication phenomenon and one that allows many forms and styles of communication.

THE WORLD WIDE WEB AND THE MASS MEDIA

Technology

Although the Internet has been in existence since the 1970s, the recent introduction of user-friendly Web browsers has been accompanied by an explosion in the number of users exploring this unique medium. The World Wide Web is truly a revolutionary creation. It is technologically a separate and unique medium, yet it shares many similar properties with traditional media.

In the traditional competitive arena, each medium offers advantages and strong points over the others. Radio is convenient and portable and can be listened to while the audience is engaged in other activities. Television is visual and captivating, and print is absorbing and can be read anytime, anyplace. And now the Web offers many of these same advantages. The Web can be listened to while attending to other activities, graphic and video displays make it attention-grabbing and compelling, and information is archived for future retrieval, and thus can be read anytime.

Although the Web's advantages over conventional media have been emphasized, the Web in some ways falls short of television, radio, and print media. The Web is not portable; people cannot carry it around with them or take it to the beach as they can a newspaper, radio, or television Walkman. Although wireless modems, wireless networks, and hand-held computers will eventually lead to more portability, presently, to use the Web a wired Internet connection is required; people cannot just add batteries and raise the antenna. Neither video nor audio is delivered as clearly on the Web as on television and radio, and it takes longer to download an electronic page than to turn a printed one.

Content

The ways content is delivered by the broadcast and print media in their non-electronic forms are distinct from one another. Yet, when on the Web, radio and television sites deliver audio, video, and text, and online newspapers can be read, seen, or listened to, blurring the distinctions among the media.

Traditional radio, television, and print content are constrained by various factors. Radio and television content is limited to the amount of available airtime, and print by the number of pages. These restrictions disappear on the Web. There are no space constraints or time limits. Cyber-delivered news and entertainment are not confined to seconds of time or column inches of space, but are free-flowing, with lengths determined by the writers or Web page designers. The Web, however, is limited by bandwidth. **Bandwidth** is the amount of data that can be sent all at once through a communication path, such as a telephone line. It may be useful to visualize bandwidth as a water faucet or a pipe. The width of the faucet or pipe determines the amount of water and the speed at which it can flow. Similarly, bandwidth determines the amount of data that can electronically flow throughout the Net, but it affects the speed of information flow more than the amount of content allowed. Bandwidth limitations are becoming less of a concern, especially with the growing trend toward fiber optics. The Web stands out from other media because it is the only one that has the capability to present content as a combination of text, graphics, audio, and video.

Despite some of its disadvantages, the Web is turning traditional information delivery systems upside-down and sideways as an increasing number of individuals and corporations rush to establish a Web presence. Not only are information providers familiarizing themselves with the Web and adjusting to its uniqueness, but so are receivers. The number of individuals using the Web has exploded since 1994 as people flock to this easy, convenient means of accessing almost any information they need.

The decentralized nature of information dissemination on the Web means that it may not have used traditional methods of source-checking, editing, and establishing accuracy and credibility. Generally, when using traditional media, people are aware of the information source. Broadcast and print fare are generally written and produced by networks or independent producers, professional musicians, or credentialed journalists. Audiences rely on these sources and believe them to be trustworthy, accurate, and objective. But how reliable and accurate is Web information, especially when posted by an unknown source? Many Web sites are posted by credible and known sources such as CNN and NBC. However, anyone can produce Web pages, so source credibility comes into question. How much credence should be given to a page describing a movie star's antics or a news event that has been posted by an unknown person in an undisclosed location? Web users need to sift through cyber-information very carefully, be cautious before accepting conjecture as truth, and be wary of using Web sources as a substitute for academic text, traditional books, or other media that check sources and facts for accuracy before publication.

Characteristics of Traditional Mass Media

There are many different types of communication technologies, such as the printing press, television, radio, and the telephone. Each of these is best suited for specific communication situations: the telephone for interpersonal messages over distances, television for broadcasting messages to a large, geographically diverse audience, and radio for airing local information. Each medium can be differentiated from another by the following characteristics: audience, time, display and distribution, distance, and storage (Bonchek, 1997; Pavlik, 1996).

AUDIENCE   Media differ in their ability to reach varying audience sizes simultaneously. For example, radio and television are single-source media that reach large audiences simultaneously, while others, such as the telephone, are intended to reach only one receiver at a time. The Internet has the capability of reaching people all over the world simultaneously. For example, thousands of Web users can access the same site at the same time. Other Internet applications, such as e-mail, are designed to reach one or several receivers at a time.

TIME   Media can be differentiated according to whether information is transmitted and received in an asynchronous or synchronous manner. With asynchronous media, there is a time delay between when the message is sent and when it is received. Newspapers, books, and magazines, which are printed well in advance of delivery, are asynchronous media, as are videotapes, CDs, and films. Since letters hold messages until they are read, they too are considered asynchronous.

With synchronous messages there is no perceptible delay between the time messages are sent and the time they are received. Synchronous messages from media such as television, radio, and telephone are received almost instantaneously after transmission. Though a telephone call is a synchronous form of communication, an answering machine that stores messages until retrieved is asynchronous.

Some Internet resources are asynchronous and others synchronous. The Web, e-mail, listservs, and Usenet Newsgroups are all asynchronous because messages are stored until accessed by receivers. Conversely, Internet chat forums and virtual conferences, where users type in messages simultaneously and directly to other users, and Internet telephone, where interaction occurs simultaneously as users literally talk to each other via the network, are synchronous modes of communication.

Along with synchronicity comes interactivity. Often interactivity is thought of as the simple act of selecting from a menu of choices presented by an interactive television system or a CD-ROM. Interactivity, however, involves more than just making a choice. It is a two-way communication of "reciprocal influence" between a source and receiver. In other words, feedback influences subsequent communication (Pavlik, 1996, p. 135). For example, when participating in an Internet chat discussion, responses can instantaneously be modified depending on feedback. Interactive parties alternate between being the source and the receiver. Telephone calls and face-to-face communication are highly interactive. With new technologies, such as CD-I (Compact Disc-Interactive), interactivity comes into play as each user determines which information will be displayed and in what order.

Not all synchronous media are interactive. For instance, radio or television broadcasts are synchronous but are not considered interactive. Listeners can call radio request lines and viewers can participate in television talk shows via the telephone, but these are really more feedback mechanisms than true interactivity.

DISPLAY AND DISTRIBUTION   Media differ in the way they display and distribute information. *Display* refers to the technological means (video, audio, text) used to present information to audiences or individual receivers. *Distribution* refers to the method used to carry information to end users. This can include over-the-air broadcasting, coaxial cable, or electrical power lines. For instance, television presents audio and visual images that are either broadcast over the air, carried by coaxial or fiber optic cable, or delivered via satellite. Radio is an audio-only medium transmitted by the airwaves. Newspapers and magazines are text-based printed media that are distributed by physically transporting them from the source to the receivers.

The Web displays audio, visual, and textual information distributed from one computer to another via a complex network of telephone lines and cables. The Web, thus, displays and distributes information using a combination of technological means and electronic methods.

DISTANCE   Media transmit messages over varying distances; some are better suited for long-distance delivery and others for local transmission. Printed media need to be physically transported to their destinations; this can be cumbersome and expensive over long distances. Electronic media deliver messages through the air waves, telephone lines, cable wires, satellites, and fiber optics, giving them a time and cost advantage when transporting information over long distances. The Internet is the ideal distance medium. Information can be posted by anyone from anywhere in the world and be retrieved easily and quickly by someone living across the planet.

STORAGE Storage technology is limited to those media that have electronic means of housing large amounts of information. CD-ROM and computer hard drives have the capacity to store millions of bits of data, whereas newspaper publishing offices typically have limited space for storing back issues, and television stations must rely on small videotape libraries.

The Internet utilizes the process of digitization to allow almost limitless storage capabilities. The process of digitization transforms analog signals (continuous waves) into a binary or discontinuous signal that can be compressed (reduced) and thus more easily stored and sent. With Internet data storage, large amounts of information can be archived and retrieved for later use, and users do not have to rifle through torn pages or warbled video and audio tapes to find the information they are seeking.

Characteristics of the Web

So far the Internet has been discussed as a combination of various mass media. Modes of communication and physical characteristics of each medium are brought together on the Web, resulting in an electronic convergence of the mass media. **Convergence** has been defined as the "coming together of all forms of mediated communication in an electronic, digital form, driven by computers" (Pavlik, 1996, p. 132).

The Web facilitates convergence of both mass and interpersonal communication. The Internet can be a one-to-one medium (e-mail), a one-to-many medium (discussion groups and listservs), a many-to-one medium (through the selection of stored information), and a many-to-many medium (mass-marketed Web sites).

Easy medium can be uniquely characterized using the factors of audience, time, display and distribution, distance, and storage. For example, television serves a homogeneous audience, is nonsynchronous and noninteractive, displays audio and video information via over-the-air broadcasting and cable for long distance delivery, and information can be stored for later use on videotapes.

The Internet, however, does not readily lend itself to these same characterizations, because it blurs the boundaries that distinguish one medium from another. The Internet can reach a geographically diverse mass audience, or messages can be tailored and sent to individuals. Traditional media content is displayed as either text, graphic, audio, video, or in some cases a combination of two or three modes; the Internet presents content in all four viewing modes. Some Internet resources are asynchronous (i.e., listservs, e-mail, Web sites), while others are synchronous (i.e., discussion groups, Internet telephone). Additionally, some Internet applications are interactive, while others, such as Gopher, which lacks hypertext, are not. Lastly, the Internet is ideal for transporting information over either long distances or just next door.

The Internet has evolved into a new interactive mass medium. It is a convergence of many of the characteristics of traditional media molded together into one unique medium. It is doubtful that the Internet's creators foresaw either what it would eventually become, and is still becoming, or the tremendous impact it has had, and is having, on traditional mass media and on communication in general.

There are many media specialists who claim that traditional media will soon be replaced with new electronic delivery systems. Ted Turner and Michael Crichton, author of *Jurassic Park* and other best-sellers, have both proclaimed that "old" style media, especially newspapers, are dinosaurs on their way to extinction in the age of new communication technology (Pavlik, 1996).

History, however, tells a different tale. Throughout the ages, new media have never caused the demise of existing media. Radio did not erase print media from the face of the Earth, and television did not replace radio. Newer media have, however, eroded existing media audiences and thus their revenue bases. For older media to survive, they have had to adapt to the new competitive environment. Adaptive strategies include creating specialized uses targeted to more narrow audiences, increasing services, and recycling existing content into new formats (Pavlik, 1996). By delivering their content online, traditional media are adapting to the Internet. The Internet is a means for media to extend their existing services, to add new services, and to repackage their content. The Internet, thus, is augmenting existing media rather than replacing them.

HISTORY OF THE INTERNET AND THE WORLD WIDE WEB

The word *Internet* is a combination of the prefix *inter,* meaning "between or among each other," and the suffix *net,* short for "network," defined as an interconnecting pattern or system. An inter-network or internet, (small *i*) can refer to any "network of networks" or to any "network of computers" (Bonchek, 1997; Krol, 1995; "Yahoo! Dictionary Online," 1997). However, the Internet (capital *I*) is the specific name of the communication network that is composed of hundreds of thousands of interconnected computers that freely exchange information with each other worldwide (Groves, 1997; Pitter, Amato, Callahan, Kerr, & Tilton, 1995).

Contrary to the belief that the Internet is a 1990s phenomenon, this electronically networked system was actually envisioned in the early 1960s. Paul Baran of the Rand Corporation conceptualized sending messages via a system of networked computers. In 1964, Baran approached the U.S. government with a formal proposal outlining the need for a decentralized communications network in the event of a nuclear attack.

During the decade of the Cuban Missile Crisis and the Vietnam War, the U.S. government used Baran's idea to experiment with ways to transmit military research among their agencies by linking computers housed in various geographic locations. By 1970, the **Advanced Research Projects Agency (ARPAnet)** was created to advance computer interconnections.

In the early 1970s Stanford University was a site of early Internet development. Vinton Cerf and his colleagues researched and developed the communication protocols that would later be used for transmitting information across the Internet. Cerf's pioneering contributions to network technology earned him the title "Father of the Internet." Through ARPAnet and research conducted by several other companies and individuals over the last three decades, interconnectivity, packet-switching technologies, and transmission protocols were developed that allow the Internet to function as it does today.

The network established by ARPAnet soon caught the attention of other U.S. agencies who saw the promise of an electronic network as a means of sharing information among research facilities and schools. In the mid-1980s, the National Science Foundation took on the task of designing an expanding network that became the basis of the Internet as it is known today. At the same time, Tim Berners-Lee and a group of scientists in the European Laboratory of Particle Physics (CERN) were developing a system for worldwide interconnectivity that was later dubbed the World Wide Web.

Tim Berners-Lee, often referred to as the "Father of the World Wide Web," developed the Web as a means of sharing scientific information. Berners-Lee, who had a background in system design, wrote the Web software as an "Internet-based hypermedia initiative for global information sharing" ("1995 Kilby Young Innovator," 1997). Berners-Lee earned a degree in 1976 from Oxford University, where he built his first computer with a soldering iron, a data processor, and an old television set ("Tim Berners-Lee Bio," 1997). Berners-Lee is currently the director of the World Wide Web Consortium at the Laboratory for Computer Science at the Massachusetts Institute of Technology (MIT).

Prior to the development of the Web, Internet information was retrieved by conducting a series of complicated steps and commands to locate data, make remote connections, and download data to a local computer. The process was difficult, time consuming, and required an in-depth knowledge of Internet commands. Primarily due to its laborious retrieval system, limited accessibility, and scientific content, the Web was largely out of the public eye until 1993, when the Web browser Mosaic was developed by students at the University of Illinois. Headed by undergraduate Marc Andreessen, Mosaic was designed to allow users to access and share Web-based information without having to master difficult commands or interfaces.

Andreessen, whose early interest in computers started with a Commodore 64, was paid all of $6.85 per hour while working as a part-time programmer for the university. After graduating, Andreessen headed to California's Silicon Valley, where he was soon courted by Jim Clark, founder of Silicon Graphics. With Clark's financial backing and Andreessen's know-how they came up with the idea of enhancing and improving Mosaic. Together they founded Netscape Communication Corporation in 1994, and Netscape Navigator, an enhanced Web browser, was born shortly thereafter.

HOW THE INTERNET AND THE WEB WORK

Though it may sound confusing, the Internet's components and how they work together to deliver information can be mapped out in a fairly easy-to-understand manner. The Internet operates as a **packet-switched network.** This means that the Internet takes bundles of data and breaks them up into small packets or chunks that travel through the network independently. It is kind of like when someone moves and dismantles their stereo system and moves the tuner and CD player in the car, but puts the speakers in the back of the truck. The stereo is a complete unit, but when transporting, it is more convenient to move each part separately and then

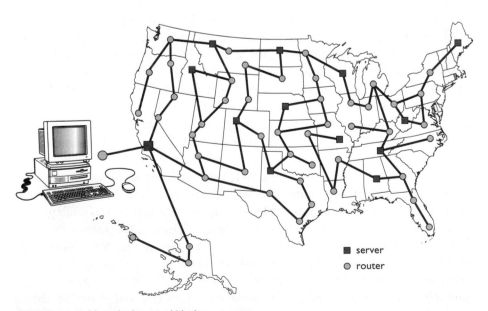

■ server
● router

FIGURE 1.3 How the Internet Works

reassemble all of the components when it gets to its new location. Briefly, that is how the Internet works, except it disassembles data rather than stereo systems and reassembles the whole unit at its destination point.

When packets of data are transmitted, they are mixed in with all of the other packets of data, transferred to other computers, resorted, and finally sent to the addressed computers. Because the Internet is commonly accessed through telephone lines, many believe it to work similarly to a telephone company. However, it actually operates like the U.S. Postal Service (Krol, 1995). When transmitting data (either letters or electronic bits) users do not have a dedicated piece of the network. Telephone connections set aside dedicated lines for each call so that only the caller and recipient are connected at once. Otherwise telephone calls would be a jumbled mess reminiscent of the old party lines. Unlike a dedicated telephone connection, the Internet allows many senders' messages to be transmitted on the same line at the same time. And like the U.S. Postal Service, the Internet mixes everyone's messages together, sends them off to another computer, like a regional post office, resorts all of the messages and then distributes them to various localities until they are finally delivered to their final addresses.

Data flow through the Internet via interconnected computers. For instance, an e-mail message originates on a computer known as the **client** and is addressed to another computer, also known as a client. From there the message gets sent to the originating client's **server.** Servers are powerful computers that provide continuous access to the Internet. The server houses data to be transmitted to the Internet and receives data from the Internet. The server then sends the packets on to a router. **Routers** are simply computers that link networks together on the Internet, and again, can be thought of as regional post offices. Routers sort each packet of data until the entire message is reassembled, and then transmit the electronic packets on either to other routers or directly to the addressee's server (similar to a local post office). The server holds the entire message until an individual directs his or her client computer to pick it up (Krol, 1996).

For data transmission to be successfully completed, servers and routers need to know where on the Internet to send the data. This is accomplished through **Transmission Control Protocols (TCP)** that define how computers from different manufacturers running different software communicate with each other on the Internet. There are many different brands of computers using various operating systems, so for these very different computers to transfer information among each other electronically they must follow **Internet Protocols (IP).** Think of IP as a set of road maps that tell the U.S. Postal Service drivers which streets to take to get to the regional and local offices. TCP is the set of rules that moves smaller packets into an IP file until all of the data bits are together. IP then tells routers how to reassemble the data packets and sets the rules for addressing the data so the routers will know where to send them. Each computer has its own Internet address, and

TABLE 1.1 Comparison of HTTP, WAIS, and Gopher Network Information Systems

	World Wide Web (HTTP)	Gopher	WAIS
Text	YES	YES	YES
Menus/graphics	YES	YES	NO
Hypertext	YES	NO	NO
Text search	YES	YES	YES
Reference to other servers	YES	YES	NO

Source: Berners-Lee, Cailliau, Luotonen, Nielsen, & Secret, 1994

each address has a corresponding numerical-only address (which users usually do not see) that the routers read so they know to which computer to send the information (Krol, 1995).

By the end of 1997 most routers were processing about 100,000–500,000 messages per second. However, to keep up with the ever-growing flow of Internet information, routers should ideally forward about five million messages per second. To help increase the flow of information through the Internet, two teams of researchers from Washington University in St. Louis have devised a new method of processing Internet data packages. The process of transmission along the Internet is expedited by altering the way routers read and sort IP addresses, and thus, e-mail and other electronic data will fly through the Internet at speeds up to ten times faster than the current pace. As of January 1998, four companies were close to signing licensing agreements with Washington University to market the new application (Allen, 1998).

There are several types of Internet protocols:

HTTP (Hypertext Transfer Protocol): Set of rules for transferring hypertext (World Wide Web) documents. All Web addresses begin with http://

WAIS (Wide Area Information Service protocol): Defines the rules for accessing a text-only index of Internet databases

GOPHER: Protocol used for accessing a text-only menu-based Internet system

FTP (File Transfer Protocol): Set of rules and application program that transfer data files from one computer to another

TELNET: Terminal emulation protocol used when logging into other computer systems on the Internet (Krol, 1996).

CONNECTING TO THE INTERNET

Internet Service Providers

The connection between a home or office computer and the Internet is established by an **Internet Service Provider (ISP),** a company that provides Internet access to computer users. The number of ISPs in the United States and Canada almost tripled from about 1,500 in 1995 to approximately 4,100 by mid-1997. ISPs each service an average of 1,800 customers (The Internet Index, 1997a; 1997b). According to a consumer survey reported in *PC World,* the two most important ISP services are fast, reliable connections with no busy signals, and reliable e-mail delivery in less than five minutes (Grimes & Perdue, 1998). According to the consumer research firm Odyssey, eight out of ten ISP subscribers say they are unhappy with their service and 62 percent switched to a new provider within a single year (Petrozzello, 1997).

Individuals who wish to access the Internet do so by subscribing to an ISP. Usually for a small monthly fee, subscribers make a local call to the ISP whose modem connects the subscriber's computer to the Internet. The ISP provides customers with the software needed to access the Internet and gives customers a special telephone/modem number to call that links customers' computers to the ISP's servers. ISPs provide servers for storing and transmitting Web-linked data and the T1 phone links to the Internet. A **T1 line** has the capacity for transmitting huge amounts of data from the ISP's home base to the Internet. Most ISPs charge customers either a monthly flat rate or by the number of minutes each user spends online.

All ISPs must register their Internet server's address. Since 1993, Network Solutions, Inc., has been operating **InterNIC,** the main registry of Internet addresses. Until late 1995, the federal government paid for the IP address registry. However, each ISP now pays a $100 annual fee, and the government picks up the registration tab only for educational and governmental institutions. Recent data show that only about one-half of the domain name registrants have paid the required fee (The Internet Index, 1997a). *The Deadbeat List* compiles the names of commercial sites that were suspended by InterNIC for not paying their registration fees.

Internet Addresses

Serving as the central Internet address registry is only one of InterNIC's functions. It also sets Internet rules, assigns servers IP addresses, and organizes registrants into the following categories: universities, businesses, networks, military, government, and organizations. These categories are signified by a three-letter code—**first-level domain extender,** or **top-level domain (TLD)**—that is added to the end of each address. These are as follows:

com: commercial	mil: military
edu: education, university	net: a network support company
gov: government	org: nonprofit and nongovernmental organization

Every person or computer given access to the Internet is assigned an Internet protocol (IP) address. IP addresses are unique to each user and serve as a locator. When a server receives a request for information, it knows by the IP address where to send the requested data.

Internet addresses, also called the **Domain Name System (DNS),** are structured in the following way: user name@host.subdomain. For example,

bkaye@genericU.edu

The "user name" is the name of the person who was issued Internet access, though many people choose to use nicknames rather than their given names. The "@" literally means "at." Host.subdomain is the user's location. In this example, the location is genericU, which, in this case, stands for a fictitious university. The "edu" is the first-level domain, which is always the last element of an address and indicates the host's type of organization. In this case, "edu" indicates that genericU is an educational institution.

The number of Internet addresses (domains) has increased tremendously. In March 1995, there were about 52,500 domains registered with InterNIC. One year later, InterNIC was recording that same number of registrants per month. By December 1996, there were almost 900,000 registered domains (Murphy, 1997; Ramstad, 1996). By 1997 the number of domain names was increasing by an extraordinary 85,000 new registrations per month (The Internet Index, 1997a).

Domain Name Disputes

Trademark policy, copyright law, and intellectual property attorneys work closely with Network Solutions, Inc., to set policies for domain name and trademark or logo use. Besides domain name disputes, Network Solutions resolves other issues, such as when someone may use a trademark or logo that does not belong to them on their Web page, such as a teenager who adorns his homepage with a trademarked graphic of Bart Simpson.

In many instances, trademark disputes are often settled between the concerned parties themselves without involving Network Solutions in the battle. Generally, large companies more often than not prevail in their claims for exclusive trademark rights. For example, a private citizen posted an Elvis Presley Web page filled with sound clips of hit songs and photographs of the late rock and roll legend. Elvis Presley Enterprises claimed its trademark and copyright protections were being infringed upon by the unofficial page and requested that the page be withdrawn from the Web. The page was subsequently taken off the Web after the owner received a cease-and-desist order ("The Letter," 1994).

InterNIC also sets policies for resolving domain name (Internet address) disputes. For instance, say a person named Nancy Francine Little has the Web address www.nfl.com, but then the National Football League decides it wants that address. InterNIC's policy gives priority to the trademark holder. In other words, InterNIC would be likely to give Nancy's address to the NFL, which holds the trademark.

Often domain name disputes are not easy to resolve and drag on for some time. In these situations the domain name is put on hold and cannot be used until the matter is resolved. For example, when the District of Columbia Information site was registered as "dc.com," Warner Bros. complained to InterNIC that the "dc.com" name infringed on its trademark for DC Comics. The domain name was put on hold pending resolution (Agmon, Halpern, & Pauker, 1996).

Another domain name dispute involved Warner Bros. and Roadrunner Computer Systems. Warner Bros. wanted to post its animation pages as roadrunner.com, but that address was already being used by the computer company. Although it is customary to place domain names on hold, in this case the computer company successfully petitioned an exemption, and was allowed to keep its address until an agreement was reached. Eventually Roadrunner Computer Systems prevailed and retained their address, while Warner Bros. simply put a hyphen in the URL to get www.road-runner.com.

There are instances where individuals intentionally register a domain name to prevent the trademark holder from posting a Web site under that same name. The New York Times Company paid an undisclosed sum to an individual for the domain name "nyt.com." The long distance company Sprint briefly held the domain name "mci.com," and a student registered for the name "Windows95.com." "Domain name grabbing" has in some cases been used as a deliberate attempt to extort money from the trademark holder (Agmon, Halpern, & Pauker, 1996).

To circumvent domain name grabbing, many companies are buying up the rights to names just to keep others from having them. For just $100 per name, Bell Atlantic, which also owns the telephone company Nynex, bought the names "bellatlanticsucks.com," "bigyellowsucks.com," and "nynexsucks.com." Proctor & Gamble is trying to stay ahead of unofficial and parody Web sites by registering names such as "underarm.com," "badbreath.com," "dandruff.com," and "diarrhea.com." On the other hand, many companies claim that there are just too many derogatory names, too many parody Web sites, and too many Web sites in general to bother with snatching up whichever names the companies think that unfriendly Web site creators may want use ("Companies Buying Internet Addresses," 1997).

One of the latest domain name issues concerns "stealth URLs" whose slight variations of well-known site addresses are intended to trick confused users into visiting the sites. For example, "whitehouse.gov" is the official presidential URL, whereas "whitehouse.com" surprises many online users with its sexually explicit material. Bad typists who add a second "r" to "Motorola.com" will find themselves staring at nude photos. As expected, several lawsuits are pending to outlaw URLs that snare unsuspecting visitors and thus increase their number of hits by taking advantage of poor spellers and inexperienced Web users (Rambler, 1998, p. 88).

A Solution for Domain Names Problems

Network Solutions has been under contract with the National Science Foundation, which oversees the Internet. Network Solutions' contract with the NSF was scheduled to expire in March 1998 (but was extended six months) opening the doors for competitors to enter the domain name registration business. The Internet Assigned Names Authority (IANA) has proposed that other entities be allowed to issue new top-level domain names. Several companies have already begun registering domain names for certain subsets of the market. American Convergent Technologies issues community-based domain names, and Internet Domain Names records domain names for companies outside of the United States. Network Solutions aims to hold on to its dominance in the domain name business with its introduction of WorldNic, a center of online registration services marketed to nontechnology and small businesses ready to get on the Web (Martinez, 1997; "Sorting Out the Identity," 1996).

As new companies join in the domain name business, the astronomic number of domain name registrants and increasing infringement on trademarks has impelled a consortium of international organizations (International Ad Hoc Committee—IAHC) to create and add seven new top-level domains (TLDs) to the existing list. The following is a list of proposed domains:

firm: business or company sites

shop: vendors or other sites offering products for sale

Web: WWW information specific sites

arts: cultural and entertainment sites

rec: recreation-oriented sites

info: information providers

nom: personal sites

The additional domains will give similarly named enterprises in different lines of business greater flexibility in using their company names in their online addresses. For example, Acme Insurance could have the domain "acme.firm," the Acme Travel Agency could be known as "acme.rec." Acme Hardware could operate as "acme.store," and the Acme Guide to Museums as "acme.arts" ("New Top Level Domains," 1997).

It was initially anticipated that the seven new domain names would be in use by February 1998. However, as of spring 1998, there was still some question as to whether the proposal will go into effect as planned. At first, many were concerned that the original proposal restricted new domain-registering companies from adding more domain names to the system (Rodger, 1998b). Additionally, many corporations, fearing that trademark protection would be more difficult to enforce, were against adding any new domain names (Harmon, 1998).

In late January 1998, the Clinton Administration released its "Green Paper" that supports handing government control over domain names to a competitive market. However, the administration has proposed establishing a nonprofit organization that would oversee many groups who register addresses under existing domain names. Additionally, the government does not support the seven new domains proposed by the IAHC. Instead the Green Paper calls for a gradual phasing in of "five new domains under five new registries" (Harmon, 1998; Rodger, 1998a, p. 7).

Internet experts and the government largely agree that registration of domains should be competitive and that additional domain names are sorely needed. What is in dispute, however, is how a competitive registration system should be handled, how many new domains should be allowed, and who has authority to select the new domains. It is largely believed that these issues will be settled by the end of 1998; however, that may be an optimistic prediction.

NAVIGATING THE WORLD WIDE WEB

Net Browsers

The World Wide Web is an Internet application that provides text and graphics and in many cases audio and full-motion video. The Web browser **Mosaic** was the first system that allowed Web users to travel easily from one site to another merely by pointing and clicking on icons or hot buttons. Since Mosaic's introduction, many other Web browsers have become available; Netscape Navigator (commonly referred to as "Netscape") and Microsoft Explorer are the most notable. Although newer Web browsers operate similarly to Mosaic, they have added features that make Web browsing much easier than the earlier version. With Netscape, "the Web has exploded into a user-friendly, do-it-yourself hypermedia publishing system that's likely to change the way many of us look at the way we distribute information . . ." (Himowitz, 1995, p. C1).

Web browsers present online information in a readable form. They do this by interpreting the formatted commands of the Web programming language, **HTML**

(**Hypertext Markup Language**), and reconstructing the text and graphics online. Coined in 1962, **hypertext** is "non-linear text, or text that does not flow sequentially from start to finish" (Pavlik, 1996, p. 134). Hypertext electronically links text, graphic, video, or audio documents from one document to another or from one computer to another (Krol, 1996). Browsers are platform-independent, meaning they interpret Internet data regardless of the type of computer the documents were created on or are being sent from. A Macintosh computer, for example, can send a hypertext document to an IBM machine. Hypertext frees authors and readers from the constraints of linear text and allows them to explore different pathways through a written work. Movement between hypertext documents occurs in a nonlinear or nonsequential manner. For example, when reading a hypertext document one can easily start on page 2, then jump to relevant information on page 15, then to page 8, and so on. Hypertext allows readers to pick and choose the parts of documents they wish to look at rather than following the text in a linear fashion, such as with books, which are written to be read sequentially.

One professor likes to explain the nonlinear nature of hypertext using the example of a student who created a Web page about every city he stopped at during a cross-country bicycle trip. If the student wrote his travel diary as a magazine article, he would more than likely organize the piece as a linear document meant to be read in chronological order. Although readers are always free to skip around any printed text, the meaning may be missed if not read in the order meant by the author. However, with hypertext links in mind, the author may design a Web site in a nonlinear manner, so that readers can start where they want and find out about the bicyclist's adventures in any given city without losing the continuity of the entire trip.

Hypertext Markup Language

HTML is the World Wide Web programming language. It consists of a series of commands that tells browsers how to display the text and graphics. If a document to be posted on the Web consists of varying font sizes and styles, with some text that is boldfaced and perhaps centered, the text must be formatted in HTML before it can be interpreted by a Web browser. For example, if the document title "A Rose Is a Rose" is to be displayed in boldface, then the commands (**tags**), <b> </b>, would be inserted before and after the title, respectively: **<b>A Rose Is a Rose </b>**. If the title is to be displayed in the center of the computer screen, then the HTML "center" tags would be added. **<center><b>A Rose Is a Rose</b> </center>**. The first set of commands within the brackets alerts the browser to present the text centered and boldfaced. The set of bracketed commands containing a slash tells the browser to stop displaying the text in the designated style.

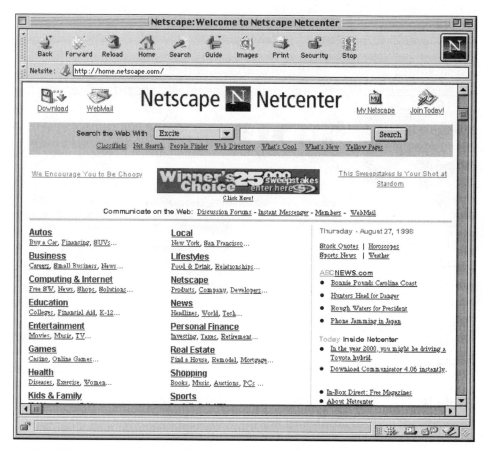

FIGURE 1.4 Netscape's Homepage

Many HTML commands are used in designing a Web page. These designate font style, size, and format, tables, page design such as centering, justifying, indents, color, the placement of graphics, and so on. Web page authors determine how their documents will look online by formatting the page using the proper HTML commands to be read and interpreted by the browser.

While surfing the Net, users are often drawn to a particularly well-designed Web page and may wonder how the page is HTML formatted. It is possible to see how Webmasters created their pages by viewing the page's "source." In Netscape, HTML source codes can be seen by clicking on the "View" pull-down box in the Netscape tool bar, then clicking on the "Document Source" option. For more information about HTML, see *A Beginner's Guide to HTML,* or any other HTML over-

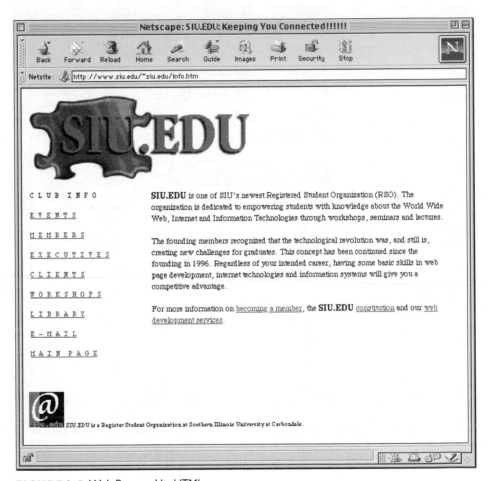

FIGURE 1.5 Web Page and Its HTML

view available on the Web or in most bookstores. Figure 1.5 is an example of a browser-displayed Web page and its document source.

Java

Years after its May 1995 introduction, Java remains the hottest cyberspace programming language around. Created by *Sun Microsystems,* Java has opened the Web to a whole new world of animation. Until Java, Web pages were generally without movement. But now, Java can be used to design Web pages with rotating 3-D images, graphics that move around a page, interactive games, spreadsheets, and other dynamic applications. Java transforms Netscape into more than just a Web

SIU.EDU Web page HTML source code

```html
<!DOCTYPE HTML PUBLIC "-//W3C//DTD HTML 4.0 Transitional//EN">
<HTML>
<HEAD>
<META HTTP-EQUIV="Content-Type" CONTENT="text/html; charset=iso-8859-1">
<META NAME="GENERATOR" CONTENT="Mozilla/4.07 [en] (Win98; I) [Netscape]">
<TITLE>SIU.EDU: Keeping You Connected!!!!!!</TITLE>
<!-- Page designed by Nora Ferguson-Buhlig at Southern Illinois University at
Carbondale -->
<!--Copyright (c) 1997 by SIU.EDU at Southern Illinois University at Carbondale-->
</HEAD>
<BODY BGCOLOR="#FFFFFF" LINK="#003399">
<IMG SRC="images/bar1.jpg" >
<TABLE BORDER=0 >
<TR>
<TD VALIGN=TOP WIDTH="170">
<PRE>C L U B  I N F O
<A HREF="events.htm">E V E N T S
</A><A HREF="members.htm">M E M B E R S
</A><A HREF="execs.htm">E X E C U T I V E S
</A><A HREF="clients.htm">C L I E N T S
</A><A HREF="workshp.htm">W O R K S H O P S
</A><A HREF="library.htm">L I B R A R Y
</A><A HREF="email.htm">E - M A I L
</A><A HREF="index.htm">M A I N  P A G E</A>
</PRE>
</TD>
<TD VALIGN=TOP><B>SIU.EDU</B> is one of SIU's newest Registered Student
Organization (RSO). The organization is dedicated to empowering students with
knowledge about the World Wide Web, Internet and Information Technologies
through workshops, seminars and lectures. 
<P>The founding members recognized that the technological revolution was, and
still is, creating new challenges for graduates. This concept has been continued since
the founding in 1996. Regardless of your intended career, having some basic skills in
web page development, internet technologies and information systems will give you a
competitive advantage. 
<P>For more information on <A HREF="join.htm">becoming a member</A>, the
<B>SIU.EDU</B> <A HREF="constit.htm">constitution</A> and our <A
HREF="service.htm">web development services</A>. </TD>
</TR>
</TABLE>
<P><IMG SRC="images/lillogo.gif" > <FONT SIZE=-2>SIU.EDU is a Register
Student Organization at Southern Illinois University at Carbondale.</FONT>
</BODY>
</HTML>
```

page browser; with Java, Netscape acts like a computer-within-a-computer able to interpret and display dynamic Web functions.

Java language is based on FORTRAN C++ programming language with some modifications. Associated with Java are **applets,** applications written in Java language. Also making the news is HotJava, a Java-based Web browser that reads and displays Web pages and runs applets. However, as of late 1997, HotJava was still in the demo stage and not yet available for Macintosh computers.

Those who do not have the foggiest idea of how to write a Java program, but still desire an animated Web page, can try **JavaScripting.** Unlike Java, which is a programming language, JavaScripting is a fairly easy-to-use scripting language developed by Netscape. Microsoft, which is embroiled in stiff competition with Netscape, has developed its own JavaScript "dialect" that works best on Microsoft's own Web browser, Internet Explorer.

JavaScripting is a set of commands, embedded within an HTML document, that produces Web pages emulating Java-programmed interactivity and animation. JavaScripting is written as part of the HTML document to enhance Web pages. Many books are available on beginning JavaScripting, or turn to the Web for online instructions like *Introduction to JavaScripting*.

JavaScripting can be used to create dynamic Web pages similar to those created by Java programming. Animated graphics that rotate and fly around pages, hot buttons or links, simple calculating spreadsheets, and forms and surveys can all be created with JavaScripting. JavaScripting is becoming a popular all-around Web-design tool, whereas Java programming tends to be reserved for pages that contain more complicated animation, games, forms, and spreadsheets that require the browser to read data and produce output files.

Java-enhanced pages have many advantages over standard HTML-based Web documents. Primarily, Java adds life and dimension to Web pages with moving objects and interactivity. Java, JavaScripting, and HotJava have caused quite a stir in the cyber-community as more and more enhanced pages are popping up and transforming the Web into an exciting, dynamic, and interactive medium (Holden & Webster, 1995).

Moving around the Web

HOT LINKS AND BUTTONS   Using a Web browser to navigate the World Wide Web is as easy as point-and-click. There are two primary ways to navigate the Web. Web pages are connected to each other via hot links, which consist of hidden HTML commands that tell the browser to find a particular Web page that is housed on an interconnected server. Users can travel from Web site to Web site by simply clicking on **hot links** or **buttons,** which are displayed as either highlighted text or as icons.

The second method of navigating the Web is by entering a Web site's specific location, known as a **Uniform Resource Locator (URL).**

UNIFORM RESOURCE LOCATOR The URL is a document's specific location on the Web. Think of it as street where every building has a unique address. URLs generally take on the following standard form:

> **Protocol://host/path/filename**

For example, consider the Web pages pertaining to American Trans Air. This is a commercial airline based out of Indianapolis, IN. Its Web site can be found at:

> **http://www.ata.com/about_ata/index.html**

Here is how to decipher this location: "http" stands for **hypertext transfer protocol,** which means that the set of rules governing the transmission of a hypertext document will be followed. The three *ws* after the first two slashes signify the World Wide Web, which means the requested information is posted on a Web-linked server. "ATA" means that the page was created by ATA; "com" means that ATA is a business or commercial site. The part of an address before the first slash will be the site's main homepage, or frequently a menu page of links to other Web pages. Therefore, the URL for ATA's homepage is

> **http://www.ata.com**

To continue with the example, "about_ata" is the name of a Web page that is linked to ATA's menu page. "Index" is linked off the "about_ata" page and is the company's official page with information about ATA. "Htm" means it is a hypertext document created on a Windows-based, non-Macintosh computer.

Here is how to decipher another URL for an ATA homepage.

> **http://www.halcyon.com/integra/ata.html**

This page is hosted by Northwest Nexus, an Internet service provider that uses "halcyon" as its domain name on URLs. The page is posted on the server in a file called "integra," "ata" is the name of a subfile that is an "unofficial" home page for American Trans Air, and "html" means that the site was created on a Macintosh computer.

Bookmarks

Traveling around the Web can be like walking through a hedge maze. It is easy to lose track of which pages have been visited and which pages are linked together. Hansel and Gretel dropped a trail of bread crumbs to find their way back home, but unfortunately, the birds ate the bread crumbs and the two children ended up captive

FIGURE 1.6 American Trans Air Homepage

in the old witch's goose pen. To keep Web users from losing their way, browsers act as a trail of bread crumbs by keeping track of the pages that have been visited. On Netscape Navigator, clicking on the main menu's "Go" option brings up a list of recently visited Web pages in the order that they were accessed. Visitors can quickly revisit pages they accessed earlier in their browsing session and bounce back and forth among several pages. The "Go" button, however, only lists the Web sites visited during the active Web session. In other words, once users quit Netscape the list of visited pages is not stored in memory. However, an ongoing list of favorite sites can be stored from one Web session to another through **bookmarking.**

Similar to a bookmark placed between pages of a novel, Web bookmarks guide users to pages they want to revisit. Bookmarking serves as an alternative to writing

BOX 1.1 DECIPHERING A URL

URL	Web Page
http://www.ata.com	ATA's home page
http://www.ata.com/about_ata	A page entitled "About ATA"
http://www.ata.com/about_ata/index.htm	The official ATA home page with information about the airline

down URLs of favorite pages. Simply clicking on the "Add Bookmark" option under the "Bookmarks" option in the main menu bar saves the page for future access. The URL of the page that is currently visible on the screen is stored along with the page's title.

Users have the flexibility of arranging their bookmarks in many different ways, such as alphabetically, or in folders sorted by topic. Pulling down on the "Window" option on Netscape's main menu bar and then clicking on "Bookmarks" opens a window containing a list of bookmarked sites. Folders can be created by clicking on the "Insert Folder" option under "Item" in the main menu bar and then dragging the title of the site into the folder. Bookmarked sites are alphabetized by highlighting the list and clicking on "Sort," which is found under "Item" in the main menu bar.

Internet Explorer's tool bar labels bookmarks as "Favorites." IE users can add favorite pages and open pages from the "Favorites" pop-up menu, from which users can also edit their "Favorites" lists and organize their "Favorites" using the "New Divider" and "New Folder" options.

Bookmarking sites is so easy to do that the list can grow very quickly. It is surprising how long the list can become just by adding one or two sites during every Web session. Before too long users may find themselves spending too much time searching through their lists seeking a specific site. Bookmarked titles are much easier to look through and select if arranged in some logical order.

SELECTING A WEB BROWSER

Selecting a Web browser is a matter of personal preference. Web browsers all operate in the same basic manner, though some have benefits that others do not, and some work best with certain types of computers. Generally, browers that take up less hard disk space and operate at fairly quick speeds are less troublesome than those that are large and inefficient. A cumbersome browser may take significantly longer to

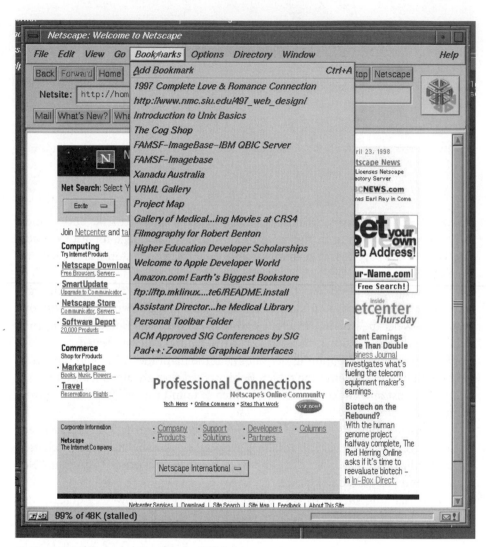

FIGURE 1.7 Example of Bookmarked Web Sites

download pages and may often result in "bombing out" and other connection problems, especially on pages that carry new components like audio, video, and Java features.

Security has recently emerged as an important criterion for selecting a browser. A strong browser keeps computers safe from viruses and protects users from hackers and other unwelcome invasions of privacy. Many users also look for browers that have cross-platform ability, meaning that they can be used with Windows, Windows 95, Windows NT, Macintosh, and other operating systems. Additionally, browsers that support an integrated e-mail system allow users to send or receive messages without having to keep closing the Web and opening the e-mail window. With an integrated system, copying, attaching, composing, and sending messages are available in one package.

Although there are many browsers, a market share between Netscape Navigator and Microsoft's Internet Explorer will be examined. Until the August 1995 unveiling of Microsoft's new Windows 95 operating system, which includes Internet Explorer, Netscape was used by about 80 percent of the people who connect to the Web, especially Macintosh users (Ortiz, 1996). Increasing competition from Internet Explorer and other browsers that provide their software for free—Netscape charged $49.95—had eroded Netscape Navigator's market share to about 70 percent in mid-1997 (Shaw, 1997). By early 1998, Netscape was the browser of choice by slightly less than six out of ten users, while Internet Explorer was holding an almost 40 percent share, twice the percentage from a year earlier (Green, 1998; Guglielmo, 1997; Guglielmo, Whitestone, & Babcock, 1998; Hafner & Meyer, 1998).

Internet Explorer has quickly been diminishing Netscape's dominance, much to the dismay of Netscape and the United States Department of Justice. At issue is whether the Windows 95 operating system and Internet Explorer are one integrated application, as Microsoft claims, or whether they are two separate products, as the Justice Department contends. According to the Justice Department, forcing computer makers to install the browser software as a condition for installing Windows 95 undermines consumer choice and is in violation of a consent decree that the company signed in 1995. In October 1997, Attorney General Janet Reno issued Microsoft a cease-and-desist order and a one-million-dollar-a-day fine until the company stops preinstalling their Web browser on computers with Windows 95. Microsoft insists that it is acting lawfully and is not in violation of the 1995 decree that allows the company to integrate new features into its operating system.

Although the suit has not been entirely settled, Microsoft conceded its resolve to keep Internet Explorer part of Windows 95. In January 1998, Microsoft reluctantly agreed to allow computer manufacturers to temporarily install Windows 95 without being forced to include Internet Explorer. In response to Microsoft's decision and in an attempt to win back its market share, Netscape announced it will no longer charge customers for its browser, and it will release the source code so anyone with some know-how can make improvements (Levy, 1998).

With the impending release of Windows 98 the pressure was on to resolve the case. Windows 98 more tightly integrates its browser with the operating system, making it more difficult to separate the two functions (Glass, 1998; "Consumers Win," 1998; Glass, 1998; Markoff, 1998). In July 1998 the Washington, D.C. circuit court handed Microsoft at least a partial victory when it overturned the preliminary injunction against the company, freeing "Microsoft to bundle what it likes into its operating system—Web browsers, ham sandwiches, whatever—as long as it demonstrates some 'plausible' benefit consumers can't get any other way" (Hirsh, 1998, p. 50). In other words, the judge ruled that Microsoft did not violate the 1995 consent decree and stated that the browser could be considered to be an integrated part of Windows. Two days after the decision, Microsoft launched the long-awaited Windows 98.

Despite the latest ruling, Microsoft is not out of the woods. There are still at least two federal antitrust suits and complaints from as many as twenty states that claim Microsoft intentionally used its Windows monopoly to stomp competitive browsers out of the marketplace. Many legal experts regard the pending Microsoft antitrust case as a watershed event, and that regardless of the outcome, the case could set new rules and standards of competition for the computer industry (Hirsh, 1998; "Microsoft Probe," 1997; Rodger, 1997; Tedesco, 1997).

ONLINE SERVICES

Online services, such as America Online (AOL), Prodigy, and CompuServe, are proprietary companies that provide information that they think will be of interest to their subscribers. Although proprietary services usually provide their customers with access to e-mail and the World Wide Web, they primarily provide access to online databases. Online databases are posted by the government and by companies such as Consumer Reports, Grolier's Encyclopedia, and others that make their information available electronically. It is a daunting task for individuals to attempt to access about 7,000 existing electronic data bases, so online services make it easy by giving subscribers links through one main provider and by packaging the databases in an easy-to-use system (Berkman, 1994).

The depth of database information and content varies from one service to another and depends on the monthly fee. Many online services charge a flat monthly fee, sometimes as low as $19.95, for unlimited use. However, this plan is quickly losing favor among services whose customers spend hours and hours online tying up phone lines and making it difficult for others to log on. On average, Internet users spend sixteen to eighteen hours online per month, and it costs most online services 90 cents to $1.80 an hour to keep a customer connected. So if they charge only $19.95 a month, services start losing money when customers remain online for more than eleven hours ("Flat Rates," 1997).

Often media-based content is provided by online services. AOL provides full-text online versions of *The Chicago Tribune* (which owns 10 percent of AOL), *San Jose Mercury News,* and *Time* magazine. The *San Jose Mercury News* also posts classified advertisements on AOL. The publications furnish the electronic versions to online publishers (Otte, 1994). The financial arrangements between content providers and online services are often based on connect-time revenue, which is the amount charged to subscribers for electronic access. Typically, the content provider receives 10–25 percent of an online service's connect-time revenue, and in the case of AOL, providers also earn a percentage of revenue from member subscriptions. In exchange, content providers contract for exclusivity on the online service for an agreed-upon length of time (Bixby, 1995).

Many online services now include browsers that give subscribers access to the World Wide Web. Additionally, most proprietary services act as servers, allowing subscribers to post personal homepages on the Net. For example, AOL offers subscribers between two and five megabytes of space on its server, and Compuserve subscribers can get about five megabytes of space for their personal homepages (Grimes & Perdue, 1998).

The earliest and most popular online services, AOL, CompuServe, and Prodigy, have been joined by Microsoft Network and others. AOL acquired CompuServe in mid-1997, but continues to operate it as a separate entity. AOL members tend to be younger with lower annual incomes than CompuServe subscribers, who tend to be higher-income entrepreneurs. By keeping the two entities separate instead of merging them, AOL hopes to satisfy its CompuServe members who may resist joining AOL. Many CompuServe supporters perceive AOL as an inferior service (Gengler, 1997; McChesney & Edwards, 1997).

AOL leads the way in online services with nine million subscribers and $1.7 billion in revenue ("Block May Be Big," 1997). CompuServe and Microsoft Network both follow with about 2.5 million members. All three providers leave Prodigy in the dust with about one million subscribers (Barlas, 1998; "Direct Satellite," 1996; Kanell, 1997).

Since its inception, Prodigy tended to attract more older people and family subscriptions (Bixby, 1995), which may have accounted for its low revenues and small subscriber base. However, Prodigy's 1996 acquisition by International Wireless from IBM and Sears, and subsequent infusion of funding, together with its new alignment with the Web searching service Excite may help boost Prodigy's market share and revenues. Under the terms of their agreement, Excite promises to provide Prodigy subscribers with personalized Web content, such as sport scores and television listings. In return, Prodigy will stop developing its own content and will no longer promote any searching service other than Excite on its Web page (Barlas, 1998; Poletti, 1996; "Prodigy, Inc., Secures," 1997).

SUMMARY: THE INTERNET AND THE WORLD WIDE WEB

The Internet has been in existence since the 1970s, but for about two decades it was used primarily by government and academic researchers adept at accessing information through a series of complicated commands. The advent of the first Web browser, Mosaic, which brought hypertext to the World Wide Web, sparked a surge of interest in the Internet. The general public has been quick to embrace this new medium and to learn how to "surf the Net." Although new users are warily paddling their way around the Web, the learning curve is relatively flat, and the inexperienced quickly get comfortable and easily caught up in this new wave of information technology.

There are seven major network resources available on the Internet: Gopher, WAIS, e-mail, listservs, Usenet Newsgroups, chat forums, and the World Wide Web. Currently, e-mail is the most widely used Internet function, though the Web is catching on strong. The Web's strong appeal stems from a similarity to other media. The Web presents information as text (like newspapers and books), as graphics (like magazines or photos), as audio (like radio), and as video (like television and movies). It is a medium that has the potential to satisfy everyone's media needs. Not only is the Web an excellent vehicle for accessing information, but it also allows anyone to be an information provider. Anyone can create a Web site and display whatever information they want in whatever manner they choose. For the first time in media history, many people can communicate to a mass audience without government regulation, licensing requirements, or steep costs.

Like television in the 1950s, the Internet is still in the early stages of development. Technological changes are breeding new Web developments and innovations that are happening with lightning speed. As the Web continues to evolve and more features and functions are added, it will continue to impact traditional mass communication and mass media.

CHAPTER LINKS

ABC—http://www.abc.com

America Online—http://www.aol.com

A Beginner's Guide to HTML—http://www.w3.org/Markup

CNN Interactive—http://cnn.com

CompuServe—http://world.compuserve.com/

Dharma and Greg—http://www.abc.com/primetime/dharma_and_greg/index.html

Introduction to JavaScripting—http://www.siu.edu/~siu.edu/javascript/

Microsoft Network—http://www.msn.com

Netscape Navigator—http://home.netscape.com/

National Public Radio—http://www.npr.org/programs/morning/

Prodigy—http://www.prodigy.com/

PointCast Network—http://www.pointcast.com
Sun Microsystems—http://www.sun.com
TV Guide Online—http://www.tvgen.com/

REFERENCES

Aboba, B. (1993, November). How the Internet came to be. In *The online user's encyclope-dia.* Reading, MA: Addison-Wesley.

About one in four adults has access. (1996). *1996 National omnibus survey.* University of Maryland Survey Research. [Online]. Available: Alishaw.sccf.ucsb.edu/~survey1/

Agmon, J., Halpern, S., & Pauker, D. (1996). *Introduction to domain name disputes.* [Online]. Available: http://www.law.georgetown.edu/lc/internic/recent/rec1i.html

Allen, W. (1998, January 4). WU inventions make data zip along the Net. *St. Louis Post Dispatch,* pp. A1, A12.

American Internet user survey. (1997). *Emerging technologies research group.* [Online]. Available: http://etrg.findsvp.com/Internet/findf.html [1998, January 7].

Angell, D., & Heslop, B. (1995). *The Internet business companion.* Reading, MA: Addison-Wesley.

Barlas, P. (1998, January 28). Search engines add value to lure advertisers. *Investor's Daily,* p. A8.

Berkman, R. I. (1994). *Find it online.* New York: Windcrest/McGraw-Hill.

Berners-Lee, T., Cailliau, R., Luotonen, A., Nielsen, F. K., & Secret, A. (1994). The World Wide Web. *Communications of the ACM. 37* (8), 76–82.

Bixby, D. (1995). *Annual Review of Communication.* International Engineering Consortium. Vol. XLVIII.

Block may be big winner in swap. (1997, September 9). *Raleigh News and Observer,* p. D4.

Bonchek, M. S. (1997). *From broadcast to netcast: The Internet and the flow of political information.* Doctoral dissertation, Harvard University. [Online]. Available: http://institute.strategosnet.com/msb/home.html

Caruso, D. (1996, January 29). Technology. *New York Times,* p. C3.

Cleland, K. (1996, August 5). Chat gives marketers something to talk about. *Advertising Age, 67* (32), 22.

CommerceNet and Neilsen Research. (1995). The *CommerceNet/Neilsen Internet demo-graphics survey: Executive summary.* [Online]. Available: http://www.commerce.net/information/surveys/

Companies buying Internet addresses for the names. (1997, December 30). *CNN Interactive.* [Online]. Available: http://cnn.com/TECH/9712/30/Internet.names.ap/index.html [1998, January 7].

Consumers win under partial Microsoft settlement, Computer-makers can remove IE browser if they choose (1998, January 22). *CNN Interactive.* [Online]. Available: http://cnn.com/TECH/9801/22/microsoft/index.html [1998, January 28].

Croal, N., & Stone, B. (1996, May 27). Cyberscope: More sites. *Newsweek,* 10.

Direct satellite online drive burgeoning arena. (1996, August 19). *Advertising Age, 67* (34), S10.

Eager, B. (1994). *Using the World Wide Web.* Indianapolis, IN: Que Corporation.

Fahey, T. (1994). *Net.speak: The Internet dictionary.* Indianapolis, IN: Hayden Books.

Flat rates for Internet not paying off, firm says. (1997, January, 11). *St. Louis Post Dispatch,* p. 25.

Gengler, B. (1997, February). Suddenly everyone's an ISP. *Internetwork, 2* (8), 45.

Glass, A. J. (1998, April 7). Justice, Microsoft trying to make a new deal. *San Francisco Chronicle,* p. C2.

Green, H. (1998, January 19). Has Netscape hit the "innovation ceiling"? *Business Week,* 69.

Grimes, B., & Perdue, L. (1998, January). ISPs you can count on. *PC World, 16* (1), 146–55.

Groves, D. (1997). *The Web page workbook.* Wilsonville, OR: Franklin Beadle.

Guglielmo, C., Whitestone, R., & Babcock, C. (1998, January 12). Can Netscape fly without a parachute? *Inter@ctive Week,* 48–49.

Guglielmo, C. (1997, December 22). Netscape launches browser campaign. *Inter@ctive Week,* 7.

Gunther, J. (1997). Introduction to JavaScripting. [Online]. Available: http://www.siu.edu/~siu.edu/javascript

GVU's sixth WWW user survey. (1996). Georgia Institute of Technology's Graphic and Visualization and Usability Center. [Online]. Available: http://www.cc.gatech.edu/gvu/user_surveys/papers/9610-release.html

GVU's seventh WWW user survey. (1997). Georgia Institute of Technology's Graphic, Visualization and Usability Center. [Online]. Available: http://www.cc.gatech.edu/gvu/user_surveys/survey_1997

Hafner, K., & Meyer, M. (1998, January 19). Sharing the blame. *Newsweek,* 51–52.

Harmon, A. (1998, February 2). U.S. plan on Internet names lacks support from users. *New York Times: CyberTimes.* [Online]. Available: http://www.nytimes.com/library/cyber/week/020298domain.html [1998, February 2].

Hedges, C. (1997, February 9). Now TV interrupts Milosevic's programming. *New York Times,* p. E5.

Herz, J. C. (1995, November 30). What a wonderful Web it could be. *Rolling Stone,* 22.

High performance computing and communications: Hearing before the committee on science, space, and technology. U.S. House of Representatives, 103d Cong., 2d Sess. 1 (1994).

Himowitz, M. (1995, February 1). "Come into my Web," said Prodigy to a guy. *St. Louis Post Dispatch,* p. C1.

Hirsh, M. (1998, July 6). A big win for Chairman Bill. *Newsweek,* 50.

Hoffman, D. L., Kalsbeek, W. D., & Novak, T. P. (1996a). *Internet use in the United States: 1995 Baseline estimates and preliminary market segments.* [Online]. Available: http://www.2000.ogsm.vanderbilt.edu/baseline/1995.Internet.estimates.html

Hoffman, D. L., Kalsbeek, W. D., & Novak, T. P. (1996b). *Internet and Web use in the United States: Baselines for commercial development.* [Online]. Available: http://www.2000.ogsm.vanderbilt.edu/papers/Internet_demos_july9_1996.html

Holden, G., & Webster, T. (1995). *Mastering Netscape 2.0.* Indianapolis, IN: Hayden Books.

How the Web was won. (1998, January 17). *Web Wonder Inc. homepage.* [Online]. Available: http://www/Webwonderinc.com [1998, January 17].

Internet eats into TV time. (1996, January). *St. Louis Post Dispatch,* pp. 6C, 8C.

Internet history. (1996). *Silverlink LLC.* [Online]. Available: http://www.olympic.net/poke/IIP/history.html

The Internet Index. (1997a, February 15). Open market. [Online]. Available: http://www.openmarket.com/intindex

The Internet Index. (1997b, September 10). Open Market. [Online]. Available: http://www.openmarket.com/intindex

Kanell, M. (1997, September 28). Internet commerce. *Atlanta Journal and Constitution,* p. 1G.

Kardas, E. P., & Milford, T. M. (1996). *Using the Internet for social science research and practice.* Belmont, CA: Wadsworth.

Krol, E. (1995). *The whole Internet.* Sebastopol, CA: O'Reilly & Associates.

Krol, E. (1996). *The whole Internet,* academic version. Adapted by Bruce Klopfenstein. Sebastopol, CA: O'Reilly & Associates.

The letter. (1997, November 10). [Online]. Available: http://sunsite.unc.edu/elvis/manatt.html

Levy, S. (1998, February 2). Microsoft's moment of truce. *Newsweek,* 6.

Liberatore, K. (1998, January 20). So what's Yahoo! got to do with it. *MacWorld.* [Online]. Available: http://macworld.zdnet.com/netsmart/features/searchin.links.html [1998, January 20].

Marc Andreessen, co-founder of Netscape. (1997). *Jones telecommunications and multimedia encyclopedia homepage.* [Online]. Available: www.digitalcentury.com/encyclo/update/andreess.htm [1998, January 21].

Markus, M. L. (1990). Toward a "critical mass" theory of interactive media. In J. Fulk & C. Steinfield (Eds.), *Organizations and communication technology* (pp. 194–218). Newbury Park, CA: Sage Publications.

Markoff, J. (1998, January 28). Gates goes on the offensive during Silicon Valley visit. *New York Times.* [Online]. Available: http://www.nytimes.com/library/cyber/week/012898microsoft.html [1998, January 28].

Martinez, M. (1997, December 15). Domain name registrations co. ready for rivals. *Advertising Age 68,* 44.

Maudlin, M. L. (1995). *Measuring the Web with Lycos.* [Online]. Available: http://lycos.cs.cmu.edu

McChesney J., & Edwards, B. (1997, September 9). *Morning Edition.* Washington, DC: Public Broadcasting Service.

McGarvey, J. (1996, January). Latest net survey: 9.5 million active surfers. *Inter@ctive Week,* 9.

Microsoft probe to explore new frontiers. (1997, October 23). *St. Louis Post Dispatch,* p. 8B.

MIDS. (1995). Third MIDS Internet demographic survey. Matrix Information and Directory Services, Austin, TX. [Online]. Available: http://www3.mids.org/ids3/pr9510.html

Minister living alone gets on-line aid after seizure. (1996, February, 22). *CNN Interactive.* [Online]. Available: http://cnn.com/TECH/9602/Internet_rescue/index.html [1998, January 7].

Murphy, R. (1997, January 17). The InterNic year in review. [Online]. Available: http://rs.internic.net/nic-support/nicnews/jan97/txt/yearinreview.txt

Murray, J. A. E., Bradley, H., Craigie, W. A., & Onions, C. T. (1989). *The Oxford English Dictionary.* 2nd ed. Oxford: Oxford University Press.

National Academy of Sciences (1995). *Evolving the high performance computing and communications initiative to support the nation's information infrastructure.* Washington, DC: National Academy of Sciences.

Network Solutions, Inc. (1995, November 23). NSI domain name dispute policy statement (World Wide Web). [Online]. Available: http://rs.internic.net/domain-info/internic-domain-4.html

Neufeld, E. (1997, May 5). Where are audiences going? *MediaWeek, 7* (18), S22–S29.

New top level domains and registries proposed. (1997, April). *Internet Marketing & Technology Report, 3* (4). Carlsbad, CA: Computer Economics, Inc., 8.

1995 Kilby Young Innovator. (1997). [Online]. Available: http://dc.smu.edu/kilby/Berners.html

No need to phone. (1998, January 26). *Newsweek,* 15

O'Reilly survey sets U.S. Internet size at 5.8 million. (1995). Sebastopol, CA: O'Reilly Publishing. [Online]. Available: www.ora.com/research

Ortiz, C. (1996, August 21). Browser battle. *St. Louis Post Dispatch,* p. 5C.

Otte, P. (1994). *The information superhighway: Beyond the Internet.* Indianapolis, IN: Que Corporation.

Pavlik, J. (1996). *New media technologies.* Boston: Allyn and Bacon.

Peters, R., & Sikorski, R. (1997, June 20). How to use Usenet. *Science, 276* (5320), 1893–94.

Petrozzello, D. (1997, December 15). Image boost, choices key to "cablenet." *Broadcasting and Cable,* 105.

Pitter, K., Amato, S., Callahan, J., Kerr, N., & Tilton, E. (1995). *Every student's guide to the Internet.* San Francisco: McGraw-Hill.

Poletti, T. (1996, July 29). Prodigy merges with investor International Wireless. *Reuter Business Report.* Available: Lexis-Nexis.

Prodigy, Inc., secures $179 million in funding through private placement. *Business Wire, Inc.* Available: Lexis-Nexis.

Rambler, M. (1998, March 2). Shocking discoveries. *Newsweek,* 88.

Ramstad, E. (1996, August 26). Traffic cop: InterNIC keeping movements in sync on Internet. *St. Louis Post Dispatch*, p. 5C.

Registration services. (1998, February 5). InterNic homepage. [Online]. Available: http://rs2.internic.net/rs-internic.html [1998, February 12].

Rodger, W. (1997, December 22). Judge asks M'soft to explain itself. *Inter@ctive Week*, 7.

Rodger, W. (1998a, February 9). Clinton's domain plan stirs pot. *Inter@ctive Week*, 7.

Rodger, W. (1998b, January 12). IANA may hold the cards in domain name game. *Inter@ctive Week*, 7.

Shaw, R. (1997, August 25). Netscape's latest offers more from TV sites. *Electronic Media*, 10, 34.

Sorting out the identity crisis. (1996, November 11). *MediaWeek*, 33.

Spangler, T. (1998, January 19). More choices coming for your domain-name dollar. *WebWeek*. [Online]. Available: http://www.Webweek.com/current...structure/19980120-dollar.html [1998, January 20].

Taylor, C. (1997, July 5). Net use adds to decline in TV use; Radio stable. *Billboard*, 85.

Tedesco, R. (1997, October 27). DOJ acts to deter Microsoft 'Net dominance. *Broadcasting and Cable*, 47.

Tim Berners-Lee. (1997). *Peking University homepage*. [Online]. Available: http://www.pku.edu.cn/on_line/w3html/people/Berners-Lee-Bio.html

Tim Berners-Lee Bio. (1997). *World Wide Web consortium homepage*. [Online]. Available: http://www.w3.org/People/Berners-Lee/Longer.html [1998, January 21].

Tittel, E., & James, S. (1995). *HTML for dummies*. Foster City, CA: IDG Books.

Tolhurst, W. W., Pike, M. A., & Blanton, K. A. (1994). *Using the Internet*, special edition. Indianapolis, IN: Que Corporation.

Vinton Cerf. (1994, June). *Computer Sciences Corporation homepage*. [Online]. Available: http://www.csc.com/csc_vanguard/bios/v_cerf.html [1998, January 17].

Web founder: Tim Berners-Lee. (1996). [Online]. Available: http://www.cytex.com/mitsc/sp96/sp96kcet.htm

What's your daily dose? (1997, November 18). *PC Magazine*, 9.

Why Internet Advertising. (1997, May 5). *MediaWeek, 7* (18), S8–S13.

Yahoo! Dictionary Online (1997). [Online]. Available: http://www.zdnet.com/yil/content

CHAPTER
TWO

SEARCHING THE WEB

Growing up without a father was difficult for Dora Luna. Born to immigrant parents, Dora knew only that her father had gone back to his native Mexico to find work, but then never returned home to her and her mother. Although she often thought about her father, she did not have the slightest clue of how to locate him. Then thirty years later, she found him through the Web.

At a friend's office one day, Dora accessed the Web for the first time. While surfing, she stumbled on a site that specifically searches for people. She impulsively entered her father's name, and much to her amazement, a few seconds later she had his address and phone number in Ciudad Juarez, Mexico. That evening Dora and her father were tearfully reunited on the telephone, and a month later both hugged and cried when he arrived in Los Angeles for a visit. Dora's father had never even heard of the Internet, but calls it miraculous. Dora agrees.

("California Woman Finds," 1997)

Every day millions of Americans in search of information and entertainment are turning on their computers and connecting to the World Wide Web. Most likely, a Web session opens with a browser's homepage, and then, all too often, users ask themselves, "Now what do I do?" "How do I find what I'm looking for?" and "Can I trust the information I find?"

The Web is an intricate information retrieval system that can befuddle even the most experienced users. Unlike a library where the Dewey Decimal System determines the location of books and periodicals, or a television guide where program listings are laid out in an easy-to-read grid, the Web cannot be viewed or mapped out in its entirety, and often users find it difficult to find the information they are seeking. There are Web "maps" available that show the interconnections among major categories of sites, but these are very general and are like a map of the United States that shows the interstate highways but not any of the other roadways. Such a map is not very useful. To many, searching on the Web is like taking all of the books from the country's libraries and throwing them into one pile, and then trying to find information about Tom Sawyer. Good luck!

To facilitate Web traveling, "search services" were developed that categorize the millions of Web sites for easy access. Users merely enter key search terms for a list of clickable links to sites that are likely to contain the information they are seeking. There are many strategies that can be used to narrow searches to specific information and lessen the chances of getting a list of thousands of links.

Chapter 2 begins with a discussion of the credibility of online sources and using the Web for research, including a section about citing Web sources for research papers. Next, it traces the development of search services and search engines, discusses how they work, and gives tips for online search strategies. Further, since many students are learning to use Web-posted information for writing research reports and other classroom assignments, this chapter directs Web users to communication-related sites and to other Web resources.

TRUSTING WEB SOURCES

The credibility of information posted to the Web is of great concern. Though much of what is found on the Web is accurate and reliable, there are many Web sites that contain false and misleading information. Searches do not differentiate between trustworthy Web sites and those that lack credibility. Users must cast a critical eye to the Web if they are to become confident consumers of Web information.

A Web page can be created by almost anyone who has access to a server and has some rudimentary knowledge of HTML. The Web is a largely unregulated medium where editorial content can be posted without verification. Though a Web page may look as though it comes from an official or legitimate source, a campaign analyst once warned that its author may be some guy named Joe typing away in his basement in Dubuque. As more people begin to rely on the Web as a primary source of information, its credibility becomes of fundamental concern, especially if "Joe from Dubuque" creates a site that appears as trustworthy as those posted by the news media or other official sources (Noble, 1996).

Public perception of the news media's credibility has dropped considerably during the 1990s. By 1997 people were as likely to believe what they heard from a lawyer or a Congressperson as what they heard from a newspaper reporter ("News Junkies, News Critics," 1997). In the face of declining confidence in the mass media, a pertinent concern is the degree of trust in online information from unknown sources as well as from well-known sources such as the *New York Times Online*. Credibility is crucial if the public is going to continue to embrace and accept the Web. If people do not trust or believe what they see or hear in the traditional media or from online media sources, they are less likely to pay attention to it (Gaziano, 1988). The public's lack of trust in information obtained from the Web could keep it from becoming a major source of news and information. For the Web to become a true competitor of traditional media sources, the public must view it as a trustworthy and believable medium.

Public Trust in the Web

Although many studies have looked at the public's perception of trustworthiness and believability of traditional media sources, credibility levels of Web information are just beginning to be assessed. When judging political candidate information, one study found that almost three-quarters of the respondents reported Web pages as more in-depth than television and slightly more than four out of ten respondents said the Web was less biased than television (Brady, 1996). Another study revealed that slightly more than half agreed that information found on the Web is accurate and believable ("One-in-Ten Voters," 1996). When comparing online media sites, such as newspapers and television networks on the Web, to their traditionally delivered counterparts, online sources were consistently judged more credible (Johnson & Kaye, 1997). Other research, however, shows that more people trust sources such as CNN and the *New York Times* than the Internet. Web credibility is a new issue, and before a clearer picture of the public's level of trust in the Web can emerge, much research is still needed.

While evidence remains scarce on whether individuals perceive the Web to be credible, several analysts have examined whether Internet information *should* be judged as trustworthy as traditional sources. An assumed strength of the Web—"that it is a freewheeling, unregulated outpost of opinion and expression—might also weaken its value as a credible information source" (Johnson & Kaye, 1998, p. 326). While traditional news sources and other organizations and companies are held to both rigorous professional and social standards and pressures to provide accurate and unbiased information, Web sites posted by Joe from Dubuque are not subject to such constraints (Calabrese & Borchert, 1996; Starobin, 1996). Additionally, many parody sites, which look like the ones posted by legitimate or official sources, have cropped up on the Web. Well-designed parody sites may mislead users, especially Web novices, into believing they are visiting official sites when in fact they are not. Even more experienced Web users may land inside a parody site, just past the opening page that may post a disclaimer.

Messages from Usenet and other discussion forums may be deemed even less believable than Web sites. Standards for judging a source's believability include the source's expertise and bias, as well as the receiver's prior knowledge and impressions of a source. It is unlikely that discussion participants have much knowledge of each other; thus, careful examination of supporting data, believability, and presentation is crucial.

Evaluating Web Content

Pierre Salinger, former press secretary to President Kennedy, learned a hard lesson when he mistook theory and speculation for truth. In July 1996, TWA Flight 800 inexplicably exploded and fell into the Atlantic Ocean. After many months of public speculation, the cause of the explosion was still unknown. Salinger announced he had obtained a document from French Intelligence sources that purported the plane was downed by a U.S. military missile, a fact the article claimed the government was covering up. Based on this information, Salinger publicly accused the government of concealing the cause of the crash. It was soon discovered that Salinger's document was identical to one that had been floating around several Internet newsgroups and was probably started by conspiracy theorists who had little knowledge of what happened to the plane and were just speculating based on media reports. Salinger was publicly belittled by the government and media for not checking the source of his information and for blindly believing what was on the Internet.

In response to the Salinger incident, a *New York Times* article mused that theorizing and talking about plane crashes have been happening for years, but they used to be called gossip (Wald, 1996). Now, with the Internet firmly in place, public speculation in the form of newsgroups, e-mail, or Web sites has taken on greater credibility. Many experts share the belief that people seize on Internet information as true because of a basic distrust in conventional media.

With careful evaluation of Web content, users do not have to fall victim to false information or unscrupulous sources. People are bombarded every day with so much information that in an instant they choose which messages to ignore, which to pay attention to, and which to believe. Generally, message credibility is weighed against a set of criteria set by each individual. Some people will only believe what they see on television, others believe only what they read in daily newspapers, while others put faith in the supermarket tabloids.

Verifying Web Content

The amount of unregulated content posted on Web pages requires users to assess critically the information they come across. Users cannot assume that just because information is on the Web that it is true, accurate, or reliable. The following are tips for evaluating the credibility of Web pages.

1. The Web page's URL should be carefully read and deciphered. The first part of the URL is the host's name, which tells where the information is coming from, though not necessarily who is the author. For example, if the host's name is nbc.com, then the NBC network is hosting the page. Once the host is known, users can decide if it is a reputable and legitimate source.

2. The content on many Web sites, especially those posted by the news and entertainment media, is editorially reviewed before going online. Often, news and other information is first written for print, television, or radio, and then transferred to the Web. Much of this information is subject to editorial standards and review.

There are many Web-only magazines and journals that do not have a non-online counterpart. Many of these are reputable and editorially reviewed. However, many "zines" are fly-by-night operations posting questionable content. If in doubt about the reliability of information, the site's manager can be e-mailed and asked for the editorial review policy and the authors' backgrounds.

3. All too often, Web users mistake the date they accessed the page, or the posting day, for the date the document was originally published online. Careful scanning of the page will often uncover the day the information was current, the day it was posted online, and the last time the page was updated. Many online news sources post the day's current information and will archive events in chronological order by date. The correct citation date is the date on which the event was originally published on the online site from which the information is being retrieved.

On many Web sites the publishing day is not always obvious. For instance, the text of a speech that Bill Clinton gave in July 1995 could be posted on the Web in April 1997. A novice researcher who accesses the page in November 1997 may inadvertently use either the access day or the posting day as the day Clinton delivered the speech, or may confuse the day the speech was delivered with the online publishing date.

Another Web site operator may post a news story that begins, "Two grizzly bears escaped from the city zoo this morning striking terror in nearby neighborhoods." If the operator neglects to post the dateline, readers will not know when the escape occurred and may mistakenly use the date they accessed the story as the publishing date. Or they may use the date the page was last updated as the day the escape actually occurred.

Web pages should be carefully scanned for the date the information was current, the date the information was posted, and when or if the information was last updated. Pertinent dates can often be found at the bottom of the page, or near a document's title, or in the URL itself. For example, the publishing date of an article that appeared in *Advertising Age* online is listed as part of the URL. The last part of the URL shows that the article was published on August 22, 1997:

http://adage.com/ns search/interactive/daily/archives/19970822

4. Information should be obtained directly from the primary source and not from a Web site operator who wrote his or her own interpretation of the original material. For example, researchers interested in information about the weather phenomenon El Niño should look on the *National Weather Service* homepage, or other meteorological sites operated by scientists and weather experts, and not on a college student's online term paper site.

The Web makes it easy to check the primary source of information. For example, if an online document contains data that was originally reported by the *National Association of Broadcasters*, the researcher should verify the document's accuracy by going directly to the NAB's page and looking up the data. Often, hypertext icons and buttons within online documents will link researchers directly to the original source.

5. Several sources should be checked to verify Web content. Information obtained from a Web site should be compared to information obtained from other sites and non-online sources. All sources of information should be verified experts and reliable authorities on the researched topic.

Citing Web Sources

Although often highly dreaded, written papers are required of students in many college-level courses. The Web can often make the process of researching and gathering information easy, fun, convenient, and less time-consuming. Information that is gathered and used in a paper must be attributed to its original source, whether a book, journal, magazine, or Web page. For example, any information taken from the FCC's Web site must be attributed to the FCC, and it must be specified that the information came from its Web site and not from another type of publication.

Online sources can be easily moved from one Web address to another, and are often done so without informing Web users or providing a link to the new address. Therefore, it is especially important that complete citation information is recorded, so that others can easily retrieve the same document if needed. For example, an older citation listed an outdated URL for *The Internet Index*, a resource for Internet trivia. Apparently, the site shortened its URL and thus could no longer be found at its original address. However, because the citation also listed the author's name, a quick name search on Alta Vista brought up listings of several of the author's sites, including the new URL for *The Internet Index*.

BOX 2.1 ELECTRONIC STYLES: EXAMPLES OF APA AND MLA

1. APA: Magazine Article

Style:

Author. (year, month day). Article title. *Magazine, Volume*. [Medium]. Available: URL [Date of access].

Example:

Cuneo, A. Z. (1997, November 17). Holiday shopping could spur booming Web commerce. *Advertising Age, 68*. [Online]. Available: http://adage.com/ns-search/interactive/daily/archives/19971117/id19971117-12.html [1997, December 15].

2. MLA: Magazine Article

Style:

Author. "Article Title." *Magazine Title*, (Date): Number of pages or paragraphs, or n. pag. (for no pagination). [Medium]. Available: URL. [Date of Access].

Example:

Cuneo, Alice. "Holiday Shopping Could Spur Booming Web Commerce." *Advertising Age*, (17 November 1997): n. pag. [Online]. Available: http://adage.com/ns-search/interactive/daily/archives/19971117/id19971117-12.html [15 December 1997].

Source: Li & Crane, 1996

There are many different styles that can be used for documenting in-text citations and reference lists. Styles set by the American Psychological Association (*APA*) and *Modern Language Association* (MLA) are commonly used in the field of communication. Each organization publishes a manual and has a Web site describing proper styles for documenting online and non-online sources. *Electronic Styles: A Handbook for Citing Electronic Information* and *Online! A Reference Guide to Using Internet Sources* are excellent books for citing online materials using several different styles, including APA and MLA.

USING THE WEB FOR RESEARCH

Research usually begins with a question and the desire to know more about a subject or to discover something new. Research also often begins with trying to solve a problem or finding a new way to do something. Just asking the questions "who," "what," "where," "when," "why," and "how" initiates inquiry. Though many people, especially students, cringe at the word *research*, most people conduct research in their everyday lives without consciously thinking of it as research. Looking in the newspaper for movie listings, price comparison shopping, and calling for airline schedules are just a few examples of the kinds of research people engage in quite frequently.

Knowing how and where to find information saves countless hours and much exasperation. Research has been defined as "systematic inquiry," meaning that proper and thorough examination should be conducted methodically, or step by step (Rubin, Rubin, & Piele, 1996). The subject of inquiry should be as narrow as possible and proper terminology should be used when needed. Knowing which resources are most likely to yield relevant information is vital, as is knowing where to find resources.

With over 150 million pages of information, the Web is an excellent and convenient source of information. Knowledge of search tools and strategies aids users in retrieving documents about most any subject they wish, often without having to go to the library or finding other printed sources. Full-text articles and other information are available online from newspapers, magazines, journals, books, nonprofit organizations, government agencies, online library collections, bibliographic databases, press releases, biographies, almanacs, yellow page listings, and many other helpful resources, such as Usenet Newsgroups, listservs, and discussion forums. Additionally, scholarly publications and papers are appearing online and some are even distributed solely on the Web.

Although there are millions of documents available on the Web, it is still a supplement and not a replacement for traditional sources. Many books, articles, and other pieces of information are not available on the Web and may never be posted online. Copyrighted books and papers, many academic journals, historic works, statistical information, and other items are not available online. Although many traditional sources have established online sites, they often offer only limited versions and abstracts of their printed content and may charge a fee for the full-text versions even if available.

Search Services

Many Internet users would be lost without search services that hunt for online information. Search services spare users the agony of clicking through hundreds of Web sites without direction. Searching services have become so popular that they are now the preferred method of finding online information by almost three-quarters of all Web users. The remaining users find online information and Web sites as provided by the media, friends, and relatives, and by linking from one site to another.

Searching services are generally made up of a database of Web sites and a search engine that provides the capability of searching online indexes. Though the

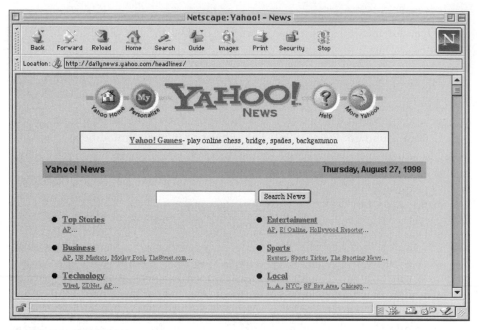

FIGURE 2.1 Yahoo! Homepage

term **search engine** is commonly used as an overall term describing search services, it is only one part of the many features provided by the service. For example, the search service Lycos uses a search engine called PURSUIT; Yahoo!'s search engine is licensed from Open Text; while Harvest uses several search engines (Courtois, Baer, & Stark, 1995; Standard & Poors, 1996). Although Yahoo!, Alta Vista, and other similar search services are commonly called search engines, this book will refer to them by the more appropriate description *search services,* especially since many, such as Yahoo!'s City Maps section that displays road maps of U.S. cities, offer benefits in addition to searching.

Yahoo!

Yahoo! was one of the first Web services that provided users with the capability of searching for online information. In April 1994, two Stanford University electrical engineering graduate students, David Filo and Jerry Yang, casually started compiling lists of their favorite Web sites. As the list grew longer, they started categorizing the sites and later subcategorizing, working from their campus trailer office. Pretty soon, the pair had created a kind of Yellow Pages for the Internet that kept doubling, tripling, and quadrupling in size and was increasingly popular with Stanford's students. Dubbed *Yahoo!* (Yet Another Hierarchical Officious Oracle), the list became one of the first Web searching tools and found a home on Stanford's computers, but only for as long as Filo and Yang were students. Along came Marc Andreessen, one of the creators of Mosaic and Netscape Communications, Inc., who envisioned Yahoo! as a tool to facilitate and boost Web use. He set up Yahoo! so it could be accessed from Netscape's main menu page, taking its popularity beyond Stanford's students.

Yahoo! ranks as one of the most popular search services, averaging close to 60 million page views per day ("Yahoo! Reports," 1998; "Yahoo!'s U.S. Audience," 1997). Boasting a large database, Yahoo! organizes over 230,000 Web site listings in fourteen major categories, and in about 16,000 hierarchical subcategories. Like most all search services, Yahoo! does not charge users for its service but rather derives its revenue by selling space on its Web pages to over 250 advertisers (Standard & Poors, 1996; Tedesco, 1996; "Yahoo! In the Black," 1997).

In April 1996, Yahoo! began trading on the NASDAQ exchange with an initial public offering of $13 per share, which generated approximately $35 million in net proceeds (Standard & Poors, 1996). What started as a hobby became a full-time and very lucrative job for Filo and Yang, who never did finish their Ph.D.s, but became multimillionaires instead. Now worth about $140 million each, they recently gave Stanford University $2 million to endow a chair in the School of Engineering ("Chief Yahoos," 1997).

Yahoo! is certainly not the only Web searching service available. Others include Lycos, Alta Vista, and Web Crawler. Though they all provide Web searching capabilities, they differ in their search methods and in the additional services they may offer.

How Search Engines Work

When selecting a search service it is important to keep in mind that not all search services, their search engines, and the databases they search are the same. Techniques for database searching and indexing, and retrieving and displaying results, may differ. Also, the availability of advanced searching strategies may vary, and few have the capability of exhaustively looking through the entire Web. Commonalities and differences among searching services are discussed below.

DATABASE CONSTRUCTION   Most Web databases are automatically compiled using programs called **spiders, worms,** and **robots,** just to name a few of the more popular terms. These programs find and identify Web pages to index and add to the database. A few Web pages employ manual indexing and abstracting and some allow Webmasters to submit their own pages to the database (Courtois et al., 1995; Yuwono & Lee, 1996).

EASY-TO-USE SEARCHES   Most search engines provide easy-to-use forms on which users enter key words and phrases. Subject categories help users narrow their search terms and strategies, and advanced searching capabilities increase the chances of a more relevant results list. Additionally, some services, like Alta Vista, even link users to their page containing search strategies and tips.

ORDER OF ENTRY   Many search engines do not require search terms to be entered in their proper order. For example, on Lycos, entering "pig latin" as a key search term is the same as entering "latin pig." However, Excite and Alta Vista, for example, require the exact order of entry. Some search engines allow search terms to be entered as phrases. In many cases the order of entry is crucial. For example, "All you can eat" is not the same as "Can you eat all" on Alta Vista and Yahoo!, but the two phrases yield similar results on Excite and Lycos. Knowing the proper way to enter terms for each search service significantly improves the chances of finding relevant documents.

NUMBERED SETS   Web search engines do not provide for the reuse of previously numbered search terms or data sets. In other words, the entire search query must be entered in one statement. For example, the search term "children and television and cartoons" must be entered as one phrase, rather than separately, as allowed by many bibliographic databases such as Dialog.

TRUNCATION   To *truncate* literally means to "lop off" or to "shorten." This means that several variations of a word are searched. In some cases, users need to signify with an asterisk how they want the search term truncated. For example, "telecommu*" will yield results containing the words *telecommute, telecommuting,* and *telecommuter.* Often search terms are shortened or automatically truncated by default. For example, the search term "computerize" may be truncated to "computer," and thus documents containing the words *computer* and *computerized* would be retrieved. Conversely, suffixes are often added to shorter search terms. For example, the search term "solar system" could yield documents containing the terms *solarium, systematic,* and *systematize.* Also, many search engines will find shorter words within a longer word. For example, entering the term "cuss" could yield documents containing the word *concussion* (Courtois, 1996; Ding & Marchionini, 1996).

FIELDS   Some databases will search different fields of HTML documents. A field is the part of the document in which the search term appears, such as the URL, header, title, and text. Some search engines will produce a list of documents that include the search term only if it is included in certain fields, such as the URL or the title. Other search engines will produce an output list that includes documents in which the search term appears in the text and in other fields.

RELEVANCY RANKING   Each search service sets its own criteria by which to rank and display search results. Output varies from one service to another but generally all provide links to primary sources. There are several ways to rank the results list. Most Web search engines use **relevancy ranking,** which displays the documents in the order of most likely relevance as determined by criteria set by each search service. The criteria used are usually a combination of the number of search terms contained within each document, placement of terms within the document, and a weight assigned to words within a topic. For example, if the search term "whale" is entered, the search engine may also seek out documents containing the word *cetacean* (another word for whale), and items containing the most occurrences of the words *whale* or *cetacean*. Also, documents in which the search terms are closer to the beginning of the article will often appear at the top of a relevancy-ranked output list (Courtois et al., 1995; Ding & Marchionini, 1996; Zorn, Emanoil, & Marshall, 1996; Tenopir, 1992).

CUSTOMIZED RESULTS LIST   Many search engines allow users to customize the output by specifying the number of retrieved items to display. Rather than receiving a list of one hundred Web sites, a searcher can limit the display to just the ten most relevant items. Other search services go a step further by allowing users to set a relevancy threshold score so only items meeting the specified threshold criteria are displayed (Courtois et al., 1995).

DIRECT LINKS AND OTHER FEATURES   Most every search engine lists the most relevant Web sites with a short description of the page's content. Each description contains a clickable link for direct access to the source.

"What's New" pages, "Frequently Asked Questions (FAQs)," and searching tips are also featured on many search service sites, accessible through direct highlighted links. Additional features include news headlines, links to shopping and entertainment resources, and U.S. city maps and driving directions.

Searching Strategies

Effective Web searching takes finesse and a knowledge of techniques. All too often searches yield thousands of documents, and at other times none at all. Understanding and employing proper search strategies can save frustration, hours of time, and a walk to the library. Keep in mind that every searching service is slightly different. A strategy that works on one search engine may not work on another. It is a process of trial and error to discover which searching functions are supported by which services. Ineffective searches can be easily avoided by checking each search service's "help" pages before beginning to search. "Help" pages outline the various search

BOX 2.2 COMMON BOOLEAN OPERATORS

Operator	Search Syntax	Result
AND	Trees AND Forestry	Documents about trees and forestry
OR	Sprites OR Elves	Pages about sprites or elves
NOT	Homer NOT Alaska	Any Web page about anyone or anyplace named Homer, except Homer, Alaska
NEAR	Cigarettes NEAR/10 smoking	Articles containing the word *smoking* within ten words of *cigarettes*
ADJ	Movie ADJ Stars	Documents that use the term *movie stars,* but not those that contain the words *movies* and *stars,* such as in the sentence "Drive-in theaters are great for watching movies under the stars," because the terms *movies* and *stars* are not adjacent to each other.
*	comput*	Articles containing words beginning with the letters *comput* such as *computer, computers, computerize,* and *computate.*

methods used by the service and generally guide users and give them tips for successful search strategies.

BOOLEAN LOGIC Most search services support the use of **Boolean operators** that narrow and customize searches. Boolean operators are terms that define the relationship between the search words and terms. Operators such as AND, OR, NOT, NEAR, FOLLOWED BY are commonly used for specifying searches. For example, entering the name "Homer" will yield a list of thousands of documents including any Web page about anyone named Homer, including Homer Simpson, and information about the town of Homer, Alaska. A specific search for Homer Simpson should be entered as "Homer AND Simpson." Taking the search one step further, using *nested Boolean*—"Homer (NOT Alaska OR Simpson)"—will result in documents containing the name "Homer" but not those containing "Simpson" or "Alaska."

COMPARING SEARCH QUERIES Several researchers tested and compared the specific search syntax required by Alta Vista, Excite, and Lycos (Chu & Rosenthal,

1996). The researchers developed ten reference questions (search terms) and constructed each as proper search queries for each of the three search engines. Some of the search terms consist of a single word, some require Boolean operators, some test truncation and case-sensitivity, and while most deal with general themes, some concern specific topics. Using Chu and Rosenthal's method, new search terms were constructed and proper search syntax was compared among Alta Vista, Excite, Lycos, and Infoseek. The search terms and the corresponding syntax required by each of the three search services can be found in Box 2.3.

Using Search Services

Besides Yahoo!, Alta Vista, Excite, and Lycos, there are many other search services available on the Web. As mentioned earlier, though each service provides searching capabilities, each differs in the way the searches are conducted and in the items retrieved. Following are descriptions and listings of some of the more popular search services currently available.

ALTA VISTA   Introduced to the Web in December 1995, Alta Vista has emerged as one of the top Web searching services, and as of January 1998, it indexes the full text of over 50 million Web pages and is accessed 23 million times each day (Harding, 1997; Liberatore, 1997). Alta Vista allows Boolean, term and phrase, proximity, and field searching, and right-hand truncation requiring an asterisk. The service also conducts natural language searches, such as "What is the state flower of Florida?" Although many search services claim to read natural language queries, they yield more pertinent results if the search term is as succinct as possible. Using the previous example, entering only the words "state flower of Florida" is more likely to result in closer matches than "What is the state flower of Florida?"

Order of display is determined by relevancy ranking. Phrases can be searched by enclosing them in double quotes and searches can be specified by field. The results list can be configured for either compact or detailed display with items presented in groups of ten (Chu & Rosenthal, 1996; Courtois, 1996; Zorn et al., 1996).

The search service also lets users customize their search by choosing from among twenty-five languages. The service will return search results and Web pages published only in the specified language. Other features include finding linking pages, searching within a range of dates, and image searching.

EXCITE   As part of the new generation of search tools, Excite has given many a cause to celebrate. Excite's database is updated weekly and is loaded with 50 million fully indexed Web pages, categorized within about twenty major headings (Harding, 1997; Liberatore, 1997).

One of its finest features is its ability to "concept" search for synonyms and related terms rather than just matching the search terms. For example, researchers

BOX 2.3 SEARCH TERMS AND PROPER SYNTAX FOR ALTA VISTA, EXCITE, LYCOS, AND INFOSEEK

1. Search Term: NAACP
   Alta Vista[1]: NAACP
   Excite/Lycos[2]: NAACP
   Infoseek: NAACP

2. Search Term: television violence and children's programming
   Alta Vista: "television violence" + "children's programming"
   Excite/Lycos: television violence and children's programming
   Infoseek: "television violence" + "children's programming"

3. Search Term: Internet and children
   Alta Vista: Internet + children
   Excite/Lycos: Internet children
   Infoseek: Internet children

4. Search Term: American journalism history
   Alta Vista: "American journalism history"
   Excite/Lycos: American journalism history
   Infoseek: American journalism history

5. Search Term: schizophrenia in teenagers
   Alta Vista: schizophrenia + teen*
   Excite/lycos: schizophrenia teen*
   Infoseek: schizophrenia + teen*

6. Search Term: interactivity
   Alta Vista: interactivity
   Excite/Lycos: interactivity
   Infoseek: interactivity

7. Search Term: Columbia Broadcasting System
   Alta Vista: "Columbia Broadcasting System"
   Excite/Lycos: Columbia Broadcasting System
   Infoseek: Columbia Broadcasting System

8. Search Term: Web in schools
   Alta Vista: Web in schools
   Excite/Lycos: Web in schools
   Infoseek: Web in schools

1. Alta Vista uses a "+" (plus sign) in place of the operator "AND" and a "−" (minus sign) in place of "NOT."
2. In every one of these cases, Lycos and Excite had identical syntax (Chu & Rosenthal, 1996).

FIGURE 2.2 Search Services

found that inputting the search term "intellectual rights" uncovered documents about the topic that contain related terms such as "software piracy" and "copyright law," even if the items do not actually contain the exact search term (Chu & Rosenthal, 1996, p. 129). Boolean operators are limited to AND and OR with more weight assigned to terms using AND.

Excite keeps a staff of professional journalists on hand to write lively, witty descriptions and reviews of 150,000 Web sites (Courtois, 1996; Liberatore, 1997). As an added feature, Excite automatically generates abstracts of each Web page it indexes (Chu & Rosenthal, 1996).

INFOSEEK GUIDE   One of the forerunners in Web searching, InfoSeek was chosen in 1995 by *PC Computing* as the best Internet search tool (Courtois, 1996). InfoSeek claims to search 11.5 million sites, and bills itself as the most selective, most current, and most popular Web database (Liberatore, 1997). InfoSeek provides access to eight other databases, most providing full-text output.

InfoSeek's database of over one million Web pages, along with FTP and Gopher resources, is partially updated weekly, with thorough revisions each month, and purports to delete duplicate URL entries (Zorn et al., 1996). For complicated searches, InfoSeek provides special operators such as capitalization for proper names, hyphens, or double quotations for adjacent searching, square brackets for proximity searching, plus and minus signs for AND and NOT operators, and commas to separate terms not usually adjacent to each other (Courtois,

1996; Ding & Marchionini, 1996; Liberatore, 1997). InfoSeek also deciphers natural language questions but works best when the search term is as concise as possible.

Users can specify whether to search through all Web pages or only pages that have been reviewed. InfoSeek uses a complex relevancy ranking scheme to give the first one hundred hits for each search, displaying ten finds per screen.

LYCOS   Another popular search service, Lycos boasts a database covering more than 95 percent of the Web, including FTP and Gopher files. The name *Lycos* is derived from the first five letters of the Latin word for wolf spider, *Lycosa Tarentula*. Using its own patented technique, Lycos spiders locate and index the most popular sites and refresh its database daily with full updates every two months. In January 1996, *PC World* named Lycos the best Web search service. Originally designed at Carnegie Mellon University, Lycos was purchased by America Online and became Lycos, Inc. Rather than indexing full text, Lycos extracts a document's title and the smaller of either the first twenty lines of text or one-fifth of the article (Chu & Rosenthal, 1996; Courtois, 1996; Ding & Marchionini, 1996).

Lycos recognizes Boolean logic, and simplifies the process by providing a clickable menu of operators. Truncation is automatic and can be broadened by adding a dollar sign after the search term, which increases the relevancy score of words built on the term's root. Truncation can be turned off by adding a period after a search term (Courtois, 1996; Liberatore, 1997). Phrase and adjacency searching are not supported and order of entry is unimportant (Courtois et al., 1995). Users set the minimum relevancy score by selecting the "match level" for their search. A "close" or "strong" match restricts the search to the most relevant hits, while a "loose" match results in less relevant items.

Searchers select from among four display formats: output, summary, detailed, and standard. With summary format, results are displayed as titles and clickable links. The standard format generally includes the title, abstract, URL, and file size. Detailed output includes descriptions, abstracts, URL, file size, ranking score, words matched in page, and links to outside resources. Users also get to select the number of hits to display (1–99,999) (Courtois et al., 1995).

WEBCRAWLER   Online since April 1994, WebCrawler has since been purchased by America Online. WebCrawler identifies and retrieves primary Web resources despite having a smaller index than other search services. WebCrawler is a user friendly searching aid and is a great place for Web novices to learn basic searching techniques.

Searches are easily conducted through pull-down options boxes accompanied by subject headings. Boolean operators are supported, and users can specify display as title or as summaries and can limit the number (10, 25, or 100) of documents to retrieve. Using relevancy ranking, WebCrawler determines the order of retrieved items by the number of times the search terms appear in the document (Courtois et al., 1995; Courtois, 1996).

YAHOO!   Though not as powerful as other search aids, Yahoo! is popular among Web users. An abbreviated Yahoo! subject directory is easily and conveniently accessed by clicking the "Net Directory" button on Netscape's homepage.

Yahoo! only indexes titles, URLs, and comments, limiting its overall capability. Users can opt to limit a search to a specific topic area, and the Boolean operators AND and OR are supported; however, phrase searching and field specifying are not supported. Additionally, searchers choose the number (100, 200, 300, or unlimited) of retrieved items to be displayed.

A major benefit of Yahoo! is its hierarchical classification scheme that allows users to browse subject headings as an alternative to keyword searching. Yahoo! guides users to the newest items that have been added to their database by identifying them with brightly colored icons.

Yahoo!'s new feature, My Yahoo!, is a personalized guide to the Web that encourages visitors to input their interests and geographic locale in return for personalized information such as local weather and sports reports. My Yahoo! managers position it as a tool that facilitates one-to-one relationships with its customers (Tedesco, 1996).

CUSI, SUSI, and Meta Searching

CUSI (Configurable Unified Search Index), SUSI (Simultaneous Unified Search Index), and Meta (meaning comprehensive or fundamental) are three commonly used terms for consolidated Web databases used for one-stop searching. Users simply enter a search term and choose the databases to be searched. Although CUSI services only search one database at a time, SUSI and Meta services such as Meta-Crawler, search several databases simultaneously. Additionally, these services access many Internet indexes such as WAIS, and Usenet FAQs. The convenience of searching several databases from one service is the primary advantage of using consolidated services. However, they tend to take longer to produce an output list and do not indicate if a database is down and unsearchable.

Consolidated services generally support their own searching syntax and Boolean operators. Users have the advantage of searching the Web through one outlet without having to bother learning the searching syntax of each individual service.

Online Directories

Searching services are similar in that they all use search engines to locate information. However, some services, such as Yahoo! go beyond simply looking for sites;

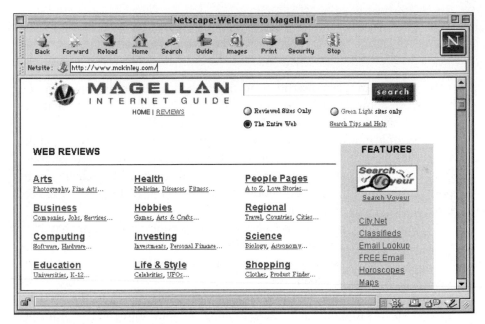

FIGURE 2.3 Magellan Web Page

they are also directories that categorize information by subject areas. Searches via directories can be conducted through the Web at large or within a specific category such as "entertainment" or "medicine." Nondirectory search services, such as Alta Vista, look for information throughout the entire Web. The output lists produced by directories often differ from those posted by nondirectory sites. For example, entering the search term "Prodigy" in Alta Vista yields a list of 34,393 sites. If a searcher is specifically looking for information about the online information provider Prodigy, then he or she must wade through thousands of URLs containing information about the company as well as those about the rock group named Prodigy, or personal pages on the Prodigy site, or any other sites that use the word *prodigy*. In contrast, Yahoo! delivers two overall categories (entertainment/music, and business and economy) containing the term *Prodigy*. Searchers interested in the online service provider company select sites from the business category, while users looking for information about the rock group would click on the music category.

Magellan is another example of a directory that searches the Web and categorizes and provides summaries of over 40,000 Web sites and brief descriptions of another two million sites. The directory, which is owned by Excite, rates each site based on its own set of criteria and informs users of the site's intended audience, its producer, and whether the site contains adult material (Rafter, 1996; Maloney & Goldblatt, 1996).

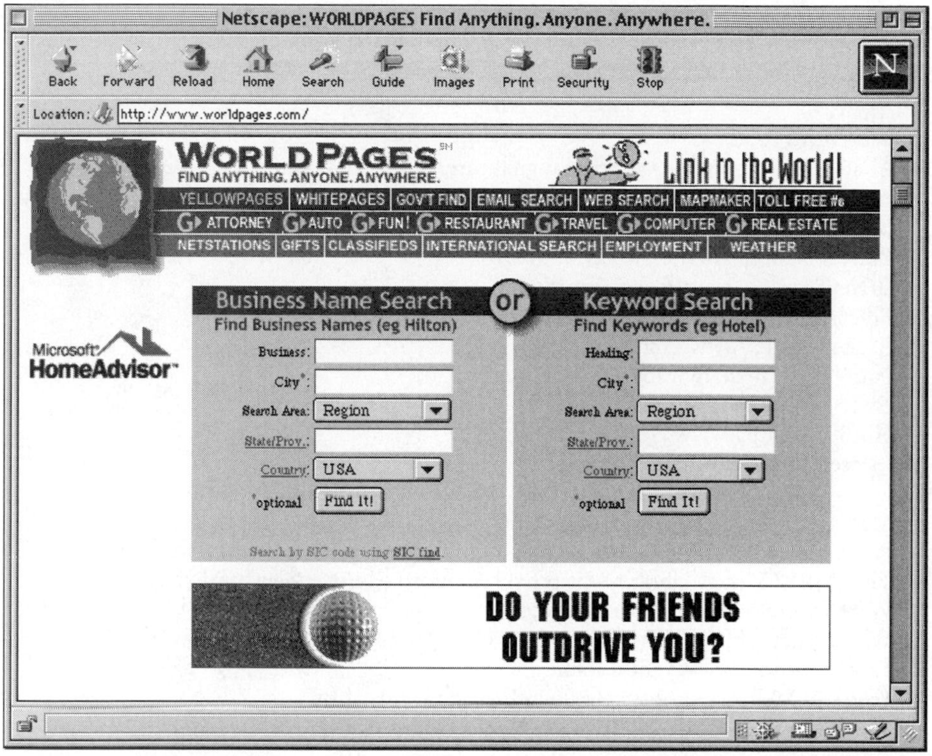

FIGURE 2.4 WorldPages

Searching for People

Many Web sites function as directories of home addresses, telephone numbers, and e-mail addresses of thousands of people around the world. These directories are designed exclusively for searching for people. The *Four-11* Internet White Pages site searches e-mail address and telephone book listings from around the world. *WorldPages* is another international directory of personal e-mail addresses, home addresses, and telephone numbers. The site will also search for government and business listings and Web pages.

Conducting a Search

Suppose students in a mass communication course are required to write a short paper about Microsoft owner Bill Gates. The Web is an excellent resource that can be used along with books and magazines and, in some instances, in place of printed material. Step-by-step instructions for looking up Bill Gates using Alta Vista follow:

BOX 2.4 SEARCH SERVICES AND DIRECTORIES

Searching Tools
Alta Vista—http://www.altavista.digital.com/
Ameritech's Internet Yellow Pages—http://yp.ameritech.net/
Big Yellow—http://s17.bigyellow.com/
BizWiz—http://www.bizwiz.com/bizwiz/
C/Net Search—http://www.search.com
Einet Galaxy—http://galaxy.einet.net/galaxy.html
Excite—http://www.excite.com
Four-11—http://www.four11.com/
GoTo—http://www.goto.com/
HotBot—http://www.HotBot.com/
Infoseek—http://infoseek.com/
Lycos—http://lycos.cs.cmu.edu/
Magellan—http://www.mckinley.com/
Point—http://www.pointcom.com
The WWW Virtual Library—http://vlib.stanford.edu/overview.html
WebCrawler—http://Webcrawler.com/
WorldPages—http://www.worldpages.com/
Yahoo!—http://www.yahoo.com/
YelloWWWeb Pages—http://yellowwWeb.com/index.htm

Search Engines for Usenet Newsgroups
Deja News—http://www.dejanews.com/
Inktomi—http:inktomi.berkeley.edu
Starting Point—http://www.stpt.com/

CUSI, SUSI, Meta Search Services
All-In-One Search Page—http://www.albany.net/
Dogpile—http://www.dogpile.com/
Find-It!—http://www.iTools.com/find-it/
MetaCrawler—http://www.metacrawler.com
NetSearch—http://www.uznet/uzu/sch000.html
SavvySearch—http://www.cs.colostate.edu/~dreiling/smartform.html
W3 Search Engines—http://cuiwww.unige.ch/meta-index.html

To List Pages on the Web
Submit It!—http://www.submit-it.com/

1. Go to the Alta Vista homepage at http://altavista.digital.com

2. Enter the following search phrase: Bill+Gates

3. Click on the type of search desired. Options include searching for documents written in English and form of display.

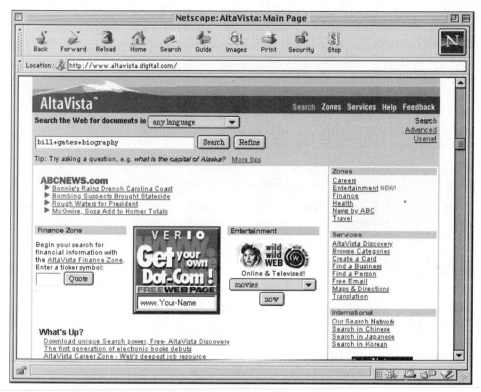

FIGURE 2.5 Step-by-Step Search Using AltaVista

4. Click on the "search" button.
5. The results are printed in the order of relevancy.

The search for Bill Gates yielded 91,927 documents. Topping the list are lampoon sites with titles such as "Bill Gates Is the Devil" and "Bill Gates Goes to Heaven." To limit the search to biographical information, follow the same steps as above except enter the search term as Bill+Gates+biography. The refined search resulted in a list of twenty-four documents about Bill Gates's life.

Selecting a Search Service

Experimenting with searches is a good way for individuals to decide which search tool best meets their needs. Entering the same search terms with different search services and comparing the results produced by each is a good way to assess features, capabilities, and performance, and to determine if some search engines are better suited to particular subject areas than others. Users can quickly become proficient

TABLE 2.1 Comparison of Web Searching Services

	Alta Vista	Excite	InfoSeek	Lycos	Yahoo!	WebCrawler

Fields Indexed	Full-text	Full-text
		URL
		URL refs.
		  summary
			Full-text
			URL
			URL refs.
				20 lines text
				URL
				URL refs.
				100 weighty
				  word
					URL
					Title
					  comments
						Full-text

Search Method						
Querying/Browsing	Query	Query & Browse	Query Limited browse	Query Limited browse	Query & Browse	Query & Browse
Typing/Selecting	Query	Typing & Selecting	Typing	Typing & Selecting	Typing & Selecting	Typing & Selecting
Search Capabilities						
Boolean search	Yes	Yes	Equivalents of AND, OR, NOT NEAR	No	AND, OR	AND/OR
Bound phrases	Yes	No	No	No	Yes	No
Nested Boolean	Yes	Unknown	No	Unknown	Unknown	Unknown
Case sensitive	Limited	No	Yes	No	No	No
Concept search	No	Yes	Yes	No	Yes	Yes
Exact matching	Yes	Almost	Almost	Yes	Yes	Yes
Field search	Yes	No	No	No	Yes	Yes
Multiple search sets	No	No	No	No	Yes	Yes
Proximity search	Yes	No	Yes	Yes	Yes	Yes
Truncation	Yes*	No	No	Automatic	Yes	Yes
Weighted terms	Yes	Yes	Yes	Yes	No	No
Output						

Display	No limit
	Up to 10
	  per screen
		No limit
		Up to 10
		  per
		  screen
			Up to 100
			10 per screen
			One format
				No limit
				20, 30, or 40
				  per screen
				Three formats
					10, 25,
					  100, 500
						100 default

Relevancy ranking	Can specify	Yes	Yes	Yes	No	No
Update Frequency	Daily	Unknown	Daily	Weekly	Varies	Daily

Source: Chu & Rosenthal, 1996; Courtois et al., 1995; Ding & Marchionini, 1996; Zorn et al., 1996

in Web searching by investing a small amount of time in trying out various search services and searching strategies. Learning how to use search tools properly can save time and frustration in the long run.

Following is a list of hints and suggestions for searching the Web.

1. The unique features of each search service should be studied. Help screens should be used if needed, and instructions and examples carefully read and followed. "Frequently Asked Questions" pages posted by most services are generally very helpful.

2. It is unlikely that one search service will fulfill every need. Users can expedite their searches by becoming comfortable and proficient with several databases and learning which is most appropriate for the specific types of information they are seeking.

3. The more narrow the search the more relevant the results. It can take a long time to look through the results list for just the right information. Learning to use Boolean operators effectively will decrease the likelihood of getting a results list of thousands of irrelevant documents.

4. Most searching services are very busy handling thousands of requests each minute. Though most have the capability for handling a large number of requests, searches may take less time if conducted during off-peak hours such as late at night.

5. It can be beneficial to try new search services and check on previously used ones for updates and new features. New search services frequently crop up, and some of these become mainstays of the Web while others come and go within a short time (Courtois et al., 1995).

Push Technology

The Web is so jam-packed full of news and information that even the most seasoned users can feel overloaded. Even the creator of Netscape Navigator admits that the Web is adding to information overload. Marc Andreessen asserts that "manually searching the Web is not a sustainable model, long term" (Cortese, 1997, p. 95). Enter push technology.

Push technology is like "letting your fingers do the walking," but in the case of the Web, letting your software do the searching. Information has been pushed to consumers for a long time, but "pushing" has only lately become technologically feasible on the Web. Subscribing to a magazine or newspaper that comes directly to your mailbox or doorstep is an example of "push," whereas going to the newsstand to purchase the latest issue is "pull." Receiving mailings of Eddie Bauer catalogs is "push," going to the mall store is "pull." Direct mail advertisements and television are "push" delivery systems; the information is pushed to consumers even if not requested (Levy, 1997).

Jumping on the push technology band wagon is easier than most people think. The process starts by downloading push software which is available on many Web sites such as the *PointCast Network,* known for its innovative work on push technology. Users register for push services and fill out an online form customizing their news and information preferences. The software then searches through the content and retrieves and delivers the requested items directly to the subscriber's computer. Users are signaled when news is updated and new information is delivered. Early 1997 estimates placed the total push audience at about two million, with an annual growth rate of close to 200,000 new subscribers per month (Shaw, 1997a).

Designed to look like a real pager, *CNN Interactive*'s "shockwave pager" alerts customers of breaking news and headlines every half-hour. *InfoBeat,* a push service, gathers news from sources such as Reuters, Tribune Media Services, and ESPN, and delivers it directly to subscribers' e-mail boxes. The service selects and edits the stories, categorizes them by topic, and then sends out the e-mail newsfeeds to requesting clients (Crotty, 1997).

Though news, sports, and weather are the most likely types of requested information, many marketing and advertising applications are making use of push technology. Constantly updated apartment rental listings are pushed by *Rent Net,* a Web-based relocation service covering about 1,000 cities.

Dubbing itself the next generation of push sites, Netscape's Netcaster delivers information to home computers through "channels" that users "tune in." Netcaster, which operates only with Netscape Navigator 4.0 and later versions, pushes content from providers, such as Disney, CNNfn, ABC News, and others, to their clients' computers as often as the client specifies (e.g., hourly, daily, or weekly). Netcaster subscribers have access to more than seven hundred channels of Web site content from many companies, including Nickelodeon, MTV, TV Guide Entertainment, and Hearst Home Arts. A Netscape spokesman claims that Netcaster "is for all those who are interested in providing a channel or set of dynamic content, much like a newspaper, assembled by professional content aggregators" (Rodriguez, 1997). Netcaster content providers benefit by amassing information from users who must register to use the application (Finnie, 1997; "Netcaster Channel," 1997; Rodriguez, 1997; Shaw, 1997b; Tedesco, 1997).

Push services are being welcomed by many news and information hounds as well as by content providers, such as CNN Interactive. At first, some Web site operators looked upon PointCast and other push services as competitors, and saw little reason to provide them with content. Web site operators expressed concern about viewers accessing content through a push service rather than from the original source. For example, pushing someone a news item that was originally published by *USA Today* could decrease the likelihood of that person going to the *USA Today* Web site for that information. Web site managers have discovered, however, that affiliating with a push service can actually bring additional traffic to a Web site by providing links to more information. A short news item provided by CNN Interactive, but pushed by PointCast could, for example, direct PointCast subscribers to the CNN Interactive site by linking the item to an in-depth story (Shaw, 1997a).

Daily news and information pumped in a steady stream to subscribers' computers may one day become the primary method of receiving Web information. Searching services may be left for retrieving specialized information sought on a one-time basis. Many people who fear getting lost in a murky pit of information are relieved to know that there are new, simpler ways of retrieving Web content.

Other Internet Resources

Listservs and Usenet Newsgroups are two online resources that can yield helpful and interesting information. A primary advantage is the interactive quality of posting and receiving messages and the continuing dialogue among many participants. Many fascinating viewpoints, opinions, and articles, which can be enlightening and useful, are found in these discussion-type groups. Listservs and Usenet Newsgroups were briefly described in Chapter 1, and the following sections provide brief instructions on how to use each for research.

LISTSERVS   A listserv is a group e-mail forum where subscribers post and receive messages en masse. Listservs provide an arena for exchanging messages pertaining to a specific topic. There are thousands of listservs covering thousands of topics, such as dog grooming, cooking, gardening, and computer programming. Many listservs accept subscriptions from the general population of Web users. Some, however, are available only to specific groups, such as employees of a company, or students in a class. Many professors establish listservs as a means of disseminating information to their students and promoting discussion among students outside of the classroom.

Using Listservs   A person interested in subscribing to a listserv can locate one of interest through almost any search service. When "listserv" was entered into AltaVista, it retrieved 273,800 items. Rather than perusing this list, a follow-up search using the term "list+of+listservs" yielded thirteen documents that include lists of listservs or other instructions on finding a listserv. Clicking on the listserv of interest will bring up instructions for subscribing, and for sending and receiving messages. Only subscribers may send out electronic messages via the listserv, and those messages are delivered only to other subscribers.

In many ways listservs are more conducive to researching a subject than newsgroups. Listservs' topic areas tend to be more specific than newsgroups', and subscribers generally have a more genuine interest in the topic area. A student interested in classroom applications of multimedia probably will be overwhelmed with the knowledgeable information received from a "multimedia-related" listserv.

Subscribing to Listservs   Subscribing to a listserv usually entails sending a request to the listserv manager. Each listserv has its own specific instructions to follow and a precise way of wording the subscription request. For example, ShopTalk, a broad-cast industry listserv, can be subscribed to as follows:

1. Send an e-mail message to ShopTalk at listserv@listserv.syr.edu.

2. In the body of the message, "subscribe SHOPTALK" should be typed along with the user's first name and last name (all on the same line). For example:

subscribe SHOPTALK John Doe

3. New subscribers are e-mailed a notice of verification and instructions for unsubscribing. It is wise to keep the "unsubscribe" instructions handy for when needed.

Members of SHOPTALK receive messages via e-mail from other listserv members. In the case of SHOPTALK, the messages revolve around radio and television happenings, personalities, and important events. Subscribers are free to respond to messages and to start their own lines of inquiry.

USENET NEWSGROUPS   **Usenet Newsgroups** function similarly to nonelectronic bulletin boards, where messages are posted and can be read by anyone who finds them. Often messages on bulletin boards in grocery stores or laundromats are organized by subjects such as "lawn services," "babysitting," "houses for rent," or "lost and found." Newsgroups are also organized by topic. There are thousands of electronic newsgroups categorized in various subject areas. Some of the more popular areas follow:

alt	alternative and miscellaneous topics
comp	computer-related issues
humanities	arts and literature-related postings
news	current event messages
rec	recreation-oriented
sci	science topics
soc	social issues, behavior, and culture
talk	discussions of various issues and problems

Students seeking information and discussion about the subject "Internet and privacy" probably would post messages either to the "talk," "news," or "comp" newsgroups. The "sci," "soc," and "news" newsgroups are probably the best forums for debate surrounding the ethical issues of cloning.

Newsgroups are posted on Usenet, which is a worldwide network that is not actually part of the Internet but is accessed through the Internet. Usenet was developed in 1979 and is its own network housed at Duke University (Ackerman, 1996; Kurland, 1996; Kardas & Milford, 1996). Newsgroups can be good starting points

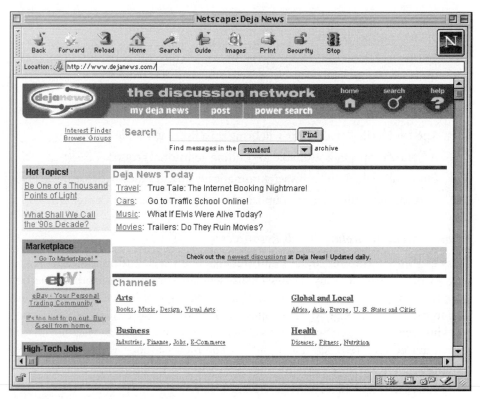

FIGURE 2.6 Deja News Homepage

for conducting research, because many participants will give suggestions on where to find additional information. Newsgroups are also a great way to gather public opinion about certain topics and events. Finding newsgroups has been made much easier by search services such as *Deja News*, which specialize in linking users to newsgroups of interest.

Using Usenet   The newer versions of the browser Netscape Communicator 4.05 has a very simple yet effective feature for logging into Usenet or joining discussion groups. This version of Netscape makes it much easier to join Usenets than older versions of Netscape Navigator.

1. Open Netscape and click on the "Communication" button found at the top of the page.
2. Go to Collabra Discussion Groups or press "Ctrl 3."
3. "Message Center" window will appear and give a prompt to enter account information.

4. After entering e-mail address, name, and other information, users can then open the Message Center.

5. To open, click on the "Discussions" button on the component bar found at the lower right corner of a Netscape Communicator window.

6. Click on the "Subscribe" button on the toolbar of the Message Center window.

7. The "Subscribe" dialog box will bring up a list of available groups.

8. A "Search" option is available for finding additional groups.

9. Once subscribed, the browser automatically updates messages for the users.

10. Posting and replying is accomplished through the Message Center window.

Communication-Related Web Resources

Mass communication researchers and students often seek information that is specific to their areas of study. Professionals, scholars, universities, and associations have constructed Web sites that provide information specifically related to the study of communication. Many of these sites act as information centers as well as networking venues. Some sites provide listservs and e-mail addresses as forums for discussing current research and trends in communication. Generally, these Web sites make excellent starting points for researching communication-related topics.

The Scholarly Electronic Publishing Directory points users to scholarly articles, documents, books, and other materials. Supported by the University of Houston libraries, this online bibliographic database provides links to online sources, a table of contents, and a search engine that supports several Boolean operators. Materials can be downloaded in Word files and Acrobat file formats.

The Communication Institute for Online Scholarship (CIOS) developed Comserve, a searchable index of abstracts and full-text articles taken from 29,000 bibliographic references from sixty-five communication journals and publications. Many of these are available only by paying a small yearly membership fee. However, many bibliographies, conference and job announcements, grant and fellowship opportunities, and other items of interest in the field of communication are available free of charge.

The Communication Studies and Journalism Resources created by Nanyang Technological University (NTU) in Singapore provides hundreds of links to national and international communication and journalism-related sites and newsgroups.

American Journalism Review's comprehensive site includes 4,500 links to newspapers, magazines, broadcasters, and news services worldwide.

Students interested in radio broadcasting will be delighted to find *The MIT List of Radio Stations on the Internet*. Listed are links to thousands of radio stations that have created a Web presence.

The *RhetNet, Cyberjournal of Rhetoric and Writing* publishes articles devoted especially to rhetorical implications of the Internet. This University of Missouri–hosted site focuses on merging scholarly conversation relating to rhetoric and writing with new technology.

The *American Communication Journal* is a Web-only scholarly refereed journal that is published by the American Communication Association. The journal made its online debut in September 1997, with its first issue devoted to interactive scholarship. The journal, however, is not limited in scope and publishes works from a variety of methodological perspectives ranging from rhetorical to communication theory to new communication technologies. Full-text journal articles are available free of charge to anyone.

The *Electronic Journal of Communication* is an academic journal available only online. First electronically published in 1990 by the Communication Institute for Online Scholarship, the quarterly journal publishes original works from various areas of communication studies.

The *Journal of Electronic Publishing* focuses on the electronic publishing business. The journal focuses on issues related to digital publishing, including the economics of the industry, international electronic transmission, and other related topics. The journal does not publish a printed version; articles are available only online.

Often professional and academic organizations post Web sites geared toward professionals, academics, and students. The communication-related scholarly associations providing Web sites include the *American Communication Association, Association for Education in Journalism and Mass Communication, Broadcast Education Association, National Association of College Broadcasters, National Communication Association,* and the *Southern States Communication Association.*

Generally, these sites provide information pertaining to upcoming conferences, journal submissions, grants and fellowships, and in some cases conference paper abstracts and text, and links to resources for teaching and research in communication.

Other Web Resources

Other reference materials such as dictionaries, almanacs, factbooks, Yellow Pages, maps, and other databases can be accessed on the Web. Rather than using a search service, researchers can go directly to the source for expedient fact finding. For example, U.S. census data can quickly be scanned by going online directly to the *Bureau of Census.*

Legal cases can be looked up on the *Federal Register's Table of Contents* and the *Federal Trade Commission's* site, and the latest telecommunication and Internet legislation is updated on the *Federal Communications Commission's* Web site.

Merriam-Webster publishes several of its dictionaries online, and *OneLook Dictionaries* will check any of ninety-four dictionaries for word definitions and origins. OneLook Dictionaries specializes in "hard to find," obscure, and industry-specific words that may not appear in general dictionaries.

SUMMARY: GETTING THE MOST OUT OF THE WEB

For many users the Web is an extraordinary medium that brings the world to them with the click of a few buttons. For other people, the Web is a huge tangled mess of interconnections that lead to useless and unreliable information. Developing an understanding of the Web and its content and learning how to use search services properly are the keys to a positive experience with this new medium.

Many people are under the impression that online information is easy to find and that searching the Web takes less time than looking through traditional sources. However, with millions of online documents and no Dewey Decimal System equivalent to rely on, searches often lead from one dead end to another. Learning how search engines work and knowing how to enter search terms properly makes Web traveling much more enjoyable and much less frustrating. In the long term, mastering several preferred search services will save countless hours of time that can be wasted by jumping around from one search site to another and, simply because the search is being conducted incorrectly, never finding what is being looked for. Also, bookmarking favorite and frequently used sites eliminates having to conduct a new search with each online session.

Using the Web to conduct research can be tricky if users do not know whether they are accessing an original source or someone's interpretation of information posted by an original source. Knowing how to decipher a URL tips users to the host and source of a site.

Web-posted information must be carefully scrutinized for accuracy, reliability, and credibility. Many sites, such as those created by well-known and trustworthy media outlets, demand that information go through an editorial review before being presented to the online public. Other sites, however, are not so careful, and much of the information floating around cyberspace needs to be evaluated before being taken as the final word.

In all likelihood the Web is here to stay. Granted, many changes and new features are yet to come, and years down the road the Web may bear little resemblance to its current state. To understand the Web of the future, users need to understand the Web of the present. A strong grasp of search engines and services and an understanding of the origins of Web content can transform an ordinary user into a Web-savvy user who knows how to get the most out of the Web.

CHAPTER LINKS

American Communication Association—http://www.americancomm.org/

American Communication Journal—
http://www.americancomm.org/~aca/acj/acj.html

American Journalism Review—http://www.newslink.org/

APA Style—http://www.uvm.edu/~xli/reference/apa.html

Association for Education in Journalism and Mass Communication—
http://www.aejmc.sc.edu

Broadcast Education Association—http://www.beaWeb.org/

Bureau of Census—http://www.census.gov

CIOS—http://www.cios.org

CNN Interactive— http://www.cnn.com

Communication Studies and Journalism Resources—
http://www.ntu.ac.sg/ntu/lib/commun.html

Deja News—http://www.dejanews.com

Electronic Journal of Communication—http://www.cios.org/www/ejcmain.htm

Electronic Styles: A Handbook for Citing Electronic Information—
http://www.uvm.edu/~xli/reference/espub.html

Federal Communications Commission—http://www.fcc.gov/

Federal Register—http://www.access.gpo.gov/su_docs/aces/aces140.html

Federal Trade Commission—http://www.ftc.gov

Four-11—http://www.four11.com

InfoBeat—http://www.infobeat.com

Information Express—http://www.express.com

International Communication Association—http://www.icahdq.org/

The Internet Index—http://www.openmarket.com/intindex

Journal of Electronic Publishing—http://www.press.umich.edu:80/jep

Merriam-Webster Online—http://www.m-w.com

MIT—Radio Stations on the Internet—http://wmbr.mit.edu/stations/list.html

Modern Language Association—http://www.mla.org

National Association of College Broadcasters—http://www.hofstra.edu/~nacb/

National Association of Broadcasters—http://www.nab.org

National Communciation Association—http://www.natcom.org/

National Weather Service—http://www.nws.noaa.gov

New York Times Online—http://www.nytimes.com

OneLook Dictionaries—http://www.onelook.com

Online! A Reference Guide to Using Internet Sources—
http://www.smpcollege.com/online-4styles~help

PointCast Network—http://www.pointcast.com

RentNet—http://www.rentnet.com

RhetNet, Cyberjournal of Rhetoric and Writing—http://www.missouri.edu/~rhetnet

The Scholarly Electronic Publishing Directory—http://info.lib.uh.edu/sepb/sepb.html

Southern States Communication Association—http://ssca.net

World Pages—http://www.worldpages.com

REFERENCES

Ackerman, E. (1996). *Learning to use the World Wide Web.* Wilsonville, OR: Franklin Beadle.

Brady, D. J. (1996, November). *Cyberdemocracy and perceptions of politics: An experimental analysis of political communication on the World Wide Web.* Paper presented to the annual Conference of the Midwest Association for Public Opinion Research, Chicago, IL.

Calabrese, A., & Borchert, M. (1996). Prospects for electronic democracy in the United States: Rethinking communication and social policy. *Media, Culture and Society, 18,* 248–68.

California woman finds her long-lost father, credits the Internet for reunion. (1997, November 9). *St. Louis Post Dispatch,* p. A11.

Chu, H., & Rosenthal, M. (1996). Search engines for the World Wide Web: A comparative study and evaluation methodology. *Proceedings of the 59th American Society for Information Science annual meeting, 33,* 127–35.

Chief Yahoos endow engineering chair at Stanford. (1997, March 20). *St. Louis Post Dispatch,* p. 8C.

Coates, J. (1996, November 10). Bogus news crowds the Internet, and many mistake stories for fact. *St. Louis Post Dispatch,* p. 5B.

Cortese, A. (1997, February 24). A way out of the Web maze. *Business Week,* 95–101.

Courtois, M. P., Baer, W. M., & Stark, M. (1995, November/December). Cool tools for searching the Web. *Online,* 15–32.

Courtois, M. O. (1996, May/June). Cool tools for Web searching: An update. *Online,* 29–36.

Crotty, C. (1997, February). All news, all the time. *MacWorld,* 173–76.

Ding, W., & Marchionini, G. (1996). A comparative study of Web search service performance. *Proceedings of the 59th American Society for Information Science annual meeting, 33,* 136–42.

Dowe, T. (1997, January). News you can abuse. *Wired,* 113.

Eager, B. (1994). *Using the World Wide Web.* Indianapolis, IN: Que Corporation.

Finnie, S. (1997, November 4). Netcaster. *PC Magazine Online.* [Online]. Available: http://www.zdnet.com/pcmag/features/Webcast/Webcastr2.htm

Gaziano, C. (1988). How credible is the credibility crisis? *Journalism Quarterly, 65,* 267–78.

Harding, W. E. (1997, June). How to find it on the Web. *Journal of Accountancy,* 69–72.

Johnson, T. J., & Kaye, B. K. (1998). Cruising is believing?: Comparing Internet and traditional sources on media credibility measures. *Journalism and Mass Communication Quarterly.* 75(2) 325–340.

Kardas, E. P., & Milford, T. M. (1996). *Using the Internet for social science research and practice.* Belmont, CA: Wadsworth.

Kurland, D. J. (1996). *The 'Net, the Web, and you.* Belmont, CA: Wadsworth.

Levy, S. (1997, May 12). The Internet gets pushy. *Newsweek,* 84.

Li, X., & Crane, N. B. (1996). *Electronic styles: A handbook for citing electronic information.* Medford, NJ: Information Today.

Liberatore, K. (1997, June 5). Rating the search engines. *MacWorld.* [Online]. Available: http://macworld.zdnet.com/netsmart/features/searchin.review.html [1998, January 20].

Liberatore, K. (1998, January 20). So what's Yahoo! got to do with it? *MacWorld.* [Online]. Available: http://macworld.zdnet.com/netsmart/features/searchin.links.html [1998, January 20].

Maloney, J., & Goldblatt, H. (1996, December 9). Yahoo! still searching for profits on the Internet. *Fortune,* 174.

Metcalfe, R. M. (1996, December 16). Alta Vista sets sights on complete 'net products and IPO. *InfoWorld, 18* (51), 42.

Netcaster Channel. (1997, October 29). *Fast Company.* [Online]. Available: http://www3.fastcompany.com/Web/netcaster.html

News junkies, news critics. (1997, January). *Roper Center homepage.* [Online]. Available: http://www.newseum.org

Noble, P. (1996, July). Net the vote. *Campaigns & Elections,* 27–33.

One-in-ten voters online for Campaign '96. (1996, October). *Pew Research Center Survey of Technology.* [Online]. Available: http://www.people-press.org

Peters, R., & Sikorski, R. (1997, June 20). How to use Usenet. *Science,* 1893–94.

Rafter, M. (1996, March 13). Web search tools so advanced they even search other tools. *St. Louis Post Dispatch,* p. 8C.

Rodriguez, K. (1997, April 15). Netscape pushes out Netcaster. *Inter@ctive Week.* [Online]. Available: http://www.zdnet.com/intweek/daily/970415a.html [1997, November 4].

Rosenberg, S. (1996, November 12). Blame it on the Net. *Salon Magazine.* [Online]. Available: http://www.salon1999.com/media/media961112.html

Rubin, R. B., Rubin, A. M., & Piele, L. (1996). *Communication research: Strategies and sources.* Belmont, CA: Wadsworth.

Search engines most popular method of surfing the Web. (1997, April 16). *CommerceNet/ Nielsen media survey.* [Online]. Available: http://commerce.net/news/press/0416.html [1997, October 27].

Shaw, R. (1997a, February 17). Giving sites a push to wider exposure. *Electronic Media, 16* (8), 10.

Shaw, R. (1997b, August 25). Netscape's latest offers more from TV sites. *Electronic Media, 16,* 10, 34.

Starobin, P. (1996, May 25). On the square. *National Journal,* 1145–49.

Standard & Poors stock reports. (1996, July 18). *Yahoo! Inc.*

Tanaka, H., & Hannah, D. (1995, March 20). Super cyber surfers. *Newsweek,* 43–44.

Tedesco, R. (1996, July 29). Excite's new engine points at Yahoo's pole position. *Broadcasting and Cable,* 57.

Tedesco, R. (1997, August 18). Netcaster ships with broad net. *Broadcasting and Cable,* 51.

Tenopir, C. (1992). Online databases. *Library Journal, 117* (10), 94, 96.

Wald, M. L. (1996, November 10). Cyber-mice that roar. *New York Times,* sect. 4, p. 5.

Wolfe, M. (1995). *Netguide.* New York: Michael Wolfe & Company.

Yahoo! in the black. (1997, October 13). *ComputerWorld, 31* (41), 31.

Yahoo! reports fourth quarter and 1997 fiscal year end financial results. (1998, January 14). *Yahoo! homepage,* press release. [Online]. Available: www.yahoo.com/docs/pr/release141.html [1998, February 16].

Yahoo!'s U.S. audience surpasses 25 million, outpacing leading broadcasting and print media. (1997, November 10). *Yahoo! homepage,* press release. [Online]. Available: www.yahoo.com/docs/pr/release131.html [1998, February 16].

Yuwono, B., & Lee, D. L. (1996). WISE: A World Wide Web resource database system. *IEEE Transactions on Knowledge and Data Engineering, 8* (4), 548–54.

Zorn, P., Emanoil, M., & Marshall, L. (1996, May/June). Searching: Tricks of the trade. *Online,* 15–28.

During the Bosnian War, the Internet became the citizens' primary conduit of information. The war in former Yugoslavia destroyed many communication facilities in that country, including radio and television stations and the telephone system. Many of the remaining media were forced by the government to cease operating. While Belgrade's radio station B-92 was shut down for only three days, others were silenced for much longer periods of time. The destruction of these communication infrastructures escalated the breakdown of dialogue between the different ethnic groups and fueled hatred and distrust among the peoples.

Scholars, members of humanitarian organizations, students, and peace-seeking individuals searching for ways to bring the warring factions together ingeniously set up a system of communication using the Internet. Without other forms of mass communication, the Internet became the primary means of reaching a sizable number of Bosnia's inhabitants. Forums such as Sarajevo Online served as a venue for intellectuals, politicians, artists, students, and others to talk candidly and openly about their views and differences of opinion. Organizers of the online dialogue view the Internet as a means of increasing understanding among the various ethnic groups and as an alternative communication route toward lasting peace.

CHAPTER THREE

INTERNET RADIO

Some people dream of being a DJ or owning a radio station, but for many reasons they think it is an impossible dream. But guess again. With Internet radio, DJs or station owner "wannabes" can fulfill their broadcasting desires. With RealAudio software, a microphone, and an Internet connection, anyone can be on their way to creating their own Web "radio" station and becoming a global "netcaster." Getting into the Internet radio business is much less expensive and a whole lot easier than buying an over-the-air station or competing with hundreds of DJs for a couple of hours of broadcast time.

On the other hand, some people are not in the least bit interested in producing cyberaudio. For them, Internet radio is a great way to listen to favorite tunes or to a top radio station even when far from its broadcast area. From online radio stations, visitors can listen to live music and news, find out what is going to be played over-the-air and online, and read DJ biographies.

Internet radio is catching the ears of Web users and is fast becoming a viable alternative to over-the-air broadcasting. By virtue of Web technology, cyber-radio can offer so much more to its audience than traditional stations, which are limited by signal range and audio-only output. Online radio delivers audio, text, graphics, and video, satisfying a range of consumer needs.

THE GROWTH OF INTERNET RADIO

Live Internet audio was born on September 5, 1995, when Progressive Networks transmitted the Seattle Mariners and New York Yankees game online. The next day, SW Networks cybercast Mario Cuomo's speech live from a National Association of Broadcasters' convention. Real-time music debuted a few months later on November 20, when a Vince Gill concert from Nashville was cybercast live on MCI's Telecom Web site. The concert was also simulcast over the TNN cable network and syndicated to radio stations across the nation, giving it the distinction of being the "first-ever triplecast" (Taylor, 1996, p. 6).

The University of Kansas made history on December 3, 1994, when its student-run radio station, _KJHK-FM,_ was among the first stations to go live on the Internet twenty-four hours a day. Imagine the thrill of taking music requests from someone listening in from Australia, or the excitement generated just by knowing listeners are tuning in from around the world (Petrozzello, 1995a). With support from AudioNet (now known as broadcast.com), an online broadcast network, Dallas station _KLIF-AM_ entered the record books on September 9, 1995, as the first commercial radio station to netcast live continuous programming (AudioNet, 1997).

Stations that were among the first to establish an Internet presence have paved the way for others to follow. Small- to medium-market and college stations generally led the way to the Internet (Noack, 1996), and their success stories quickly spread throughout the radio industry as stations eagerly connected to the Net. As of January 1998, more than 100 radio networks and more than 4,000 of the nation's 11,000 radio stations have created some sort of Internet presence; approximately one-quarter of the Web stations have educational or noncommercial formats, followed by about 11 percent that favor album-oriented rock. Of the online radio station sites, slightly more than 500 offer some form of real-time netcasting by transmitting audio or video clips of programming.

The rise of Internet radio somewhat mirrors the development of over-the-air radio. Early wireless radio was dominated by amateur (ham) operators using specialized crystal sets to transmit information to whomever could pick up their signals and would take the time to listen. However, operating a receiving set was difficult and expensive, the reception was poor and full of static, and the sets themselves were large and cumbersome, leaving only a small audience of technologically advanced listeners. In the early days of radio the technologically adept were the first to gravitate toward the new medium. In the late 1990s, those people who are computer- and network-savvy are the ones producing and tuning into cybercasts. Also, the bandwidth limitations and slow processor and modem speeds of Internet radio lead to long downloading times, frustrating many who would otherwise become regular users and keeping them from adopting this new medium, just as difficult-to-use radios with poor audio output once kept the general public from experiencing the airwaves.

Over-the-air broadcasting caught on and grew into an influential medium only after professional stations, most notably KDKA in Pittsburgh, began transmitting news and a regular schedule of music and talk programs, and radio receiving sets were mass manufactured. Now, the popularity of Internet radio is increasing as radio station Web sites increasingly transmit a regular schedule of music and programs. Also, as users become more familiar with the Web in general and learn where to find the radio programming of their choice, and as computer and Net technology become less expensive, easier to use, and deliver better sound quality, cyber-radio may one day become as popular as over-the-air stations.

Just as the Internet is often viewed negatively today, early over-the-air radio was once heavily criticized as a corrupter of youth and the instigator of moral decay. Woodrow Wilson once proclaimed radio information to be the "poison of revolt, the poison of chaos" (Lubar, 1993, p. 222). Yet, as more people turned to radio for news and information and relied on it as a credible source, criticism waned and the public embraced radio as a new communication device. During the years of the Depression many people could not afford to buy newspapers, and neighbors hovered around public radio sets in stores and offices to hear the news. Franklin D. Roosevelt, realizing the power of radio to connect the country, began broadcasting his well-known and eagerly awaited "fireside chats." Just as FDR foresaw the potential of radio to boost his chances of re-election, all of the major presidential candidates in the 1996 campaign used the Internet to reach out to their constituencies.

Today, over-the-air radio is a major force around the world and is heavily relied upon for music, entertainment, and news. Many radio stations are taking technology and models of broadcasting to the Internet. Some radio station Web sites are merely promotional vehicles for their over-the-air counterparts, with Web pages consisting of on-air personality biographies, playlists, audio shorts of new songs, and community calendars. Other stations, however, are reaching out to listeners beyond their signal areas by cybercasting live and archived news and music.

Over-the-air radio use is slowly decreasing among listeners who use the Internet. Several studies found that 5 to 13 percent of Web users reported that the amount of time they spend listening to over-the-air radio has decreased as a result of using the Web (American Internet User Survey, 1997; Bromley & Bowles, 1995; Kaye, 1998). This could suggest that the more time users spend on the Internet the less time they have to devote to other media use, such as radio listening. The decrease in radio listening could also be the result of Internet radio supplanting over-the-air radio use. Although only a small percentage of people have reported listening to the radio less since becoming Web users, if this trend continues it could have quite an impact over time on the size of traditional radio's audience.

Other studies, however, contend that the Internet and radio are compatible media, as both can be used in tandem, and that Internet users tend to be heavy radio listeners. Almost nine out of ten online users regularly tune in to radio, and 42 percent are considered heavy listeners (Taylor, 1997). Web users can easily listen to over-the-air radio while surfing the Net, and users can listen to many online audio programs while performing other computing tasks.

To attract large audiences of listeners to Internet radio, computer and network technology will have to improve and become as easy and inexpensive to use as broadcast radio is today. Internet radio and online radio should consider simulcasting more often to increase their listening audiences and lessen the competition between the two media.

INTERNET RADIO VERSUS OVER-THE-AIR RADIO

Benefits of Internet Radio

There are several reasons why Internet radio has the potential to be better than broadcast radio. First, Web audio files can be listened to at anytime regardless of

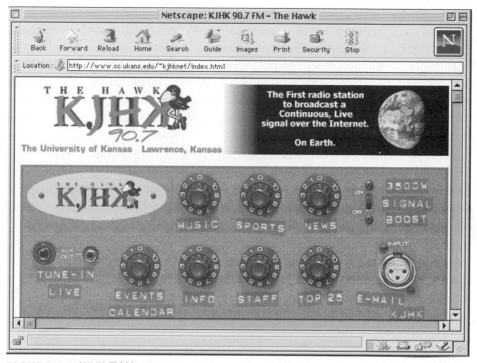

FIGURE 3.1 KJHK-FM Homepage

when they were first "aired." Users are not tied to a broadcast schedule where listeners have to tune in at the time their program is being broadcast; they can listen to archived files whenever they choose. Although some **netcasts** and **cybercasts** (Internet radio broadcasts) are live, when radio programs and newscasts are stored on servers available to listeners anytime this is known as **audio-on-demand;** users demand it, users get it.

Second, netcasts can be listened to from anywhere in the world regardless of the place of origin. Instead of tuning into a local broadcast radio station for regional news and programs, Web users can hear netcasts from across the United States or from as far away as Finland. Net fans in California can tune into Michigan State University's or many other universities' Web sites for cybercasts of sporting events. MSU was one of the first universities to provide online audio of its athletic games, and many others have since followed suit (McKee, 1996).

Third, not only can online users listen to radio, but they can see it too. Song lyrics, rock bands in concert, and news can be seen via text, graphics, or video, opening up a wide range of possibilities never before available to traditionally delivered radio stations. Listeners are not bound to an audio-only delivery system.

Last, the ability to listen to broadcast radio while doing other things is an advantage and has contributed to its popularity. Much to the Internet's benefit, new technologies allow **multitasking,** the ability of users to listen to an audio program while performing other computer tasks and even while surfing the Web. Now, rather than having to wait for an audio file to download before listening, users can hear music or news as the audio streams through the computer's speakers at the same time they are working on a word-processing document or accessing Web information.

With millions of people in slightly more than two hundred countries connected to the Internet, the potential audience for Web radio is almost limitless (Sullivan, 1996). Soon it will be commonplace for executives, university professors, students, and almost anyone to work on their computers while tuning in to radio stations halfway around the world.

Challenges of Internet Radio

The sound quality of Internet radio is a formidable barrier to widespread adoption. The clarity of cybercast audio largely depends on the type of Internet connection used. Many users still access the Web with 14.4 kbps (thousand bits per second) modems, which causes choppy delivery with dropped syllables and words, and makes the audio difficult to decipher. Additionally, high treble and low bass sounds are diminished as the data squeeze into the available bandwidth. With a 14.4 kbps modem, the sound quality is similar to AM radio. With data rates of 28.8 kbps and higher, the sound becomes similar to FM mono radio. With high-speed cable modems, increased bandwidth, and direct Internet access becoming more widespread, Web listeners will soon hear audio that is of FM stereo and even CD-quality sound.

Another challenge that cybercasters face is the significant delay many users experience when downloading audio files. For example, Internet Talk Radio's former program, *Geek of the Week,* was a 15-minute netcast. Without new audio software, it took almost two hours to download the program using a 14.4 kbps modem (Quittner, 1995). In addition, most online radio stations cannot accommodate more than a few hundred simultaneous listeners. If listeners are tying up the connection while downloading large audio files, they inadvertently block others from accessing the station. Many server, home computer, and bandwidth limitations need to be overcome before online stations can reach unrestricted numbers of listeners.

Though faster Internet connections are easing downloading delay, audio clarity still suffers. Audio is lost as it is compressed and cut from CD quality of 40,000 bps to Internet quality of 1,000 bps. Though the Internet is complementary with the spoken word, it is less than ideal for music (McKee, 1996).

Of the most problematic obstacles to widespread adoption of Internet radio is its lack of portability. Cyber-radio cannot be taken to the beach, a baseball stadium, the park, or the gym, as can battery-operated radios. Portability, however, may not be a stumbling block to widespread use for long. In the not too distant future satellite-delivered Web technology promises to beam the Internet directly into cars, where people tend to do most of their radio listening. This system is still in an experimental stage and not available to the general public ("Listening While Driving," 1998; "Online on the Go," 1997). With other new applications, such as **Audible Audio,** Internet music programming is becoming more transportable. With Audible Audio, radio listeners can now download their favorite programs and play them back whenever they want, and from whatever location they please. Online audio is no longer as tied to the computer as it once was but is now transportable via a Walkman-like device. Designed by Audible Audio, the system works by downloading audio that can be played back either through a computer or through a portable, pocket-sized Audible Player that holds up to two hours of programming that takes about thirty minutes to download using a 28 kbps modem. *Audible Audio*'s Web site provides thousands of hours of audio of popular radio programs, speeches, books, magazines, and other periodicals and sources. After paying a little less than $200 for an Audio Player, users need only put on their headphones to take their audio with them wherever they go (Audible Audio, 1998).

REAL-TIME AUDIO: WHAT IT DOES

RealAudio was the first application to bring real-time audio-on-demand over the Internet. Because of this, millions of users have the capability of receiving AM-quality radio transmissions on their computers. ESPN Sportszone features live play-by-play broadcasts of NBA games over the Internet. National Public Radio delivers their programs *All Things Considered* and *Morning Edition* over the Web, and by clicking on ABC RadioNet's Web site, which was one of the first to integrate Real-Audio capabilities, users hear hourly newscasts live or at any other time they please. Media companies using RealAudio on their Web sites include *CBS, NPR, ABC Radio Networks,* and *Time, Inc.* CBS's *Up to the Minute News* uses audio clips for its headlines. Additionally, in the first six months of 1996, the amount of live audio programming available on the Web jumped by 400 percent (Taylor, 1996).

Since the introduction of RealAudio, hundreds of radio stations made the leap from broadcast to netcast. Progressive Networks claim that close to 180 stations are using its technology, with only about ten of those featuring Web-only content. The others retransmit or simulcast over-the-air broadcasts ("Web music," 1997). Using RealAudio, AM and FM commercial radio, public radio, and college stations envision larger audiences thanks to a technology that has moved them from providing prerecorded audio clips to transmitting live, real-time audio in continuous streams. **Streaming** technology shoots data through the Net in a continuous flow,

FIGURE 3.2 ABC Radio Networks Homepage

so information is displayed on a user's computer before the entire file has finished downloading. Streamed audio and video selections can be played as they are being sent, so users do not have to wait for the entire file to download.

One of the best features of RealAudio is that it does not require computer expertise to use or expensive hardware upgrades to install. RealAudio software loads onto existing servers and stores audio information to be netcast in real time and in higher sound qualities. Thus, with RealAudio, die-hard audio fans do not have to wait hours for a program to download but can hear it immediately. RealAudio also contains a multimedia element that allows the incorporation of sound with images and text over the Web.

Since RealAudio's 1994 introduction, several other companies have developed similar audio-on-demand applications. Though less popular than RealAudio, *StreamWorks, Internet Wave Selections,* and *TrueSpeech* are software applications that deliver radio transmissions over the Internet in an audio-on-demand format (Berniker, 1995c).

Though sound on the Internet has been available since the mid-1980s, the long downloading time has kept it from gaining mainstream popularity among users. Before real-time capabilities, a 15-minute program could take hours to download and would eat up 30 megabytes (MB) of hard drive space. For audio files to travel quickly through the Internet, they need a larger bandwidth than is currently available through telephone lines.

To broaden narrow bandwidths, RealAudio has gone beyond Internet Transmission Control Protocol (TCP) by developing **User Datagram Protocol (UDP)**. In Chapter 1, this book discussed how TCP moves data across the Internet by breaking bits of information up into small packets and then reassembling them into a larger packet once all of the elements reach their destination. At each stop along the way computers must "talk" to each other to verify that all of the information has been received. This communication takes up valuable bandwidth. UDP works in a similar fashion to TCP, but it assumes that all of the packets of information have arrived at their destination; if any data bits are lost, a built-in buffer will fill in the blanks by analyzing the data in the other packets, instead of using up precious bandwidth to "talk" to other computers looking for the missing bits of data.

The audio system developed by the company StreamWorks transmits sound files using standard TCP, but to hasten delivery uses the **MPEG (Motion Pictures Experts Group)** compression scheme commonly used for transmitting graphic files. **Compression** squeezes files down to about one-tenth their original size (Stauffer, 1997). Data that are compressed move through a network at faster speeds and take up less hard drive storage space. MPEG is a consortium of engineers who have been working together since the late 1980s to set world standards for digital compression of audio and video (Grant, 1996; Pavlik, 1996). *VocalTec,* another Internet technology company, also uses TCP to send audio, but it has developed its own compression software to work within narrow bandwidths (Rossney, 1996). What this means is that instead of the typical "download then play" routine, compression occurs in near real time. Computers compress and play the data at near the same time, involving less waiting.

As more companies begin offering real-audio technology and investing millions of dollars in research and development, standardization and cooperation are becoming increasingly necessary. Led by Progressive Networks, thirty-eight large companies (e.g., Hewlett-Packard, Apple, and IBM) have agreed on a new standard, dubbed **real-time streaming protocol** (RTSP), which will speed up the downloading process, especially for large amounts of data. Many people anticipate that RTSP will become the Internet's primary audio programming protocol, just as HTML is the text programming protocol. As of mid-1998, the RTSP proposal is waiting approval from the Internet Engineering Task Force (Rafter, 1996a).

Still other protocols are being researched. Most Internet audio is delivered point-to-point, like a telephone call, but new technologies like **multicasting** allow one file to be sent out to multiple receivers, increasing the listening audience (Stauffer, 1997).

FIGURE 3.3 RealAudio Homepage

REAL-TIME AUDIO: HOW IT WORKS

To send an audio message across the Internet, a cybercaster needs the portion of *RealAudio* software known as the **Encoder.** To receive audio over the Internet, Web users need to download the RealAudio **Player** decoder application.

RealAudio Encoder

Internet audio encoders digitize an audio file so it can be sent out in data packets and played on the Web in real time (Jessell, 1995). Cassettes, CDs, records, and simple voice recordings can be made and edited using computer software such as Adobe's Premiere, Sound Edit Pro, Sound Edit 16, Sound Forge, and Pro-Tools. The sound file is then "encoded" into a RealAudio file ready for playback on the Web. The RealAudio encoder uses a buffering scheme to send digitized binary audio in a stream of continuous sound to a computer with a RealAudio Player. RealAudio encoders are available for downloading free of charge on RealAudio's Web site.

RealAudio Player

Incoming digitized audio sent from a server with real-time capabilities is played by the RealAudio Player through the computer's speakers. After a user clicks on an audio icon, it takes only from one to ten seconds before a musical selection is heard—a vast improvement over two-hour downloads without RealAudio technology. Using RealAudio, listeners can play a selection as it downloads, or they can store it for later retrieval when they can fast-forward, rewind, and pause their audio selections.

Using RealAudio Plus, an enhanced version of RealAudio Player, users can preset buttons to access their favorite RealAudio sites quickly, scan hundreds of live radio stations without having to wait for graphics to download, and receive customized live and prerecorded audio programs ("Progressive Networks Launches," 1996).

Free copies of audio player software are available from RealAudio and many other sites that provide links to RealAudio's homepage. Downloading RealAudio Player takes a few minutes and uses up only about 300K of hard disk space (Rafter, 1996b). As of December 1997, about 30 million free copies of RealAudio Player have been downloaded onto personal computers since its 1995 introduciton, and the number of daily downloads has risen to about 70,000 ("RealNetworks' Real-System," 1997).

NETCASTING NETWORKS

Many over-the-air radio stations belong to **radio networks.** Networks supply stations with programming, news, and network commercials. Stations benefit by receiving high-quality, expensive-to-produce programs, and attracting a listening audience that they would otherwise not be able to satisfy with their own local programming. There are many over-the-air radio networks, most notably Westwood One and ABC. Many of these networks have created Web sites for their member stations. Additionally, new Internet-only radio networks have been formed to assist radio stations with developing online sites.

ABC RadioNet provides live-breaking events, weather, sports, and news from Washington, entertainment news (including audio movie reviews), and links to _ABC World News Tonight_ and _This Week,_ along with many other features. Additionally, ABC RadioNet cybercast live the O. J. Simpson trial verdict and President Clinton's 1996 State of the Union address (Taylor, 1996). Other examples of online radio programs include _CBS Radio Networks Online,_ which offers live news feeds and other features, and _Bloomberg Information Radio,_ uses Streamwork technology

FIGURE 3.4 Examples of Some Radio Stations on the Web

to deliver live newscasts, financial reports, and other information from its premiere station, WBBR-AM, New York (Pack, 1996).

Radio networks that specialize in a talk format are also finding their way onto the Web. *Taylor Satellite Talk Radio* (TST), beamed to subscribing homes with a satellite dish, expanded its service to the Web, however, the network recently shut down its Web site. While online, Internet users chose among fifteen topic-related programming channels. Some nationally recognized personalities carried by TST included Dr. Laura Schlessinger, politician Jerry Brown, and Dr. Derrick DeSilva. By connecting to the Internet, listeners tuned in to national talk radio shows that might not air on a broadcast station in their area, and they listened to the programs free of commercial interruptions (Petrozzello, 1995c).

CYBERCASTING RADIO STATIONS

Broadcast Stations on the Web

Broadcast radio stations excel on the Internet by becoming local information providers to those users who are unable to pick up the over-the-air signal. Beyond local news and sports delivery, a station's Web site can be the primary source of community information and community ties. Users can tune into their favorite station's Web site to find information about which songs are the most popular in the area, which CD stores are having sales, which bands are playing at which clubs, which bands are looking for new members, and other items of interest. Information posted by a radio station does not have to be limited to music. Radio Web sites compete with local newspapers by providing local news, movie listings, and information about art exhibits, plays, and other community events.

Web radio is also used as a tie-in to promotional events. For instance, _KIIS-FM_ in Los Angeles used its Web site to show live still images of a benefit event and concert it sponsored. Of the station's 1.8 million listeners, only 17,000 could attend the concert in person, so the Web site was added to make listeners feel like they were part of the show (Taylor, 1996).

Radio station Web sites vary considerably. While many contain splashy graphics, video, and live and archived audio, others contain only text-based information. Some stations use their Web sites for selling promotional merchandise such as T-shirts, pencils, and coffee mugs emblazoned with the station's logo and call letters.

Experts recommend that radio stations build Web sites that go beyond simple DJ biographies. A radio Web site should include a station profile, photos of on-air personalities, a program schedule and playlist, short downloadable audio files, and, most important, an e-mail address for visitors to send in requests and comments. Most listeners never get to see radio personalities or even the inside of a station. A Web page is a great way to boost a station's image, differentiate the station from its competitors, and bring listeners closer to the station by offering them an inside look into the everyday operations.

Internet radio is a big boon to local stations. Rather than having their reach limited to the audience within their broadcast signal range, stations "netcast" to a large global Web audience. For example, a student from Baltimore who is attending college in San Diego and wants to know what's going on in his or her hometown simply needs to connect to the Web and click on Baltimore station _WBAL-AM_, which broadcasts its audio over the Internet twenty-four hours a day. Through the Web, information about all of the happenings in Baltimore can be netcast to a dorm room in San Diego, or anywhere in the world.

Additionally, station revenues can be enhanced by offering advertising packages that include both airtime and space on the Web page. Stations benefit by the extra advertising dollars, and advertisers benefit by reaching an audience beyond the station's signal area. Radio station revenue brought in through advertising on Web sites is expected to leap from $200 million in 1996 to $2 billion by the close of the century (Borzillo, 1996).

Houston's _KHMX-FM_'s Web site includes an online listener survey where approximately twenty-five song clips are available for sampling. Visitors are asked to fill in their opinions of each song. The station offers T-shirts and other giveaways to promote the site and encourage the audience to participate in the survey. Since the Web is a global medium, and the stations want to know what local listeners want to hear over the airwaves, survey participants are asked to enter their places of residence so researchers can analyze the local responses separately (Atwood, 1995).

Among the thousands of radio stations that have established a Web presence are *WPSL-AM*, cybercasting from Port St. Lucie, Florida, and San Diego's *Star 100.7*, entertaining with songs from the '80s and '90s in a variety of audio formats. Bellevue Washington's rock station *KISW-FM* has been recognized as one of the best online sites in several surveys. The site is loaded with contests, games, music news, DJ biographies and photographs, concert and ticket information, and RealAudio CD demos. The site is designed to entertain and provide its visitors with useful information. The station's promotions director claims that attractive graphics are not enough to lure visitors to Web sites. He claims that a good mix of online personality and lifestyle-oriented information combined with links to other music sites is what makes their site so popular (Borzillo, 1996). These are just three examples of stations that can be found on the Web using the directories of online radio that have sprouted up on the Net to guide users to cybertunes.

The following is a listing of just a few of the many guides to cyber-radio: *Airwaves Radio Station Page, MIT List of Radio Stations on the Internet,* and *Radio Online.* Additionally, a printed reference guide to over four hundred stations on the Web, *Passport to Web Radio—1997,* includes listings of live programs and sportscasts (Comarow, 1997).

INTERNET RADIO PROGRAMS

Internet radio is the beginning of "alternative radio. Any format is game, from classic rock to Slovenian dance music, when there is a worldwide audience" (Steinert-Threlkeld, 1996, p. 19). Clicking on any of the many cyber-radio sites lets music and news flow across the world.

Countless news sites that originate in many countries are available on the Web in many languages and in many combinations of text, audio, graphic, and video formats. News of all types, whether international, national, local, entertainment, sports, or business, can be had at the click of a mouse. The *Dow Jones Investor Network* offers economic news and information and a six-month archive of audio interviews and conferences with financial experts.

Some radio sites retransmit portions of their over-the-air programs on the Net, others produce programs for online use only, and still others netcast a combination of retransmitted programs and Internet-produced ones.

Webbies tuning in to *Ann Online,* an Internet-only talk show, interact with the program's hostess, Ann Devlin, through an online chat room, or via e-mail. Listeners can also post messages and comments on the site's electronic bulletin board. *Definitely Not the Opera,* produced by the *Canadian Broadcasting Corporation,* distributes sound clips over the Internet of its regular broadcast program, and uses Internet technology to produce interviews. The interviewee speaks into a com-

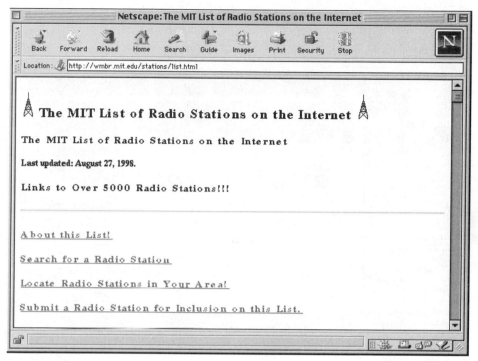

FIGURE 3.5 MIT List of Radio Stations on the Internet

puter through a microphone attached to a sound card, resulting in a ready-to-air digital audio file that is transmitted over the Internet to the producer's studio. This process increases the audio quality of telephone interviews, and cuts down on expensive production and travel costs (Strangelove, 1995).

Where many audio sites and stations provide a variety of music and news to suit most people's tastes, other sites offer very specific types of music in an attempt to reach a small target audience, also known as a **niche** audience or **niche marketing.** With niche marketing, products and services are directed toward an audience whose members share similar interests and needs or other characteristics, such as age or purchasing patterns. By targeting their consumers, companies and vendors can customize product features to best meet their audience's needs and thus attract advertisers who want to get their message to the same niche audience. Niche marketing, widely used in the non-online world, has made its way to the Web. The "All Grateful Dead, All-of-the-time" Web site and sites that feature only heavy-metal music are examples of niche audio on the Internet. The heavy metal band Megadeth was the first on its block to launch a Web site with *Megadeth Arizona*. Way back in 1994, Megadeth was cyberconnecting with its fans on a site that would soon become

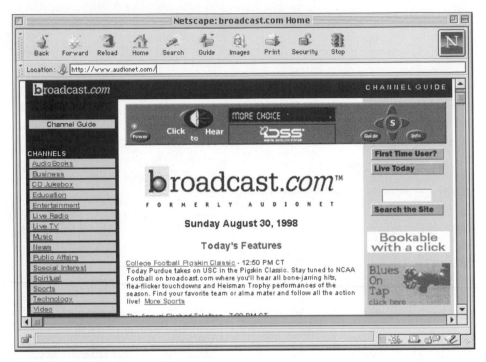

FIGURE 3.6 Broadcast.com Homepage

a model for other groups. Band member Dave Mustaine views the group's site as a promotional outlet, declaring, "Much as people want to say, 'I love playing music,' it's a business ... and when a record company finds a new way to skin a cat, everybody gets in on it" (Levine, 1998, p. 59). Specific target audiences are also drawn to sites with offerings such as foreign language and religious programs, Swedish rock, and Hawaiian songs ("Web Music," 1997).

There are hundreds of audio programs available on the Net. Web users merely need to use any online search engine or radio program guide to get the time and place of a live program or a long list of URLs on which audio files reside. Guides to radio on the Net can be found at several locations throughout the Web, most notably on *C/NET Radio* and *PC World Online News Radio*. Both sites list dates and times of live radio netcasts.

Web-Only Radio: Networks and Stations

Many Internet radio sites exist only on the Web and do not have an over-the-air counterpart station. A cyberstation can be established for as little as $10,000 in software and equipment, compared to well over $250,000 for a low-powered rural broadcast AM station. Plus, cyber-radio does not require licensing, nor is it subject to government restrictions.

The defunct Internet Multicasting Service (IMS) earned the distinction of being the first cyber-only radio station when it premiered *Geek of the Week* on April Fools' Day, 1993 (Pack, 1996). IMS's *Radio on the Internet* site had grown into a multifaceted audio-on-demand archive containing files on a wide variety of topics and including a key-word search mechanism. Three years after pioneering cyber-radio, IMS disbanded and is no longer available online.

NetRadio Network creates its own original programming for the Net rather than creating Web sites for existing broadcast stations. Claiming to be the first Web-only broadcasting outlet, NetRadio sent out its debut cybercast in October 1995 ("Web Music," 1997). NetRadio offers sports, weather, news, and other fare, and by using Microsoft Windows 95, selections can be customized for direct access to favorite programs (Stauffer, 1997).

Broadcast.com is another example of an Internet-only radio network. In early 1997, the network consisted of sixteen Web-only radio stations and 250 broadcast stations that listeners tap into for music, sports, news, and other programs. Broadcast.com claims its infrastructure allows the most simultaneous listeners (up to 15,500) on the Internet (AudioNet, 1997; Steinert-Threlkeld, 1996, p. 19). Additionally, the network's coverage of Super Bowl XXXI events drew over 500,000 listeners worldwide (AudioNet, 1997). Though users can archive programs and news that aired previously, broadcast.com notes that it is the live events that draw the largest audiences. Broadcast.com's goal is not to compete with existing over-the-air stations but to find new listeners who cannot pick up the stations' signals. Broadcast stations that sign on with the network are provided with a server and Internet connections. By mid-1997, broadcast.com had signed 167 stations and anticipated that by the end of the year it would have added about thirty more stations (Steinert-Threlkeld, 1996).

There are many Internet-only audio broadcasts, stations, and networks on the Internet. In some cases, Web sites function as a combination of an online directory, station, network, and program site. For example, RealAudio's service, *Timecast*, provides links to radio broadcasters, live concerts, and other programs. Users can customize their own news packages from among several options such as national or world news, entertainment, business, and sports (Stauffer, 1997).

CYBERMUSIC

Audio-on-demand transforms the Internet into an excellent platform for marketing music to the public. Major recording labels have established Web sites promoting their newest releases with downloadable audio and video samples. Often unique

BOX 3.1 MÖTLEY CRÜE CYBERJAM

Imagine the anticipation that rushed through the concert audience as Mötley Crüe vocalist Vince Neil announced that something special was about to happen—a cyber-jam. The band was about to embark on a techno-journey where none had gone before.

The Chicago concert site was linked to a television station in Detroit where a die-hard Mötley Crüe fan was anxiously awaiting his chance to play along with the band. Linked through fiber optic technology, the fan and the band jammed to "Anarchy in the U.K." Concertgoers were treated to the live band and to the fan who appeared on a large screen that was positioned above the stage. When the fan hit the first note the audience let out a roaring cheer that gave the Mötley Crüe bassist "the chills."

Mötley Crüe is keeping heavy metal alive through RealAudio netcasts, Web-based chats, and online ticket sales. Their *Swine Interactive Network* site follows the band's "Mötley Crüe vs. the Earth tour" with photos, RealAudio songs, and a "crowd-o-meter" that registers audience applause from the various concert venues.

Source: Levine, 1998.

and newer selections of music are available on these sites than on traditional radio stations. The Spanish-language version of Madonna's "You'll See" is available on *Warner Bros. Records'* Web site, and *Atlantic Records* cyber-released Tori Amos's "Caught a Little Sneeze" several weeks before distributing it to radio and retail stores. As a bit of Web trivia, there are over seventy Tori Amos Web sites, making her one of the most popular Web personalities. As broadband technology improves, record labels plan to create their own music-video programming for the Web, potentially offering users specific types of music sites, such as all-rap or all-alternative sites (Atwood, 1996a).

Loud Records and BMG Entertainment launched a new cybercast show, *Loud Radio,* featuring well-known DJs spinning their favorite tunes (Atwood, 1996b). Even live concerts have made their way to the Web. House of Blues New Media and Progressive Networks have teamed up to attract the hip-hop crowd to their Web site, *LiveConcerts.com*. The site uses Progressive Network technology to cybercast live musical performances from House of Blues venues across the country. Live-Concerts.com and other Web sites (e.g., *SonicNet, imusic, MediaCast,* and *L.A. Live*) that contain links to live concerts are competing for music fans who may not otherwise get to see new bands on television or hear new music on the radio. Also, Paradigm Music has teamed with the Microsoft Network (MSN) to provide online music programming for MSN's Web show, *MSN OnStage* ("Paradigm Teams with," 1997).

Through the Creative Musicians Coalitions, *Child's Touch,* and Harber Brothers' Productions, *KinderNet,* children's music has found its place on the Web with specially designed sites to attract young consumers with selections from Disney and other providers of children's entertainment. At these sites, young visitors find CDs and cassettes for sale, artist biographies and photos, and downloadable samples of a wide variety of songs. KinderNet claims its site is like "radio with pictures" (McCormick, 1996, p. 52).

INTERNET RADIO AND THE FEDERAL COMMUNICATIONS COMMISSION

By mid-1998, Internet radio was still not regulated by the Federal Communications Commission (FCC). The FCC has not stipulated any licensing requirements for Web radio stations (Steinert-Threlkcld, 1996). In other words, Internet radio is truly uncensored radio. Adam Curry, former MTV-VJ, turned to the Internet with *Rave Radio* in part to have a music show free of FCC regulations. "In cyberspace we can create programs no radio station would touch. Internet radio offers complete freedom for both the artist and the producer" (Strangelove, 1995, p. 36). For example, Rave Radio can play "Let Me Be in Your Underwear," which uses the "seven dirty words" that the FCC prohibited from the broadcast airwaves (Strangelove, 1996). The regulations that prevent radio stations from airing certain "dirty words" do not affect the Internet. While this may not mean much for stations that play music almost exclusively, it may allow an Internet radio station to play music with some four-letter words, candid interviews, or comedy albums with adult material. One note of caution, however. If a server is "owned" by a public institution such as a university, school system, or library, content posted by individuals may be under some scrutiny.

As RealAudio gains acceptance and becomes more popular among Internet users, the music industry is becoming concerned with copyright abuses. At issue are users downloading songs, storing them for repeated use, and playing them back without paying for the rights. When a music file is downloaded, in effect it makes a copy of the recording. However, because of the poor playback quality, Internet radio is generally viewed as ideal for sampling music and as a promotional tool rather than as a substitute for CD purchases ("Entertainment and Technology Strategies," 1998).

The 1995 *Frank Music Corporation v. CompuServe* case was settled by requiring "managers of CompuServe's forums to pay a full mechanical royalty each time a song was downloaded through its network" (Siegel & Stein, 1997, S4). The mechanical royalty pertains to music that is downloaded and stored. However, with new audio streaming techniques, music can be listened to in real time but is not necessarily stored on computer hard drives. Thus mechanical royalties cannot be applied to streamed selections. Streamed music that is not recorded is considered a public performance by the music licensing organizations, ASCAP (The American Society of Composers, Authors, and Publishers) and BMI (Broadcast Music, Inc.). At issue is whether a public performance license should be required for audio streaming. Of course, ASCAP and BMI insist that any music played over the Internet should be licensed, and therefore they are in the process of developing appropriate licensing regulations and are negotiating terms with Web site operators. However, it is impossibly difficult to police the Web and catch every site that cybercasts audio without a license (Siegel & Stein, 1997).

In addition to looser licensing regulations, the Internet is not subject to ownership restrictions. Presently, the FCC prohibits an entity from owning more than eight broadcast radio stations in a single market (*Broadcasting and Cable Yearbook*, 1996). Though Internet broadcasting is not under FCC restrictions as yet, there may come a time when stations may not be able to operate online without licenses and may face ownership restrictions.

For the time being, Internet radio is not as restrictive as broadcast radio. Anyone interested in delivering radio programming over the Web has much more freedom than their over-the-air counterparts. Online radio producers should be cautioned that the freedoms they now enjoy may be curtailed in the not-too-distant future.

PRODUCING AN INTERNET RADIO SHOW

An Internet radio show can be produced in much the same way that a broadcast radio show is produced, but the signal path from sound source to audience is quite different. A broadcast signal starts from a microphone, tape source, or CD. This signal is then sent to an audio mixer for processing (if necessary), then to a broadcast transmitter. In most cases the audio signal comes from the source as an analog signal, and remains an analog signal throughout the path from origination to processing to transmission to reception. The exception to this is sound that originates from a CD or DAT (digital audiotape) player. These sounds are on the recording medium in digital form, then transformed to analog form for processing and transmission. Internet radio follows a somewhat different path.

Internet Radio Signal Path

Internet radio sound can originate from the same sources as broadcast radio sound: microphone, tape source, or CD player (for nostalgia fans, vinyl LPs can also be used). Once the sound signal leaves the sound source, a number of different things must happen. First, the sound signal must be converted from an analog signal to a digital file. This process, known as digitizing, is similar to dubbing, but converts the analog sound to binary 0s and 1s in a digital file in a computer. Once the signal is digitized, it is stored in one of several different formats, a process known as encoding. This part of the process can be accomplished in two ways. One way is to use a dedicated piece of hardware called an *encoder*. This device does only one thing: convert analog signals to a particular style of digital format. A second way to effect this same process is to enter the analog signal into a computer that has the appropriate sound card and software that will convert the analog signal to a particular digital format. Currently, the most popular format for storage is MPEG-2 Layer 3, which has a file extension of .mp3.

This process of encoding compresses the information, so that a large amount of audio information can be stored in a small amount of space with as little sound degradation as possible. The machine that stores the digital audio files should be a computer dedicated for this use, or a computer that has software and an audio card that will enable it to accomplish this task as well as perform other tasks. It is preferable, however, that a dedicated computer be used. This component in the signal path is known as the live encoder, and it makes the compressed digital audio information available to another computer known as a *server*.

The server for audio can be a standard server that would also provide text and graphics to clients on the Web. Special software on this server allows more than one listener to be connected to the site at the same time. A special, dedicated server can also be used for the purpose of providing multiple feeds for numerous listeners. This type of server is known as a **replication server.** It expands the capacity of the first server and can provide a geographic dispersion of the audio file. It takes one signal from the first server and duplicates it many times. **IP Multicast** is a technique for signal replication that would occur in the Internet itself, thus making a powerful replication server unnecessary.

Listeners who connect to the radio Web site must have the capability to translate the digital audio files into sounds. This is accomplished by using the appropriate software, like RealAudio Player. The software decodes and decompresses the digital information and sends it to a sound card in the computer. The **sound card** changes the digital information into an analog signal that is fed to speakers. The result of this process is sound similar to that from a radio.

Types of Audio File Transfer

Sound information in a server can be sent in two ways: downloading and streaming. *Downloading* occurs in a format that will be stored as a digital file in a client's computer for later use. This style of signal transfer is simple downloading, much the same way as graphic or text files would be transferred. The extension often associated with this type of audio file is .wav.

When audio signals are compressed, the compression ratio affects sound quality. The higher the compression ratio, the more the sound signal degrades. This becomes a trade-off. High compression files are transferred quickly, but the sound is not as good as lower compression files that take longer to send and download. Even with a high compression ratio, downloading is slow and somewhat dissatisfying to people who expect a Web site to operate similarly to broadcast radio. When they get to the site, they want to hear sound immediately. This does not happen. While this wait may be acceptable when the listener has ordered prepackaged music, it is just not radio.

A solution to the long download time has been created with the technique of *streaming* the audio information as it reaches the listener's computer. When a signal is streamed, it starts decoding a signal as soon as it is received and plays it almost immediately. The computer continues to receive the signal, playing it shortly after reception, until the file has ended. The combination of streaming the audio signal and IP Multicast has brought the concept of Internet radio closer to a functional reality.

Program Delivery

Internet radio is capable of delivering live radio through the use of streaming. Any program material such as music, talk, news, or drama that can be transmitted on a broadcast station can also be sent live on the Internet. The production process is the same in Internet radio as broadcast radio. The difference, as mentioned above, lies in how the signal is processed after production and then sent to listeners. Internet radio does offer some distinct programming advantages over live radio. Internet radio can provide on-demand programming, either with regular "live" radio that is streamed, or programming that has been prepackaged or that was already transmitted and stored for reuse. Prepackaged programming is flexible in that it does not have to be prepared for any particular "airtime." It is made available when it is ready to be transmitted. This could be a special program like a thirty-five-year retrospective of the careers of the Rolling Stones. The program could take months to produce and then simply be made available to listeners who click on the "Rolling Stones Retrospective" button on a Web site. News programs could be produced and made available at certain times during the day. Excerpts from a live concert that was sold out can be made available for listeners who click on the appropriate button or menu item.

Producing an Audio File

As with any type of media production, there are many levels of quality. Usually skill and good equipment can lead to high quality production. This is true of producing audio for the Internet. Regardless of the high quality of a computer or the caliber of the encoding software or hardware, the audio can only be as good as it was when it was originally created. Although some noisy recordings can be cleaned up and improved in production, remember an old saying about the handling of information by a computer: Garbage in, garbage out. Just because the setup for audio recording for the Internet is expensive and sophisticated does not necessarily mean that the audio will sound good. There is no substitute for good, clean sound.

At the very basic level, a digital sound file can be recorded with a computer running Windows 95 or 98 and some type of sound input, e.g., a microphone. Find the Sound Recorder program, start it and select "New" under the "File" option. Click on the "Record" button (it has a red circle on the button) and create sounds like speaking, playing music, or sound effects into the microphone. When recording is completed, click on the "Stop" button (it has a rectangle in it). The file can be modified by clicking on "Effects" and selecting either "Increase or Decrease Volume," "Increase or Decrease Speed," "Add an Echo Effect," or even "Record in Reverse." Audio files are saved the same as any other type of file, but with the .wav extender, such as "Test1.wav."

Sound editor programs, like shareware Goldwave Sound Editor, are used specifically for editing the quality or quantity of an audio file. The RealAudio Basic Server shareware prepares sound files for streaming on the Internet through a process of encoding. Using the proper software and following the procedures results in audio suitable for the Internet. Producing over-the-air quality work is similar to producing audio for the Internet, except more sophisticated tools are required to create broadcast quality sound.

SUMMARY: WHERE DOES INTERNET RADIO GO FROM HERE?

Internet radio is relatively easy to set up, inexpensive to maintain, and netcasters can play and say whatever they want, making cyber-radio an ideal medium for those who dream of reaching a global audience and who have visions of radio free of government regulations.

It is likely that by the turn of the century there will be more Internet radio programs than over-the-air stations (Strangelove, 1995). As one online radio executive said, "We are at the beginning of a new age in radio marked by the gradual acceptance of new technology" (Petrozzello, 1995a, p. 34).

Web radio is just one of many uses of Internet audio. Other possible applications include corporate information systems, Web kiosks, long-distance training and education, and audio libraries. As bandwidth increases, and modem connections get faster, "Internet radio will have the effect of turning cyberspace into a multimedia social environment" (Strangelove, 1995, p. 37).

CHAPTER LINKS

ABC RadioNet—http://www.abcradio.com

Airwaves Radio Station Page—http://www.airwaves.com

All Things Considered—http://www.npr.org/programs/atc/

Ann Online—http://www.annonline.com

Atlantic Records—http://atlantic-records.com

Audible Audio—http://www.audible.com

Bloomberg Information Radio—http://www.bloomberg.com

Broadcast.com—http://www.audionet.com

Canadian Broadcast Corporation—http://www.radio.cbc.ca/

CBS—http://www.cbs.com

CBS Radio Networks Online—http://www.cbsradio.com

Child's Touch—http://www.w2.com/

C/Net Radio—http://www.news.com/radio/index.html

Dow Jones Investor Network—http://www.dowjones.com/

imusic—http://www.imusic.com

Internet Wave Selections—http://www.vocaltec.com/

KHMX-FM—http://www.khmx.com

KIIS-FM—http://www.kiisfm.com

KinderNet—http://www.kindernet.com/

KISW-FM—http://www.kisw.com

KJHK-FM—http://www.cc.ukans.edu/~kjhknet/index.html

KLIF-AM— http://www.570klif.com/

L.A. Live—http://www.lalive.com

LiveConcerts.com—http://www.liveconcerts.com

Loud Radio—http://www.loud.com

MediaCast—http://www.mediacast.com

Megadeth Arizona—http://hollywoodandvine.com

MIT List of Radio Stations on the Internet—http://wmbr.mit.edu/stations/list.html

Morning Edition—http://www.npr.org/programs/morning/

National Public Radio—http://www.npr.org

NetRadio Network News—http://www.netradio.Net/

PC WORLD Online Radio—http://www.pcworld.com/news/newsradio/

Radio Online—http://www.radio-online.com

Rave Radio— http://www.rave-network.com

RealAudio—http://www.RealAudio.com

Sarajevo Online—http://www.worldmedia.fr//sarajevo/index.html

SonicNet—http://www.sonicnet.com

Star 100.7—http://www.histar.com/home.html

StreamWorks—http://www.xingtech.com

Swine Interactive Network—http://www.generationswine.com

Taylor Satellite Talk Radio—http://www.tstradio.com

Time, Inc.—http://pathfinder.com/time

Timecast—http://www.timecast.com

TrueSpeech—http://www.dspg.com/

VocalTec—http://www.vocaltec.com/

Warner Bros. Records—http://www.wbr.com

WBAL-AM—http://www.wbal.com/

WPSL-AM—http://www.wpsl.com/

REFERENCES

ABC RadioNet will be first to provide live news broadcasts on the Internet. (1995, October). *Information Today,* 50.

American Internet user survey. (1997). *Emerging technologies research group.* [Online]. Available: http://etrg.findsvp.com/Internet/findf.html [1998, January 7].

Atwood, B. (1995, May 20). KHMX Houston survey on the Web. *Billboard,* 96.

Atwood, B. (1996a, February 17). Desktop broadcasting. *Billboard,* 79–80.

Atwood, B. (1996b, June 22). DJs pump up the volume on "Loud Radio." *Billboard,* 76.

Atwood, B. (1996c, August 17). New Web site a ticket to live music. *Billboard,* 70.

Audible Audio. (1998, January 7). *Audible Audio homepage.* [Online]. Available: http://www.audible.com

AudioNet. (1997, February 4). *What is AudioNet?* [Online]. Available: http://www.audionet.com/about/

Berniker, M. (1995a, July 31). CBS the latest to use RealAudio. *Broadcasting and Cable,* 32.

Berniker, M. (1995b, October 30). NBA gets on Web with Starwave's ESPN SportsZone. *Broadcasting and Cable,* 74.

Berniker, M. (1995c, October 30). RealAudio software boosts live sound, music onto the Web. *Broadcasting and Cable,* 67.

Borzillo, C. (1996, September 28). Web sites promote station identities. *Billboard*, 91–94.

Broadcasting and cable yearbook. (1996). New Providence, NJ: R. R. Bowker.

Bromley, R. V., & Bowles, D. (1995). Impact of Internet use on traditional news media. *Newspaper Research Journal, 16* (2), 14–27.

Comarow, A. (1997, January 27). Radio waves. *U.S. News & World Report*, 73.

Crotty, C. (1996, October). The revolution will be netcast. *MacWorld*, 153–55.

DeJesus, E. X. (1996, February). Toss your TV: How the Internet will replace broadcasting. *Byte, 21* (2), 50–60.

Entertainment and technology strategies. (1998, January). *Forrester Research*. [Online]. Available: http://www.forrester.com [1998, April 24].

Grant, A. E. (1996). *Communication technology update* (5th ed.). Boston: Focal Press.

Hedges, C. (1997, February 9). Now TV interrupts Milosevic's programming. *New York Times*, p. E5.

Jessell, H. A. (1995, July 31). EZ sees money in the Net. *Broadcasting and Cable*, 31.

Kaye, B. K. (1998). Uses and gratifications of the World Wide Web: From couch potato to Web potato. *The New Jersey Journal of Communication, 6*, 21–40.

Levine, R. (1998, February). Heavy meddling on the Web. *The Web Magazine*, 58–59.

Lubar, S. (1993). *InfoCulture: The Smithsonian book of information age inventions*. Boston: Houghton Mifflin.

McCormick, M. (1996, May 4). Kids' music gets a Net boost. *Billboard*, 52.

McKee. (1996, February, 21). Sound bytes: Sites with sounds hit the Internet.

Merli, J. (1998, January 5). Listening while driving most popular. *Broadcasting and Cable*, 40.

Miles, P. (1997, September). Never off-air, never off-line. *Talk*, 6–7.

The MIT list of radio stations on the Internet. (1998, January 5). [Online]. Available: http://wmbr.mit.ecu/stations/list.htm

Noack, D. R. (1996, June). Radio, radio: Radio stations are blooming on the Internet as the Net becomes a radio medium. *Internet World*. [Online]. Available: http://www.webweek.com [1997, February 3].

Noack, D. R. (1997, November). CBS prohibits radio station Webcasting. *Editor & Publisher*, 42.

Online on the go. (1997, November 26). *Newsday*, p. CO3.

Pack, T. (1996, December). Radio-activity on the Web. *Database*, 38–45.

Paradigm teams with Microsoft Network for online music programming. (1997, February 5). [Online]. Available: http://biz.yahoo.com/bw/97/o2/05/y0007_y00_23.html

Passport to Web radio. (1997). Annual Report. Penn's Park, PA: International Broadcasting Services.

Pavlik, J. V. (1996). *New media technology*. Boston: Allyn and Bacon.

Petrozzello, D. (1995a, September 11). Radio + listeners: A match made on the Internet. *Broadcasting and Cable*, 34.

Petrozzello, D. (1995b, January 23). Radio on the Internet: University of Kansas station puts twenty-four-hour broadcast online. *Broadcasting and Cable,* 159.

Petrozzello, D. (1995c, July 31). Talk radio network goes on the Web. *Broadcasting and Cable,* 35.

Petrozzello, D. (1996a, April 8). Radio on the Internet: Study pinpoints heavy users. *Broadcasting and Cable,* 44.

Petrozzello, D. (1996b, April 22). Radio urged to interface with Internet. *Broadcasting and Cable,* 46.

Programming resources. (1998, February 13). *RadioSpace home page.* [Online]. Available: http://www.radiospace.com/programmingresources.htm

Progressive Networks launches RealAudio player plus. (1996, August 18). *RealAudio homepage.* [Online]. Available: http://www.realaudio.com/prognet/pr/playerplus.html

Quittner, J. (1995, May 1). Radio free cyberspace. *Time,* 91.

Rafter, M. (1996a, October 30). Progressive Networks wants to drown out all other Web sounds. *St. Louis Post Dispatch,* p. 5C.

Rafter, M. (1996b, January 24). RealAudio fulfills Web's on-line sound promise. *St. Louis Post Dispatch,* p. 13B.

RealNetworks' RealSystem 5.0 experiences rapid market adoption. (1997, December 10). *RealNetwork Homepage,* press release. [Online]. Available: http://www.real.com/corporate/pressroom/pr/50momentum.html

Rossney, R. (1996). Don't touch that dial. . . . *New Scientist,* 36–38.

Siegel, H., & Stein, D. J. (1997, November 3). Music performance rights on the 'Net: Continuing uncertainty over "cybercasting." *New York Law Journal,* S4.

Stauffer, T. (1997, January–February). Radio free Internet. *Websight,* 47–49.

Steinert-Threlkeld, T. (1996, January 29). Will the Web be all ears? *Inter@ctive Week,* 19–20.

Strangelove, M. (1995, January). Internet radio. *Online Access,* 36–37.

Sullivan, R. L. (1996). Radio free Internet. *Forbes,* 44–45.

Taylor, C. (1996, June 8). Real-time audio livens radio stations Web sites. *Billboard,* 6.

Taylor, C. (1997, July 5). Net use adds to decline in TV use; Radio stable. *Billboard,* 85.

Vaughn-Nichols, S. J. (1995, October). Radio comes to cyberspace. *Byte, 10* (20), 46.

Webcasters by format as of January 1, 1998. (1998, January/February). *Manager's Business Report,* 4.

Web music networks take programming beyond radio dial. (1997, January 13) *USA Today Online.* [Online] Available: http://www.usatoday.com/life/cyber/tech/CT555.htm

CHAPTER FOUR

TELEVISION
ENTERTAINMENT

While many fans are guffawing at the antics of the characters on Comedy Central's television program South Park, *the network is frowning at the antics of some of the program's fans. The animated series' wise-mouth, controversial, but lovable characters have captured the hearts of many devoted viewers who cannot seem to get enough of the program, even though it is aired five nights a week. To satisfy cravings for* South Park, *more than 250 "unofficial" program Web sites have sprouted up, many of which feature full 30-minute episodes and other bootlegged video.*

At first, Comedy Central asserted that streamed video does not show South Park *at its best and was rather chagrined that so many sites had appeared. The network claimed that the "unofficial" Web sites were not needed because the program airs so frequently and because the network operates its own Web site that contains* South Park *pages. The* South Park *section accounts for about 40 percent of Comedy Central's site traffic, and the site is so popular that four million chat messages were exchanged during the first two weeks of October 1997.*

Comedy Central soon realized that South Park's *skyrocketing popularity may in part be attributed to the Web. Since many cable systems do not carry the network, many viewers' first introduction to the raucous program was on the Web. Acknowledging the value of the Web as a promotional medium and as an alternative to television, Comedy Central has recently stopped discouraging the postings of unofficial Web sites, although many of these sites are in violation of copyright laws. The renegade* South Park *sites are proving to be too valuable to the continuing popularity of the program for the network to take any legal action to protect its copyrighted materials.*

For rabid South Park *fans, the Web has become a supplement to the television program. Viewers have an online venue where they can get their* South Park *fix twenty-four hours a day, seven days a week. And the Web has proven to be a satisfying substitute for those who cannot get the program through television.*

(Galetto, 1997; Gegax, Rosenberg, Rhodes, Gill, & Angell, 1998)

THE WEB AND TELEVISION ENTERTAINMENT

Many ardent fans have long hailed television as the ultimate form of entertainment. Television shows are delivered directly to homes, content is individually controlled by the push of a button or flick of a switch, and most programming is available twenty-four hours a day, seven days a week, covering every imaginable subject and gratifying most every need. Yet, despite all the benefits derived from watching television, the viewing public is increasingly looking to the television industry and new technologies for ways to boost their viewing pleasure.

Over-the-air broadcasting was once the primary means of receiving programming. Though cable was established early on in the life of television, it did not take hold with viewers until the 1970s. Since then technologies have given rise to newer means of program delivery. Direct Broadcast Satellite (DBS) transmits hundreds of channels direct from a satellite to a viewer's receiving dish. Multichannel Multipoint Distribution Service (MMDS) is often referred to as "wireless cable" because programs are delivered via microwave transmissions rather than by underground cable. As the installation of fiber optics progresses, digital cable, with the capability of delivering five hundred or more channels and interactive communication between viewers and televised information, is on the horizon.

Added to these systems is a new way of delivering television entertainment: the Web, in the form of PCTV, WebTV, and other television/computer hybrid systems. The viewing public's curiosity has turned toward this system that can deliver both traditional televised fare and the Web through one living room appliance, which is actually a television set and a computer combined.

Though Web technology cannot currently netcast an entire half-hour episode of a broadcast program without taking days to download, eventually, traditionally delivered shows will be available via the Web. Meantime, the Web is primarily a promotional vehicle for the networks' broadcast programs and their Web-only programming fare.

This chapter begins with a short history of the development of information delivery systems, including the Web. Next, television audience characteristics and theories of television viewing and their applicability to the Web are discussed. Examples of broadcast and cable network's uses of the Web and Web-only programming round out the chapter.

TELEVISION DELIVERY SYSTEMS

Television signals were first transmitted over the air, and viewing choices were limited to the number of channels that could be picked up by rooftop antennas. Later, cable and various satellite delivery systems were developed, increasing the number of channels and programming options. The viewing audience is increasingly turning to newer delivery systems, including the Web, for entertainment and information.

Broadcast

In the early days of television, broadcast programming was limited to a few channels that aired only during select hours, usually in the evening. Eventually, the three television networks—ABC, CBS, and NBC—became the mainstays of broadcasting, and along with a few independent stations, they began airing programs almost twenty-four hours a day. For many years, the viewing audience and industry executives were satisfied with this three-network, all-day broadcasting arrangement. The three broadcast networks dominated television and reached their peak in 1978, when they drew 93 percent of the viewing audience to their prime time programs. Both the introduction of the Fox broadcasting network in 1987 and the gaining popularity of cable television precipitated the decline of the three major networks. In the twenty years since their heyday, ABC, CBS, and NBC have experienced an almost 40 percent drop in their share of the prime time viewing audience.

Cable Television

Cable television was originally developed to carry programming to areas that could not receive over-the-air broadcast signals. Prime candidates for cable were valley towns surrounded by mountains that blocked signals emitted from television antennas in nearby cities. Until the late 1970s, broadcasting and cable benefited from each other. Broadcasting benefited from cable, which primarily delivered over-the-air programs via coaxial cable to an audience that was otherwise unable to receive broadcast signals, and cable had the advantage of delivering first-rate network programs that in turn attracted viewers, and thus increased the number of cable subscribers.

Cable television came on strong during the 1980s when HBO and Ted Turner's CNN and superstation WTBS began airing **cable specific programming,** which is original programming produced for cable delivery. Since then, slightly more than three hundred cable programming services and channels (e.g., The Golf Channel, The Sci-Fi Channel) have become available to subscribers (*Broadcasting and Cable Yearbook,* 1996). By 1996, increased program options had enticed almost seven out of ten households to subscribe to cable (Pavlik, 1996). Cable programs now compete head-to-head with broadcast shows for advertising dollars and ratings.

Multichannel Multipoint Distribution Service

In addition to cable delivery, **Multichannel Multipoint Distribution Service (MMDS),** or wireless cable as it is also known, increases viewers' programming choices by delivering shows via short-range microwave transmission to households that cannot receive cable but want to watch more than just over-the-air channels. MMDS is most often used and is most effective in urban areas where over-the-air signals are blocked by large buildings.

Direct Broadcast Satellite

Direct Broadcast Satellite (DBS) is slowly making its way into many of the nation's homes. DBS technology has improved since the 1980s, and now, thanks to video compression, users can choose from hundreds of channels that are beamed up to a satellite transponder (receive/transmit units on satellites) and sent directly to a subscriber's receiving dish. The number of households with DBS systems has not grown as quickly as projected. Major drawbacks to DBS are expensive equipment, a monthly subscription fee, and the absence of local over-the-air broadcast programming. Nevertheless, as the system gains in popularity by delivering a large number of programs, such as all NFL games, via satellite, it increasingly competes with over-the-air and cable programming.

High Definition Television

High Definition Television (HDTV) has long held the promise of being the television of the future. Prototypes were developed in Japan as early as 1964, but HDTV research was delayed in the United States until the 1980s, when scientists, the television industry, and the FCC agreed to work out various technical issues.

HDTV utilizes 1125 lines per screen, compared with 525 lines on standard television sets. The added lines improve the resolution and quality of televised images. HDTV pictures are as crisp and sharp as 35-millimeter motion pictures. Watching HDTV is almost like being there: viewers watching experimental digital telecasts claim to discern individual blades of grass, the seams of a spiraling football, five o'clock shadows on batters in the on-deck circle, and every laugh line and wrinkle on an actor's or actress's face (Mitchell, 1998).

The amazing clarity and detail delivered by HDTV is presented in a more rectangular form than nondigital television. The shape of the television screen is called the **aspect ratio,** which is the proportion of screen width to screen height. The aspect ratio of standard televisions is four units wide by three units high, yielding an almost square shape. HDTV has an aspect ratio of sixteen units wide by nine units high, closely resembling a rectangle or the shape of a movie theater screen. The new aspect ratio, combined with the increased number of lines per picture, means that HDTV viewers see a remarkably clear and colorful picture that can be viewed at a wider angle. HDTV is comfortably viewed starting at distances of only three times the height of the screen, and from farther distances without blurring or picture distortion. HDTV is also broadcast in stereo sound.

By government decree, digital television broadcasts will be available to half of U.S. households by the end of 1999 and to every home by the year 2002 (Mitchell, 1998). Despite the availability of digital broadcast signals, the road to widespread consumer use is expected to be a slow and winding one as industry experts and the FCC debate several major issues. Most pressing is the cost of digital television sets. HDTV sets are anticipated to hit the consumer market with a price tag between $7,000 and $12,000. Due to the extremely high costs of the sets, the FCC insists that HDTV broadcasts be compatible with existing non-HDTV sets, so viewers with standard sets would still be able to receive HDTV broadcasts. Additionally, current analog broadcasting is scheduled to be phased out by the year 2006, forcing consumers to purchase a digital set or a digital converter box for their old televisions (Mitchell, 1998). Compression schemes, sound quality, interlaced scanning, and other technical concerns must still be agreed upon and approved by the FCC before HDTV becomes commonplace in living rooms across America.

Interactive Television

While cable, MMDS, and DBS compete directly with over-the-air programming, these delivery modes are also in competition with each other and with new technologies that offer viewers choices beyond simply watching television programs. Television that offers more active program viewing has been envisioned since the 1960s, and actual two-way communication, where viewers interact with their television sets instead of just receiving messages, has been in development for over two decades. Throughout the country different interactive systems where users can "talk" to their television sets to complete banking, shopping, and other transactions have been tested, some with more success than others. High subscription rates, limited options, and low public demand have curtailed the growth of interactive television.

Despite earlier obstacles, interactivity is still highly sought after and, with the establishment of the information superhighway, has become the buzzword of the 1990s. There is much discussion regarding the factors that constitute true **interactivity.** Some argue that interactivity is simply selecting from a television menu of options or choosing movies on demand. Others, however, present a more complete view of interactivity, "in which everyone . . . can be both a source and receiver, just as anyone using a telephone can place or receive a call. In a telecommunications context, interactivity means two-way communication between source and receiver, or more broadly, multidirectional communication between any number of sources and receivers. In a broadest sense, interactivity simply means a process of reciprocal influences" (Pavlik, 1996, p. 135).

WEB DELIVERY SYSTEMS

The Web and Interactivity

Interactive television systems present viewers with a limited menu of interactive options. People who use interactive television systems are just receivers who input their preferences, but are not providers of information. Users react to the information provided by the cable company and interact via feedback mechanisms; however, users do not provide information that is available to other users on the system.

The Web, on the other hand, transcends interactive television. It has emerged as a system of information delivery where users receive, provide, and interact with information and with other users through Web pages, newsgroups, and other discussion forums. Additionally, an almost limitless amount of data provided by thousands of sources is available at the click of a mouse. Interactivity through hypertext is at the core of using the Web. The Web is an interactive medium with the potential of carrying traditionally televised fare and thus competing with the television industry for the viewing audience.

Intercasting

The Web and television are growing closer together as more sophisticated technologies emerge. There are many indications that the two technologies will eventually unite, making it unnecessary for a household to have both a traditional television set and separate computer with access to the Web.

The convergence of television and computers is possible through intercast technology. The word *intercast* is a combination of the "Internet" and "broadcasting." **Intercasting** makes it possible to receive both television signals and the Web both over a television set and through a computer (Hamilton, 1997; Proffit, 1997).

Intercast technology was designed by Intel Corporation. Intercasting works by inserting Web data into television programs via the vertical blanking interval (VBI). On older model television sets, the VBI was visible as the black lines that rolled by when the vertical hold was improperly adjusted. On newer televisions, the VBI is invisible and its broader bandwidth allows data, such as closed-captioned text and the Web, to be inserted into the television signal itself.

Set-Top Boxes, PCTV, and Hybrid Systems

The Web can be accessed through a standard television set that is connected to a special set-top box. Set-top box systems, such as Microsoft-owned WebTV, are bringing the Web into the living rooms of those who feel more comfortable looking at a television screen than a computer screen. These systems are marketed to consumers who are television viewers aware of the Internet, and maybe even curious about it, but who do not own a computer, and are not about to buy one. However, it seems that early adopters of WebTV are not necessarily part of the targeted computer illiterate; 40 percent already own a computer (Mermigas, 1998; Yovovich, 1998).

A WebTV competitor, ViewCall America, owned by NetChannel, focuses on the television and entertainment aspect of set-top boxes by dubbing themselves a "television service provider" (TSP). NetChannel's box allows up to six people to customize content (Tedesco, 1997e). Although NetChannel offers all Internet functions, the company purposely downplays the Internet and even lists it last on its on-screen menu of entertainment options (Tedesco, 1997d).

Television is enhanced by set-top box systems. Through a telephone line connection and a set-top box, television is no longer just television, but is an entertainment center that delivers the Web and many Internet functions, including e-mail, along with traditional programs. Newer versions of set-top models, such as WebTV Plus, split the television screen, so that viewers can surf the Net at the same time they are watching a program (Hafner, 1997; Wildstrom, 1996; Zelnick, 1997). With WebTV Plus, users can also download video and data onto the system's hard drive (Tedesco, 1997b). Even though only 150,000–300,000 WebTV boxes had been sold by the end of 1997, Jupiter Communications forecasts that by the end of 1998 there will be five million "Internet enabled televisions" in consumers' homes (Colman, 1997; Taylor, 1996a, p. 9; Yovovich, 1998).

"Internet Television" and "PCTV" are two commonly used terms that refer to the reception of both television signals and the Web over a computer. A cable connection and special intercast plug-in card for the computer combine to bring television signals to a computer at the same time Web pages are being viewed. However, Web pages are limited to ones that are directly related to the television program being shown. For example, when an MTV program is on, users can only access a limited number of MTV-related Web pages.

Both PCTV and Web-enhanced television possess inherent disadvantages as they endeavor to deliver the quality of two media in one package. PCTV-delivered television programs suffer from poorer quality video than programs transmitted to a television set. Additionally, Web surfing is tied to the companion television program and not the Web at large (Proffit, 1997). Set-top boxes offer snail-paced Internet access through standard telephone line connections. In an effort to speed up Internet access, newer versions of WebTV pre-download popular television-related Web sites and store them in the set-top box's hard drive for quick retrieval while viewing televised fare. This helps somewhat, but real-time connections remain painfully slow.

Monitor resolution is another drawback to both PCTV and set-top systems. Most computer monitors possess a sharp resolution that makes them ideal for up-close viewing. Television screen images are not as sharp as computer images, but are ideal for viewing video across most living rooms. However, text-rich Web pages and many graphics may be too small, and thus too difficult, to discern at more than a few feet away from the set unless displayed on a large screen monitor, and even then the low resolution may make some enlarged text and graphics appear fuzzy (Gross, 1997; Wildstrom, 1996).

Net computers (NC) or Internet computers are low-cost computers made for the primary purpose of accessing the Internet. A Net-only computer could become a viable consumer product by the end of the century. These limited-capacity computers are designed for people who would like to navigate the Net using a computer, but do not have the money to purchase a complete computer system. For around $500, an NC is little more than a central processing unit (CPU), wireless keyboard, screen, and modem through which a user would access the Internet. More sophisticated prototypes would allow users to perform other computing tasks by accessing software from the server's computers. When users finish using a program, the software remains on the server, eliminating the need for hard drive storage (DeJesus, 1996; Meyer, 1995; Tedesco, 1996e).

With computer prices dropping and complete second-hand computer systems selling for close to the price of a new NC, analysts believe many consumers would balk at paying for a computer that really is not a computer. NCs are designed primarily for accessing the Internet, but other computing tasks can be carried out by tapping into a remote storage network. Consumer behavior specialists doubt that users would feel safe storing their data on a network. Most users want the security of knowing their data is sitting in their computer hard drives or backed up on floppies, a security they would have to forego with an NC (Hafner & Levy, 1996). NCs were heavily hyped in 1995 and 1996, but by the end of 1997 they had hardly made a dent in consumer awareness or in the marketplace (Vonder Haar, 1997).

Several companies are working on other ways of delivering the Internet and television by taking the best of computers and the best of television and rolling them into one home entertainment device. Compaq's PC Theatre is just one example of a computer/television appliance capable of transmitting both the Web and television programs. PC Theatre consists of a complete computer, a 36-inch TV/computer monitor, wireless keyboard, remote control device, and Internet connection. Through this type of hybrid television/computer, it is possible to surf the Web at the same time a television program is being watched. Additionally, the system has a remote control and wireless keyboard for short- or long-distance viewing, and the large screen monitor displays high-quality video and Web page text ("A Marriage of Convergence," 1997; Bertolucci, 1997). Hybrid systems were generally priced between $2,000 and $4,000; however, in November 1997, the Cyrix Corporation demonstrated new sophisticated home entertainment devices that are anticipated to sell for around $1,000, excluding the monitor. In general, the public has been slow to purchase hybrid systems, which are generally perceived as being too complex and too expensive (Clark & Carlton, 1997; Hof, 1997).

Cable Modems

In addition to PCTV, set-top boxes, and hybrid systems, other advances are delivering Web data to television sets. Cable modems can be configured to deliver the Internet to a computer or to a television set at speeds up to 80–100 times faster than by telephone lines (Haddad, 1997; Tedesco, 1997e, 1997f). However, modem access is delivered from the same cable system, so the more users logged on at the same time, the slower the transmission speed (Tedesco, 1996e).

Major cable MSOs (multisystem operators), such as Tele-Communication, Inc., Continental Cablevision, Time Warner Cable, and Comcast Cable, are beginning to offer Internet access to their cable television subscribers. Cable MSOs join with computer companies, such as WorldGate, to launch cable television–based Internet services. WorldGate provides the Internet connection, and the cable company loads the required Internet software into the cable television converter box (Brodsky, 1997; Hafner, 1997; Lee, 1997; Zelnick, 1997). A click of the remote control device signals the cable company to transmit the Web pages associated with the television program that is being watched (Brodsky, 1997).

Although cable modems hold the promise of transmitting quick Web data, high monthly prices and the non–fiber optic infrastructure of many cable systems are current barriers to widespread adoption. Cable modems are also up against consumer feelings of general dissatisfaction with cable companies. Many consumers would prefer to have as little to do with their local cable companies as possible, which may further hamper the adoption of cable modems. According to Odyssey research, almost one-quarter of cable subscribers feel their service is "not good," and only three out of ten report "very good" service (Petrozzello, 1997). Nevertheless, cable modems are projected to be in 3.4 million U.S. homes by 1999, and cable Internet services offered to 90 percent of the population by 2006 (Tedesco, 1996e; Van Tassel, 1997).

As WebTV, PCTV, computer/television hybrids, and cable-modem based delivery systems vie for their share of the market, the television and computer industries will continue to forge ahead with new improvements and innovations that will lead eventually to an affordable all-in-one system that delivers both television programs and the full range of Web sites and Internet applications.

TELEVISION, THE WEB, AND AUDIENCE USE

Audience Fragmentation

Cybercasting, information delivery on the Web, differs from television's model of "broadcasting" where programs are expected to appeal to millions of viewers. Cable television introduced **narrowcasting,** where topic-specific shows appeal to smaller but more interested and loyal audiences. The Net takes narrowcasting a step further by targeting information to smaller groups and individuals and delivering it straight to home computers or even to pagers and cell phones. The Web is becoming a "personal broadcast system" (Cortese, 1997, p. 96).

Although broadcast and cable television networks primarily use the Web as a promotional vehicle for their televised programs, some networks have created special Web-only programs and Web-only versions of existing television shows. Examples of some of these "Webisodes" are given later in this chapter when cyber-programs are discussed. Time spent on the Web is time that may be taken away from watching television, thus decreasing viewership and further adding to the erosion of network ratings.

Just as radio's audience was encroached on by broadcast television, and, in turn, broadcast television viewers were drawn to cable, the Web has slowly been attracting users at the expense of other media, especially television. Although the Web is not yet as visually compelling as television, 18 to 37 percent of Web users report watching less television now than before becoming Internet users (Bromley & Bowles, 1995; "Internet Eats into," 1996; Kaye, 1998; "Why Internet Advertising," 1997), and households that subscribe to AOL watch 15 percent (seven hours each week) less television than average (Taylor, 1997; Tedesco, 1997c). Meanwhile, Nielsen Media Research data reveal that 1.3 million fewer people watched prime time television during the February 1997 sweeps period than in the same period in 1996 (Taylor, 1997). Although Nielsen denies that the Internet is directly responsible for the loss of television viewers, it is initiating a new project to study home computer and Internet use. The project is based on the company's television measurement service, but instead of using meters, special software will track participants' online use (Tedesco, 1997d).

BJK&E Media concurs with Nielsen that the Internet is not responsible for the loss of television viewership. BJK&E Media claims that while online users watch less television than nonusers, the difference is not attributable to the Internet, but to other lifestyle preferences. Additionally, when television use is examined by time of day, Internet users tend to watch less daytime programming, but just as much prime time and late-night fare as nonusers (Ross, 1997).

The Web is in the competitive arena as media vie for an already fragmented audience. Advertising costs are largely based on the size of the audience reached. In the early days of television, viewership was mostly shared among three major broadcast television networks, which were and still are fiercely competitive, because even a small percentage gain in the number of viewers means millions of dollars of additional advertising revenue. Cable television, which often offers sixty-plus channels, only serves to further fragment the viewing audience. Now, as viewers increasingly subscribe to cable and satellite-delivery systems and turn to the Web as a source of information and entertainment, the size of television's audience is eroding further, and with it, potential advertising revenue. To help offset audience loss and to retain current viewers, most networks have established Web sites on which they promote their programs and stars, and offer visitors insights into the network and the world of television. The 1997 season debut of NBC's *ER* was heavily promoted through traditional television ads, as well as through a weeklong online chat component that was available on the program's Web site. As one executive said, "The more they talk about it, the more they watch it" (Krol, 1997, p. 40). Clearly, many Internet and television program executives view the Net as a means of attracting viewers to televised fare. Additionally, the networks charge for advertising on their Web sites. Web advertising is much less expensive than television advertising, and therefore Web advertising revenues do not, at least for now, make up for any lost television ad revenues caused by a declining audience.

The number of television viewers who turn their attention to the Web is increasing daily. The Web gives users more information and entertainment choices than do typical broadcast programs. The Web's growing audience, its offerings of hundreds of thousands of Web sites, and its potential for attracting advertising revenue all combine to further bolster the Web as a viable information delivery system.

Remote Control Devices

Browsing through Web pages is in many ways similar to watching television: users face a screen displaying text and graphics, which in some instances also includes audio and video components. Switching from Web site to Web site is in some ways similar to changing television channels. When Internet users wish to switch from one Web site to another they may do so by typing in a known Web address (URL— uniform resource locator) into a pull-down window. Web users may also switch from site to site by using a mouse simply to click on a hot link, or they may browse sites by clicking on Netscape's Back or Forward buttons, which function similarly to the up and down arrow keys on television remote control devices.

For true "Net potatoes" or mouse potatoes, a cordless Internet controller lets users kick back and surf the Web from as far as thirty feet away from their computers. With a quick click of a button a user can scroll through pages, go back to a previous page, or select a bookmark. An Internet controller frees users from the confines of a chair and keyboard and allows them to travel through the Web while sitting on the couch or lying on the floor.

Even the "lingo" of Web browsing is borrowed from television. Commonly used terms such as *surfing* and *cruising* and *browsing*, which are used to describe traversing from one Web site to another, are also descriptors of television channel-switching behavior.

Instrumental and Ritualistic Use

The Web is still very much a novelty medium. Though there are many experienced users, most are just now beginning to dabble in this intricate network. The more the Web is used, the more likely people will develop different styles of use, as they have with television.

Two primary ways of viewing television have been identified. **Instrumental viewing** tends to be goal-oriented and content-based; viewers decide to watch television with a certain type of program in mind. **Ritualistic viewing** is less goal-oriented and more habitual in nature; viewers watch television for the act of watching without regard to program content (Rubin, 1984). The Web easily lends itself to both the television models of instrumental and ritualistic viewing. Users may begin their Web sessions seeking specific information, paying attention to content and actively moving from site to site with a clear goal in mind. On the other hand, users may get on the Web just to pass time, and thus explore sites by randomly clicking on hot links. For many, the Web is quickly becoming a habit, something they just do on a regular basis. Although the Web commands attention and cannot be used as mindlessly as television, new Web technology and design will one day allow more passive use. Viewers' attention will be held longer on each screen, decreasing the need for active scrolling and site switching. More compelling and lengthier video and audio promise to keep users' eyes on the screen for longer periods of time. Larger monitors will present greater amounts of information on the screen without scrolling. Additionally, Web pages are increasingly being designed with hyperlinks to other Web pages or specific areas within a page, further decreasing the user's need to scroll.

Selecting Television Programs and Web Sites

The television remote control device (RCD) has altered existing television viewing patterns. RCDs have enabled individuals to establish their own creative patterns of television channel selection. For example, some viewers may quickly scan through all available channels, while others may slowly sample a variety of favorite channels before selecting one program to watch (Heeter, D'Allessio, Greenberg, & McVoy, 1988). Prior to the advent of RCDs, viewers generally chose a program from among several options and tended to watch it through its entirety. Viewers often stayed tuned to the same channel throughout the viewing session, watching commercials and whatever programs were on the network's lineup. Now with RCDs, viewers zap commercials, watch two or more programs simultaneously by quickly switching back and forth between channels, and channel surf.

Viewers tend to surf through the lowest channels (2–13) on the dial more often than the higher-numbered channels (Bollier, 1989). Unlike television, however, the Web does not have prime locations on its "dial." Therefore, one Web site does not have inherent location advantage over any other site (Levy, 1995). However, sites with short domain names are easier to type in and remember, and thus they may be accessed more frequently than their counterparts with longer URLs ("A TCP/IP," 1993).

Similar to television, online push services are being organized as "channels." Once users have registered for a service, they specify the channels and topics they are most interested in. Models of Web channels include information grouped into major categories such as news, sports, weather, entertainment, and so on. Users can "surf" within specific topic areas rather than through the Web at large, or wait for the push service to send them items pertaining to selected topics.

As users become more experienced and adept at making their way around the Web, customized styles of Web cruising could emerge. Many users may explore only one level beyond a site's opening page, while other users may feel compelled to delve through more information by clicking on links that take them three and four levels deep into a site. Others still may only look through a set of favorite sites. Just as television program selection patterns warrant study, research probing Web site selection patterns could uncover interesting and helpful information for site designers.

Channel and Web Site Repertoire

RCDs, along with cable television, have fostered individual **channel repertoire,** which has been defined as a subset of channels, out of the total number of available channels, that viewers watch on a regular basis (Heeter et al., 1988). Most viewers watch an average of 10–12 channels on a regular basis, regardless of the number of channels offered by their cable systems (Ferguson & Perse, 1993; Heeter, 1985).

Establishment of a repertoire of channels suggests that viewers tend to watch a small selection of "favorite" channels. Although Web use is still in its infancy and users are exploring a wide range of sites, it is likely that experienced users will eventually create their own repertoire of Web sites. Information overload is affecting many Web users, who often feel overwhelmed by the huge selection of Web sites. Many Web and computer experts vow that the public wants the Web to be as easy to use as their televisions, and they want just a few good sites to choose among (Cortese, 1997). One Web executive admits to having only about a half-dozen sites that he visits on a regular basis (Taylor, 1996b). Web users' repertoire could consist of a limited set of Web sites, probably bookmarked, that would be the first accessed during a Web session and would be visited more frequently than other sites.

Web cruising styles and Web site repertoire are likely to be affected by push technology. Users can register with one or more push sites and wait for requested information to be transmitted to their computers. Push technology diminishes the need to surf the Web and access many different sites when searching for specific information.

Using the Web as Television

The Internet is a new medium that is changing the way people receive and provide information and is altering existing media behaviors. The Web attracts thousands of new users daily. For some, the Web will always be a supplement to existing media, but for others the Web may become a primary medium, the one they turn to first for news, information, and entertainment. For some, the Web will become a necessity, for others a habit, and still many more will consider it a luxury. Web novices may closely attend to the screen, giving close thought to their Internet travels. More instrumental uses may give way to ritualistic use as experienced Web cruisers quickly scan bookmarked sites just to pass the time or to keep their mind off other things.

People tend to use WebTV to enhance their overall television viewing experience rather than as another way of using their computers. Entertainment is the primary reason for using WebTV, and it is also the primary motivation for watching traditional television (Rubin, 1981; 1983). Furthermore, with WebTV people can be entertained while relaxing with friends and family members, and most people prefer that to sitting alone in front of a computer screen (Tedesco, 1997c).

Many Web site managers strive to emulate television in their presentation of content. AOL sought guidance from MTV creator, Bob Pittman, and the late Brandon Tartikoff, former NBC programming executive. Additionally, Microsoft Network is planning on introducing new sites in "seasons," and pulling those with low ratings (Levy, 1997).

Just as new television technologies gave rise to new viewing patterns and uses, Web technologies are also altering Web use. Undoubtedly, the new Internet remote control devices will foster new Web site changing patterns, and perhaps even increase the amount of use because of added comfort and convenience. Soon full-motion video and wider fiber optic bandwidth will team to bring broadcast and cable program episodes to the Web, further refining, changing, and influencing users' motivations, patterns, and amount of Web use.

TELEVISION AND THE WEB: CONTENT

The World Wide Web is still in the early stages of development, similar to television in the 1950s (Bimber, 1996). Early television programs were largely adapted to the new medium from radio. Programs such as *Amos 'n' Andy, Life of Riley, The Guiding Light, You Bet Your Life,* and *The Lone Ranger* all had their origins in radio, as did many other shows televised in the 1950s. Eventually, industry executives and writers took advantage of television's strong points and began producing shows that were not rooted in radio. The visual aspects of television, set designs, location shoots, tape delay, and other production advantages all led to the creation of new, exciting, dynamic shows and program genres not possible within the confines of radio. Similar to television adapting programs from radio, much of what is seen on the Web is adapted from other media.

Many Web sites, especially those created early on, are primarily made up of text taken directly from the pages of newspapers, magazines, and brochures, radio and television scripts, and other sources. In other words, some Web sites merely display what has already been aired or printed using traditional methods.

Among the most popular Web sites, besides search engines, are the ones containing television-related topics. Several sites, such as *ESPN SportsZone, MTV Online,* and *The X-Files* receive more than 200,000 hits each day (Berniker, 1995c; "Netmation's 100 Most Popular," 1997; Tedesco, 1997e). Each of the big three television networks (ABC, NBC, CBS) and dozens of cable channels tried out the Web for the first time in 1994 (Mandese, 1995a), and many others have since established Web sites. Web users can read about the week's lineup of guests on *Late Night with David Letterman,* chat with "cyberpals" about whether a favorite soap character really died, and discuss what they like or hate about certain programs. By accessing television program sites, the Web audience sees photos of their favorite television stars, reads about upcoming episodes, listens to television programs' theme songs, and hears characters spewing popular lines, such as Homer Simpson's "Doh," or Beavis and Butthead's well-known and widely imitated laugh.

Because of the advent of newer technologies, avant-garde Web pages are filled with eye-catching text, audio, and graphics. News and information are still often taken from traditional sources but are adapted more specifically to the Web. Text is edited and rewritten for visual presentation and screen size, and short summary versions may be linked to longer detailed ones. Bold graphic illustrations, audio and video components, and interactive elements enliven Web pages and give them a television-like appearance.

Although television programs in their entirety are not yet available on the Web, short promotional video clips of episodes can be viewed on some network sites. Bell Laboratories is experimenting with new image and audio transmission software that stores video and text transcription on the Web within minutes of a television program's conclusion. The software uses content-based sampling that delivers still video images, and with more advanced technology, full-motion video in parallel with the text. A program with a few hundred still images and a one-hour hypertext transcript can be stored on one floppy disk. If television viewers miss an episode of a program such as the *News Hour with Jim Lehrer,* they will be able to access the Web site and "see" the program in its entirety (Rupley, 1996).

Before online content can widely become as compelling and visually interesting as television, the industry's Web sites need to shift from a promotional emphasis to a content emphasis, but that is an expensive proposition. Many industry analysts concur with MTV's senior vice president Matt Farber, who claims that when Web sites start "charging millions for an online ad," then the Web will become as important as television and can justify "proportional investment in content creation" (Shaw, 1998, p. 18).

Without the time and space constraints that plague traditional media, Web authors and designers are free to expand their offerings and produce Web-only material and Web versions of traditionally delivered fare. The Web is exploding with sites that complement traditional offerings but also offer unique content not found elsewhere. Electronic magazines and newspapers, and online soap operas and talk shows are just a few examples of original content. The Web is a unique medium where original and adapted content live side-by-side.

Broadcast Networks on the Web

The Web is creating new programming outlets for cable and broadcast networks. Almost every television network has a cyberspace presence. Although Web sites were once seen as promotional vehicles, online "channels" containing original and adapted content are evolving.

Web users flock to television-related Web sites. The four major broadcast networks' homepages include entertainment, news, sports, personality, and programming information with sound bites, video clips, and interactive applications. Networks tout their programs, draw visitors to upcoming episodes through short video segments, encourage fan participation, spark interest through interactive games, and in some cases, offer original "online programs."

ABC *ABC.com* has cyberpages for *ABC Prime Time, ABC News, ABC Sports, ABC Soaps, ABC Radio,* and *Good Morning America.* ABC's Web site offers users programming information and schedules, summaries and descriptions of segment packages for their public affairs programs, lists of upcoming guests on talk and interview shows, downloadable audio, video, and program transcripts, and news updates.

CBS *CBS, Eye on the Net* claims 1.2 million hits (visits) per week to its site, and features information about its television programs, including specials and children's shows. Visitors can link to programs such as *Late Show with David Letterman, Late Late Show with Tom Snyder,* and *CBS News,* which delivers up-to-the-minute news (Berniker, 1995b; Mandese, 1995b).

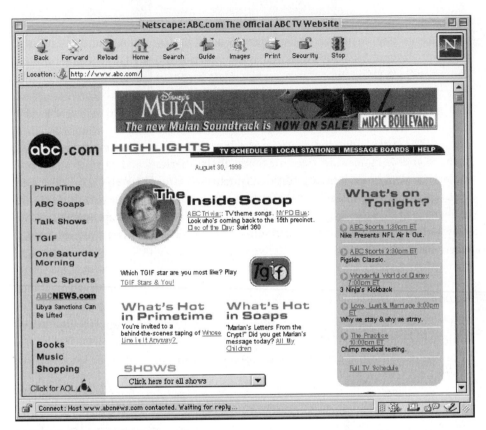

FIGURE 4.1 ABC-TV Homepage

In 1995, CBS switched from Prodigy to AOL as its cyber-content carrier. The network made an "open-ended financial arrangement" with an option to renew with AOL. CBS's cyberpresence on AOL boosts the proprietary service's aspirations of becoming the leading source of television and media online information (Berniker, 1995b).

NBC On NBC TV's home on the Web—*NBC.com*—visitors enjoy previews of new programs. NBC, hoping to attract a younger, upscale audience to its programs, promotes its fall television lineup on the Web.

More than the other three major networks, NBC considers the Web as an online business. NBC has gone beyond a basic network Web site by uniting with the Microsoft Corporation to create *MSNBC*, a news and information Web site. NBC is planning to form other partnerships to compete head-to-head with major Web sites such as ESPN SportsZone (Berniker, 1995d; Ross, 1996).

FOX   The Fox network launched its Web site, _FoxWorld,_ in 1995. It features program information, sound bites, video clips, and interactive original Fox programming. This site is heavily into promotion and has a "Fox Kids" area and in-depth summaries of past episodes of its television programs, with emphasis on _The X-Files._

Cable Networks on the Web

Like the broadcast networks, cable networks see value in establishing a Web presence. Cable networks tend to have smaller audiences than their broadcast counterparts, and thus they are striving to reach new viewers through the Web. Smaller, less popular cable networks such as the Sci-Fi Channel created their own cybernetworks on the Web to promote themselves to potential viewers who do not have access to the cable channels.

Dominion, the Sci-Fi Channel's cyperspace site, is more than just a promotional site for the network's television programs. It is an "online home base for science fiction." The Web site connects science fiction fans to shopping, sci-fi news, and samples of sci-fi programs. The Sci-Fi Channel's parent company, USA Networks, claims an average of 14,000 hits per day on the network's homepage, and averages 759 daily hits directly to _Dominion_ (Walley, 1995, p. 14).

Comedy Central Online includes a daily humor page consisting of song parodies, sketches, characters, and comedy bits. The material is updated daily by the network's Web writers. The interactive comedy group, NET//WITTS, includes syndicated radio personalities "Dr. Dave" Kolin and James Justice.

The Food Network serves up a Web menu of recipes and other goodies on its _CyberKitchen_ site. Diet and health information, food-related news, and links to restaurants give visitors plenty to whet their appetites over.

Lifetime Online serves up a range of the latest health information, including sports and fitness. A section devoted to parenting includes advice from physicians and a "Dad's Diary" written by a new father.

Nick-at-Nite and TV Land Online is the ultimate destination on the Web for fans of classic TV. Nostalgia buffs are treated to photos and audio and video clips from television favorites such as _The Brady Bunch, Happy Days,_ and _Laverne & Shirley._ Visitors can also enjoy a wide variety of games, sweepstakes, and polling. This site strives to attract younger viewers who watch classic television and people who enjoyed the original airings.

PBS Online's sophisticated site mirrors its television network's highbrow content. Audio clips and transcripts of _Frontline_ and _The NewsHour with Jim Lehrer_ are offered along with an online news hour. Links to PBS's children's shows delight children who visit online with their _Sesame Street_ pals.

FIGURE 4.2 Nick at Nite Homepage

Online networks encourage repeat visits by frequently updating and revitalizing their Web sites. The *Discovery Channel Online* chooses a theme such as history, nature, or science and technology for each day of the week. Keeping Web sites fresh, dynamic, and interesting is challenging and requires an extensive labor force. *MTV* and Discovery Online and other cable networks hire staffs just to design and update their Web sites, and they also employ numerous freelance writers, reporters, and producers who are primarily responsible for Web content (Hall, 1996).

The cable networks discussed previously are just a smattering of the large number of cable television networks that have established Web sites. Generally, broadcast and cable network sites heavily promote their televised fare, but also may offer visitors links to fan clubs, star biographies, recaps of past episodes, previews of upcoming episodes, audio and video clips, and in some instances games and other fun activities. Network sites act as extensions of their television networks and as ways to reach out to and interact with the viewing public.

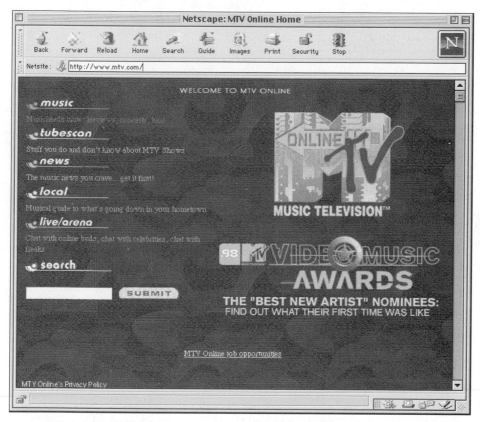

FIGURE 4.3 MTV Homepage

TV Entertainment Sites

UTV, the *Ultimate Television Network,* aspires to be the "ultimate TV Web site, celebrating TV's past, present and future" (Reidman, 1996, p. 21). The site includes "Daily TV" and "TV Daily News," from which visitors can download broadcast clips and access Nielsen Media Research. The "Ultimate TV List" includes about 6,000 links to various television program Web sites and to about five hundred network, cable, and local television station homepages. In its first three months online, 9,500 television enthusiasts registered to participate in the site's chat rooms (Taylor, 1996a). UTV is jammed full of all kinds of television-related information that will keep even the most die-hard television aficionados happy.

Sony Pictures Entertainment has launched one of the most encompassing entertainment sites on the Web. The site is billed as a "major interactive entertainment complex" featuring audio clips of musical artists, an online jukebox, soap

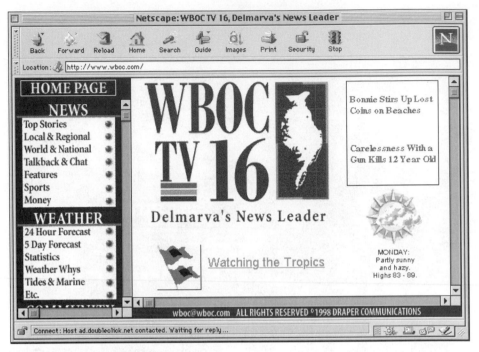

FIGURE 4.4 WBOC-TV Homepage

opera tie-ins, and game show sites such as *Jeopardy, The Dating Game,* and *Wheel of Fortune. Police Story* recants true crime stories in interactive interviews and provides pertinent case information, staged reenactments, and chats with forensics experts. Sony supports more than just a Web site that features television programs; it also covers other entertainment media such as music and theatrical movies (Ross & Johnson, 1997).

Television Affiliates with Web Sites

According to the Ultimate Television Network, as of mid 1997 slightly over seven hundred U.S. television stations had found homes on the Web. The stations offer a range of information such as local news, weather, community calendars, and community events.

Television Broadcasters' Web Sites, by James Rea, is a 500-page research report that is considered to be the Web's "equivalent to the Holy Grail" (Freeman, 1996, p. 23). The report is a thorough assessment of Web sites produced by television stations and broadcast and cable networks. Among the stations receiving high accolades for Web creativity is CBS affiliate *WBOC-TV.* The Maryland station's Web

FIGURE 4.5 KPIX-TV Homepage

site includes a tristate newsletter. Station *KGTV-TV* in San Diego ties its Web site in with its owner McGraw-Hill's *Business Week* magazine and with ABC News, offering a mix of radio and business features. Landmark Communications' Las Vegas online *KLAS-TV8* posts a "city guide" that is described as "a cross between an electronic yellow pages and hotel visitor's guide" (Freeman, 1996, p. 23).

KCPQ-TV, Seattle, targets children with its array of games, jokes, and other fun Web activities. For adults, sports and news are tops and the site's "Most Wanted List" has led to the capture of many criminals. Weather watchers can track the latest hurricane with animated Doppler radar on Tampa's *WFLA-TV*'s Web site. This site includes a list of links to local media, the school system, and area physicians. It even has "quick eats," links to online food ordering.

KPIX-TV, San Francisco, capitalizes on its claim that one-quarter of Internet users live within its broadcast signal range. The station, along with KPIX-FM, presents a lively page filled with news, weather, traffic, and other local information. Additionally, users can download demonstration software available as a special deal from software companies that advertise on the KPIX site.

Hundreds of other network television affiliates and independents have established unique, interesting, and lively Web sites linking visitors with local news and weather and community services and events. These sites enrich a station's image and can draw the affiliate closer to its audience through e-mail and other avenues of interactivity.

CYBERPROGRAMS: NETWORK AND WEB-ONLY

Although many of the network sites are promotional vehicles featuring the networks' televised fare, some sites also create and netcast original Web-only programs. Web-only programs add a new dimension to the sites by offering unique, interactive entertainment not possible using other media. Following is a sampling of broadcast and cable network shows and how they are promoted on the Web. Also, examples of Web-only programs illustrate the emergence of new forms of entertainment made possible through Internet technologies.

Children's Programs

The PBS program *The Magic School Bus* drove onto the information superhighway with a Web site specifically designed to be easily accessed by children. Summaries of past episodes highlight difficult words that, when clicked, bring up a dictionary, and the Art Gallery link features drawings by kids who visited the site. The site contains many amusing and interesting activities that stretch children's imaginations and spark their curiosity.

Children's Web-Only Programs

The popular afternoon program *Bill Nye the Science Guy* has spun *Nye Labs* in cyberspace. Nye Lab visitors can download audio clips, participate in fun online experiments, and also e-mail in requests for scientific information. The PBS network requires producers to create separate Internet applications of its programs. Nye Labs is an example of online interactive content that is different from the televised version.

Universal Cartoon Online Network (UCON) is still on the drawing board but plans to provide more than just cartoons on the Web. The site's creators want UCON to be "just as accessible as TV" (Parets, 1997a). In addition to cartoons, the site will provide online games, movies, and a science fiction series with many different story lines depending on which character users choose to follow.

Dramatic Shows

One of television's most popular programs, *The X-Files* brings UFOs, La Chupacabra, and other life mysteries to the Web. Along with typical promotional items about the characters and actors, the site provides links to the show's fan club and to summaries of every episode ever made. The site, which draws over one million visitors per month, sees a lag in activity whenever *The X-Files* airs on television, but as soon as the episode concludes, site usage goes back up (Tedesco, 1997c).

On Showtime's *The Outer Limits* homepage, devout fans can download up to four 60-second segments of recent episodes of the sci-fi program. *The Outer Limits* site also includes summaries of past episodes and a page where visitors rate the episodes.

The companion Web site for the television program *People's Court* gives viewers the chance to play attorney. The site presents 3-minute online summaries of each case the night before the program airs. *People's Court* visitors examine the facts and send in their verdicts, some of which will be used on the air.

Web-Only Drama

NBC's first try at original Web programming is based on its television program, *Homicide: Life on the Street*. Linked from NBC's Web site, *Homicide: Second Shift* features a cast of characters who are not featured on the televised version of the show. Users become sleuths in each "Webisode" and participate in crime-solving investigations by looking through crime scene photos and other evidence. NBC producers are further merging the on-air program with its online counterpart with appearances by Second Shift Lt. Walter Neal on the television program. The cyber-lieutenant and the television detectives will team up in an investigation. Although a small online audience and video streaming limitations preclude a true crossover of on-air and online programs in the near future, in the long run producers plan to move some of the characters and storylines from television to the online world (Ross & Jensen, 1997; Tedesco, 1996a, 1997a).

Game Shows

Versions of the popular game shows *Wheel of Fortune* and *Jeopardy* are available on the *Sony Pictures Entertainment* site. The television programs *Jeopardy* and *Wheel of Fortune* are produced by Columbia TriStar, a Sony Pictures Entertainment company. Sony promotes the games on its Web site. On both game sites, Web contestants get to play individually at any time of the day and compete for recognition on the daily "Top Ten Players" list. Eventually, players will compete for prizes donated by corporate sponsors. Additionally, Columbia TriStar's *Rock & Roll Jeopardy* can be found online.

Talk and Entertainment Programs

E! (Entertainment Television) teamed with the computer network C/NET to form a jointly owned Web entertainment network featuring gossip and other show biz

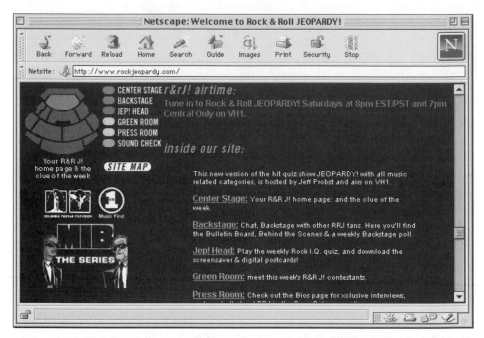

FIGURE 4.6 The Rock & Roll Jeopardy Web Site. © 1998 Columbia TriStar Interactive. All rights reserved. Visit the Sony Pictures Entertainment Web site at www.spe.sony.com.

news. *E! Online* focuses on entertainment news, celebrities, movies, and television programs. The site comes across primarily as a promotional vehicle for the network's television programs. An E! Online executive claims the Web site is "a perfect extension of our brand. We have an existing viewing base and can cross-promote the Web site on our twenty-four-hour network. It makes perfect sense to us with the geometric growth of the Web" (Clark, 1996, p. 10). E! Online has its own editorial, advertising, and technical staffs but relies on their cable network newsroom for reports of current events. E! Online complements the E! cable network, has nominal production costs, and draws its audience from existing cable viewers (Clark, 1996). At first E! Online plans to be totally advertiser supported, but later it plans to charge fees for certain premium content (Cuneo, 1996).

Letterman's Top 10 list and the best lines from his daily monologues can be accessed from the *Late Show with David Letterman* homepage for chuckles any time of the day or night. *Late Show with David Letterman*'s Web site features a list of upcoming guests, ticket information, biographies of David Letterman and his staff, and lists links to many unofficial Letterman Web sites.

Web-Only Talk and Entertainment Programs

As would be expected, *MTV Online* is a cool, hip-hop site featuring video and audio clips of the latest music releases as well as television program reviews. The site also offers news headlines and behind-the-scenes production glimpses. Linked from MTV Online is *Yack Live,* an online chat service where Web users' comments are scrolled across the television screen.

As with broadcast and cable programming, Web shows come and go. Tim Conway, Jr. (the actor's son), bet on the Internet as the perfect venue for his nightly talk show, *Late Net.* Netcast nightly from a Santa Monica storefront, *Late Net*'s guests included actress Talia Shire and Dodger manager Tommy Lasorda. The program, however, can no longer be found on the Net (Haring, 1997).

Web-Only Informational Programs

The *Discovery Channel Online* produces original multimedia stories exclusively for its own Web site as well for the *Learning Channel*'s online page (Hall, 1996). A Discovery Communications executive strategizes that people probably will not come to the Web page just "to see the same thing they can see on TV. We have to give people a reason to go online every day and we also want to open up the Web to people who wouldn't otherwise go online. Original programming does that" (Parets, 1997a).

The award-winning Discovery site presents a different theme every day, such as "History Monday" and "Nature Tuesday," complete with photographs, downloadable audio and video, bulletin boards, and original stories with which users interact, because "people don't want to just read a lot of type on screen" (Parets, 1997a). "Letters from the Road," which showcases American subcultures with reports about offbeat events and people, encourages visitors to provide tips for future stories.

Discovery's *Animal Planet* presents "Pet Talk," a forum for pet owners and animal lovers, and "Animal Bytes," a synopsis of the current month's programming. The site includes many other sections that give visitors insights into the world of animals.

Web-Only Reality Programs

HBO brings "reality TV" to the Web with its program *III:am.* The show documents life on Manhattan streets at 3 A.M. An HBO video crew hangs out on street corners capturing the lives of sleepless people who roam about at that hour of the night. Later, the interviews are transcribed, the video edited, text and graphics laid out and formatted into HTML language and posted on the Web site. Visitors to *III:am* are

FIGURE 4.7 WhirlGirl Homepage

likely to see stragglers such as seventeen-year-old Alice, with pierced lip and dreadlocks, talking about what she is doing out at that time of the morning (Goff, 1996).

Web-Only Adventure Programs

WhirlGirl is a Web-only adventure series that follows the exploits of a twenty-something superhero in the year 2040. Similar to a television show, new episodes are introduced on a weekly basis with "airings" at 8:30 P.M. on Sundays. Created by Visionary Media, the weekly, advertiser-supported series is targeted to individuals 15–35 years of age. Among the first carriers of *WhirlGirl* are the games sites *GameZone* and E-Pub's *Amused* and the music site BMG's *BUGjuice* (Spring, 1998). *WhirlGirl* promotions air on several major-market television stations. Visionary Media's president expresses a strong belief in the Web as a programming outlet for all types of media.

Following the television syndication model, Visionary Media is Web syndicating *WhirlGirl* to other sites in exchange for advertising revenue. Visionary Media has signed up five Web sites to carry the program and will continue adding "affiliates" until the combined weekly number of page views hits about four million, a cap set by the company to avoid excessive competition for *WhirlGirl* viewers among the affiliates. The deal between Visionary Media and its affiliates is similar to a television barter split. Affiliated sites benefit from the deal by gaining a new audience attracted to *WhirlGirl* and from selling banner ads with the program. Visionary Media benefits by increasing exposure to the program and by receiving a percentage of the affiliates' advertising revenue (Spring, 1998).

Visionary Media sees Web syndication as a way to increase its audience and thus attract television syndicators to adapt the online program to a televised companion show. Visionary Media executives claim that the online adventure series will make it to television only when *WhirlGirl*'s average monthly hits increases to about three million (Schneider, 1997; Shaw, 1997b).

Network Soaps Online

Web surfers find their favorite soap operas online packed with information about the stars, plots, gossip, and behind-the-scenes action. Soap addicts can tune to the largest soap site on the Web, *Soap City*, designed and operated by Columbia TriStar Interactive Productions. Part of Sony Pictures Entertainment site, *Soap City* delivers in-depth storylines, cast information, character biographies, and archived summaries of daytime soaps dating back twenty-five years and more. In addition to weekly updates of all currently aired soaps, addicts can chat with other die-hard fans about who is sleeping with whom and whether an upcoming marriage is sure to be a disaster (Martin, 1995; Khalili, 1997a).

Melrose Place brings its nastiness online with links to the "Ultimate Melrose Party" and to "Melrose Magazine." The party link brings up ideas for throwing parties à la Melrose style and tells visitors how to set up for a *Melrose Place* watching party. "Melrose Magazine" is full of tidbits of information about the plots, characters, and actors.

Cybersoaps

Online, anyone can become a soap opera character by playing a part on a cyber-drama, a soap opera made just for the Internet. Emotional wretchedness comes alive through e-mail and chat forums on "programs" such as *Lake Shore Drive*, replete with twenty-something-year-old characters living in Chicago.

In *Virtual Dorm*, real-life college students play out their traumas before real-time virtual cameras placed in their dorm suites. Through audio and video images, users vicariously cook dinner, study, eavesdrop on lovers' quarrels, or just hang out with the "characters." *Virtual Dorm* prides itself on combining the best of a Web

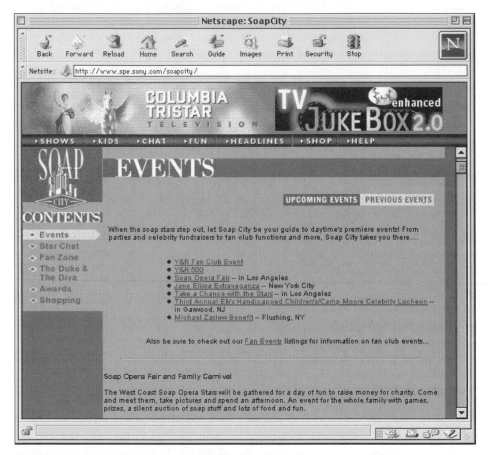

FIGURE 4.8 Soap City Homepage. © 1998 Columbia TriStar Interactive. All rights reserved. Visit the Sony Pictures Entertainment Web site at www.spe.sony.com.

site with the best of a chat room by offering a daily journals section in addition to live images (Marx, 1995).

It is anticipated that the Web will one day become as essential as television is today for accessing entertainment and information. Cyberdrama producers are betting that as interactivity increases and technology improves, online soaps will be as addicting as their broadcast counterparts. After all, cybersoaps are just as exciting as televised ones and are full of similarly outlandish plots involving baby-switching, adultery, murder, and even exorcism and UFO abductions.

The first and most popular cyberdrama, *The Spot,* set in Los Angeles, features the sex lives of the young and beautiful. Launched in June 1995, *The Spot* has attracted up to 40,000 users daily. The site contains daily photos, journal entries, and interactive goodies where, for instance, users can dress a character in different bikinis (Grumann, 1996; Hall, 1997b; Parets, 1997a).

American Cybercast, creators of *The Spot* and other online programs, has hired a former Columbia Pictures executive to pattern its programs after a television network. The company's slogan, "The revolution won't be televised," is based on its belief that the Web will one day compete with traditional television viewing (Hall, 1997b, p. 18).

American Cybercast has, unfortunately, discovered the pitfalls of an online venture. It filed for bankruptcy under Chapter 11, after foundering under a lack of advertising revenue despite support from such heavy-hitters as Toyota and VISA. Internet experts acknowledge that strong content, coupled with advertisers who draw a target audience, makes for a successful and profitable Web site. So far, online soaps have largely appealed to teenagers and those in their early twenties. Almost one-half of *The Spot*'s audience belongs to the under-the-age-of-twenty-six crowd. A young audience is not one that typically has money to burn, and advertisers have been slow to buy space on a cybersoap Web site. Regardless of its financial situation, *The Spot* pioneered cybersoaps, a new Web genre that many strive to imitate (Jensen, 1997).

Other Webcast Programs

Broadcast and cable outlets are not the only ones sponsoring and creating Web programming. Microsoft sponsors a monthly interview show, *Encarta on the Record,* hosted by journalist Linda Ellerbee (Croal & Tanaka, 1996). On the cybercast Ellerbee explores important issues with invited guests and encourages the online community to join in the debates.

GrapeJam, a Web series featuring the comedy troupe "The Grapes," was conceived as an interactive television show, but instead of waiting to pitch the program to the networks, the producers took it to the Web. It is anticipated that "The Grapes" will eventually make it to network television, and if so, the Web site will be used to enhance the television show with additional story lines and by facilitating interaction between fans and characters (Parets, 1997b).

Simulcast Programs

The Broadcast Production group is aiming to bring a magazine-style program, "Internet Live," to television and computer screens simultaneously. The weekly half-hour show will be made up of short segments on topics such as Internet news, lifestyles and general information. The simulcast format represents a "paradigm shift" for television and the Internet (Tedesco, 1996d, p. 76).

On its Web site, TBS simulcast thirteen days of James Bond movies, with running commentary. With "one eye on the TV and one eye on the Web," Bond fans were treated to about 150 trivia items per movie. As movies were being aired on television, the Web site ran tidbits of information that matched each scene, and pointed out bloopers, such as when the supercool agent's shoe was untied. TBS is planning monthly offerings of programs that synchronize over-the-air broadcasts with online information (Vonder Haar, 1998).

Showtime got a knock-out punch when it posted a "score-at-home" Web site during the Mike Tyson versus Frank Bruno fight in March 1996. An on-screen promotion was flashed during the bout encouraging viewers to score the fight on the Web site. Immediately, the site was inundated with so many people trying to connect that the server crashed after thirty seconds. Much to their relief, Showtime had the server up and running ten minutes later. While investigating the incident Showtime discovered that close to four out of ten viewers watch television and use their computers at the same time (Brown, 1997; The Internet Index, 1998). Further inquiry uncovered that between 40 percent and 58 percent of households that own both a computer and a television set keep both in the same room (Vonder Haar, 1998).

ONLINE TV/WEB LISTINGS

NetGuide Live

TV Guide-type listings are now available on the Web. *NetGuide Live* is an hour-by-hour grid listing Web events taking place in real-time. *NetGuide Live* users can, for example, read CNN headlines, then link to the CNN site for more detailed news. Eventually, *NetGuide Live* will create "channels" or areas devoted to entertainment, business, and sports. *NetGuide Live* developer CMP Media expects the hourly listings to be the focus of the service, thus giving rise to scheduled programming on the Web. In addition to the Web listings, *NetGuide Live* also offers a search engine, reviews of about 50,000 Web sites, new Web item summaries, and lockout capabilities for objectionable pages. *NetGuide Live* was developed under the code name "Gulliver" as competition for the floundered "iguide," created by News Corporation, publisher of *TV Guide*. Although *NetGuide Live* competitors include Yahoo!, Web Crawler, and other search engines, CMP Media claims that with its site's broader offerings and Web listings "the competition is in a way something that doesn't exist yet" (Johnson, 1996, p. 4).

Television Program Guides Online

Since 1953, when *TV Guide* debuted, it has become one of the most widely read weekly magazines and now flaunts an annual circulation of slightly over 13 million (Block, 1997; Kerwin, 1998). Many viewers cannot turn on the television without first consulting the magazine, and others plan a whole week of viewing in advance with their *TV Guide*s in hand. More than just a compilation of program listings, *TV Guide* is a big influence on a program's success. A favorable review in *TV Guide* guarantees a large audience, whereas a mediocre write-up can doom a show from the beginning.

Using its popular name and good reputation, *TV Guide*'s entertainment network (TVGEN) has launched *TV Guide Online*. The site provides visitors with complete television program listings. Claiming three million page views per month, *TV Guide Online* offers unique features, such as a daily TV column, trivia games, and program discussion groups. Additionally, program listings can be customized for individual viewers. For instance, a viewer living in Peoria, Illinois, can request program listings with the correct channel numbers for his or her area. Viewers can also specify their favorite program types, from which *TV Guide Online* customizes listings for each individual's viewing preferences. *TV Guide Online* does not charge for any of its services; instead it generates revenue by selling advertising space to such companies as Yahoo! and American Express.

TV Guide insists that the online and printed versions complement each other and do not compete for the same audience. The two versions attract audiences with different demographics. Many *TV Guide* subscribers are unlikely to access *TV Guide Online,* and electronic users are unlikely to subscribe to the printed *TV Guide.* With more than five hundred channel choices looming in the near future, it is hard to imagine the bulk and weight of a printed *TV Guide* containing all of those program listings. *TV Guide Online* is a practical alternative to a cumbersome printed guide (Memom, 1996).

TVGEN recently teamed with WebTV, agreeing to provide its online content to WebTV viewers. TVGEN's entertainment site posts interactive *TV Guide Online* listings and customized viewing schedules, as well as movies, music, news, and sports information from Fox Sports Online and Fox News ("The TV Guide Entertainment," 1997; Spring, 1997).

TV Guide Online is not the only television program listing site on the Web. *TV Guide* has company in the form of sites such as *The Gist,* which also claims three million page views per month. In addition to customizable program listings, The Gist provides celebrity interviews, a best shows of the day list, news items, and soap opera summaries to its 200,000 registered users (Hall, 1997a).

E! Online's movie finder is a dream come true for film buffs who are alerted to upcoming broadcast and cable movies. Users select which movies they plan to see, up to ten days in advance of the airings, and just to be sure they do not miss their selections, they get a "Remind Me" e-mail message a day or two in advance of showtime (Avallone, 1997).

Online television program listing sites are expensive to produce and are labor-intensive, requiring daily updates and changes. Though many other sites, such as

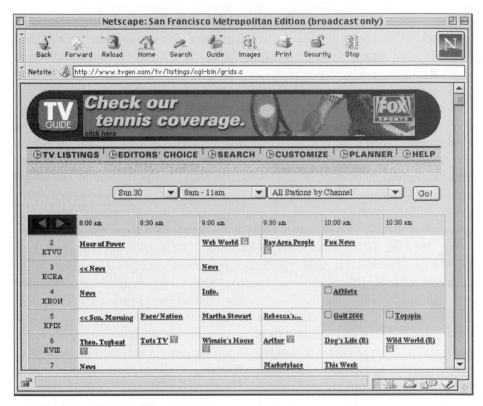

FIGURE 4.9 TV Guide Online Homepage

Yahoo! and *City Search* have considered offering local listings, until now they have left that job to others.

THE WEB ON TELEVISION

So far this chapter has focused on the media's appearance on the Web. However, in 1996, the Web made its debut on television. The computer network *C/NET* has joined with GGP, a San Francisco–based syndicator, to produce and distribute television programs devoted entirely to the World Wide Web and new technology (Spring, 1996).

The San Francisco–based computer company is a leader in integrating television programming with a network of sites on the Web. C/NET excels in providing information about computers, future technology, and the Internet. The company was founded on the belief that "television and online media are perfect and necessary complements" (C/NET, 1996). C/NET was started to be a twenty-four-hour cable network and is expected to become one by early 1998. The company's cyber-space presence includes three of its own Web sites, and it produces E! Online, E! Entertainment TV's online site (Atwood, 1996).

Several television networks and C/NET are distributing Web-related television programs. *The Web* is a funky, magazine-style television program airing the latest in Web sites and trends. *The Edge* focuses on Web technology, and C/NET's newest program, *TV.COM,* is a half-hour journey through various Web sites. Featuring new technologies and Internet personalities, the news-magazine format show targets adults 18–54 years of age. C/NET produces new episodes on a weekly basis and finances all production costs. *TV.COM*'s hosts include *Inside Edition*'s Justin Gunn; Tracy Smith, cohost of *Channel One;* and Gina St. John, cohost of *C/NET Central* series shown on the USA Network and Sci-Fi Channel (Spring, 1996).

The idea for *TV.COM* emerged from GGP's one-time special, *Nothing but Net,* which was syndicated on about 150 television stations. The stations were so enthu-siastic about the Internet special that one-third of them asked for first shot at picking up a weekly World Wide Web program.

Television stations broadcasting *TV.COM* can promote their own Web sites during the program in 30-, 60-, or 90-second time slots. Additionally, GGP provides stations with technology segments to insert in local newscasts (Spring, 1996).

C/NET has a widely popular Web site known for news and information about computers and the Web. Its online content is closely linked to their television shows and vice versa. Though the network idea has not yet caught on, C/NET has become a powerful force in the online world, creating and promoting original Web material and producing television programs devoted to the Internet. One C/NET executive states that while television is "just a land of sound bites, the Internet personalizes the media experience." By combining television and the Internet, "viewers get the best of both worlds" (Parets, 1997b, p. 32).

SUMMARY: TELEVISION OF TOMORROW

People are in love with television and with the act of watching television. To many people, there is nothing better than coming home, flopping on the couch, grabbing the remote control and maybe some microwave popcorn, and settling down for an evening of watching whatever is on the screen. Such passive viewing can be relaxing, comfortable, and entertaining. It is unlikely that viewers will give up this pleasure no matter how much technology changes. Rather, new technologies will add to the overall viewing and entertainment experience.

The Internet, and specifically the Web, is already enhancing television. Web sites are teeming with television-related content. Networks use the Web as a pro-motional vehicle for their broadcast and cable programs. Those visiting television-oriented sites get their fill of performer biographies, fan club chat rooms, video and audio clips of past and upcoming episodes, television trivia, and many other tidbits of information. If that is not enough, there are plenty of Web-only cybersoaps, talk shows, and other program genres available. These new interactive television-like shows keep even the most Web-intent interested and amused.

Even the physical act of using the Web is becoming similar to watching television. Web users wielding an Internet remote controller can slouch on a couch, chair, or floor and flip through Web sites without having to touch a keyboard. As the Web becomes easier to navigate, it is likely that users will move from more instrumental, purposeful uses to more passive, habitual motives. Users will "turn on" the Web just to surf around looking for something interesting, instead of just connecting to the Web when they have a clear purpose in mind, such as accessing a particular site or looking for a specific item of information.

PCTV, WebTV, or hybrid systems that display both televised fare and Web content may one day replace traditional television sets. Consumers may come to view these systems as an inexpensive alternative to purchasing both a conventional television set and a home computer. The Web is moving from being an office and school information source to becoming an in-home information and entertainment source. As viewers embrace the Web in their living rooms, television executives and producers will find new ways to maximize their viewing audiences through applications that go beyond using a site as simply a promotional venue.

The Web is still in its infancy, and no one is really sure what it will be like in its mature form. What is known, however, is that the Web is having an enormous impact on the television industry and on television entertainment. If predictions hold true, the Web and television will eventually merge, offering both conventional television fare and Web-based content through one living room "set."

CHAPTER LINKS

ABC—http://www.abc.com

Amused—http://www.amused.com

BUGjuice—http://www.bugjuice.com

Business Week—http://www.businessweek.com/

CBS, Eye on the Net—http://www.cbs.com

City Search—http://www.citysearch.com

C/NET—http://www.cnet.com

Comedy Central Online—http://www.comcentral.com

CyberKitchen—http://www.foodtv.com

Discovery Channel Online—http://www.discovery.com

E! Online—http://www.eonline.com

Encarta on the Record—http://encarta.msn.com

ESPN—http://ESPN.SportsZone.com/

Fox World—http://foxnetwork.com

GameZone—http://www.gamezone.net

The Gist—http://www.thegist.com

Good Morning America—http://www.abcnews.com/onair/gma/html_files/index.html

GrapeJam—http://www.crlight.com

HBO—http://hbo.com

HBO-IIIam—http://www.hbo.com/IIIam/

Homicide: Second Shift—http://www.nbc.com/homicide

Jeopardy—http://www.spe.sony.com/tv/shows/jeopardy/index.html

KCPQ-TV— http://www.kcpq.com

KGTV-TV—http://www.kgtv.com

KLAS-TV8—http://www.klas-tv.com/

KPIX-TV—http://www.kpix.com

Lake Shore Drive—http://www.chiWeb.com/chicago/lsd

Late Show with David Letterman—http://marketing.cbs.com/latenight/lateshow/

Learning Channel—http://www.discovery.com/diginets/learning/learning.html

Lifetime Online—http://www.lifetimetv.com

The Magic School Bus—http://www.scholastic.com/magicschoolbus

Melrose Place—http://www.foxnetwork.com/melrose/index.htm

MSNBC—http://www.msnbc.com

MTV Online—http://www.mtv.com

NBC.com—http://www.nbc.com

NetGuide Live—http://www.netguide.com

Nick-at-Nite's TV Land—http://www.nick-at-nite.com

Nye Labs—http://nyelabs.kcts.org

The Outer Limits—http://www.showtimeonline.com/spotlight/serover.tin?series=-16

PBS Online—http://www.pbs.org

The People's Court—http://www.peoplescourt.com/

Rock & Roll Jeopardy—http://www.rockjeopardy.com

Sci-Fi Channel Dominion—http://www.scifi.com

Soap City—http://www.spe.sony.com/soapcity

Sony Pictures Entertainment—http://www.spe.sony.com

The Spot—http://www.thespot.com

Ultimate Television Network—http://www.ultimatetv.com

The X-Files—http://www.thex-files.com/index.htm

TV Guide Online—http://www.tvgen.com/

TV.COM—http://www.tv.com

Virtual Dorm—http://www.vdorm.com/thedorm/index.html

WBOC-TV—http://www.wboc.com

WFLA-TV—http://www.wfla.com

Wheel of Fortune—http://www.spe.sony.com/tv/shows/wheel/thanks.html

WhirlGirl—http://www.whirlgirl.com

Yack Live—http://www.yack.com

Yahoo!—http://www.yahoo.com

REFERENCES

Agee, W. K., Ault, P. H., & Emery, E. (1997). *Introduction to mass communication.* New York: Longman.

Antonoff, M. (1996, January). Broadcasting the Web. *Popular Science, 31.*

Atwood, B. (1996). C/NET sets sights on cable-TV market. *Billboard, 87.*

Avallone, L. (1997, June 16). E!'s program planner. *Broadcasting and Cable, 66.*

Berniker, M. (1995a, October 31). ABC renews exclusive pact with America Online. *Broadcasting and Cable, 68.*

Berniker, M. (1995b, July 31). CBS joins America Online, talking with Microsoft. *Broadcasting and Cable, 33.*

Berniker, M. (1995c, October 23). Intel garnering support for "intercasting." *Broadcasting and Cable, 74.*

Berniker, M. (1995d, August 28). NBC gets post position on Microsoft Network. *Broadcasting and Cable, 37.*

Bertolucci, J. (1997, July). PC Theatre takes centre stage. *ComputerLife Online.* [Online]. Available: http://www.zdnet.com/complife/buz/9707/compaqtv.html

Bimber, B. (1996). *The Internet and political transformation.* [Online]. Available: http://www.sscuf.usb.edu/~survey/poltran2.htm

Block, V. (1997, December 1). Branding pro aims to tout magazine. *Crains New York Business, 31.*

Bollier, D. (1989). How Americans watch TV: A nation of grazers. *Channels Magazine,* 41–52.

Broadcasting and cable yearbook. (1996). New Providence, NJ: R. R. Bowker.

Brodsky, I. (1997, June 23). Cable modems to the rescue? *Telephony,* 20–26.

Bromley, R. V., & Bowles, D. (1995). The impact of Internet on use of traditional news media. *Newspaper Research Journal, 16* (2), 14–27.

Brown, J. (1997). Showtime Web strategy was shaped in the ring. *Electronic Media, 18.*

Clark, D., & Carlton J. (1997, November 18). Visions of PC and TV firms compete at Comdex. *Wall Street Journal,* p. B10.

Clark, T. (1996, January 29). E!, C/NET team on show biz Web site. *Inter@ctive Week,* 10.

Cleland, K. (1996, May 13). TV game shows take a spin on the Internet. *Electronic Media,* 20.

C/NET. (1996). *C/NET homepage.* [Online]. Available: http://www.cnet.com/Community/Welcome/About/profile.html

Colman, P. (1997, December 8). Set-top scramble in Silicon Valley. *Broadcasting and Cable,* 14.

Cortese, A. (1997, February 24). A way out of the Web maze. *Business Week,* 95–101.

Cuneo, A. Z. (1996, January 29). Hollywood hits cyber high. *Advertising Age,* 27.

Croal, N., & Tanaka, J. (1996, January 29). Ellerbytes. *Newsweek,* 10.

DeJesus, E. X. (1996, February). Toss your TV: How the Internet will replace broadcasting. *Byte, 21* (2), 50–60.

Dominick, J. R., Sherman, B. L., & Copeland, G. A. (1996). *Broadcasting/cable and beyond.* New York: McGraw-Hill.

Ferguson, D. A., & Perse, E. M. (1993). Media and audience influences on channel repertoire. *Journal of Broadcasting and Electronic Media, 37* (1), 31–47.

Fischer, A. (1996, February). Weave the Web with TV. *Computer Life,* 29.

Freeman, M. (1996, August 26). So who's got the best Web site? *MediaWeek,* 22.

Galetto, M. (1997, October 27). Comedy Central not amused by Net bootleggers. *Electronic Media,* 12.

Gegax, T. T., Rosenberg, D., Rhodes, S., Gill, J., & Angell, E. (1998, March 23). The rude tube. *Newsweek,* 56–62.

Goff, L. (1996, August 26). Programming pioneer. *ComputerWorld, 30* (35), 92.

Gross, N. (1997, March 24). WebTV behind the screen breakthrough. *Business Week,* 202.

Grumann, C. (1996, February 21). Soap operas invade the Internet. *St. Louis Post Dispatch,* p. 3E.

Haddad, C. (1997, November 6). Cable modems slowly making inroads. *Atlanta Constitution,* p. D-9.

Hafner, K., & Levy, S. (1996, November 11). Next: Nothing but the Net? *Newsweek,* 88.

Haner, K. (1997, September 29). TV meets the Web. *Newsweek,* 82–87.

Hall, L. (1996, March 11). Cable broadcast online sites come into their own. *Electronic Media,* 42, 56.

Hall, L. (1997a, August 18). The Gist offers to solve problem of TV grid-lock. *Electronic Media, 15,* 14.

Hall, L. (1997b, January 20). Online soap pioneers are now on the spot. *Electronic Media, 15* (4), 18.

Hamilton, A. (1997). Couch spuds, they're all after you. *ZDNet.* [Online]. Available: http://www5.zdnet.com/anchordesk/story/story_825.html

Haring, B. (1997, January 13). New breed of talk shows up on the Net. *USA Today.* [Online]. Available: http://www/usatoday.com

Head, S. W., Sterling, C. H., & Schofield, L. B. (1994). *Broadcasting in America*. Boston: Houghton Mifflin.

Heeter, C. (1985). Program selection with abundance of choice. *Human Communication Research, 12* (1), 126–52.

Heeter, C., D'Allessio, D., Greenberg, B., & McVoy, S. D. (1988). Cableviewing behaviors: An electronic assessment. In C. Heeter & B. Greenberg (Eds.), *Cableviewing* (pp. 51–63). Norwood, NJ: Ablex Publishing Company.

Hof, R. D. (1997, March 24). Hello, couch potatoes. *Business Week,* 200–202.

Hoffman, H. (1996, November). WebTV brings access to the masses. *Computer Shopper.* [Online]. Available: http://www.zdnet.com/cshopper/content/9611/cshp0069.html

Internet eats into TV time. (1996, January). *St. Louis Post Dispatch,* pp. 6C, 8C.

The Internet Index. (1998, January 21). *Open market.* [Online]. Available: http://www.openmarket.com/intindex [1998, February 1].

Jensen, J. (1997, January 27). Net soap market sours after "Spot" creator's crash. *Advertising Age,* 34.

Johnson, B. (1996, August 12). CMP launches NetGuide Live Web site. *Advertising Age, 67* (33), 4.

Kaye, B. K. (1998). Uses and gratifications of the World Wide Web: From couch potato to Web potato. *The New Jersey Journal of Communication, 6* (1), 21–40.

Kerwin, A. M. (1998, February 23). Top magazines report lackluster results in 2nd half. *Advertising Age,* 28.

Khalili, B. (1997a, July 14). In a lather over soaps. *Electronic Media,* 12.

Khalili, B. (1997b, July 28). Nick at Nite brings TV's past to the Web. *Electronic Media,* 16.

Krol, C. (1997, September 29). Internet promos bolster networks' fall programs. *Advertising Age,* 40.

Lee, J. C. (1997, October 13). Web ready television starts making sense. *Fortune,* 158, 162.

Levy, S. (1995, February 27). TechnoMania. *Newsweek,* 25–29.

Levy, S. (1997, May 12). The Internet gets pushy. *Newsweek,* 84.

Mandese, J. (1995a, March 13). Snags aside, nets enamored of 'net. *Advertising Age,* S20.

Mandese, J. (1995b, February 6). The Web takes to the 'net. *Advertising Age,* 13.

Martin, Z. (1995, August 21). Cyberspace explosion. *Electronic Media,* 12.

Marx, A. (1995). College life: Live on the Web. *Inter@ctive Week,* 26.

Memom, F. (1996, November 4). What's on? TV listings go online. *Inter@ctive Week,* 33.

Mermigas, D. (1998, March 30). A passage to digital. *Electronic Media,* 1, 14.

Meyer, M. (1995, November 6). Is your PC too complex? Get ready for the "NC." *Newsweek,* 101.

Mitchell, R. (1998, April 20). TV's great leap forward. *U.S. News & World Report,* 47–54.

Netmation's 100 most popular Web sites. (1997, December). *Netmation Homepage.* [Online]. Available: http://www.netmation.com/

Parets, R. (1997a). As the Web turns. *Websight.* [Online]. Available: http://www.Websight.com

Parets, R. (1997b, January–February). HTTV: How cable Web hybrids are changing the way we watch TV. *Websight,* 30–32.

Pavlik, J. V. (1996). *New media technology: Cultural and commercial perspectives.* Boston: Allyn and Bacon.

Petrozzello, D. (1997, December 15). Image boost, choices key to "cablenet." *Broadcasting and Cable,* 105.

Proffit, B. (1997, January 27). Intercast brings the Web to TV. *PC Magazine Online.* [Online]. Available: http:www.zdnet.com/pcmag/issues/1602/pcmag0032.htm

Rea, J. (1996). *The television broadcaster's Web site.* TeleWeb Publishing.

Riedman, P. (1996, September 2). TV Net aims to be ultimate television Web site. *Electronic Media,* 21.

Rist, O. (1997, Winter). A marriage of convergence. *Home Entertainment,* 9–16.

Ross, C. (1996, September 4). TV networks struggle with Internet role. *Advertising Age,* S16.

Ross, C. (1997, August 11). Study offers new angle on Internet TV usage. *Advertising Age,* 14.

Ross, C., & Johnson, B. (1997, February 3). Sky's the limit for Sony's ambitious Station plans. *Advertising Age,* 40.

Ross, C., & Jensen, J. (1997, February 3). NBC to launch an online version of "Homicide" series. *Advertising Age,* 44.

Rubin, A. M. (1981). An examination of television viewing motives. *Communication Research, 8* (2), 141–65.

Rubin, A. M. (1983). Television uses and gratifications: The interactions of viewing patterns and motivations. *Journal of Broadcasting, 27* (1), 37–51.

Rubin, A. M. (1984). Ritualized and instrumental television viewing. *Journal of Communication, 34* (3), 67–77.

Rupley, S. (1996). TV shows could be the next wave in Web content. *PC Magazine.* [Online]. Available: http://www.pcmgn.com/search/1502/pcm00017.htm

Schneider, M. (1997, July 21). First the Web, then the world. *Electronic Media,* 20.

Shaw, R. (1998, March 16). Bandwidth, ads make Web TV-like. *Electronic Media,* 18.

Shaw, R. (1997a, March 17). Log in to cable. *Electronic Media,* 56.

Shaw, R. (1997b, November 10). "Whirlgirl" is online test case. *Electronic Media,* 36.

Spring, G. (1996, May 20). World Wide Web gets first show dedicated to it. *Electronic Media,* 35

Spring, G. (1997, September 8). TV Guide online turns a new page. *Electronic Media,* 10.

Spring, G. (1998, March 30). Syndication "whirls" onto the Web. *Electronic Media,* 12.

St. John, D. (1996, February). Web TV. *PC Entertainment,* 28.

Taylor, C. (1996a, November 11). Tube watchers, unite. *MediaWeek,* 9–10.

Taylor, C. (1996b, September 23). Zapping onto the Internet. *MediaWeek,* 32.

Taylor, C. (1997, July 5). Net use adds to decline in TV use; Radio stable. *Billboard,* 85.

A TCP/IP green thumb: Effective implementation of TCP/IP networks. *LAN Magazine, 8* (6), 139.

Tedesco, R. (1996a, December 9). Cable modems move from concept to reality. *Broadcasting and Cable,* 106, 108.

Tedesco, R. (1996b, December 30). C/Net, Intel plan cyber-bash at new Mediadome. *Broadcasting and Cable,* 50.

Tedesco, R. (1996c, February 5). The great cable hope. *Broadcasting and Cable,* 38–44.

Tedesco, R. (1996d, March 11). "Internet Live" shoots for simulcast. *Broadcasting and Cable,* 76.

Tedesco, R. (1996e, February 5). What's hot, what's next? The Internet PC. *Broadcasting and Cable,* 76.

Tedesco, R. (1997a, December 22). Cyberspace detective takes to the air. *Broadcasting and Cable,* 31–33.

Tedesco, R. (1997b, November 24). Internet TV face-off. *Broadcasting and Cable,* 71.

Tedesco, R. (1997c, June 2). That's intertainment. *Broadcasting and Cable,* 54–62.

Tedesco, R. (1997d, May 19). TV–'Net vendors resist the marketing Web. *Broadcasting and Cable,* 54–62.

Tedesco, R. (1997e, September 22). WebTV, NetChannel square off. *Broadcasting and Cable,* 70–71.

Tedesco, R. (1997f, January 27). Worldgate adds $11 million toward service launch. *Broadcasting and Cable,* 63.

The TV Guide entertainment network partners with WebTV networks. (1997, January 13). *WebTV homepage.* [Online]. Available: http://www.Webtv.net/HTML/home.tvguide.html

Ultimate TV—United States of America television. (1997, June 2). *Ultimate Television Network.* [Online]. Available: http://www.UltimateTV.com/tv/us [1998, April 17].

Van Tassel, J. (1997, August 11). Countdown to 2006: PC to TV. *Broadcasting and Cable,* 127 (33), 48–49.

Vonder Haar, S. (1997, December 8).The top twenty-five unsung heroes of the Net. *Inter@ctive Week.* [Online]. Available: http://www.zdnet.com/intweek/ [1998, January 14].

Vonder Haar, S. (1998, January 13). Internet-Television tie-ins tune in. *Inter@ctive Week.* [Online]. Available: http://www.zdnet.com/intweek/ [1998, January 14].

Walley, W. (1995, July 31). A match made in cyberspace. *Electronic Media,* 14.

Web notes. (1996, July 8). *Electronic Media,* 12.

Why Internet advertising. (1997, May 5). *MediaWeek, 7* (18), S8–S13.

Wildstrom, S. H. (1996, September 16). A Web surfer box for peanuts. *Business Week,* 22.

Workman, W. (1997). Cable modem makers struggle to settle standards. *Computer Shopper Online.* [Online]. Available: http://zdnet.com/cshopper/content/9701/cshp0140.html

www.Web pages/cover.story@b&c.com. (1996, October 28). *Broadcasting and Cable,* 38–54.

Yovovich, B. G. (1998, January 19). Webbed feat. *Marketing News, 32* (2), 18–19.

Zelnick, N. (1997). WebTV breaks new ground. *WebWeek,* 1, 45.

Zyskowski, J. (1995). Tuning into cable modems. *Computer Shopper Online.* [Online]. Available: http://zdnet.com/cshopper/content/9512/sgfeature/sub2/html

When nineteen-year-old au pair Louise Woodward was convicted of the second-degree murder of a child in her care, defense attorneys asked Judge Hiller B. Zobel to overturn the jury's verdict. Claiming that autopsy photographs were introduced too late into the trial, the defense requested that the judge reduce Woodward's sentence to involuntary manslaughter, order a new trial, or let Woodward go free.

Woodward's trial elicited enormous media and public interest, and millions of people in the United States and abroad anxiously awaited the judge's decision. Taking an unprecedented approach, the judge announced that he would post his ruling on the Internet rather than distributing paper copies to the media.

Originally, the judge planned to post his ruling exclusively on the <u>Lawyers Weekly</u> Web site. However, shortly after the Web site's address was made public, it experienced an overload of visitors. Fearing that a mass of online users would crash the site, the judge agreed to transmit his verdict via e-mail to about twenty-five media organizations with the understanding that they would post it on their Web sites. The judge claimed that the Internet is the fastest way to disseminate information simultaneously to a large number of people. Additionally, court clerks would be freed from the tasks of photocopying and handing out printed copies of the verdict to hordes of reporters.

Though Judge Zobel had 120 days to issue his decision, it came within one week. The media and the public were informed of the day and time the judge's ruling would come whizzing through the Internet. At about 10 A.M. on November 10, 1997, the judge was ready to transmit his opinion. The media were standing by. The public was glued to their televisions, radios, and computers. The judge hit the "Send" button . . . but alas, nothing happened.

Unbeknownst to the judge, at just a few minutes before 10 A.M., his Internet service provider lost power when Boston Edison workers disconnected the ISP's electricity while working on an unrelated problem. Electricity was restored and computers

NEWS AND SPORTS ON THE WEB

were running within thirty minutes, but by then it was too late to use the Internet. Sources close to the judge quickly leaked the verdict to the throng of frothing media who were waiting outside the Boston courthouse. By the time the judge's e-mail was up and running, the whole world knew the verdict; it was reduced to manslaughter.

Despite the judge's best intentions, technology intervened and foiled his plans. However, many experts agree that the Internet is an efficient medium for distributing legal judgments. As one attorney told reporters, "If the judge is going to issue an opinion, the thing you don't want is for some people to get it and others not." Further, a New York Times technology correspondent remarked that "the judge's idea is part of a natural progression made possible by new technology."

("Au Pair Defense," 1997; Holliman, 1997; "Judge in Au Pair," 1997; "Judge Plans," 1997)

NEWS ON THE WEB

The World Wide Web has ushered in a new age of news distribution. Prior to the development of the Web, the public was at the mercy of newspaper printing times and regularly scheduled news programs. Web technology has opened the doors for twenty-four hour news and for customized reports delivered directly to computer screens at any time of day.

Before the invention of the printing press and the advent of the first newspapers, people anxiously awaited accounts of important events to arrive by word of mouth. Unfortunately, by the time news made its way from place to place, it was often fraught with inaccuracies. With the advent of newspapers, news traveled much faster, was more credible, and more reliable. Morning papers were quickly bought up for yesterday's news, while afternoon and evening papers heralded themselves as purveyors of today's news. For late-breaking stories "extra" editions were quickly printed and distributed by newboys who ran down crowded streets yelling, "Extra, extra, read all about it."

Modern day newspapers flaunt sophisticated layouts, hard news, compelling headlines, and feature stories, but the one thing newspapers do not do is deliver round-the-clock news. The flow of information is controlled by newspaper executives who work within the capabilities of the printing press to set printing and delivery times. An eager public waits for their papers to roll off the presses. All too often, readers are ready to jump into the pages but have to wait for the paper to be delivered. Many subscribers end up coming home from work and leafing through the early morning edition, reading what is really yesterday's news.

Electronically delivered news has an inherent advantage over printed news in that it can put reports of current events on the air as soon as they happen. Stations do not have to wait to fire up their presses before conveying the latest information to their audiences. Radio and television stations often interrupt regularly scheduled programs with important news updates, and save more in-depth accounts for their daily newscasts. Families often set dinner hours around the six o'clock news, and many retire for the night after the eleven o'clock report, confident that they have heard the latest stories. The introduction of twenty-four-hour radio and television news networks has increased access to the most up-to-date news, but viewers still have to wait for the moment when a particular story of interest airs.

Now, with the Web and push technology, the news-interested public has immediate access to the latest scoops, and nearly 20 million Americans regularly take advantage of the Web to satisfy their needs to keep abreast of the latest events (Levins, 1998). Frequent updates and even customized news reports can be pushed from Web sites directly to a client's computer twenty-four hours a day, and archives of yesterday's stories are readily available for those who may have missed a report.

This chapter begins by examining the sources of Web news and the advantages and disadvantages of delivering news via the Web. Next, a brief look at the rise of newspapers, news magazines, radio news, and television news suggests the need for using the Web as a news distribution channel. Issues concerning ownership of online content and control over links, audience recall of online information, and the roles of editors and journalists are also discussed. This chapter charts the growth of Web news and wraps up with a look at the media outlets that have embraced the Web as a medium of news delivery.

NEWS SOURCES

Traditional models of mass communication are composed of the source, medium/ channel, and receiver/audience. Information flows from the source/sender to the audience, through a medium like television or radio. In the case of news, sources are commonly known as **gatekeepers** (the editorial staff or producers), who decide what news should be delivered and how it should be presented to the public. Gate-keepers then send the news through a medium such as a newspaper, television, or radio for mass distribution to the receiving audience.

This rather straightforward model has become somewhat muddied in the era of new technologies, especially when identifying the sources of news. For example, the source of a television news item broadcast on a local affiliate could be the reporter, the anchor, the news organization, the wire service, or the television network. Viewers' perceptions of sources are vital to the believability and overall credibility of the news. Many television news anchors are beloved and trusted as sources, whereas many news organizations are seen as bullies and purveyors of bad news. If an audience views their adored television news anchor as the source of a story, the story is deemed more believable than if a disliked corporation is thought to be the source (Sundar & Nass, 1996).

The same may hold true of the Web. Perceptions of the source may influence the credibility of the online news site. Typically, news editors oversee the content posted to media news sites, but the online environment also offers three additional sources of news: the technology itself, individuals, and other users (Sundar & Nass, 1996).

New media technologies, such as the Web, which offer increased choices, interactivity, and other advanced features, may themselves be perceived as the sources of information. For example, computer interfaces often select which daily news reports to place online. In these cases, the technology becomes the source. Technology as a source can be so powerful that human perceptions of the content is altered depending on the medium through which it is delivered. Although content and source are generally recognized as being separate entities, features of new media technologies blur the distinction. Therefore, many argue that "the media technology is the source" (Sundar & Nass, 1996, p. 3).

The Web is generally recognized as a medium with many different sources. Visitors to Web sites receive information posted by others. Almost anyone with a knowledge of HTML and access to a server can be a news source. Thus, receivers of online news also double as sources of news. Though at first this may seem contradictory, the very nature of interactivity allows receivers to act as sources. When individuals access Web sites they select which information to receive. The very act of interacting and selecting creates the perception of self as a source provider—people are choosing which information to provide for themselves (Sundar & Nass, 1996).

Just as news sources can affect receivers' perceptions of traditionally delivered news, assessments of online news content are also influenced by sources. In an experimental study, subjects reacted differently to identical news stories depending on their perceptions of who was the source of the communication. Though the sources' identities did not affect the general credibility of online news, they did influence liking, quality, and representativeness of each story. Online news stories that were selected by news editors consistently received lower ratings in liking and quality than identical stories selected by other users. When computer technology and users, other than the subjects themselves, were identified as sources, subjects liked the stories more and rated them as higher quality and more representative than when they themselves acted as sources by selecting the same story (Sundar & Nass, 1996).

Early research identifying the types of online sources furthers the understanding of source effects on Web-based news. It is suggested that perceptions of the quality of online news may be influenced by users' perceptions of the sources of the news, just as traditional news sources influence audience judgments of non-online news. Perceptions of sources may in part explain user preferences and the selection of one news site over another.

DELIVERING NEWS ON THE WEB

News editors and publishers have been experimenting with the Web as a news delivery channel since the Web's advent. Many immediately recognized the advantages of delivering news online and distributing stories globally. Others, however, remain more cautious, largely concerned about losing traditional media audiences to the online world. Although evidence indicates that some Web users are turning to this new medium as their primary source of news, online information still largely acts as a supplement to conventional media sources rather than as a replacement (Bromley & Bowles, 1995; Kaye, 1998).

Advantages of Online Delivery

The Web frees newspaper and electronic news editors from the constraints of time and space. Most news organizations gather more information than they have room to print or time to air. The Web presents a "bottomless" news hole, as stories no longer have to be shortened to fit into a set number of column inches or written to fill a small number of seconds (Niekamp, 1996, p. 1). Online news can be written as a summary version with links to in-depth versions and to related stories. Hyper-linked stories give visitors to online sites greater control over the news they receive by allowing users to select reports they find most interesting.

The Web is a global venue for local news reports. Curiosity seekers, news buffs, and those far away from home tie into online local newspapers and television and radio stations. The Web connects people to hometown news no matter where in the world they are living. For example, during the two days following the 1996 Halloween riots at Southern Illinois University at Carbondale, the number of daily hits on the college newspaper Web site rocketed 438 percent. Alumni, concerned parents, students, and others turned to cyberspace for the local point of view and in-depth coverage of the event ("Access Statistics," 1996).

Late-breaking news can be added to the Web almost instantaneously, and stories can be updated and amended as needed. Online archives of yesterday's news ease the minds of news junkies who no longer have to worry about missing a television newscast or the day's newspaper. Additionally, Web news is richly presented in audio, text, video, and graphic formats. Where radio is bound to audio, television to audio and video, newspapers to text and graphics, the Web is boundless in its presentation. Radio news on the Web is presented visually, television news with text, and newspaper stories with audio. The characteristics that distinguish conventional media from one another fade on the Web.

Consumers of Web-delivered news revel in selecting items of interest from international, national, regional, and local sources at any time of day or night. Additionally, the Web promotes active consumption of news through the selection of various versions of stories and presentation formats, and through other hypertext interactions. Subscribers to push technology are kept on the cutting edge of daily news and information with updates flowing to their computers throughout the day.

Disadvantages of Online Delivery

Despite many benefits, catching the news on the Web is not always as convenient or pleasurable as turning to more traditional sources. Many prefer watching the news while eating dinner or lying in bed, and many die-hard newspaper fans love the feel of newsprint and the portability of a paper. Old habits are hard to break, and many will never be broken. It is hard to imagine crossword puzzle purists typing letters into the squares, rather than writing them in using their favorite pen. It is very

BOX 5.1 WEB SITES' COVERAGE OF PRINCESS DIANA'S DEATH

The sudden and tragic death of Princess Diana punctuated the Web's importance as a news medium. The media coverage of the events surrounding the beloved Princess's accident was deemed thorough and in-depth by traditional standards. However, the coverage was limited to the amount of available air time and print space allowed by editors and producers. Many viewers and readers who desired more information about the accident and about Diana's life turned to the Web.

Over the 1997 Labor Day weekend, activity on the major news Web sites increased dramatically. *CNN Interactive* claimed 4.3 million page views on the night of the accident. *ABCNews* reported 2.9 million page views in the two days following Diana's death. *MSNBC* announced that the number of people who accessed its site doubled from normal levels, and *FoxNews* claims the tragedy drew a single-day record high number of visitors.

By using the Web, mourners could link to in-depth information about Diana's life and family, and to many stories surrounding the car crash, the subsequent investigation, and Diana's funeral. Additionally, many sites offered audio and video clips of the tragedy and some even provided chat forums for people to express their thoughts and emotions. A FoxNews director probably echoed the thoughts of many media experts when he commented that "the Web can do what TV can't." A CNN Interactive official believes that with "a big story like this . . . random access ability is invaluable. . . ." And an ABC News vice president remarked that they have created a "complete news-on-demand site, and this was the kind of story it was designed for."

Source: Tedesco, 1997l

difficult to get people to change from their primary source of news to an alternate medium. Additionally, many find the Web too difficult to use, and they do not see the advantages of making a steep financial investment in a home computer, modem, and software to obtain information they can already get from television, radio, and newspapers.

Web content is often criticized for being largely the same as the printed or broadcast versions. Often content is first written for the traditional version of the medium supporting the Web site, then simply "repurposed" or copied with little variation and placed on the Web (Gimein, 1996, p. 10). News broadcasts and printed material often appear word for word on the broadcaster's or newspaper's Web site without taking the capabilities of the new medium into account. However, the ratio of original news to repurposed content seems to be on the rise. By early 1998, 20 percent of online newspapers were carrying half original content and half repurposed stories, compared to a year earlier when only about 7 percent of netpapers could make that claim (Noack, 1998).

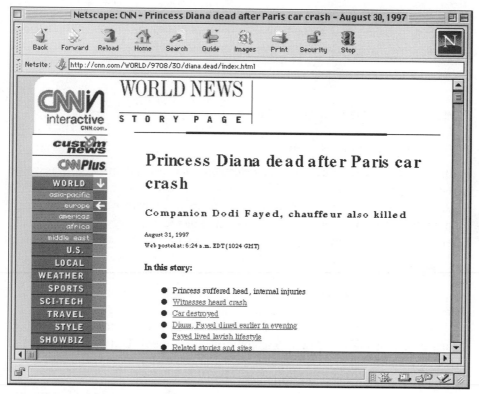

FIGURE 5.1 CNN News Site Featuring Diana Stories

News writing for broadcast differs from writing for print, but as of yet, it has not been determined which style best suits the Web, nor has a new style of online writing evolved. An executive with the *San Francisco Chronicle* asserts that newspapers should go beyond putting their existing content on the Web. "There should instead be new forms of communication . . ." that use many of the properties of newspapers, but are adapted to the online environment (Hipschman, 1995).

Although the Web has made inroads as a viable news medium, it still has a long way to go before it diffuses through the general population and becomes a major news delivery system. Clearly though, the Web is adding new dimensions to news delivery made possible through hypertext. Conventional media are establishing Web sites and eagerly posting news stories to draw new and varied consumers. Newspapers, news magazines, television, and radio heartily go beyond their technological confines of time, space, and mode of presentation by creating Web sites filled with colorful graphics, compelling audio and video, and hypertext versions of stories to satisfy their customers' needs. The motivations driving traditional media to the Web, the Web's impact on news, and the ways in which the Web is used to enhance non-online media may best be understood within the context of the development of the news media and the news-consuming audience.

HISTORY OF NEWS DELIVERY

From Newspapers to Netpapers

Before the days of newspapers and later electronic delivery systems, news was spread by word of mouth. Often, it would take weeks and even months or years for the latest news to spread from person to person. In times before the written word, events were often documented using a system of pictographs carved into cave walls. Later pictographs gave way to an alphabetic system of writing. Stone and clay tablets served as writing surfaces, and though heavy and cumbersome, they could be carried from place to place. More portable means of distributing the written word were needed, leading to the development of papyrus and parchment (tanned skin of a sheep or goat), and eventually to paper.

With the exception of early Chinese block writing, there was not an adequate means of producing more than one copy of a document. Until the invention of Gutenberg's printing press, scribes would laboriously copy document after document, but it was a tedious and time-consuming venture. In 1455, after many years of experimenting and toiling, Johannes Gutenberg printed two hundred copies of a 42-line Bible. More important, the Gutenberg printing press led the way to the explosive growth of books and the advent of newspapers.

At first, newspapers were mere one-sheet reports of important events, but later the American colonial presses began printing up to four pages of news. Early newspapers were seldom up-to-date or accurate, and distribution was slow, as the papers were carried by horses, boats, and by foot. Literacy was rare, and even for the educated few who could read, the papers were largely too expensive for frequent purchase.

In the mid-1800s several East Coast newspapers collectively known as **"The Penny Press"**—named after the price of a single issue—attracted many new readers with big bold headlines, sensational stories, and high drama. Readers were so fascinated by detailed accounts of crimes and other sordid stories that newspaper readership jumped dramatically. Newspapers were no longer a bastion for the elite but now reached out to the masses. By the turn of the twentieth century, the number of weekly papers tripled, and there were more daily newspapers than there are now at the close of the century.

In the 1900s, reporting standards became more stringent. Sources were checked for accuracy, editors strove for impartial and objective accounts of events, reporters were educated, trained, and knowledgeable, and newspapers recognized their responsibility and power as advocates of causes and social and economic reform.

Today's newspapers pride themselves as sources of reliable and credible news. Often in-depth, investigative, and interpretive reporting are the mainstays of big city, influential newspapers. Newspapers are visually more exciting and easy to read, with color photographs, subject sections, tables of contents, catchy headlines, and concise well-written stories covering a wide variety of subjects and news. Yet, the number of newspapers published and newspaper readership continue to decline.

The number of U.S. daily newspapers has dropped from about 2,600 in the early 1900s to just about 1,520 in 1996. Newspapers are also dealing with waning readership, especially among the younger population. Faced with increasing competition from broadcast news outlets and online sources, overall newspaper readership has slowly declined. In 1996, only about six out of ten adults read a newspaper daily (Consoli, 1997). Added to the challenges of printing a daily paper is the soaring cost of newsprint. Many publishers are being propelled to the Web as a means of distributing news for relatively low set-up, maintenance, and distribution costs. Additionally, the Web attracts a larger, more diverse audience, and it reaches out to those who generally ignore traditional newspapers.

NETPAPERS Major newspapers that have found their way to cyberspace include the *Boston Globe, Los Angeles Times, San Jose Mercury News, San Francisco Chronicle, Chicago Sun Times, New York Times,* and *USA Today.* By late 1997, between 40 and 60 percent of the nation's daily U.S. newspapers had established a Web presence, representing a 300–400 percent increase from late 1995, when only about 150 newspapers were online ("NAA Survey," 1997; "Online Newspaper Statistics," 1997). Additionally, of the one hundred daily newspapers with the largest circulation in the country, all but five have launched cybersites either on the Web or through an online service such as AOL (Consoli, 1997).

Some newspaper prognosticators envision a time when all news will be electronically transmitted to subscribers' home computers or WebTVs via push technology. Many blast the death of paper and ink and remain steadfast in their opinion that "netpapers" will remain supplementary to printed versions. In the meantime, many claim that establishing complementary online news services is needed to ensure newspapers' strength and to keep up with a changing market (Rogoski, 1995).

In addition to delivering news, a Web site serves as a promotional vehicle for the newspaper. A contemporary-looking site improves a newspaper's image and attracts new readers to both the online and printed versions (Singer, 1996). Visual continuity between the printed and Web issues reassures online readers that they are getting the same quality of news as those buying the paper off the rack. The *Wall Street Journal* and the *New York Times* are two examples of newspapers that have designed their netpapers with the overall layout, type face, and headline styles mirroring the printed issues (Reid, 1996).

FEE-FOR-SERVICE NETPAPERS Some media companies are betting that consumers will pay a small fee in exchange for articles and other items of information. Just as telephone callers are charged each time they dial local or long distance information service, Web users must pay each time they download a document. These "microtransactions" of usually less than one dollar are charged to users' credit card or telephone bills. Although less than one-tenth of media sites' revenues were derived from microtransactions in 1996, the revenue potential is enormous, especially as microtransaction billing services become more efficient and easy to implement (Hodges, 1996a).

As publishers are experimenting with ways to profit from their Web sites, some, such as the *Wall Street Journal Interactive,* have learned the hard way that few people are willing to pay a flat fee for online news retrieval. Within a few short weeks of implementing an annual subscription fee, the number of registrants to *WSJ*'s Web site plummeted from 600,000 to 30,000 (Tedesco, 1996). This happened in late summer 1996; the number of registrants rebounded to 100,000 a few months later when Microsoft picked up the tab for subscribers who use Internet Explorer as their browser (Gipson, 1997; Hodges, 1996b). By the end of 1997, the *Wall Street Journal Interactive* claimed about 150,000 subscribers, the most of any subscription-based site on the Web ("The Top Twenty-five," 1997; Snyder, 1998).

The *San Jose Mercury News* had a big bite taken out of its Web site when it tried to charge its users a monthly fee for customizable news services. The *Mercury Center* was stung by a 40 percent drop in usage as a result of its monthly fee requirement; however, 10,000 subscribers opted not to cancel (Moran, 1997; Noack, 1997b). The *Mercury Center* continues to charge online users $4.95 per month, and less for those who also subscribe to the printed newspaper. Technology-interested subscribers who live beyond the newspaper's circulation area seem willing to pay the monthly fee for industry-specific news that comes from the heart of Silicon Valley.

Online newspapers are learning that while readers are not willing to pay for general information that can easily be obtained from other sources, they seem to be more likely to open their wallets for exclusive, current information that has a wide appeal but is not readily available elsewhere. Users are also willing to pay for old or archived news that may be difficult to find through other sources. Newspapers such as the *Wall Street Journal* have a marketable online product that is more likely to attract paid subscriptions than most hometown papers that post wire service news and focus on local events.

Fee-for-service systems are not solely dependent on subscriptions for producing online profits. The Newspaper Association of America announced that in 1996 slightly more than one-third of online papers generated revenue mainly through display and classified advertising, providing Internet access and Web site hosting, and charging for subscriptions and premium services ("NAA Services," 1997).

PRINT JOURNALISTS IN AN ONLINE WORLD   The transition from printed news to online news can be complicated. Journalists who are accustomed to drawing in readers through well-written prose are concerned with reports becoming diluted within the splash of eye-catching graphics and video. Interviews with newspaper journalists uncovered varying opinions about newspaper Web sites. Many fear that the need for increased computer literacy will freeze them out of jobs and that the abundance of incredible and unreliable information found on many Web pages will eventually darken online newspapers' reputations. Other reporters are concerned about the lack of monetary and human resources for developing and maintaining netpapers. One or two daily deadlines are a thing of the past as cybernews requires continual updating, a responsibility that lays heavy on reporters (Singer, 1996).

With twenty-four-hour-a-day updates, newspaper Web sites are depending more on wire services than ever before. Printed newspapers such as the *New York Times* or the *Washington Post* typically run about 10 percent wire material, but almost one-half of online news stories are direct from the wires. While many editors and journalists abhor the idea of using wire stories, it is debatable whether the public even discerns a difference. Although many editors object to heavy reliance on the Associated Press wire service, others find the low-cost AP feeds more than adequate for online non-local news coverage. Online newspapers are taking a "rip and read" approach to breaking news, similar to that which television and radio have traditionally relied upon. Additionally, many major newspapers are opting for preprocessed, Web-ready feeds; thus, they all end up featuring the same AP story (Kirsner, 1997).

In addition to using wire feeds to fill their online sites, many reporters are using the Web as a source for news. The fourth annual Media in Cyberspace study found that almost half of the reporters who were surveyed said they surf the Web daily in search of news. Additionally, about one in ten journalists rely on newsgroups and e-mail lists as their primary sources of information (Noack, 1998).

Many journalists believe in the power of content and claim that the nature of their work will remain the same regardless of the method of delivery, especially as most Web content is repurposed from the printed editions. Additionally, many reporters look forward to being relieved of space constraints and the struggle of squeezing complicated stories into a few columns of space.

The interactive nature of the Web facilitates communication between reporters and readers, leading to a new style of journalism that humanizes reporters in the eyes of a more involved audience. E-mail links to reporters set up an "electronic dialogue" between journalists and their readers (Jackson, 1995, p. 60). "Readers have unprecedented access to reporters and editors, and journalists enjoy the opportunity to learn with lightning speed what their audience is thinking on a variety of issues" (Wolff, 1994, p. 62).

The integration of daily newspapers and the Web will bring journalists and the public in closer contact, provide more comprehensive news, and enhance reports through graphics, audio, and video. Publishers, editors, journalists, and readers have many reasons for hoping that newspapers and netpapers can live happily side by side.

From Printed News Magazines to Online News Magazines

The term *news magazine* was coined in 1923 by Henry Luce and associates when they founded *Time* magazine. *Newsweek* and *U.S. News & World Report* have since been established and now rank with *Time* as the most well-known news magazines published today. News magazines publish in-depth reports of important current events, aided by compelling photographs. Additionally, news magazines analyze and interpret the news, report on important persons, and keep their readers abreast of politics and social trends.

At the close of the nineteenth century, magazines were a highly respected and well-read medium. Many stories were beautifully written literary marvels full of descriptive prose, and others were hard-hitting political and social critiques. Muckraking, an early form of investigative reporting, was largely responsible for attracting new readers. Ida Tarbell's landmark investigative piece exposing Standard Oil Company's unscrupulous business practices set off renewed interest in muckracking and was behind the sudden increase in magazine circulation. Muckrakers uncovered political and corporate corruption, called for birth control and the abolition of child labor and sweat shops, and were proponents of other social and economic improvements.

The concept of news magazines arose out of the need for a vehicle to disseminate in-depth national news. In the early 1920s, general interest magazines dominated the scene. Although national news was carried by most major newspapers, there was not a venue for reaching those who did not have access to a large daily paper. News magazines flourished until the 1970s, when increased competition from television and other sources began to erode readership levels. Although *Time, Newsweek,* and *U.S. News & World Report* boast a combined circulation of almost 10 million, which represents a slight increase in circulation over the last two decades, news weeklies are experiencing a general downward trend in readership. Newsstand sales have dropped nearly 25 percent, and the bulk of lost readers are college-educated people between 25 and 40 years of age, news magazines' primary target group. These lost readers are also the group most likely to turn to the Web for news and information.

Like newspapers, magazines are searching for innovative ways to reach their target audiences. Cyberspace offers news and other specialty magazines the opportunity to gain new readers and attract those who stopped buying the printed issues. Hundreds of magazines have established Web sites. The content ranges from promotional pieces to full-text articles. By combining text, graphics, video, and audio, online news magazines present up-to-date information, news, and sports scores in a vibrant, lively, intriguing, and interactive format. Faced with many of the same challenges as newspapers, news magazines look to the Web as means of increasing readership, boosting a favorable image, and creating new avenues of revenue.

From Over-the-Air Radio to Net Radio

Until the passage of the Radio Act of 1927, radio was largely an unregulated medium operated by anyone knowledgeable enough to use (and often to build) a transmitter and other broadcasting equipment. In the early 1930s, government regulation and the Great Depression contributed to the decrease in the number of radio stations. The Federal Radio Commission's efforts to clear the radio airwaves of interference led to the decline in the number of stations allowed to broadcast. The Depression fostered a growing number of radio listeners as people came to depend on radio as a prime source of news and entertainment, and as a way to forget about their economic woes.

Throughout the 1920s and the following two decades, several radio networks formed. While some networks quickly disbanded, others thrived. By the end of the 1940s, CBS, NBC, ABC, and the Mutual Broadcasting System emerged as the four major radio networks. NBC's Blue network (which later became ABC) originated regularly scheduled newscasts in 1930. Listeners tuned in by the droves to Lowell Thomas's 15-minute nightly newscast, which set off a competitive war between radio and newspapers. Newspaper publishers feared that their readers would stop buying newspapers and would instead get the news free over the radio. As a means of self-protection, newspapers blocked broadcasters' access to the major news agencies. Fighting back, CBS set up its own news service that was quickly suspended as the press continued to pressure radio by instituting the Press-Radio Bureau to dole out tidbits of news to broadcasters. Additionally, CBS and NBC finally agreed to limit newscasts to two 5-minute daily segments of reports that were sent from the Press-Radio Bureau. Eventually, independent radio news services began appearing on the scene and the major newspaper news bureaus began providing news to radio broadcasters. The stage was now set for ongoing competition between newspapers and radio newscasts.

The audience for radio news was further boosted during World War II, when H. V. Kaltenborn and Edward R. Murrow mesmerized millions with their colorful and descriptive commentaries and live reports of the fighting. Radio's heyday was short-lived. The end of the war and the explosive growth of television led to a downturn in radio listenership. Radio news became limited to hourly news briefs and a few public affairs and information programs. Radio took a back seat to television until the late 1950s, when rock 'n' roll barged onto the scene and created a need for all-music formats. As rock 'n' roll was driving parents across America crazy, FM's advanced audio quality was quickly becoming the mainstay of radio. Eventually, all-music stations came to prefer broadcasting on FM, while AM was deemed more appropriate for news and talk programs. However, noncommercial community, college, and public radio stations offering a mix of music and news programming are broadcast on the FM band between 88 and 92 megahertz. For example, National Public Radio's *All Things Considered* and *Morning Edition* are well-known national news programs that are found on the FM band.

Today, FM radio enjoys about three-quarters of all radio listening, while AM radio is suffering from small audiences and low profit margins. The most economically healthy AM stations tend to be those that broadcast news and talk programs in major metropolitan areas. Radio stations are expensive to purchase and operate, causing many independents to sell out to ownership groups and duopolies in which more than one station in a market is owned by the same individual, group, or corporation. With many AM and FM stations in a single market, competition among stations for advertising dollars and listeners is fierce.

Radio stations are also in stiff competition with television and newspapers. Yearly Roper polls indicate that the number of people who turn to radio as their primary source of news has declined from about 35 percent in 1960 to about 14 percent in 1997 ("Key Results of the Roper Survey," 1997). Moreover, media consumers consistently judge radio news as less credible than television news and newspapers. Diminishing levels of credibility and listenership, and heavy competition between radio and television news stations and newspapers have propelled many radio stations to seek ways of attracting new listeners while striving to maintain their current audiences.

Web radio allows programmers to circumvent high costs, licensing, and burdensome regulations. Cybercasters are free to provide news and information in a largely unregulated environment. As with other media that are online, a Web radio news site acts as a promotional vehicle and draws new listeners to both the online and broadcast versions. Where traditional local news broadcasts are confined to a limited signal area, online news reaches a global audience. Local news can be accessed by those living across the country bolstering the outlet's audience and its image.

From Television News Broadcasts to Netcasts

Entertainment programs dominate the television programming landscape. Early news and information programs such as *See It Now* featured in-depth looks at then-current issues, such as the atomic blast tests and the McCarthy hearings. The *Today Show* debuted in 1952 with an original mix of entertainment sprinkled with the daily news. Early news gathering by television outlets was hindered by cumbersome cameras and poor means of delivering video accounts of events. Viewers of regularly scheduled newscasts were largely subjected to "talking head" close-up shots of anchors. Occasional glimpses of live news footage helped break the monotony. Nightly newscasts were only fifteen minutes in length until 1963 when they were increased to thirty minutes. Subtracting time set aside for commercials and network promotions leaves a half-hour newscast with about twenty-two minutes to devote to news— less information than a single page of text in a standard-sized newspaper.

Television news took a step forward in the eyes of the public with its coverage of President John F. Kennedy's assassination. Within five minutes of the shooting, the major networks had interrupted their regularly scheduled programming to deliver up-to-the-minute news about the President's condition. All scheduled programs were preempted for the next four days as mourning Americans sat riveted in front of their televisions watching and waiting for news summaries and updates. The President's funeral drew a 93 percent viewership, the highest ever for a single event.

Aided by smaller, more portable cameras, videotape, satellite relay systems, movable satellite uplinks, and other technological improvements, television news brought the Vietnam war into the living rooms of millions. Coined the "first television war," courageous journalists on the front lines gave Americans first-hand accounts and close-up looks at the horrors and triumphs experienced by our armed forces overseas. The television coverage had a tremendous impact on the collective conscience of those at home, and it was indirectly responsible for antiwar protests.

Television's spellbound coverage of important events such as the 1969 moon landing, Watergate, and the Iran Hostage Crisis, along with the debut of news programs such as *60 Minutes* and the general improvement in the quality of network and local newscasts, elevated television as a reputable and reliable source of news. By 1992, almost seven out of ten Americans reported using television as their primary source of news, and deemed it far more credible than either newspapers or radio news.

Ted Turner's Cable News Network gave birth to twenty-four-hour news formats. Turner was determined to make CNN successful despite his many critics. Called the "Chicken Noodle Network" by its many skeptics, Turner insisted that viewers were news hungry and yearned to access information at any time of the day. As predicted by Turner, CNN soon became an enormously popular and highly respected network that has won many prestigious awards for its coverage of important events. CNN's subscriber list tops 75 million U.S. households. The network also originates *Headline News,* a twenty-four-hour network of news briefs with updated sports scores that scroll across the bottom of the screen, and *CNNfn,* which focuses on financial and business news.

Importantly, CNN showed that the appetite for television news is strong and that half-hour newscasts scattered throughout the day leave the audience unsatisfied. CNN and other new twenty-four-hour cable television networks are limited in the amount of news they can deliver. There is only so much information that can be packed into the time allotted for each news segment. With the exception of some major news features, television news is generally not as in-depth as newspapers. However, cybernews can be updated all day, and it can be written as short briefs and as in-depth stories, advantages not available to traditional media. Additionally, since neither ABC, CBS, nor NBC have twenty-four-hour news outlets, establishing Web sites puts them in direct competition with twenty-four-hour cable news networks. The Web has becoming increasingly important to television news, especially to the networks, as an alternative means of distributing around-the-clock information surrounding the latest events.

NETCASTING   As with print media and radio, television stations that establish Web sites get the added advantage of promoting their non-online news sites. Several analyses of television Web sites found that stations tend to provide programming information, news anchor biographies, and other promotional material online. Additionally, stations use the Web to distribute overflow news that cannot fit into local newscasts. This serves to heighten a station's image as a reliable news provider.

At this time, there is little worry that the Web is stealing viewers away from television news programs. With online video delivering only three frames per second, compared to television's thirty frames per second, it is unlikely that anyone will mistake Web news video for the real thing. However, online technology is improving so rapidly that in the near future it is highly likely that Web video will closely resemble a television broadcast, increasing the concern that Web news is cannibalizing the television audience (Tedesco, 1997g).

COMING TOGETHER ON THE WEB

Media Characteristics

Unique differences between the media disappear on the Web. On the Web, newspapers and news magazines are no longer primarily text media, radio an aural medium, and television a visual medium. All media have the capability of providing news using graphics, text, audio, and video. News requiring visuals can adequately be illustrated on a radio netcast, and an important piece of audio can be played on a netpaper.

The advantages and disadvantages of using each medium in its conventional form fade away on the Web, and each medium is put on an equally competitive playing field. The Web audience's motivations for selecting one news Web site over another become less clear than when a person chooses a printed newspaper over a television news broadcast. Traditionally, media are differentiated from one another by mode of presentation, depth of content, ease of access, portability, and convenience. However, in cyberspace, no one medium has an inherent advantage over another. Cybernews is presented in the same manner using graphics, text, audio, video, and hypertext links, regardless of which medium is operating the site.

Dr. John Pavlik, one of the country's leading authorities on communication technologies, identifies three stages of online news content. The first stage involves posting repurposed content taken from printed or over-the-air counterparts. This format currently dominates online news delivery. An emerging second stage augments repurposed information with original content written and designed specifically for Web delivery. The third stage rethinks "the nature of a 'community' online and, most important, a willingness to experiment with new forms of storytelling." For example, the *New York Times* is experimenting with new imaging techniques that would allow users to "explore a 360-degree field of vision," giving them the "experience of 'entering' a live or recorded news event, or to see a still or moving photo in three dimensions" (Pavlik, 1997, p. 36).

Regardless of whether news is generated by an electronic or printed medium, online content delivery is evolving as the Web is recognized as a distinct medium. Traditional ways of reporting and presentation are giving way to new dynamic and interactive methods that hold promise for engaging and drawing new audiences to the Web.

Editorial Standards

It is acknowledged that the structure of the Web lends itself to in-depth news coverage and to original content that cannot fit into a newspaper's limited space or squeezed onto a few seconds of airtime. However, just because the technology allows for detailed coverage, debate is raging whether online news should deliver content that would not be printed or aired on its traditional counterparts.

When the *Bakersfield Californian* published a three-part series on child abuse, its editors decided to omit the horrendous details of autopsy reports of children who died as a result of parental or caregiver abuse. However, the "shocking" reports were posted on the newspaper's Web site. In Texas, the online version of a newspaper ran a picture of an aborted fetus that did not run in the printed edition. The *San Antonio News Express* posted online several photographs taken at President Clinton's second inaugural ceremony that were not included in the printed version. One such photograph was of a woman wearing a Clinton mask and holding an anti–Bob Dole bumper sticker that included an obscenity.

Many journalists and editors consider the online posting of controversial content an editorial double standard and believe that print guidelines for "taste and space" should be applied to the Web. Others, however, contend that while there are clear rules of what is appropriate to print, no such guidelines exist for the Web.

Further, since online users seek out Web content and can choose what they wish to see, they are not unwitting viewers of controversy. Therefore, online guidelines should allow more freedom of expression than those governing printed news. As one former news editor put it, "There are a number of things we do online that would turn hair white on the print side" (Noack, 1997a, p. 99).

As more media use the Web as a supplement to their traditionally delivered versions, it is likely that the double standard dispute will escalate as editors and electronic news producers struggle with the issue of what is appropriate online content. Future online news may reflect traditional media standards, or it may develop its own set of guidelines for dealing with controversial and objectionable material.

Media Preferences

It is largely known why certain people prefer one traditional medium over another, but the motivations behind selecting one Web news site over another are still speculative. Perhaps preference comes from users' existing beliefs, attitudes, and perceptions of traditionally delivered versions and news sources. Or perhaps a discerning Web audience makes its selections based on careful examination of the cybernews options. As consumers sift through the multitude of Web sites, they are developing Web surfing habits and site preferences. Online media are having a difficult time distinguishing themselves from their competitors. Media sites are turning to brand awareness to motivate consumers to select one site over another, such as *CBS SportsLine* over *ESPN SportsZone.* The media aim to transfer their strong brand names, such as ABC, NBC, and CNN, to the online environment. Internet experts speculate that early adopters of the Internet were not brand sensitive, but rather, they tried out many different sites and returned to the ones they liked the best, regardless of the site's originator. Those who are more Web tentative tend to be brand loyal and stray toward known sites. In other words, a Web surfer who regularly watches *CNN* on television is more likely to access *CNN Interactive* than another Web news site. Pending research, the degree of brand loyalty on the Web is conjectural. Regardless, media companies are launching promotional campaigns with the hope that brand loyalty will drive consumers to their Web sites (Haring, 1997).

Pleasing the Web audience is a key to creating sites that will be competitively advantageous over other online venues. *CNN Interactive, Washington Post, USA Today, New York Times,* and *NandO Times* (*Raleigh News and Observer*) were named the favorite news sites of 1996 by almost 33,000 Web surfers who responded to a straw poll posted on American Journalism Reviews' *News Link* page.

The Web presents a unique opportunity for news purists who wish to learn about daily events without the intervention of news editors and organizational policy. Rather than accessing edited netpapers or television netcasts, many people prefer to go directly to the source. Although cumbersome to use, *Reuters* and *Associated Press* are among several wire services that provide live feeds online. Netpapers such as the *Tampa Bay Tribune* and the *Washington Post* provide links to the wire service's feeds, and a slimmer version of Reuters' feed is available through *Yahoo!*

Effectiveness and Recall of Online News

Although there are many benefits to cybercasting, some media experts are unsure of its effectiveness, and they express concern about how well people remember online news. For many years researchers have been comparing the levels of recall of print and electronic media, but in recent years, computers, and more specifically the Web, have also been examined. Generally, news is recalled more completely if read from a newspaper than if heard on the radio or watched on television. When the text of news stories is placed on computers or on the Web, levels of recall are similar to that of newspapers, and are higher than radio and television. This suggests that similar thinking processes take place when people read newspapers and when they use the Web. Computers and the Web are largely print-based and require reading, which aids recall more so than do audiovisual and audio-only news (DeFleur, Davenport, Cronin, & DeFleur, 1992; Sundar, Narayan, Obregon, & Uppal, 1997).

Compiling Online News

Web sites that do little more than compile news taken from other news sites are springing up all over the Web. Much to the dismay of some major news organizations and media companies, these news compilers provide links to other news sites and display stories framed within their own sites. For example, visitors connected to *TotalNews* can access copyrighted information posted by CNN Interactive, *USA Today*, or any other online news site without having to go directly to each individual site. *TotalNews* frames the information and acknowledges its sources; however, the major news organizations object to this practice, stating that *TotalNews* benefits from their material by selling advertising on its own site.

Time, Inc., CNN, Washington Post, Times-Mirror, Reuters, and Dow Jones & Company collectively filed suit against *TotalNews*, claiming that it is generating advertising revenue off news provided by the media companies. The publishers claimed they have the right to control links to their sites and how their information is posted. Framing original content changes its appearance on the page, which may lead many users to believe the content is provided by *TotalNews* rather than the linked media outlet. On the other hand, *TotalNews* asserts that its site provides a service to the news publishers by quickly and conveniently linking users directly to news sources (Williamson & Cleland, 1997).

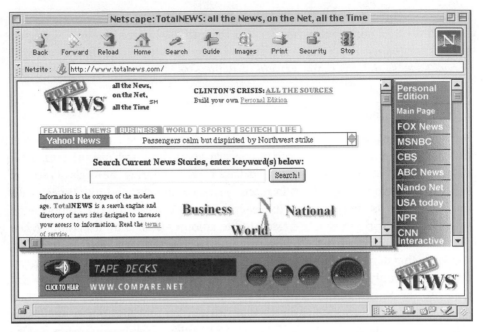

FIGURE 5.2 TotalNews Homepage

Claiming lack of funds for a proper defense, *TotalNews* settled out-of-court by agreeing to stop putting frames around news content provided by other media organizations, but it can keep a frame around its advertisements. Legal experts and Web analysts were hoping for a trial rather than an out-of-court settlement. There are many unresolved issues surrounding intellectual property rights on the Internet that may have been settled had the case gone to trial.

Other news compilers who take liberty with online news material closely followed the *TotalNews* case. *Newslinx* gathers headlines of major news stories and displays them as part of its own site rather than couched within a frame. *Newslinx* also profits through advertising sales and takes it upon itself to rewrite article headlines. Another news compiler, *Newshub,* has remained untouched by litigation, primarily because it does not sell advertising on its site or alter news headlines.

Clearly, publishers are not against others establishing links to their sites, but they are wary of others altering original content and profiting from copyrighted materials. Although the *TotalNews* settlement fell short of setting a precedent, it will at least keep other compilers of online news and content aware that they could be subject to legal action unless they clearly differentiate and attribute content to its originators (Richtel, 1997). In the long term, the settlement could impact the ownership of online content and control over hypertext links, and perhaps threaten the existence of sites that primarily act as compilers of information.

EXAMPLES OF MEDIA ON THE WEB

The Web carries thousands of newspapers, radio stations, and television stations, and many news magazines from which news can be accessed at the click of a button. These media sites differ from each other in many ways. For instance, some sites are more complex and multilayered than others. Some sites feature national and international news, while others stick with local events. And, on some sites, news is the primary focus, while on others, news is only a small part of the offerings. Following are descriptions of selected news-oriented sites that exemplify excellence in online reporting and information delivery.

Large Circulation Newspapers

NEW YORK TIMES   *The New York Times on the Web* is regarded as the most comprehensive online newspaper. Visitors can access the site for free; however, they must register and obtain a password before browsing either the text or the graphic version of the paper. Like the newspaper edition, the online edition contains international, national, and metropolitan news, and sections covering politics, business, art, science, obituaries, weather, travel, books and book reviews, and classified advertising.

The site contains several unique features, such as the AP Radio Network Newscast, and the *CyberTimes* section, which focuses on technology news that does not appear in the printed issues. The site keeps visitors up to date with audio clips, scrolling headlines, breaking news, and late news updates.

USA TODAY   The online version of this nationwide newspaper is just as colorful and eclectic as its non-electronic counterpart. *USA Today Online* carries more than 100,000 pages of news, business, sports, weather, technology news, feature stories, opinions, lifestyle and travel information, and classifieds. Archived stories cost $1.00 each to download. The site has emerged as one of the most popular general interest news sites, with a daily average of 4 million page views and 700,000 unique visitors.

WASHINGTON POST   This highly respected newspaper has carved its own niche in providing news and information on the Web. *Washingtonpost.com* presents articles taken from the daily paper's printed issue, including international news, sports, style, weather, technology, and business. Links to related information and searchable databases on restaurants, movies, videos, and other topics are available for

FIGURE 5.3 *The New York Times on the Web* Homepage

browsing. The site averages more than 700,000 page views per business day. Additionally, it features interactive areas where visitors express their views. Online discussions about important subjects such as politics and business are hosted by politicians, journalists, and other leading authorities.

Medium and Small Circulation Newspapers

SANTA ROSA *PRESS DEMOCRAT*   The Santa Rosa *Press Democrat,* located in the heart of the California wine country, localizes its online version with its "Wine of the Week" feature on the opening page, and the "Tasting Room" and "Wine Rave" pages. Area dining, lodging, and recreation, including online maps, are available for tourists and locals. The site also includes a news research center, real estate ads, and an online method for subscribing to its printed issues. The *Press Democrat*'s site is user-friendly and includes a nongraphic site map for easy traveling within its pages. The paper's online version offers much more information than it possibly can fit in its printed issues, and it reaches many more readers than its printed circulation of about 100,000 people in Northern California.

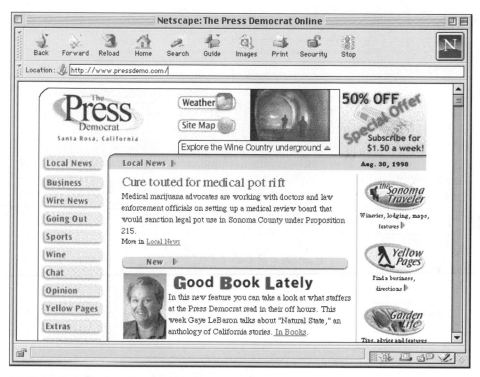

FIGURE 5.4 *The Press Democrat* Homepage

STANDARD TIMES   The presence of small local newspapers on the Web is a testament to the notion of the Web being an equal playing field for large and small newspapers. On the Web, all newspapers have the same opportunity for increasing their audiences and for generating additional advertising revenue by reaching a global marketplace.

With very little start-up money, *The Standard-Times* has built a visually pleasing and informative Web site. Based in southern Massachusetts, the *Standard Times* invites visitors from around the globe with local, state, and world news sections packaged in an easy-to-use format. Replete with bright colors, graphics, photos, and a searchable index of past issues, the site epitomizes a strong online presence and demonstrates that newspapers do not have to have deep pockets or hundreds of thousands of readers to establish a credible and attractive site.

NEW CENTURY NETWORK   The now defunct New Century Network (NCN) was brought to fruition by the efforts of nine major newspaper companies for the purpose of better serving their readers through interconnectivity. Advance Publications, Inc.,

FIGURE 5.5 *The Standard-Times* Homepage

Cox Newspapers, Gannett Corporation, Hearst Corporation, Knight-Ridder, the New York Times Company, Times-Mirror Company, Tribune Company, and Washington Post Company put their technical know-how together to form the first online newspaper network. Users benefited by quickly linking to information posted by any of the almost two hundred networked daily publications across the nation. Designating a city of residence pulled up a user's local newspaper and set it as the default site. From there, readers could connect directly from their hometown papers to any of the other networked papers for news, sports information, ticket services, home shopping, and event updates ("Going On-line," 1995; Hodges, 1997).

NCN was applauded by many newspaper experts as a great way to bring online traffic to newspaper sites and thus increase their online advertising revenue. Some industry experts believe that one of the major reasons NCN failed after about three years online is that the site did not provide visitors with an on-site search engine. The original plan called for NCN to purchase a search engine that would be "willing to co-brand its pages with news sites in exchange for new ad revenues (or perhaps licensing fees) from the newspapers" (Outing, 1998, p. 42). Instead, NCN sent its visitors to outside search services and directories that are in direct competition for local news and classified ad revenues. The major search engines are among the most popular sites and are ringing up much more advertising dollars than online newspaper sites, which rarely rank as the top most visited sites. NCN's demise could very well lead to another try by some other group of newspapers that would link their sites together and provide a customized search engine that meets the needs of the providers as well as the needs of their readers (Outing, 1998).

News Magazines

NEWSWEEK   This international newsmagazine carries original articles and features stories online, but content from its print editions is not posted. *Newsweek* online does, however, include a page devoted to previewing the contents of its latest non-electronic issue, and offers short highlights of its printed stories.

TIME   The online version of *Time* is accessible through the *Pathfinder.com* site, which provides a collection of links to well-known magazines online. *Time* online offers several international editions of its magazine, such as Asia, Canada, Europe, Latin America, and the United States. The U.S. version contains sections of national and world news, business, art, money, cinema, society and science, health and medicine, opinions, and book excerpts. Additionally, the week's cover story and other investigative pieces from the printed edition can be accessed through the online site.

U.S. NEWS & WORLD REPORT   This magazine's Web site is made up of two main sections, School Rankings and U.S. News. The former section features information about colleges, universities, and graduate schools with corresponding rankings based on specific criteria within each field of study. The U.S. News section contains articles from the weekly printed issue, including the cover story, national and world news, business and technology information, and general interest stories. Also found are late-breaking news, opinions, and a citizens' toolbox—a collection of bits of information on important issues affecting readers.

ELECTRONIC NEWSSTAND   *Electronic Newsstand* operates similarly to a traditional corner newsstand, where many different magazines can be found under one roof. Instead of searching for each source's online site, the *Electronic Newsstand* provides links to a plethora of magazines and sites about magazines. Online shopping information is also available, as are various topic-specific chat rooms and a quick search option for looking up a publication's URL. *Electronic Newsstand* is a free service that

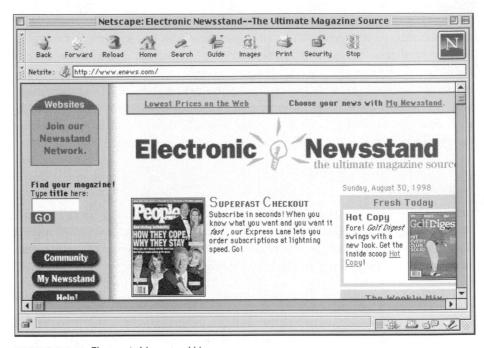

FIGURE 5.6 Electronic Newsstand Homepage

makes its money by selling advertising space throughout the site and by magazine subscriptions.

Radio News

NATIONAL PUBLIC RADIO   This government-funded radio network is relying on the Web to expand its audience. The network is reaching out to online communities and Web users to increase listenership of its highly informative and educational programs. The site is equipped with RealAudio and other interactive applications. Web users can listen to National Public Radio (NPR) newscasts and its other radio programs, such as *All Things Considered,* and many of the network's children's shows and investigative stories. Transcripts of programs are archived for future retrieval, and the site provides links to member stations, an online discussion room, and a within-site search engine.

NPR is breaking new ground by offering an audio-on-demand service, similar to Audible Audio, that allows off-line playback of audio files. The service works through the "Listen Up Player" device. The device resembles a small cassette player, and it stores digital audio files for later playback. The hand-held Listen Up Player connects to a docking device, which in turn connects to a computer to download the files. Using the Listen Up Player, users can download up to one hour of Web-based audio, and then play back such programs as *All Things Considered* or *Morning Edition,* while driving home, taking a walk, or whenever it is convenient (Levins, 1997).

Television News: Broadcast and Cable Networks

Competition between broadcast and cable networks has spurred the addition of companion Web sites as a means of increasing audience size and advertising revenue. Although the online network sites differ from one another in many aspects, such as depth of information and news customization options, they are in aggressive competition for visitors and online advertisements. The following sections give a glimpse into some of the unique features incorporated in a selection of network Web sites.

ABC *ABCnews.com* aims to give visitors the latest in breaking news by updating its site throughout the day and providing a ticker tape of news that scrolls across the screen. Designed by Starwave, the site uses the latest in RealAudio and RealVideo technologies. An extensive promotional campaign designed to bring the television audience to the Web, it features references to the Web site on the network's televised national newscasts, and on its morning news program, *Good Morning America.* ABC television viewers are directed to the network's Web site for details of late-breaking stories.

Adding to the network's news package is ABC Local Net, which connects to network affiliates across the nation. Accessed from *ABCnews.com,* Local Net debuted in January 1998 with links to thirty major-market television stations with plans to sign another hundred stations by 1999. Providing both national and local news online may lift ABC's online presence and steal visitors away from other local news sites.

CBS *Eye on the Net* is the hub of CBS Television Network programming. Up-to-date news can be accessed from the opening page; however, it does take a bit of searching to find the appropriate links. The menu page connects to network programs and projects, such as *Late Show with David Letterman, CBS Store, Primetime, Daytime, Kidzone,* and *CBS News.* The site is primarily a promotional outlet for CBS programs.

For current news, visitors must first click on the "CBS News" link that opens to a page listing all of CBS's news programs, such as *60 Minutes* and *Face the Nation.* At the bottom of the list is the link to the "Up to the Minute" promotional page that offers video, audio, and text about the television program. However, visitors are still two links away from up-to-date news. Visitors must next click on the

"Official Up to the Minute" icon to see a list of top stories, breaking news, Radio Online, and other linking pages. From there, users can finally select news stories to view.

Once visitors click and click and click their way to current news, the effort is well worth it. They get the top stories, scrolling headlines, breaking news, and news videos. Additionally, CBS Radio online provides access to live and archived programs such as the *Forbes Report, The Mary Matalin Show,* and other discussion programs.

Starting with CBS's homepage is the long road to getting current news stories. User may prefer to use a shorter route to current news by accessing the *Up to the Minute* news page directly, and bypassing the CBS homepage altogether.

Following the footsteps of its competitors, CBS has launched its own local affiliate tie-in site. *CBSnow* connects 154 affiliate stations from its site and, in turn, its affiliates link to CBSnow and the CBS homepage. *CBSnow* prompts visitors to enter their zip codes to bring up the nearest affiliate station for local news, weather, sports, and other information (Tedesco, 1998b).

NBC NBC launched its "Interactive Neighborhood" (IN), an affiliate-based Web site that connects communities with network programming and local information. At the time of its October 1997 debut, IN boasted links to forty of NBC's 210 affiliated stations. IN can be thought of as a network within the Internet. IN connects NBC affiliates' online sites to each other and to the network's homepage. IN offers visitors geographically customized news and information offered by Microsoft Sidewalk city guides, BigYellow online directories, and other content providers. Additionally, the network is encouraging affiliates to integrate their local over-the-air content with online information (Tedesco, 1997h).

For nonaffiliate news, NBC News joined forces with the Microsoft Corporation and created *MSNBC,* a dynamic, twenty-four-hour cable news venture with a complementary Web site. Playing off each other's strengths, Microsoft uses its computer knowledge to design and update the Web site, while NBC is largely in charge of content. The ultimate goal is to coordinate NBC's televised news with their online site. For example, immediately following an NBC news report, viewers can access MSNBC for more in-depth information.

MSNBC Launched in July 1996, MSNBC contains coverage of the day's events and breaking stories. Feature stories, opinion pieces, lifestyle and entertainment segments, weather updates, and sports, business, stock, and technology news are posted on the site. The site encourages user participation through chat auditoriums and e-mail interaction with company officials. NBC's affiliated stations maintain local news pages on MSNBC for those people who desire news with a local spin.

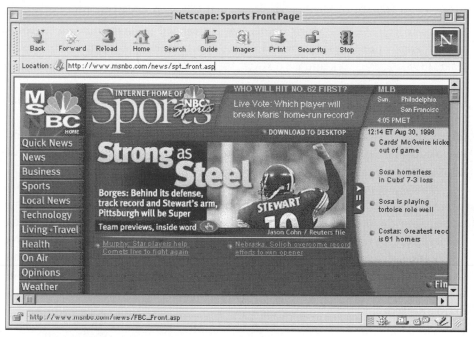

FIGURE 5.7 MSNBC Homepage

Waiting for the latest news no longer means spending hours online scanning through sites to find updated information. MSNBC pushes information by deploying "NewsAlert," a flashing icon that signals users to breaking stories. Visitors can also hop on the in-site search engine to travel directly to specific stories and other archived information.

MSNBC's "Business Video" targets corporate users with video clips and live feeds of press conferences, business meetings, and other events. MSNBC hopes to eventually sign up 50,000 subscribers to the service despite a $24.95 monthly fee.

About one year after its initial online posting, MSNBC revamped the site using sophisticated technology and design strategies to give it more of a look and feel of TV. As part of the renovation, MSNBC added more video clips and streaming of live news events (Tedesco, 1997b).

MSNBC has also announced a new stand alone site featuring sporting news and information. *MSNBCSports* content complements major sporting events airing on the NBC network, especially NFL games. With updates twenty-four hours a day, the site promises to bring up-to-the-minute action online.

Unfortunately, at about the same time the plans for *MSNBCSports* were announced, NBC was outbid by CBS for the rights to air NFL's AFC games. Nevertheless, *MSNBCSports* has plenty of other events to bring online, including professional and college baseball and basketball, college football, the 1998 Olympics, tennis, and golf. *MSNBCSports* claims that "integrated programming" is its competitive edge in an already crowded online sports market (Brown, 1998; Vonder Haar, 1998).

FOXNEWS *FoxNews Online* is neatly organized into "News," "Business," "Health," "Sports," "Technology," and "Wires" segments. Visitors are not limited just to current news, but can while away the hours looking through archived documents and video clips. The in-site key word searcher makes it easy to find current and archived articles.

    FoxNews Online was recently revamped to give it a hipper, more contemporary look. More links to major stories were added to the opening page to draw visitors deeper into the site more quickly. At the top of the homepage, a scrolling ticker flashes breaking news to lure users to the full stories, many of which contain live audio and video feed. Additionally, the site plans to coordinate its cable programs with its online site. For instance, a guest who appears on a Fox television news or talk program will simultaneously be able to field questions from viewers via the network's Web site.

CNN INTERACTIVE This pioneering online news site is a model of Web site architecture. The interface demands little and the basic organization facilitates within-site travel. Clicking on the homepage menu options takes visitors to "World News," "U.S. News," "Food & Health," "Sports," "All Politics," "Technology," "Style," "Showbiz," and "Weather." Within each topic area, visitors are presented with short one-page summaries of the day's top stories with links to in-depth versions that are often accompanied by audio, video, and graphics. For travelers or anyone sitting at home, the site provides hourly weather reports and Doppler radar updates for 3,600 cities. Additionally, users can design their own personal netcasts with the *CNN Custom News* service. Users select general areas of interest, such as weather, financial news, and so on, and the site compiles a customized program of the day's events.

    CNN Interactive plans to link its broadcast affiliate stations to the Web site to provide quick access to local happenings. As of early 1997, the "local link" program has signed on seventy of CNN's 450 Newsource subscriber stations, and hopes to get them all connected as soon as possible (Tedesco, 1997d).

    CNN considers its online version just as much of a news channel as is *Headline News* or *CNN International*. A group of about 150 employees devote their days to the online operation. News is selected from CNN's international and domestic news bureaus, as well as from the many local affiliates that provide news to CNN (Guglielmo, 1997). While CNN is only able to devote a few minutes of air time to most news events, its Web site provides in-depth coverage of most stories.

With more than 25 million page views per week, *CNN Interactive* is one of the most popular sites on the Web (Guglielmo, 1997; Pavlik, 1997). The prime users of *CNN Interactive* are upper middle-class, college-educated males between the ages of 35 and 45—demographics that mirror Web users in general. User data indicate that activity on *CNN Interactive* shoots up during the morning hours and throughout the working day, and then levels off during the evenings and weekends. Heavy daytime use suggests that the audience prefers getting online at the office where they are likely to have direct, high speed connections, and that the audience reads online news as they would a morning newspaper (Elder, 1996).

CNNfn   A spin-off of CNN, *CNNfn* devotes its Web site to financial news. "FN to GO" keeps users abreast of the latest financial news and stock market updates through a small browser window that remains open even as users travel to other sites. Claiming to be the first Web site to integrate online content with its television offerings, *CNNfn* went live in March 1996, with both broadcasts and netcasts. The Web site, which claims almost 36 million page views per month, streams its daily "Digital Jam" and "Business Unusual" programs and updates financial news twice hourly (Frook, 1996; Pavlik, 1997).

Local Television News

Many television network affiliates are building Web sites that include local news stories. Although many television stations devote their sites to promotional activities, the market is turning to these sites for news content. One such local affiliate that is reaching out to a broader audience with its Web site is WAND-TV. On the Web, the ABC affiliate is not confined to its medium-sized broadcast market. Instead, anyone from anywhere in the world can access Decatur, Illinois, local news, weather, and sports.

Newscasters recognize the Web's strength in drawing a larger and more global audience, and at the same time satisfying consumers' needs for local news at any time of the day. CBS affiliate *KEYE-TV* netcasts its four daily television newscasts. The Austin, Texas, affiliate streams the news live at 12 noon, 5, 6, and 10 P.M., and archives each netcast until the succeeding netcast goes online. The station's president claims the Web site acts as a second channel (Tedesco, 1997f).

Sporting News

ESPN SPORTSZONE   One of the most widely accessed sites on the Web, *ESPN SportsZone* features up-to-date sports scores, player and team profiles, the latest sports stories, team and league standings, archived news, and just about everything needed by rabid fans. Designed by Starwave, the easy-to-use interface allows visitors to travel quickly around the site.

Baseball fans can keep track of live games with ESPN's SportsZone Game-Tracker application. A running box score, current inning summary, live pitch count on the batter, photos of the pitcher and batter, and a graphic showing the base runners all appear on screen. Links to career and game statistics and optional audio alerts to noteworthy action are also available (Tedesco, 1997i).

ESPN SportsZone is a leader in fee-based content, reserving its in-depth stories for paying customers. One-third of its editorial content is available on a subscription basis (Hodges, 1996b).

CBS SPORTSLINE   Six months after the site premiered, CBS signed up with SportsLine USA, buying a 22 percent stake in the online venture. As part of the deal, SportsLine receives promotion time on the CBS network and the content provided to CBS sports (Galetto, 1997).

Tracking live NFL games is a snap with *CBS SportsLine*. Debuting just in time for the 1996 NFL season, the site presents a simulated playing field that is updated every thirty seconds. A helmet icon marks the ball's position on the field while the "down," "yards-to-go," "quarter," "score," and "time remaining" are displayed under the gridiron. Fans may miss the play-by-play accounts and (often annoying) color commentary heard on television, but this site is a great way to keep a visual account of games in progress. In addition to live NFL games, visitors are also treated to sporting news, updated scores, athlete biographies, sports trivia, and statistics.

Major League Baseball at first was not as willing to Webcast play-by-play action of live games. MLB has requested that teams not allow online simulcasting of contests on either *CBS SportsLine* or on team Web sites until overall policies were set. MLB insists that Webcast games should be uniformly presented and should be of high quality. Legally, broadcasting rights cover games on the Web and "the game itself is a copyrightable work. Laws governing rebroadcast on the Web are similar to those which require cable TV systems to pay local TV stations for the right to rebroadcast their programming" (Ingebretsen, 1997, p. 23).

At the 1997 team owners meeting, MLB agreed that audio and video coverage of games could be placed on a team's Web site and audio only on the team's flagship radio station's site. Additionally, MLB would work out agreements with some third-party providers, such as *CBS SportsLine* and *broadcast.com,* to carry game audio and statistics (Tedesco, 1997c). Despite Internet guidelines, online baseball struck out with many radio stations and networks, such as Westwood One/CBS radio group, that resisted carrying audiocasts of games without first renegotiating contracts to include online broadcasting rights (Tedesco, 1997k).

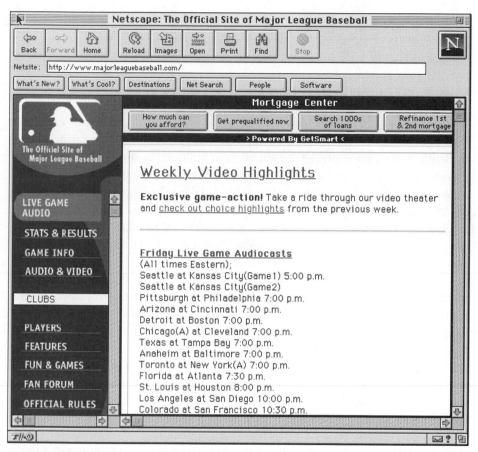

FIGURE 5.8 Major League Baseball Homepage

By opening day 1998, most MLB teams were set up to audiocast, and in some cases videocast, their games either on their own Web sites, MLB's site, or online through their local radio station carriers or other sports or audio network sites (Tedesco, 1998c).

NATIONAL BASKETBALL ASSOCIATION   When fans cannot be at a game or in front of a television set, they can tune in to *NBA.com* for video highlights of games in progress, play-by-play audio, and game stats. For $19.95, hoopsters can buy courtside seats to their home team's online games. Additionally, a desktop scoreboard flashes the latest action for supporters who are too busy with other tasks to view the online site. Even fans who have not plunked down their money can get in on the fun with audio and video game highlights (Tedesco, 1997e).

SUMMARY: ONLINE NEWS

Without doubt, the Web is fast becoming the place to find the latest news. The Web's convenient, easy-to-use interface, with many links to related information and in-depth stories, has captured the attention of millions. Enamored with push technology, many users are happy to have customized news at their fingertips. Users rejoice at the thought of getting news without picking through day-old newspapers, or desperately wading through pages of a news magazine, or anxiously hoping to catch a radio news report, or waiting until the 11 P.M. newscast airs. Newshounds simply connect to the Web to access up-to-date and customized news stories whenever they please.

Newspapers, news magazines, and radio and television news sources are finding themselves in a new competitive arena. Competition among traditional media remains strong as do the wars within each medium. The Web is a new battleground where the media compete for a fragmented audience and precious advertising dollars. Online media has to come up with new tactics to get an edge on their competition. There was a time when each medium could lay claim to depth, timeliness, and convenience, and could wield the virtues of that medium, whether it was text-, audio-, or video-based. Most news-oriented Web sites contain text, graphics, audio, and video, regardless of which medium has established the site. There is very little difference in the way content is presented on *CNN Interactive* or *USA Today Online*, though both are totally different media, one a television cable network and the other a national newspaper. The news media must concentrate their efforts in designing Web sites to draw viewers away from their online competitors, but at the same time the media must take care not to cannibalize their own non-online audience by luring viewers to the Web at the expense of traditionally delivered news fare.

The news media and journalists are trying to find their place in the world of the Web. Concerns abound that the many online sites containing unreliable and unsubstantiated news will tarnish the reputations of official news sites. Web site editors struggle over whether to post repurposed content or original material not found in their non-online issues. Control over copyrighted material and links to news sites is in litigation as more people get into the act of delivering online news.

The Web has enormous potential as a news vehicle, but many issues still need to be worked out from both the sources' and receivers' perspectives. In the meantime, most major news organizations and independent companies have established successful Web sites. Some Web news sites are getting millions of hits per month and are generating profits through advertising sales and special services subscriptions.

Web users are free to read the news in any order they like. They can scan brief reports or closely attend to in-depth stories, or they can bounce back and forth between printed and Web issues at their whim. Over the long term, online news may modify reading habits.

It is clear that cybernews is flourishing. Whether people will eventually embrace it as a primary source of news or just use it as a supplement is hard to predict, but as long as there are audiences to be gained and profits to be realized, online news is here to stay.

CHAPTER LINKS

ABC News—http://www.abcnews.com

Associated Press—http://wire.ap.org/

Boston Globe—http://www.globe.com

Broadcast.com—http://www.audionet.com

CBS Eye on the Net—http://www.cbs.com

CBS Up to the Minute—http://www.uttm.com

CBSnow—http://www.CBSnow.com/

CBS SportsLine—http://www.sportsline.com

Chicago Sun Times—http://www.suntimes.com/

CNN Custom News—http://customnews.cnn.com

CNNfn—http://www.cnnfn.com

CNN Interactive—http://cnn.com

Electronic Newsstand—http://www.cncws.com

ESPN SportsZone—http://ESPN.SportsZone.com/

FoxNews—http://www.foxnews.com/

KEYE-TV—http://www.keye.com/

Lawyers Weekly—http://www.lawyersweekly.com

Los Angeles Times—http://www.latimes.com

MSNBC—http://www.msnbc.com

MSNBCSports—http://www.msnbcsports.com

NandoTimes—http://www.nando.net

NBA—http://www.nba.com

News Link—http://www.newslink.org

Newshub—http://www.newshub.com

Newslinx—http://www.newslinx.com

Newsweek—http://newsweek.com/

The New York Times on the Web—http://www.nytimes.com

The Press Democrat—http://www.pressdemo.com

Reuters—http://www.reuters.com

San Francisco Chronicle—http://www.sfgate.com

San Jose Mercury News, Mercury Center—http://www.sjmercury.com

Tampa Bay Tribune—http://www.tampatrib.com

The Standard-Times—http://www.s-t.com/

Time—http://pathfinder.com/time

TotalNews—http://www.totalnews.com

U.S. News & World Report—http://www.usnews.com/

USA Today Online—http://www.usatoday.com

WAND-TV—http://www.wandtv.com

Washington Post—http://www.washingtonpost.com/

The Wall Street Journal—http://interactive.wsj.com

Yahoo!—http://www.yahoo.com

REFERENCES

Access statistics for www.dailyegyptian.com. (1996, October). *Daily Egyptian.* [Online]. Available: http://www.dailyegyptian.com/stats/ [1997, September 4].

Agee, W. K., Ault, P. H., & Emery, E. (1997). *Introduction to mass communication.* New York: Longman.

Allen, M. (1996, October 28). The cable news war spreads to the Internet. *New York Times, CyberTimes.* [Online]. Available: http://search.nytimes.com/Web/docsroot/library/cyber/sites/1028sites.html

Annual consumer online usage study. (1996, December). *Simmons Market Research Bureau* (1997, September 17). *USA Today homepage.* [Online]. Available: www.usatoday.com/ads/online/online03.htm

Au pair defense lawyers argue for lesser charge. (1997, November 4). *CNN Interactive.* [Online]. Available: http://cnn.com/us/9711/04/au.pair.wrap/index.html

Berniker, M. (1995, August 28). NBC gets post position on Microsoft Network. *Broadcasting and Cable,* 37.

Black entertainment television and Microsoft announce new alliance. (1996, February 6). *Microsoft homepage.* [Online]. Available: http://www.microsoft.com/corpinfo/press/1996/feb96/msbetpr.htm

Bromley, R. V., & Bowles, D. (1995). The impact of Internet on use of traditional news media. *Newspaper Research Journal, 16* (2), 14–27.

Brown, J. (1998, January 19). MSNBC on the Net ready to play ball. *Electronic Media,* 96.

Consoli, J. (1997, April 5). Good news, bad news. *Editor & Publisher,* 18–19.

Cortese, A. (1997, February 24). A way out of the Web maze. *Business Week,* 95–101.

Crotty, C. (1997, February). All news, all the time. *MacWorld,* 173–76.

DeFleur, M. L., & Dennis, E. E. (1996). *Understanding mass communication.* Boston: Houghton Mifflin.

DeFleur, M. L., Davenport, L., Cronin, M., & DeFleur, M. (1992). Audience recall of news stories presented by newspaper, computer, television and radio. *Journalism Quarterly, 69* (4), 1010–22.

Dominick, J. R., Sherman, B. L., & Copeland, G. A. (1996). *Broadcasting/Cable and Beyond.* New York: McGraw-Hill.

Elder, S. (1996, September). Anatomy of a Web site. *Yahoo! Internet Life,* 46–51.

Frook, J. E. (1996, August 19). Racing toward TV/Web integration—CNNfn, MSNBC trade blows. *Communications Week,* IA01.

Galetto, M. (1997, March 10). CBS plugs in to Internet with SportsLine deal. *Electronic Media,* 14.

Get a kick out of it. (1996, September 16). *Newsweek,* 14.

Gimein, M. (1996, June 24). Granite links with Yahoo!: Station group and Internet directory to distribute news reports. *MediaWeek, 6* (26), 10–12.

Gipson, M. (1997, September 16). *Wall Street Journal* Interactive. *Digital direct marketing letter.* [Online]. Available: http://www.netcreations.com/ipa/tester/wsj.html

Going on-line: Newspapers create firm for computer network. (1995, April 20). *St. Louis Post Dispatch,* p. 3C.

Guglielmo, C. (1997, June 2). CNN stays tuned to the Web. *Inter@ctive Week, 4* (8), 38–39.

Haring, B. (1997, August 11). Web sites strive to brand their names into users' minds. *USA Today,* p. 4D.

Head, S. W., Sterling, C. H., & Schofield, L. B. (1994). *Broadcasting in America.* Boston: Houghton Mifflin.

Hipschman, D. (1995, August). Online news, would you subscribe? *Web Review.* [Online]. Available: http://webreview.com/reviews/newsrev/index.html

Hodges, J. (1996a, November 4). Small fees add up fast for media sites. *Advertising Age,* s20.

Hodges, J. (1996b, November 4). What's holding back the drive for subscribers. *Advertising Age,* s22.

Hodges, J. (1997, June 30). New Century Network launches major Web site. *Advertising Age,* 30.

Holliman, J. (1997, November 10). Power failure delays judge's e-mail. *CNN Interactive.* [Online]. Available: http://cnn.com

Ingebretsen, M. (1997, May 12). Rhubarb over live baseball Webcasts. *Electronic Media,* 5, 23.

Jackson, D. S. (1995). Extra! Readers talk back! *Time,* Special Issue (Spring), 60–61.

Judge in au pair case turns to e-mail for ruling. (1997, November 9). *St. Louis Post Dispatch,* p. A3.

Judge plans unprecedented ruling online. (1997, November 4). *USA Today*. [Online]. Available: http://www.usatoday.com/news/nds/2.htm

Karpinski, R. (1997, October 6). The Web delivers all the news that fits—and then some. *Internet Week*, 31–36.

Kaye, B. K. (1998). Uses and gratifications of the World Wide Web: From couch potato to Web potato. *The New Jersey Journal of Communication, 6* (1), 21–40.

Key results of the Roper survey on Americans' news consumption habits. (1998, February 20). *MediaLink Worldwide homepage*. [Online]. Available: http://www.medialinkworldwide.com/roper.htm

Kirsner, S. (1997, November/December). The breaking news dilemma. *Columbia Journalism Review*, 18–19.

Levins, H. (1997, August 23). Web system offers audio news to go. *Editor & Publisher*, 36.

Levins, H. (1998, February 21). Growing U.S. audience reads news on Net. *Editor & Publisher*, 14.

Moran, S. (1996, December 1996). Print publishers pursue online, despite poor returns. *WebWeek, 2* (20), 62–63, 66.

NAA survey indicates 36 percent of online newspapers made money in 1996. (1997). *Yahoo! PR News*. [Online]. Available: http://biz.yahoo.com/prnews/97/02/07/y0026_3.html

Niekamp, R. (1996). *Television station sites on the World Wide Web*. Paper presented at the annual convention of the Association for Education in Journalism and Mass Communication, Anaheim, CA.

Noack, D. (1997a, June 21). A matter of taste and space. *Editor & Publisher*, 98–99.

Noack, D. (1997b, May 24). Paid Web site falters. *Editor & Publisher*, 27–28.

Noack, D. (1998, February 13). Newsrooms bend to Internet: Study documents widespread change. *Editor & Publisher*. [Online]. Available: http://www.mediaINFO.com/ephome/news/newshtm/stories/021398n3.htm

Online newspaper statistics. (1997, November). *Editor & Publisher homepage*. [Online]. Available: http://www.mediainfo.com/ephome/npaper/nphtm/stats.htm [1998, February 4].

Outing, S. (1998, March 14). Online newspapers' biggest mistake? *Editor & Publisher*, 42–45.

Pavlik, J. V. (1997, July/August). The future of online journalism: Bonanza or black hole? *Columbia Journalism Review*, 30–36.

Reid, T. R. (1996, August). The paperless paper. *America West*, 22, 24.

Richtel, M. (1997, June 6). Big news media companies settle with Web site in suit on linking. *New York Times*. [Online]. Available: http://www.nyt.com [1997, February 23].

Rogoski, R. (1995, June 26). All the news that fit to post. *BrandWeek*, 50–54.

Shaw, R. (1995, September 4). CNN puts all-day news on the Internet. *Electronic Media*, 3, 39.

Singer, J. B. (1996). *Facing an uncertain future: Newspaper journalists consider their place in an online world*. Paper presented at the annual convention of the International Communication Association, Chicago, IL.

Snyder, B. (1998, January 26). Online pubs explore models for paid contracts. *Electronic Media*, 36, 40.

Sundar, S. S., & Nass, C. (1996). *Source effects in users' perception of online news.* Paper presented at the annual convention of the International Communication Association, Chicago, IL.

Sundar, S. S., Narayan, S., Obregon, R., & Uppal, C. (1997). *Does Web advertising work?* Paper presented at the annual convention of the Association for Education in Journalism and Mass Communication, Chicago, IL.

Tedesco, R. (1996, October 14). Journal interactive draws 30,000 subs. *Broadcasting and Cable,* 63.

Tedesco, R. (1997a, May 19). ABCNews spotlights online depth. *Broadcasting and Cable,* 56.

Tedesco, R. (1997b, August 25). Audio, video boosting 'Net news. *Broadcasting and Cable,* 53–54.

Tedesco, R. (1997c, May 26). Baseball teams wait for the sign. *Broadcasting and Cable,* 35.

Tedesco, R. (1997d, April 28). CNN links locals. *Broadcasting and Cable,* 46.

Tedesco, R. (1997e, March 17). CNNfn, MSNBC, stream after Fox. *Broadcasting and Cable,* 106.

Tedesco, R. (1997f, June 23). KEYE-TV leads Granite online effort. *Broadcasting and Cable,* 73.

Tedesco, R. (1997g, November 3). NBA sells 'Net game packages *Broadcasting and Cable,* 62.

Tedesco, R. (1997h, October 13). NBC launches new Web network. *Broadcasting and Cable,* 56–57.

Tedesco, R. (1997i, August 18). SportsZone adds pitch-by-pitch coverage. *Broadcasting and Cable,* 52.

Tedesco, R. (1997j, April 21). TV Websites: The next generation. *Broadcasting and Cable,* 60.

Tedesco, R. (1997k, July 7). Website audio. *Broadcasting and Cable,* 48.

Tedesco, R. (1997l, September 8). Websites enhance TV coverage of princess's death. *Broadcasting and Cable,* 61–62.

Tedesco, R. (1998a, January 19). ABC boosts World Wide Web presence this week. *Broadcasting and Cable,* 94.

Tedesco, R. (1998b, January 12). CBS ready to make online move. *Broadcasting and Cable,* 110.

Tedesco, R. (1998c, March 30). MLB still planning regular Webcasts. *Broadcasting and Cable,* 34.

Top 100 Web sites—News category. (1997, December 8). *PC Magazine.* [Online]. Available: http://www.zdnet.com/pcmag/special/Web100/_news.htm

The top twenty-five unsung heroes of the Net. (1997, December 8). *Inter@ctive Week.* [Online]. Available: http://www.zdnet.com/intweek/ [1998, January 14].

Vonder Haar, S. (1998, January 13). MSNBC to launch sports-focused site. *Inter@ctive Week.* [Online]. Available: http://www.zdnet.com/intweek [1998, January 13].

Williamson, D. A., & Cleland K. (1997, March 3). Big media fights back, and the Web could lose. *Electronic Media,* 24.

Wolff, J. (1994, November–December). Opening up online. *Columbia Journalism Review,* 62–65.

CHAPTER SIX

MARKETING AND
PUBLIC RELATIONS

The sixty-eight residents of the tiny Scottish island of Eigg initiated a fund-raising Web page to save their community. The badly neglected, windswept island was put up for sale by its absentee owner in 1996. The residents partnered with the Scottish Wildlife Trust and collectively established a Web site to raise enough money to buy back their land. Thanks to the Net, word of their plight was sent "farther than it would have gone otherwise."

A donation of a little more than half of the $2.4 million goal was made by a "mystery" Web user who read about the Islanders' efforts. The generous donation helped residents take ownership of the 7,400 acre island. The community is revitalizing Eigg by fixing up weatherbeaten homes and farms, and by establishing other projects aimed at improving the overall quality of life on the island and attracting tourism to this quaint spot of land off Scotland's west coast.

("Internet Helps Scottish," 1997)

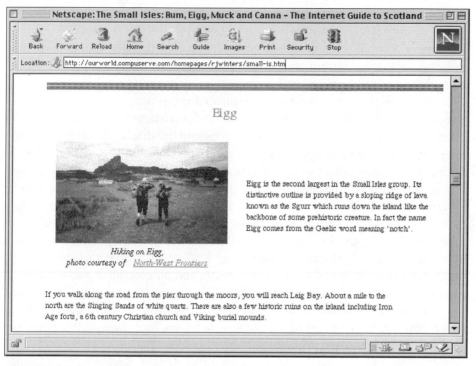

FIGURE 6.1 Scottish Island of Eigg Homepage

MARKETING ON THE WEB

Consumers all over the world are discovering that shopping on the Web is a new way to purchase goods. There is little need to fight traffic, drive from store to store, and compete for parking spaces, when comparison shopping, product demonstration, and purchasing can all be done in the comfort of shoppers' homes. Consumers are pleased with the opportunity to interact with companies, and they appreciate in the convenience of Web purchasing.

As an expanding work week cuts into leisure time, consumers spend less time shopping. The average amount of time spent on trips to the mall has decreased from ninety minutes in the early 1980s to less than one hour in the late 1990s. Moreover, slightly more than half of today's shoppers plan on further reducing the amount of time they spend in stores. With just over 50 percent of shoppers under the age of thirty-four saying that shopping is an unpleasant chore, retailers know that they must look for new alternatives to traditional methods of shopping (Kotkin, 1998).

The need to present customers with a more convenient purchasing method and the hope of increasing sales and name recognition have led many marketers, from large corporations to small mom-and-pop enterprises, to put their businesses online. Companies are taking advantage of the Web's inherent capabilities to target consumers, creatively demonstrate products, complete sales transactions, and gather demographic information. The bottom line for online marketers is to increase brand name awareness and generate sales.

The Web presents a unique opportunity for businesses. The Web reaches a global, upscale, lucrative, educated audience, and it can target customers. The Web's interface allows product demonstration, interactivity, direct communication between consumers and marketers, and point-of-purchase sales. A desire to be included in the online action induces marketers to establish Web sites. Almost 75 percent of the Web's astronomical growth can be attributed to businesses establishing cyberpresences. Each month approximately 2,000 more entrepreneurs start selling their products in cyberspace (Paul, 1996). By the close of 1996, eight out of ten of America's Fortune 500 companies had established Web presences, more than double from the prior year ("Electronic Commerce," 1997). Market analysts project that by the millennium, six out of ten large businesses and 30 percent of mid-sized companies will turn to cyberspace for marketing and business purposes (Paul, 1996).

For online businesses to thrive they need online shoppers to buy their products. It is estimated that 10 to 39 percent of Internet users have made online purchases ("Internet Shoppers Aren't Spenders," 1997; Maddox, 1997; "NCN Survey," 1997; "Online Shopping Accepted," 1996; "Simmons on Online Buying," 1996). Slightly more than two-thirds of online purchasers are males between the ages of 40 and 64, and these men earn between $50,000 and $100,000 per year. However, the Internet has a long way to go in persuading the general population of consumers to cybershop.

In early 1995, only about 1 percent of U.S. consumers bought an item through the Web. Three years later, only about 5 percent of the population were online purchasers (Bernoff, Morrisette, & Clemmer, 1998; Faust, 1996). Online shopping is increasing, albeit very slowly. A survey conducted by America's Research Group in September 1997 found that only about 3 percent of U.S. consumers feel comfortable making an online purchase, and six out of ten said they do not see themselves making an online transaction in the near future ("New Survey Shows," 1997). Lack of trust in security is the primary reason for not shopping online, followed by not being able to handle the merchandise before purchasing and lack of familiarity with the online merchant (Maddox, 1994).

Some experts, such as *Megatrends* author John Naisbitt, claim that all of the excitement about burgeoning online commerce is premature, as the Internet will not be a viable retail outlet for at least five to ten years (Faust, 1996). More people need to use the Web on a regular basis and connections to the online world need to speed up and improve in quality before online business becomes commonplace.

This chapter looks at the Web phenomenon from the marketing and public relations perspectives, beginning with the merits and shortcomings of establishing a Web site. Next, the "Four P/Four C" model of the marketing mix is examined within the context of a new technology environment. Product/consumer models, pricing/cost considerations, place/convenience functions, and promotions/communication roles and their applicability to the Web are discussed. Net security and privacy issues, including cookies technology, are covered. Chapter 6 concludes with examples of successful commercial sites, and in the latter part of the chapter, focuses on the utility of Internet resources for public relations.

To Go Online or Not to Go Online?

In many cases, the Web is a cost-effective global marketplace that is accessible twenty-four hours a day. A cyberpresence raises the curtain on new opportunities that may otherwise be missed by businesses lacking in resources. Companies on the Web can position themselves globally, expand their lines of products and services, and reach larger target audiences with less expenditure than if they accomplished these goals in a non-online environment. The Web is especially advantageous to small companies that wish to reach an international market, but cannot possibly establish a physical presence abroad or afford to print and distribute catalogs or brochures overseas.

Marketers have an unprecedented opportunity to increase sales and brand awareness online. Unlike a traditional store, the Web is not closed on Sundays, nor after 5 P.M. According to AOL, about 40 percent of online shoppers purchase goods between the hours of 10 P.M. and 10 A.M., a time period when stores are usually closed. The Web expands a company's hours of operation and its base of potential buyers as shoppers browse through cyberspace at all hours of the day and night. Product customization and "click and send" ordering further facilitate sales.

Marketers beware: Having a glitzy Web site with all of the bells and whistles is not the same as having a successful online presence. Generating sales is the foremost purpose for establishing a corporate Web site. A well-designed Web site leads visitors to product information and features, persuades them to purchase the product, and provides online ordering and purchasing forms. Similar to the shoppers who walk into a store, Web site visitors are a self-selected target audience that is already interested in the company and its offerings. It is up to marketers to persuade their customers to purchase a product before leaving the store or Web site. Just as it would be unthinkable for stores to be void of cash registers, it should be out of the question for Web sites to omit online purchasing opportunities.

Many considerations need to be taken into account before a company establishes an Internet presence. Companies can avoid wasting resources by carefully setting objectives for the site and designing the site to reach those goals. Some of the many questions that marketers need to ask include: What is the purpose of the site? Can the goals be reached? How will the objectives be measured? Who is the online audience? How can the target audience be reached? Which products will be displayed online? How will online purchases and distribution be handled? What is the budget for site design and maintenance? How many pages should be included in the site? How much interactivity should be incorporated in the site? (Janal, 1995).

Creating a Web site is a complex process that involves careful planning and evaluation. It is a dangerous mindset to assume that just because a site is there, people will come to it. A type of Web site that may be highly successful for one company may not draw an audience for another type of enterprise. Some companies may need a multilayered, in-depth, highly interactive site, whereas others may be successful with a simple, no-nonsense site. Whatever their needs, companies must take care to establish the style of site that will meet their goals and objectives, and one that matches their type of business and the kinds of products they sell.

TYPES OF COMMERCIAL WEB SITES   Generally, there are five types of commercial Web sites: the billboard, the storefront, the trading post, the library and directory, and the funhouse. These types of sites are not mutually exclusive; in other words, any site can be a combination of several different types ("Business Models for Web Sites," 1997).

A **billboard** site tends to be text-heavy and merely serves as an online brochure providing basic corporate information. Billboards contain little opportunity for interactivity and consumer feedback.

A **storefront** is usually a multilayered, product-oriented site posted for the primary purpose of generating sales. Shoppers can browse through graphic representations of items, and play back audio and video product descriptions and demonstrations. Online ordering can be done directly from most storefront sites, and feedback mechanisms keep track of customer demographics and purchasing preferences. *J. Crew* and *Gap* clothing stores, for instance, are sleek uncluttered sites featuring company information, store locations, and the latest fashions. The sites offer users three ways to purchase: online, fax, or telephone. Additionally, the customer service sections answer questions concerning ordering and returns, and other purchasing information. The Gap offers an interactive fashion design component where users get a hand in designing clothes.

Online **trading posts** serve as marketplaces where customers purchase items through a middleman who charges for services or earns a commission from each sale. For example, people who hate wheeling and dealing for a new car can turn to *Auto-by-Tel* for help with their purchases. Prospective buyers can spend as much time as they like sifting through new vehicle information, and once they have selected a car, they simply fill out an order form that is passed on to a subscribing dealer. The dealer contacts the buyer to make arrangements for delivery of the vehicle. The site is the brainchild of a former automobile dealer who was forced to close his sixteen dealerships, but instead of leaving the business altogether, he envisioned a better way to sell cars. Auto-by-Tel makes its money ($6.5 million in 1996) by charging dealers an annual, as well as a monthly, fee. Dealers make money by

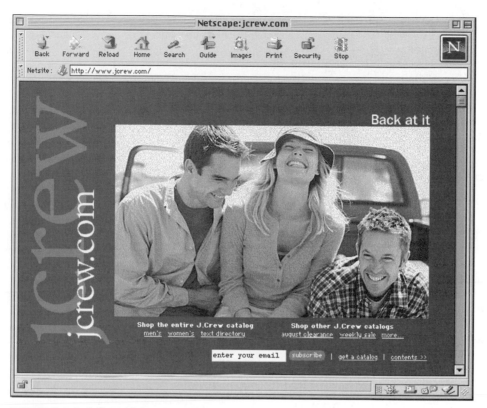

FIGURE 6.2 J. Crew Homepage

getting leads that would cost far more to attain using other means, and car buyers save themselves money by avoiding showroom markups and buying a car at no-haggle wholesale cost.

Library and directory sites serve as information storage arenas. Most news-oriented sites, such as the *New York Times,* the *Chicago Tribune,* and others that archive documents and provide direct links to information, fall into this category. Library and directory sites generate revenue through advertising sales, and sometimes through subscription and searching fees.

The search for fun and entertainment leads many young and old Web users to **funhouse** sites that are packed full of games, contests, and other interactive amusements. Most of these sites are advertiser-sponsored, while others, such as *Total Entertainment Network,* charge to play games. *The Abstract Funhouse* is an example of a free site offering games and indexes and links to downloadable shareware. Its "Laugh Riot" link brings up a list of comic strips, cartoons, and other humorous Web pages.

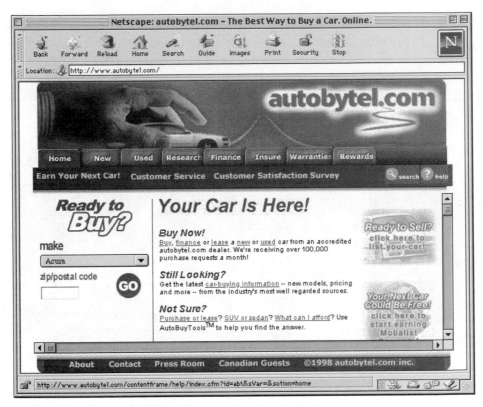

FIGURE 6.3 Auto-by-Tel Homepage

Many online commercial enterprises contain elements from several of the five categories of sites. Storefronts are notorious for their offerings of games and contests, and some libraries and directories also serve as billboard-type sites. Whatever the mix, the most successful sites are those that offer something of value to their visitors, advertisers, and sponsors, and those that encourage repeat visits ("Business Models for Web Sites," 1997).

COSTS OF ESTABLISHING AND MAINTAINING A WEB SITE Accounting for the amount of time it may take to recoup an initial investment is an important part of planning an online presence. Start-up costs vary widely depending on many factors. Companies opting to maintain their own servers can expect to pay anywhere from $5,000 to $20,000 on hardware alone, plus $1,000 to $5,000 for establishing an Internet connection, and an extra $100 to $2,000 for monthly line costs. Additionally, maintaining a server requires around-the-clock operations and troubleshooting (Hawn, 1996).

Space on an Internet Service Provider's (ISP) server usually costs about $1,000 to set up, with monthly access fees ranging from $1,000 to $2,000, and may be less burdensome for a company than owning and operating its own server (Hawn, 1996). However, many marketers believe it is much more professional for a company to have its own server and a URL such as "http://www.bookwarehouse.com" instead of "http://www.Internetserviceprovider/bookwarehouse.com." Also, the site may be easier to locate if it has the former URL rather than the latter one.

Businesses should also budget about $100 per hour for a Web site designer and consultant. Online graphic, audio, and video experts may also be needed at about the same price. Over time, maintaining and updating a Web site costs more than the initial design and start-up fees. Companies posting basic Web sites could get by with maybe one full-time employee and a few part-timers to help, but complex multilayered sites could require staffs of a hundred or more Webtaskers who command salaries ranging from $30,000 to $80,000 per year (Hawn, 1996).

Putting it all together, building a Web site can be an expensive proposition. Depending on the site's complexity and its multiplicity of layers and functions, establishing a Web site could cost anywhere from a few thousand dollars to a half-million dollars and more. In 1996, the cost for launching a billboard-type promotional site averaged about $98,000, with about another $206,000 for one-year's maintenance. In-depth content sites, such as those created by Discovery Communications, could set a company back about $1.3 million including both development and upkeep costs. Complex sites that contain an online transaction platform and many interactive components could see costs soar to close to $2 million for design and maintenance (Tedesco, 1996).

Establishing a Web site is a long-term investment and one that, in all likelihood, will take time to realize profits. Nevertheless, many marketers view the Web as a worthwhile venture for building an online presence and reputation, and they are confident that sales and profits will follow.

IS ANYONE MAKING MONEY? The Net as a commercial venue is a new concept that offers unprecedented marketing opportunity through interactivity. Even the most sophisticated analysts are unsure of which marketing approaches work best for attracting customers and building revenue. All too often, strategists simply apply old-style business plans to the Web, with dismal results. Online proprietors need to be flexible and willing to quickly implement new business strategies to ensure survival of their cyber-enterprise.

Many sites are proving that with a bit of originality and a sound plan, online commerce can be profitable, and consumers will buy products from the Web. In a June 1996 survey of 1,100 Web-based businesses, almost one-third reported they were profitable, and another 28 percent predicted they would be turning a profit within the next one to two years (Rebello, Armstrong, & Cortese, 1996; "The Real Numbers," 1997).

Amazon.com, an online bookstore, offers book lovers over one million titles for purchase, more than most stores and libraries can even dream of carrying. This literary oasis passes its volume discounts on to its customers, who show appreciation through more than $17 million in annual purchases (Rebello, Armstong, & Cortese, 1996).

Betting on music instead of books, twin brothers from Philadelphia borrowed $20,000 from their parents to start *CDNow,* an online music storefront. Raking in $6 million in sales in 1996, CDNow and other Web music stores appeal to the young, music-loving, Web-savvy generation that helped boost online sales of music to $18 million in 1996 and $71 million one year later (Bayne, 1998). Further, analysts predict Web music sales will catapult to between $1.6 billion and $2.8 billion by the year 2002 (Turner, 1997).

MTV claims its Web site has been profitable since its premiere. The network boasts of a 250 percent increase in revenue during 1997, and a 400 percent revenue increase over the site's three-year lifespan. An MTV executive believes MTV's online success is attributable to its strong brand identity (Tedesco, 1997).

Some businesses have been surprised to find that their Web sites have indirectly contributed to their profits. For example, Federal Express customers are encouraged to track the location of their packages on the company's Web site rather than telephoning a FedEx customer service representative to look up the packages' status. This online feature alone saves FedEx more than $1 million in employee-hours each month (Levy, 1997).

These are just a few examples of companies realizing profits and cost savings from their Web sites. Of course, not all Web sites are as successful, and many companies have crashed and burned online. Having the right combination of marketing and sales elements packaged in an attractive and interesting Web site can make the difference between cyber-success and cyber-failure.

THE FOUR P'S AND FOUR C'S OF MARKETING

Before products can be successfully marketed to the buying public, a marketing plan needs to be in place. Marketers formulate selling strategies to maximize company benefits and profits. Marketers need to determine which stores are best for selling their products, how many units of the product need to be sold to reach break-even costs, which color of packaging will draw the most buyers, what price purchasers are willing to pay for the product, and which promotion strategies will be most effective in generating sales. These are examples of just a few of the variables that must be considered when devising a marketing strategy.

Traditional marketing plans consist of two basic elements: the target market and the marketing mix. A **target market** is a group of customers whose shared characteristics (i.e., age, income, education, lifestyle) make them the most likely purchasers of a particular product. For example, elderly people who need a physical boost are more likely to purchase Geritol than are younger individuals. **Target marketing** is the sales effort put forth to reach the target audience. That is why Geritol can be found in stores most likely to be frequented by the elderly, and why advertisements and other promotions are directed toward the silver generation, Geritol's target audience.

A marketing mix consists of four basic elements known as the **"Four P's"**: product, place, price, and promotion. Product marketing is a complex procedure that must include creating a quality *product, placing* it in appropriate sales outlets, and establishing the proper *price* and effective *promotions.* The "Four P" model has guided marketing decisions for many years and has held up as an effective tool for generating product sales. However, newer interactive technologies and those that readily lend themselves to target marketing make it necessary for strategists to take a critical look at the "Four P's."

New communication technologies have created new outlets for product distribution and sales. Mass marketing through traditional outlets is yielding to target marketing through new electronic means. Product information and catalogs are being distributed via CD-ROMs, computer discs, videotapes, in-store electronic kiosks, interactive television, and the Internet, including the World Wide Web, e-mail, and bulletin boards. New ways of delivering information give marketers more opportunity for reaching out to consumers. Consumers are often targeted by their demographic makeup, purchasing needs and preferences, lifestyles, and other factors, and are then directly bombarded with electronic bits of product information.

Many marketing experts assert that the "Four P's" do not stand up in the new marketing environment. Therefore, the **"Four C's"** have emerged as the model for the new generation of marketers. Working in tandem with the "Four P's," the "Four C's" consist of the following elements: consumers, cost, convenience, and communication (Schultz, Tannenbaum, & Lauterborn, 1993).

The focus on *product* features has been replaced with emphasis on *consumer* satisfaction. Product manufacturing is now driven by consumer tastes, not the other way around. *Pricing* strategies go beyond profit-maximization models to include the *cost* consumers are willing to pay to gratify their needs and desires. *Place* is no longer considered a city or a store where products can be purchased, but has taken on a broader meaning that includes *conveniently* uniting purchasers with products. Old-style *promotion* through mass advertising and other one-way means has taken a backseat to interactively *communicating* with customers. The distribution of product information and the creation of brand awareness and purchasing desire develops through two-way communication, and focuses on the needs of the targeted consumers.

The "Four C" model is more consumer-oriented than the "Four P" model, and is more easily applied to new interactive technologies such as the Web. New ways of reaching customers and doing business have forced executives to rethink their old-style marketing strategies. Contemporary strategists are beginning to focus on the "Four C's" of marketing and are including the Web as an integral part of an overall marketing plan.

Integrating Product and Consumer Functions on the Web

Successful entrepreneurs are quickly realizing that the Web is more about customers than about the technology itself. The technology is most helpful when it is used effectively to build relationships between sellers and customers. Sophisticated consumers see through the hype of television-style image-building marketing, and they demand more reliable and truthful product information from the Web. In the long run, satisfying needs through a deeper level of communication leads to word-of-mouth or, in this case, "word-of-Web" marketing as loyal customers send their own persuasive messages of approval to potential buyers through online venues, such as listservs and Usenet Newsgroups.

Buyers drive the marketplace in the new marketing environment. Traditional supply and demand models fall short of guaranteeing profitability. Manufacturers cannot create demand solely through product development; rather they must rely on customer feedback to determine which products to develop. The product itself is not as important as consumers' perceptions of the item. In a highly competitive marketplace, it is often difficult for consumers to differentiate between products based on features. For instance, there is very little difference among brands of toothpaste or powdered bathroom cleansers, so companies must rely on their purchasers' attitudes and beliefs about the products. The true value of a product resides in the minds of purchasers and not in product features, such as color, pricing, and so on, that can be copied by competitors (Schultz et al., 1993).

RELATIONSHIP MARKETING   The Web's capabilities for building customer relations through interactivity are causing traditional models of mass marketing to give way to interactive marketing. From a marketing perspective, the special features of interactivity allow firms to communicate directly with individual consumers and save their responses for followup dialogue. Thus, interactivity promises a "more human face on marketplace exchanges without losing the scale economies of mass marketing" (Deighton, 1996, p. 151).

Contemporary businesses strive to build excellent products, but they must also build strong relationships with their customers. Interactive technologies foster **relationship marketing** by providing user-friendly, two-way communication interfaces. Customers are no longer merely receivers of one-way monologues, but participate in dialogues with companies where both parties learn more about each other. Relationship marketing revolves around the premise that two-way communication is vital for sustaining a relationship between marketers and consumers, and, if communication fails, then so will the relationship, and the customer will take his or her business elsewhere (Schultz et al., 1993).

Some marketing scholars support the notion that corporate Web sites must go beyond simply pushing their line of products by creating online **transaction communities** that satisfy consumers' commercial and social needs. In other words, the most successful online marketers are those who acknowledge the full range of products and services needed by their community of customers. For example, a toy manufacturer could cross-sell a range of products that satisfy the parenting community. This could include establishing hypertext links to "parenting magazines, access to book publishers, health care providers, and life insurance companies; links to brokers offering college savings plans; and even the products of competing toy manufacturers" (Armstrong & Hagel, 1996, p. 137).

Amazon.com exemplifies the meaning of an electronic transaction community. Priding itself on being more than a seller of books, Amazon.com has built a literary community by providing chat forums for readers to discuss their favorite authors and books, and space for customers to post their own book reviews. Additionally, authors are encouraged to comment on their works, and e-mail messages alert readers when new books hit the shelves. Generally, the community perspective urges cybermarketers to fully utilize the Web's capabilities to gratify a number of social and purchasing needs by linking customers to other Web and Internet opportunities.

VALUE-ADDED CONTENT Many traditional stores add little touches within their outlets to relieve the ho-hum ambiance and to add to the fun of shopping. For example, shoppers may walk the aisles to the sound of Beethoven emanating from a baby grand piano on the main floor, or they may be treated to free samples of perfume or food, or they may receive a nice thank-you note from a sales clerk, or they may rest their weary feet in a little nook filled with sofas and chairs. These extra benefits are examples of value-added components that can make shopping more enjoyable. The logic follows that if customers are having a good time, they will stay in the store longer, buy more items, and will come back more frequently.

Many online entrepreneurs follow the lead of their non-online counterparts by including **value-added content** on their Web sites. Value-added interactions, such as games and contests, may help draw visitors to sites and direct them to product and ordering information. The _Ben & Jerry's_ ice cream site epitomizes value-added content with multimedia games, puzzles, crafts, and sweepstakes. For example, children can select a cyber-pumpkin and carve a jack-o-lantern, or help Ice Cream Man fight off underwater creatures on his way to finding a treasure chest full of Phish Food®. The site is fun for adults, too, but also offers tantalizing product descriptions, ordering information, and more serious discussion concerning franchise opportunities.

Value-added content gives customers more ways to get involved with a Web site. Whether Web users are test-driving a car online, making airline or hotel reservations, guessing the number of jellybeans in the virtual jar, or playing some sort of game, they are doing something out of the ordinary, and are thus spending time on the site. Value-added content creates affinity between clients and customers, and proprietors are banking on affinity translating into additional sales.

Pricing and Cost Components of Web Marketing

The media are riddled with reports that commercial Web sites are nothing more than black holes that suck up company profits. The Web's reputation as a shaky enterprise may prove to be unfounded as cyberprofits begin to trickle into corporate coffers. It is true that many online ventures have gone bust, yet businesses continue to pour money into cyberspace with hopes that their efforts will soon pay off. The newspaper publishing group Knight-Ridder claims its thirty-two online newspaper sites cost close to $27 million in start-up and maintenance costs but only generated about $11 million in revenues in 1997. Other newspaper chains are not doing so well online either. Both the Tribune Company and the *New York Times* report losing millions of dollars on their Web operations (Neuwirth, 1997). However, a survey conducted by the Magazine Publishers of America indicates that publishers continue to support their unprofitable Web sites based on forecast claims that by the millennium they will be realizing more than ten times their 1996 revenues (Levy, 1997).

High hopes and visions of cybercash have left many online entrepreneurs disappointed in the world of online capitalism. Marketing myopia led many to believe that investing wads of cash in a flashy Web site would be enough to generate quick profits. However, many consumers are still cautiously dipping their toes into this strange new cyber-sea of commerce, forcing Web site proprietors to wait patiently for revenue streams to wash ashore (Levy, 1997).

ONLINE REVENUE MODELS   In their quest for Web profits, online proprietors are experimenting with different methods of generating revenue. Through much trial and error, four commonly used models for online revenue have emerged (Maddox, Wagner, & Wilder, 1997):

1. Direct sales: A company selling its existing products or services from its Web site;

2. Advertising: A company selling advertising space on its Web site to someone else;

3. Subscriptions: Charging users for access to content;

4. Fees for service: Charging for special services, such as downloading documents, searching, and other transaction fees.

Direct Sales   Many companies find the Web an ideal medium for selling their goods and services directly to their customers. Small businesses are especially benefiting from an online presence. Many small companies find their businesses expanding due to the Web. Without high distribution and advertising costs, geographically limited reach, and other inhibiting factors, small businesses on the Web have many of the same competitive advantages as larger companies. Some online merchants are selling goods to people from all over the world, a feat unheard of before the Web.

Advertising   No matter what the medium, advertising is a tried-and-true method of increasing cash flow. Web site proprietors are delighted that cyberspace is slowly proving itself to be an advertising-friendly medium, advantageous both to promoters and to those with space to sell. Advertisers buy an upscale, educated, targeted audience, and Web site owners are bringing in revenue from banner and classified ads. As advertising measurement and pricing problems are resolved, online advertising promises to become an excellent and profitable resource.

Subscriptions   Charging customers for access to certain content has been met with varying degrees of success and failure. Analysts are waiting for emerging trends to identify the types of content and services consumers are willing to purchase. So far, subscription-based models seem to work best on news-oriented sites. Although many consumers are still reluctant to pay for content, businesses seem eager to pay for information that will give them competitive advantages.

Business-to-business subscription services have been much more successful than those that contract with consumers. For example, *Quote.Com,* Inc., a financial data service, charges monthly fees for stock quotes, financial news, annual reports, and other business-related information that their clients are eagerly lapping up to the tune of more than $73,000 a month. Subscription-type services may be most effective in generating revenues if they deal with specialized industry-related information that is targeted to businesses rather than to individual consumers.

Fees for Service   This revenue-inducing strategy involves charging clients for such online services as searching the Web or providing server space. For example, *Industry.Net* bills itself as an online marketplace and shopping center for industry and manufacturing. Manufacturers and suppliers are charged an annual fee for maintaining a storefront on the site. Although this revenue model is not as widespread as others, it can in some instances be very profitable, as attested to by Industry.Net's claims of $20 million flowing in from its Web site in 1996.

ONLINE PRICING AND COST STRATEGIES   Many companies are now offering their products and services for direct purchase from the Web, thus cutting links out of the traditional chain of producer-to-wholesaler-to-retailer-to-consumer. Avoiding the middleman allows many companies to offer their goods at prices well below retail levels. Pricing strategists estimate that cutting out wholesalers saves consumers about 28 percent off retail prices, and leaving both wholesalers and retailers out of the chain saves a whopping 62 percent. Further, pricing models suggest that when consumers have direct purchasing access to many manufacturers of similar products, the electronic market effect drives costs down to the lowest cost producer (Benjamin & Wigand, 1995).

Offering products online calls for new pricing strategies that will significantly reduce consumer costs and at the same time will not undermine company profits. Cost/benefit ratios are taking on stronger importance as consumers may, in some cases, be willing to pay a slightly higher price in exchange for the convenience of shopping online. In the long run, online sales benefit both consumers and sellers. Consumers benefit from convenience and, at many times, price savings, and sellers benefit by offering at competitive prices goods they might otherwise have had to sell at higher prices to recoup distribution costs and other expenses.

The Web as a Place—Convenience

To many people a trip to the mall can be very time consuming and tedious, and many consumers hate the idea of running from store to store picking up product information and comparing prices. The Web is the perfect alternative for those who have money to spend but who dread the thought of stepping foot in a store. The Web is a mecca for comparison shopping, as customers are only a few simple clicks away from product features and price information that would otherwise take hours and sometimes days or weeks to find. While the Web can be a haven for those who say "Bah, humbug" to shopping, it can also feed a shopaholic's addiction by allowing bulk buying in a short span of time.

From the merchants' point of view, the Web offers companies a virtual storefront free of expensive building costs. Cyber-vendors are not restricted to a limited number of square feet of inventory space or tied to a geographic location. A Web site can house vast amounts of product and service information, reach an almost unlimited number of potential buyers, and increase overall sales with easy-to-use order forms.

WHAT WORKS, WHAT SELLS   In 1997, U.S. consumers spent $2.5 trillion in retail stores and an estimated $75 billion through catalogs (Karlgaard, 1998; Michals, 1997). Virtual stores are becoming viable distribution centers, as attested to by the millions spent on online purchases. Analysts contend that 1997 saw $2.4 billion–

$13 billion in revenue (Cuneo, 1997; Karlgaard, 1998; "Online Retail Strategies," 1998; Tedesco, 1997). By the turn of the century, it is projected that 46 million Americans will spend $16 billion–$17 billion, or about $358 each, buying products online (Cuneo, 1997b; "Electronic Commerce," 1997). Further online revenues are expected to rise to $38 billion by 2002 ("Feeding Your Head," 1998). Although still lagging behind other shopping outlets, the Internet has reaped a dramatic increase in sales since 1993, when only a paltry $200 million was spent online (Amirrezvani, 1995).

While cyberstores are a haven for some products, not all goods are selling well. Low-risk, low-cost, low-involvement products are generally the most attractive to purchasers. Books, computer hardware and software, music, and clothing were the most frequently bought items, according to a study conducted by the University of Michigan in 1995 (Amos, 1995).

The Tenagra Corporation's Web site states that products that sell best on the Web meet at least one of the following criteria:

1. The product appeals to the technologically savvy.
2. The product is a computer-related item.
3. The product appeals to a broad segment of the Internet audience.
4. The product appeals to a wide geographic audience.
5. The product is a specialty item that can be difficult to locate.
6. The product is purchased based on information, not hyperbole.
7. The product can be purchased over the Internet less expensively than otherwise.
8. The product sells for less than $20. (Sterne, 1995, p. 247)

Groceries and household goods and services are predicted to be bought online by 15 million–20 million households by the year 2007. Shoppers who are willing to purchase food and household items online have been categorized into four major groups: (1) shopping avoiders: people who dislike shopping; (2) necessity users: shoppers who for various reasons cannot physically go to a store; (3) new technologists: individuals who like the Web and are comfortable shopping online; and (4) time starved: people who do not have time to shop and are willing to spend more money on items for the convenience of shopping online. Additionally, two other groups of shoppers who need to be coaxed into buying items online are those who have time to shop and experience positive feelings from shopping, and older consumers who enjoy going to stores and generally avoid new technologies ("Supermarket for Online Shopping," 1998).

The list of successful cyber-proprietors is getting longer by the day, and many smaller businesses are finding themselves telling their own tales of Web prosperity.

Small specialty businesses generally do not have the extensive distribution channels of larger companies; thus smaller businesses increasingly rely on the Web to reach a larger audience of purchasers. *Hot Hot Hot,* a hot sauce store in Pasadena, California, claims about one-quarter of its sales are transacted over the Web. The *Tennis Warehouse,* operating out of San Luis Obispo, California, saw its overall business grow by 15 percent after it began selling tennis accessories and clothing over the Net. *Virtual Vineyards,* a California wine emporium, expects its sales to rise to over $100,000 per month. In less than two years online, *Ann Hemyng Candy, Inc.'s Chocolate Factory,* a small candy store in rural Pennsylvania, sent out more than 1,000 orders for chocolate to customers around the world (Resnick, 1996). These are just a few examples of many small companies that are reaping the benefits of selling online.

Many nationwide retailers assert that their customers use the Web to arm themselves with prepurchase information, but physically go to a nearby store when they are ready to make the buy. Macmillan Computer Publishing found that slightly more than six of every ten customers would rather buy a book from a store than over the Web. Echoing similar findings, Windham Hill Records claims that one-fifth of its Web site visitors use the information they found online to buy music from traditional stores (Maddox et al., 1997).

Manufacturers and retailers alike are stampeding to establish cyberstores. The Web has proven itself a sales center where consumers can access product information, see demonstrations, select product options, and complete sales transactions, all in a place called cyberspace.

Cyber-Promotion and Communication

PROMOTION   Before the availability of interactive technologies, promotional strategies were directed toward a mass audience, and individual consumers were treated as part of a large homogeneous group. Messages were tossed out to the public with the hope that consumers would stumble across them and be persuaded to purchase a product. Promotions are moving away from one-way messages that speak to the lowest common denominator of the mass audience toward two-way communications that address the "highest point of common interest" (Schultz et al., 1993, p. 13).

Targeting a select group of consumers became more prominent through the use of direct mail and other marketing vehicles. It is more cost-effective for promoters to target those who are most likely to purchase the company's products than to mass distribute their messages. Web technology makes it possible for marketers to identify, segment, select, and attract "smaller, more attentive and focused audiences" (Schultz, et al., 1993, p. 21).

Cyber-promoters reach their target audiences by providing consumers with around-the-clock product and ordering information. Customers are encouraged to interact with marketers through e-mail, direct response campaigns, and games and contests. Promotional tie-ins, sponsorships, discounts, and coupons abound on the Web, inducing consumers to make purchases.

PUSH MARKETING   Marketers are taking advantage of push technology as an efficient means of delivering promotions, marketing and advertising messages, new product and product improvement announcements, sales figures, and other materials to a targeted group of consumers. Push channels keep customers abreast of company and product news crucial to generating sales.

Many companies lack the resources needed to establish a push service, but they can still make use of the push concept by setting up an effective system of electronic communication. Establishing customer listservs, e-mailing product and company information and newsletters to subscribers, and contracting with external direct e-mail firms are all efficient methods of reaching target audiences. Additionally, company Web pages and other graphic material can be sent directly to customers' e-mail boxes ("Pushing the Envelope," 1997).

Direct marketing via e-mail is vastly less expensive and less labor intensive than going through the U.S. Postal Service. Savings in printing costs and postage are enough to send marketers scrambling for lists of electronic mailing addresses that have proven to be invaluable tools for reaching target audiences. Generally, e-mail lists are serviced rather than sold. For about a dime per name, Net mailing firms compile lists and take care of transmitting messages, but they generally do not sell the lists to their clients, who might in turn make them available to others (Easton, 1996).

Online connections provide marketers with a wealth of information about their consumers. Rivers of demographic, psychographic, and lifestyle information flow from customers to marketers. Savvy marketers are using detailed personal information for "time sensitive microsegmentation—marketing to the individual customer at specific points in time." For example, if "a toy manufacturer knows the birthdays and ages of children in a given household, it could market to the parents two to three weeks before the birthdays" (Armstrong & Hagel, 1996, p. 137).

While parents may appreciate a push of commercial information, many are up in arms over cybermarketers who target advertising directly to children. The Web provides a unique and unprecedented venue to reach young consumers through contests, giveaways, and flashy Web sites that entice children to enter detailed personal and purchasing information that in many instances is shared with marketing firms. Adults claim that children are vulnerable and easily influenced by the Web, especially by those sites that deftly blend advertising and content. Children who are interacting with their favorite television and cartoon characters are generally not aware that they are being encouraged to buy certain products. Worse, what young people perceive as friendship-building interactions between themselves and online characters are nothing more than sales pitches. Many parents and grassroots agencies fear that "many children may eventually become 'key pals'—the online equivalent to pen pals—with advertisements" (Branscum, 1996).

CUSTOMER FEEDBACK Satisfying consumer needs is foremost in the minds of marketers, and new product development and changes to existing goods depend on customer feedback. Companies are in close touch with online consumers through e-mail and other Web-based interactions. Manufacturing and marketing decisions are influenced by online consumers who make known their buying preferences, purchasing habits, and assessments of products. Marketers use consumer feedback to tailor products to the satisfaction of their targeted purchasers.

Consumers get a close look at products through online audio and video demonstrations. Additionally, consumers can select colors, sizes, and other options and features, and then see their customized selections before purchasing. In turn, marketers get immediate feedback concerning customer preferences that is used to improve existing products and create new goods and services. Marketers are quickly alerted to changes in customer satisfaction and buying trends, so new selling strategies can be readily formulated and put into place without delay. Prior to interactive technologies, feedback was not as direct or immediate. Consumers would often store messages for later use, leaving the marketer to wonder whether the message was received, how it was interpreted, and whether it had any impact on sales (Schultz et al., 1993).

Marketers are putting such a high value on consumer demographics, buying habits, and feedback that many are willing to subsidize Internet use in exchange for personal information. Companies such as *FreeRide* and a few others are teaming with corporate sponsors to offer free Internet access to consumers who are willing to reveal personal data and shopping and brand preferences. Additionally, individuals may be asked to purchase selected products from the site's advertisers, and to subscribe to the site's online sponsors such as *Rolling Stone* and *Newsweek.* In return, users receive proof-of-purchase coupons redeemable for credit points that go toward earning free Internet time. All parties involved benefit from this model of Internet servicing. Advertisers and sponsors benefit from sales and exposure, FreeRide benefits from corporate advertising and sponsors, and consumers benefit from free Internet access. Additionally, by earning credit points for information, credit card numbers do not have to be disclosed when making purchases, and consumers are safeguarded against online fraud (Guglielmo, 1997).

The Web adds a new dimension to promotions by providing two-way communication, thus freeing consumers from their traditional role as passive receivers of promotional messages. Through interactive technologies, audiences are more active consumers of messages and have more control over the types of information they receive, attend to, or ignore.

SECURITY AND PRIVACY ISSUES

The Web was originally conceived as a venue for posting unfettered information, with little thought given to protecting online communication. Net security became a concern with the proliferation of business and marketing, government, and other Web sites that post proprietary information. Although the Electronic Communications Privacy Act of 1986 protects electronic transmissions from interference and monitoring, it is very difficult to enforce in the Internet environment (Spar & Bussgang, 1996). Online transactions involving credit card, social security, or other identifying numbers and information have become a hotbed for computer hackers who have discovered ways to steal, alter, and delete online records and information. For example, the Air Force was not amused when hackers infiltrated its military Web site and replaced information about fighter jets with pornographic photographs ("Computer Hacker Plants," 1996). The Air Force, the Justice Department, the CIA, the Pentagon, and the Sheraton hotel chain are just a few of many government agencies and corporations that have fallen victim to hackers. According to 1995 federal law enforcement estimates, online pirates steal more than $10 billion worth of data annually, enough to send shockwaves through the cyber-community (Goldstein, 1995). While slightly more than half of all Internet users have gone online to make purchasing decisions, only about 15 percent completed the transaction on the Web ("Electronic Commerce," 1997). Many companies accommodate consumers who are still reluctant to make purchases online by promoting toll-free numbers on their Web sites.

Security and privacy concerns are often thought of as one and the same problem, but they actually deal with different issues. Security issues tend to center around tangible concerns such as protecting credit card numbers from hackers, whereas privacy issues involve trusting Web site managers to keep personal information within the site and not selling it to third-party marketers.

Tales of unauthorized credit card purchases, manipulation of payment receipts, and cybertheft have sent many online purchasers back to the malls. Repelled by the lack of security and privacy, many Web users shun cyberstores and refuse to cooperate with Web sites that request personal information of any kind.

Security

Net transactions generally involve a customer, a vendor or service provider, and a credit card company, all of whom have a vested interest in Web security. Each Web transaction requires the following elements:

1. Authentication of customer: Vendors and credit issuers need to verify that purchasers are who they claim to be.

2. Authentication of service provider: Before customers enter their credit card numbers or other personal information, they need assurance that they are dealing with a bona fide entity and not with a fly-by-night business.

3. Message integrity: Both sellers and buyers need assurance that encryption techniques are in place that protect communications from being intercepted and altered.

4. Message privacy: Marketers need to assure customers that with their encryption system messages will be retrieved and read only by the intended receivers who possess decoding software. (Blunt, 1995)

Cries for securing online information have been the driving force behind the development of information protection software. However, business losses from Internet hacking are generally less than those from telephone fraud. Due to Internet theft, businesses can expect to lose $1 for every $1,000 in revenue. In comparison, losses due to cellular telephone crimes almost top $20 per $1,000 in revenue, and losses from standard telephones hover around $16 per $1,000 (Goldstein, 1995; Noglows, 1995). Despite the reassuring reports that it is safer to conduct financial transactions on the Internet than via the telephone, many Web sites are very vulnerable to sneak attacks by hackers.

A study of more than 2,200 Web sites discovered that roughly 60 percent could be infiltrated or destroyed. Additionally, more sophisticated hacking programs and techniques could reveal security flaws in up to eight out of ten Web sites (Perry, 1997). Another survey reported that in the year prior to the study, 41 percent of the 438 organizations studied experienced some sort of unauthorized break-in of their computer systems, mostly in the form of data manipulation and alteration (Tubbs, 1996).

Marketers concerned about unauthorized intruders and wary consumers reining in the growth of online business transactions have turned to computer security experts to devise new methods of protecting cyber-information. The major credit card companies are working together to establish "Secure Electronic Transaction" (SET) standards that will "hide" credit card numbers and stop unscrupulous merchants from increasing prices after a transaction has been completed (Quinn, 1997; Shaw, 1996). While SET is still being developed, several different types of security mechanisms have been developed and instituted on many Web sites.

A **firewall** is one of the most notable systems that secures data from unauthorized individuals. A firewall is a screen that protects internal data from hackers by separating it from public information. For example, visitors to university Web pages can gain access to course descriptions, clubs and organizations, happenings on campus, and so on, but a firewall stops them from penetrating student records, faculty payroll, and other sensitive data (Paul, 1996). In the commercial world, many catalogs are freely posted online; however, firewalls are used to segregate financial transactions and credit card data from product information.

Encryption is also gaining widespread acceptance as a viable security measure. To *encrypt* simply means to put into code. Encryption software applies mathematical formulas, or algorithms, to scramble data into codes that can be deciphered only by authorized receivers with the proper translation mechanisms. Many Web sites discourage hackers by encrypting credit card numbers and other personal information (Paul, 1996).

Additional security measures entail devising a system of digital dollars. Several approaches are being tested to reduce significantly the necessity of credit card transactions. The NetCash system involves an electronic bank that issues e-mail coupons redeemable for Net purchases. Customers simply input coupon serial numbers, and then money is deducted from their NetCash accounts. Other methods include using banks as middlemen, where encoded credit card numbers cannot be decoded by a merchant but must be sent directly to the bank holding the card. The bank then decodes the transaction and relays the sales information to the merchant. This system protects credit card holders from outside parties who could use the card numbers to make unauthorized purchases.

Another system being tested involves omitting credit card numbers from the Net altogether. Customers register their credit card numbers with an electronic bank like First Virtual Holdings. When a customer wishes to make a purchase, he or she simply inputs a password onto an order form that authorizes First Virtual to make the purchase on the customer's behalf. First Virtual bills their customers directly, and sends in payment to the merchants, who do not see the purchasers' credit card numbers.

Many analysts favor a system of electronic checks, where transactions are conducted by sending instructions to transfer Internet funds, but the money has no value outside of its electronic account. Similar methods include setting up an "e-cash" account, similar to a debit card, from which purchases are deducted. A purchaser simply enters in a password and the fees are deducted from the purchaser's Internet account.

Computer experts, bankers, and proprietors are working hard to devise systems of securing online financial transactions. It is crucial for the future of Web commerce that a safe system of purchasing be developed. Customers need to feel protected from hackers and other unscrupulous parties before they can embrace the Web as a viable purchasing outlet (Mannes, 1996).

Privacy

Online privacy is a major concern for both businesses and consumers. Slightly more than one-quarter of consumers name lack of privacy as the biggest barrier to conducting online transactions, and just less than one-fifth claim it is the lack of privacy that keeps them from Net shopping ("Privacy Concerns Need to Be Met," 1997).

Therefore, in addition to taking steps to secure data, many companies are initiating online privacy policies. Web sites are beginning to post notices that display the intended use of information, identify who is collecting the data, and give users options to select which data they wish to disclose, and how the information can be used. Although efforts urging Web site proprietors to disclose privacy protection practices are under way, a check of the one hundred busiest sites revealed that only seventeen posted their privacy policies ("Web Sites Lack," 1997).

CommerceNet and the Electronic Frontier Foundation have initiated a Web-wide branding campaign to further assure consumers of Net privacy. Central to the campaign is the "etrust" label that marks the level of privacy provided by a Web site. "Trustmarks" identify sites that do not save customer data, sites that keep data only for customization purposes, and sites that do not share or sell data to outside parties.

Online "Seals of Approval"

Many would-be purchasers' concerns about online commerce stretch beyond privacy and security issues. Consumers also want to know about quality, customer service, warranties, return policies, and whether they are dealing with established, reputable firms or fly-by-night operations.

The Public Eye is a company that acts as a watchdog of Internet commerce. The Public Eye's staff of secret cybershoppers visit commercial sites to assess their overall quality based on stability, service, accessibility, warranties, and references. The Public Eye's judges look for the number of years the business has been in operation, whether a customer service 800 number and direct twenty-four-hour access to a representative are provided, the number of delivery options, and warranty and return policies. Additionally, the site posts past purchasers' impressions of merchants. Proprietors that meet the Public Eye's good business criteria receive a "seal of approval" to display on their sites. The Public Eye is hoping its mark becomes known and relied on as the symbol for excellence in Web commerce (Memon, 1996a).

The Council of Better Business Bureaus (BBB) has also initiated a seal of approval rating system to distinguish bona fide, trustworthy businesses from fraudulent vendors. To win the BBB's mark of approval, an online business must have been in operation for at least six months, have agreed to let the BBB settle unresolved customer complaints, and have provided the BBB with detailed company information (McLaughlin, 1997).

Etrust, the Public Eye, BBB, and similar branding schemes serve to strengthen consumer confidence in electronic commerce. Barriers to online interactions are crossed as consumers are assured of a site's trustworthiness. Electronic marketers should strive to earn seals of approval for their sites.

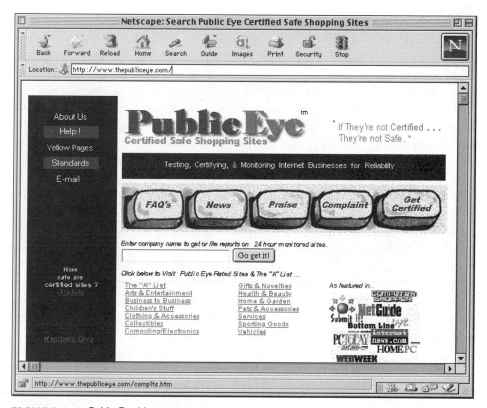

FIGURE 6.4 Public Eye Homepage

Cookies

The Web's inherent structure makes it an ideal vehicle for sending messages to targeted consumers. Push marketing, audience information-gathering techniques, and electronic two-way communications are the talk of cyber-towns as merchants and other online sellers strive to reach their customers. Many information-gathering techniques are voluntary; online visitors fill out forms, e-mail companies, and otherwise make known their shopping preferences and other personal information. However, the online community is up in arms over covert information-gathering techniques, where visitors unwittingly become marketers' guinea pigs. One of the most notorious invaders of privacy is a tool known as **cookies,** which surreptitiously stores users' Internet activities. Though it has an appetizing name, cookies are leaving a bad taste in the mouths of consumers.

Cookies work by saving information users give when they travel through a Web site, fill out a form, click on an advertisement, buy a product, or conduct other ordinary online transactions. Cookies create personal data files and user profiles that companies can use to customize their Web pages next time an individual visits the site. For example, depending on their purchasing and demographic profiles, two young men both visiting the same site may be sent different advertisements.

The primary objection to cookies is that consumers are not forewarned that their Web movements are being monitored and saved. Just think of what it would be like if every time individuals walked into department stores their identity, time and length of visit, and aisles they traveled were recorded and used to send them direct mail advertisements. Shoppers simply would not stand for such blatant intrusion, yet it is common practice in cyberspace.

New Internet tools are being developed to counteract cookies. Newer versions of Netscape Navigator and Internet Explorer give users the option of turning off the cookies tool. Existing cookies can be deleted by trashing any hard drive file called "cookies.txt." When using Netscape, users can prevent new cookies from taking hold by clicking on the "Options" menu, and then selecting "Network Preferences." Next, the "Protocols" window needs to be opened and the "Show an alert before accepting a cookie" option selected. Internet Explorer has a similar anti-cookie function that can be accessed by clicking on "View" and then selecting "Options," and marking the box on the "Advanced" tab (Wildstrom, 1996).

Also, the aptly named "Cookie.Cutter" software, a filtering approach that uses a type of intercept technology, allows users to block cookies at will. Cookie.Cutter alerts consumers to sites that use cookie technology, and thus gives consumers control over the release of personal information (Memon, 1996b, 1996c; Rigdon, 1996).

Another option for ensuring online privacy is to surf the Web using *Anonymizer*. This site works as a conduit or security agent between a Web site and a computer. The application allows users to access Web sites with utmost privacy by acting as a middleman between a user and the documents he or she wishes to retrieve. Anonymizer prevents Web sites from using cookies to track online activity and gather e-mail addresses or other Web use data.

To use Anonymizer, a Web visitor must first log onto the software's Web site and then type the domain address of the site he or she wants to visit. Anonymizer's server retrieves the document without revealing the user's identity, rewrites the document so all links are referenced through Anonymizer, then sends the document to the user's computer.

Protecting Web Site Owners

Web site proprietors have the responsibility of protecting users from breaches in privacy and security. Additionally, they have to protect the integrity of their own sites from outside interference. A Chicago-based consortium of about sixty corporations and vendors has identified nine basic threats to Web sites:

1. Data destruction: Loss of data through malicious or accidental means, and the interception of data going to or from the site;

2. Interference: Intentional rerouting of data, or spamming as an attempt to crash the server;

3. Modification or replacement: Unauthorized alteration or removal of data;

4. Misrepresentation and false use: Entering false passwords and other bogus information;

5. Repudiation: Denial of making an order or other transaction;

6. Inadvertent misuse: Accidental misuse by authorized users;

7. Unauthorized altering or downloading: Copying or downloading information without permission;

8. Unauthorized transaction: Any transaction conducted by unapproved users;

9. Unauthorized disclosure: Viewing of confidential information by unauthorized users. (McCarthy, 1997, p. 114)

In addition to the protection measures mentioned earlier, Web site proprietors are implementing alternative security methods including callback systems, one-time passwords, access control lists, receipt acknowledgment, audit trails, and challenge/response software. Marketers are also turning to copyright regulation to protect original material they post to the Web. However, it is still not clear how traditional copyright laws pertain to online material. Unregulated point-and-click downloading interfaces have kept the Net a free-for-all venue and fostered a "What's yours is mine" mentality. Online information and graphics are largely viewed as public property by many in the Internet community. Many organizations, such as the Smithsonian Institution, counter electronic theft by limiting online reproductions of their written and artistic works (Spar & Bussgang, 1996).

Enforcing online copyright regulations is often confounded by the lack of distinction between intentional and nonintentional infringements. Innocent acts, such as e-mailing parts of a Web document to a friend or downloading an article to a personal hard drive, may be seen as misuse, even though there is no commercial motive or intent to defraud ("The Accidental Superhighway," 1995). In the absence of clear online copyright protection laws, it is a good idea to place the federal copyright symbol (©) on Web sites to safeguard content from alteration and deletion and to deter others from copying original content onto their own Web sites.

MARKET RESEARCH

The Web contains a wealth of information just waiting to be tapped by researchers. It is a marketer's dream come true to travel around his or her competitors' sites, seeing which products are featured, reading in-house press releases, and gaining an intimate knowledge of what the other guys are doing. Gathering demographic data from customers and conducting mini-focus groups through online chat forums, listservs, Usenet Newsgroups, or e-mail is as easy as point-and-click.

Understanding consumers and the market and getting a jump on purchasing and lifestyle trends are crucial to the success of most businesses. Marketers delight in the waves of information that sweep across their desktops. Online libraries and directories, stock market reports, financial statements, business-related books, newspapers, magazines, and journals, minute-by-minute news updates, press releases, and other Web resources enlighten marketers to what is happening in the business world. Sharp business people view the Web as a rich resource and know how to maximize its potential as a data-gathering tool.

MEASURING SUCCESS

Part of the overall planning process involved with going online includes defining the goals and objectives of the site. Methods of measuring whether a site is living up to the company's needs and expectations need to be in place before a site goes online. It is easy to think that once the site is up and running that all of the work is complete, but that is when the real work begins. Web sites need to be continually monitored to make sure they are operating properly, and that they are accomplishing their goals. Going online is expensive and requires the dedication of valuable resources, and those holding the purse strings want to assess whether the Web is a worthwhile venture.

Simply counting the number of times a site is accessed is not a measure of marketing success. If the primary purpose of a Web site is to sell a particular item, then millions of connects will not mean much if the product goes unsold. However, counts can be an indication of the number of Web users who are aware of the site's existence and of its popularity among the online community. Although the number of times a site has been visited simply tells how many times a site has been accessed, it does not represent the number of different people who have landed on the site. Therefore, relying on the overall number of connects as a measurement of success can be unreliable and deceiving.

Counting the number of times specific pages within a site are accessed may be a more accurate accounting of which parts of the site are the most useful and interesting to consumers. Several pages may be getting the bulk of the attention while others are largely ignored. Armed with this information, marketers can quickly react to consumers' needs by changing, updating, or removing some pages (Sterne, 1995).

Most Web sites can log users' paths throughout the site. Unless a site requires users to enter their passwords at log-in, most tracking is done without establishing the identity of individual users. The options users select most frequently, paths taken to travel through the site, the depth of exploration, and other basic traversing information are often monitored and recorded for analysis. For example, if on a particular site users read about product information but most stop short of ordering a product after they read the return policy, analysts could interpret that to mean that buyers are unsure of purchasing online and need more assurance that they can return an item. This type of path analysis can tip off marketers that certain aspects of the site, product, or purchase specifications need to be altered to match consumer needs (Sterne, 1995). The retail outlet the Gap pumped its Web site full of games and other interactive promotions but was surprised when Web tracking revealed that customers spent most of their time perusing product information (Cuneo, 1997a).

A more direct measurement of online success involves analyzing sales data. The number of items sold, the types of products and models sold most frequently, the prices of the most popular items, purchasers' demographics, the number of returns, and other sales information can expose a site's strengths and weaknesses. Also, many online commercial sites are not set up to complete sales transactions; they are set up to provide information and generate leads. Web sites often provide request forms for mailings of CD-ROMs, catalogs, brochures, and other promotional materials. Many marketers measure the number of sales that are directly attributed to information obtained from a Web site to assess the effectiveness of online commerce (Sterne, 1995).

Lastly, customer feedback and electronic marketing go hand-in-hand. Consumers' remarks are very useful for uncovering any flaws in a Web site. Via e-mail and other electronic transmissions, customers often tell marketers what they think of a Web site and give suggestions for improvement and changes. Through direct feedback, marketers have a more qualitative, rather than quantitative, measurement of their site's performance.

CYBERMARKETS

Millions of dollars in sales are annually transacted through the Web. Most major corporations and many smaller companies support Web sites that include pages of product information and ordering capabilities. Often cybershoppers buy directly from manufacturers, while at other times they delight in browsing through cybermalls and online shopping networks.

The popular television station Home Shopping Network (HSN) has expanded its market through the purchase of the *Internet Shopping Network* (ISN). Shoppers flock to ISN to buy any of its 40,000 products sold by over 1,100 different vendors. In 1997, ISN launched *Computer Superstore* and *First Auction,* where computers, electronics, and other HSN goods are purchased in an auction-like format (Paul, 1996; "Internet Shopping Network," 1997).

Downtown Anywhere simulates downtown shopping as customers "walk" around town and from store to store. Set up like a virtual city, visitors interested in the arts can go to the Louvre or to Downtown Anywhere's Museum District. Information seekers can check out the Library and Newsstands, investors can make their way to the Financial District, and sports fans can go to the Arena. Shoppers can head straight to Main Street where they can go to the "Five and Dime" or to "CD Now," and order fresh Florida oranges from "The Indian River Gift Fruit Company."

There are many Web locations that provide links to electronic marketing sites and information. *The Electronic Marketing Home Page* posts hundreds of links to sites such as "Small Business Marketing," "Malls and Commercial Marketing Sites," "Academic Marketing Sites," and "Global Internet Marketing/Advertising."

An Online Catalog of Catalogs

Many retailers offer mail-order products, and many companies offer their goods exclusively through direct marketing. Catalogs benefit consumers through easy, at-home shopping, quick delivery, and money-back guarantees. As mail-order shoppers begin to discover the Web, the demand for online catalogs continues to grow. Marketers benefit from cybercatalogs by reaching their regular customers and an untapped audience of potential customers, and they save on mailing and other distribution costs. Overall, a full-blown printed catalog can cost upwards of $1 million, whereas a high-quality interactive version may cost under $200,000 (Michals, 1997).

Visitors to *The Catalog Site* find a host of their favorite catalogs under one roof. Eddie Bauer, Hickory Farms, and smaller mail-order companies such as Exclusively Bar-B-Q, Inc., and Paradise on a Hanger (for Hawaiian shirt lovers) are housed on *The Catalog Site*. Most of the site's clients produce printed catalogs, and fewer than half have established separate marketing Web sites. Launched in mid-1995, The Catalog Site lays claim to about 60,000 weekly visitors, who can scan through catalogs, check out goods on sale, request printed catalogs, and order items for themselves as well as gift certificates for others. Additionally, The Catalog Site features an online gossip page that links to catalogers' pages, and a ratings page where the catalogs are assessed according to their basic design, ease of use, originality, and other factors (Engel, 1997).

The *Buyer's Index* is a catalog search service that hooks consumers up with any of 9,000 online catalogers and Web shopping sites containing more than 21 million products. A searching tool simplifies the purchasing process for shoppers who know what product they want, but do not know where to look for it. Users

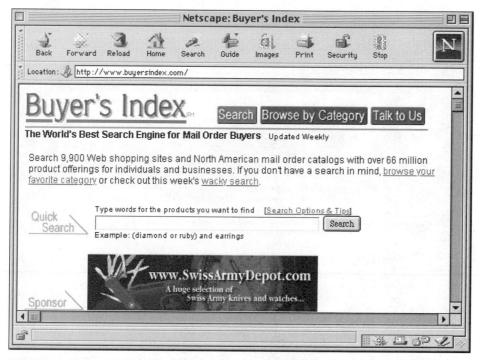

FIGURE 6.5 Buyer's Index Homepage

simply enter the type of product they want, and the search tool lists the catalogs or online sites that carry the item. Shoppers can also browse for goods within any of seventy different product categories.

TAPPING INTO THE COLLEGE MARKET

Marketers see the Web as an excellent way to reach out to the college market. College students are active consumers and an ideal audience for many products. Many college students own computers, over 80 percent use e-mail, and 94 percent have access to the Web (Croal, 1997; Rosner, 1996). Reaching this lucrative, trend-setting group takes setting up a Web site that appeals to their interests. Many marketers have done just that with collegiate sites that include news and educational information, links to scholarships and loan programs, credit card companies, spring break tours, online music and book stores, trendy clothing companies and other product outlets, contests and games, and so much more. Students from around the world are connecting to sites designed just for them, such as *Student Advantage*

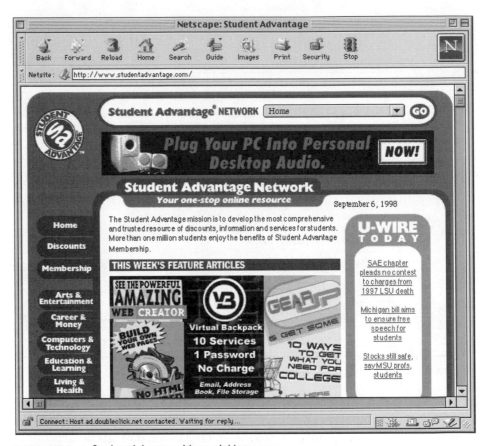

FIGURE 6.6 Student Advantage Network Homepage

Network, MarketSource's *T@pOnline,* Williams College's *Tripod,* and *College-Freshman.* The *American Express University* treats students to travel tips and guides, financial and job-seeking advice, and of course, it promotes its own credit cards.

PUBLIC RELATIONS

Public relations is often considered part of the promotions/communication function of the marketing mix. The "fourth P/C" involves publicity and promotional efforts beyond purchasing advertising space and responding to consumer feedback. The Internet has opened a new path for disseminating public relations messages to the public.

The Internet offers public relations practitioners many advantages over traditional media. E-mail, listservs, and Usenet Newsgroups are effective vehicles for direct communication among public relations agencies, practitioners, and spokespeople and their clients, the public, and the media. Web sites act as discussion forums and as bulletin boards for publicizing new products or services, posting press releases, and disseminating other news.

Typically, public relations messages flow from the source to the media, which decide whether the information is worthy of print space or airtime. Once accepted for publication or broadcast, messages are often edited, rewritten, shortened, and sometimes misinterpreted; messages received by the public are not always in their original form. However, messages transmitted directly from the source to the Internet are not subject to editing and other alterations. Using the Internet, the source behind the message has direct control over when and where to post the message and over the content itself.

Public relations and the Internet are both about interactivity and the exchange of ideas, opinions, and information. Interactivity is the common bond between the Internet and public relations. The Internet provides public relations a direct link to the public, and the public can in turn interact with public relations agencies and companies' public relations departments.

What Is Public Relations?

Public relations can be thought of as the "function that identifies, establishes, and maintains mutually beneficial relationships between an organization and the various publics on whom its success and failure depend" (Cutlip, Center, & Broom, 1994, p. 1). The Public Relations Society of America (PRSA) defines public relations as "counseling, research, media relations, publicity, employee/member relations, community relations, public affairs, government affairs, issues management, financial relations, industry relations, development/fund raising, minority relations and multi-cultural affairs, special events and public participation, and marketing communication" (Marlow, 1996, p. 1).

Public relations differs from advertising, which is the purchasing of space in print publications, or airtime of electronic media. Advertisements are created by companies or agencies that contract with various media to run the ads as submitted and on agreed-upon times and days. On the other hand, public relations material is submitted to the editorial department for approval and is printed or broadcast depending on available space or time. The media are not bound by contract to deliver public relations messages.

History of Public Relations

Some of the earliest uses of what later became known as public relations go back to early Greek and Roman civilizations, when oral communication persuaded and informed communities about governmental policies, art, and religion. Public relations is a practice that has evolved through the ages, but it was not formally recognized until the 1800s. The term *public relations* was coined in 1882 by a lawyer addressing Yale's graduating class. At that time, the term *public relations* was synonymous with the phrase *the general good* and was not used in a business sense until fifteen years later, when it was adopted by the Association of American Railroads. The 1800s also witnessed the rise of what many consider to be a lesser form of public relations—press agentry. P. T. Barnum, the world's greatest circus promoter, used hype, exaggeration, and deception to attract attention and draw crowds to his shows.

At the turn of the century, American business was in turmoil. Many were accused of unethical business practices by socially conscious muckrakers who fueled the public's dislike of large corporations. Management was in crisis and was besieged by workers demanding changes in unfair labor laws and improvements in dismal working conditions. Hired by the coal mining industry, Ivy Ledbetter Lee, who later became known as the father of public relations, ushered in a new era of company relations. Lee was instrumental in improving corporate policy and image throughout the early 1900s and for establishing basic principles of public relations. Lee believed industries should work in the public interest, should maintain open communication with employees, the public, and the news media, and should become active parts of their communities.

While Ivy Lee was developing the corporate communication aspect of public relations, Edward Bernays, nephew of Sigmund Freud, was formulating the counseling function of public relations. Drawing from his knowledge of the human mind, Bernays developed strategies to sway public opinion. Bernays counseled troubled businesses and industries with suggestions for policy changes and improvements, coupled with image-building tactics and public opinion promotions. Bernays, who lived to over the age of a hundred, left his mark in the field of public relations with his work on influencing public opinion, which has become an integral part of the practice.

As the practice of public relations has evolved, four basic roles have emerged: press agentry and publicity, public information, public persuasion, and two-way communication between an organization and its public. **Press agentry and publicity** encompass getting the word out about an organization's products or services, and they are often associated with image building and hyperbole, rather than straight factual information. **Public information** is more straightforward and strives to disseminate accurate, truthful, and unbiased information. **Public persuasion** is one-way communication that attempts to influence public opinion, attitudes, or behavior. Lastly, **two-way communication** endeavors to reach an understanding between an organization and its public through feedback and interaction (Grunig, 1984).

Public Relations and the Internet

E-mail, listservs, Usenet Newsgroups, and the Web are changing the way companies and other organizations create and reinforce their images, report on new services and products, publicize events, influence public perceptions, foster and maintain customer relations, and reach out to target audiences. The Internet is clearly changing public relations as organizations move from using hard-sell tactics to providing enticing, yet educational, information. Global accounts are no longer the realm of large well-funded agencies, as small to medium-sized public relations companies are riding the Internet to new clients. Low-cost, swift communication empowers smaller agencies to reach people around the globe, placing small agencies in direct competition with better known powerhouses (Henley, Gennarelli, Hon, & Kelleher, 1996).

The book *Electronic Public Relations,* by Eugene Marlow, puts forth the following list of uses of the Internet for public relations practitioners:

Media relations: E-mail communication with reporters and the public. Electronic distribution of news releases via e-mail and Web pages.

Issues tracking: Keeping up with the latest news and events through news wires and news service Web pages.

Electronic clipping services: Tracking story appearances in various media and other news sites.

Competitive intelligence: Keeping an eye on competitors by visiting their Web sites.

Marketing communications: Watching industry trends via industry, corporate, media, and commercial sites, listservs, and discussion groups.

Research: Developing trends, and analyzing survey data and general information.

Government affairs: Following policy through government and regulatory sites.

Employment opportunities: Recruiting and job-seeking functions through classified ad sites, industry-specific sites, and listservs.

Professional associations: Membership in various public relations organizations such as PRSA and PRSSA (Public Relations Student Society of America).

Clip art: Downloading graphics and gifs for company newsletters and electronic publications.

Technical support: Asking questions about computer or Internet-related technology.

Mailing list information: Gathering e-mail and postal addresses and phone numbers of specific publics, government officials, and members of the media.

E-mail delivery: Sending information that needs to be somewhere immediately.

Electronic water cooler: Electronic conversing with other PR practitioners through listservs and discussion groups. (Marlow, 1996, pp. 148–49)

Using Internet Resources for Public Relations Purposes

Internet resources are being applied to public relations in many ways. For instance, e-mail is being used for transmitting press releases and press kits to the media, Usenet Newsgroups for publicizing an event, and the Web for providing product and service information. While some public relations functions cut across several Internet resources, others are unique to one online resource.

E-MAIL   E-mail is effectively used for communicating between agencies and their clients, public relations specialists and the media, and organizations and their customers. Agencies and their clients can quickly send each other press releases, speeches, and other material for editing and revision. Additionally, copy alterations can be made directly on electronic files and immediately resent for approval.

E-mail facilitates media relations by pushing press releases and other publicity materials to reporters more quickly than do conventional means. E-mail messages are unintrusive, they do not require immediate attention (as does a ringing telephone), they can be accessed when convenient, and they are easily imported into word processors for editing and reformatting. Additionally, reporters can send questions and requests for more information directly to the source without having to make costly telephone calls or wait days for the U.S. Postal Service to deliver the response (Bobbitt, 1995).

E-mail protocol suggests that press releases be addressed to each reporter separately rather than sending out one message to several different media. Press releases that come in with a long string of other media e-mail addresses at the top seem too much like an impersonal mass mailing and may be purposely overlooked by the reporter. Once a novelty, e-mail press releases are in heavy competition with one another for reporters' and editors' attention. Many e-mail software packages include a feature that hides the routing list, so recipients see only their address, and not the list of others who received the same message. For example, e-mail addresses placed in Eudora's BCC (Blind Carbon Copy) field renders them invisible to the recipient.

Writing a lively and interesting headline in the subject box will set a release apart from all of the messages likely to be sitting in a recipient's e-mail box. Most

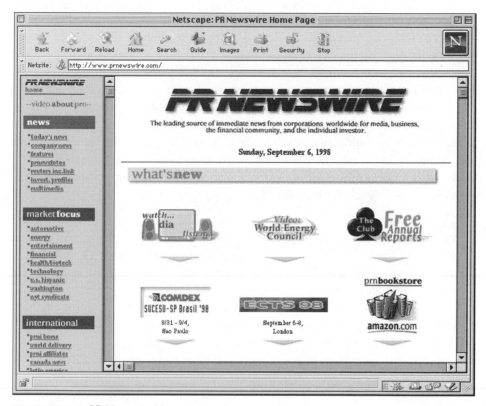

FIGURE 6.7 PR Newswire Homepage

editors and reporters do not want to spend time scrolling through a lengthy press release before getting to the gist of the matter. Electronic releases should fit on a computer screen in their entirety, usually no longer than 20–24 lines. Longer releases should be accompanied with a short summary paragraph preceding the release.

Many organizations subscribe to services, such as *BusinessWire* and *PR Newswire*, for example, that take care of distributing press releases throughout the online world. These services know the ins and outs of the Internet and the most effective places to post messages. Other services act as online "tipsheets" for specific industry-related news. For example, *Newstips* distributes tidbits of its clients' latest computer news to thousands of reporters.

URLWire, another press release service, rates some of its competitors on its home page. URLWire assesses PRNewsTarget, Gina Internet Wire, Internet News Bureau, Xpress Press, and Net News Release on costs and other criteria needed to select the most appropriate online news release service.

Those who subscribe to these services save themselves the time and resources it takes to send out releases themselves. Also, by depending on the wires' expertise, subscribers may reach a wider, more interested audience. Reporters and the public access the wire services for leads and the latest industry news.

Many organizations target markets by establishing a database of their customers' e-mail addresses and transmitting new product information, special offers, press releases, and other news to an audience already interested in the companies' lines of products. Companies should exercise care to not overload their customers with unwanted hard sales messages. Although many customers appreciate receiving new information, companies should e-mail only those customers who have expressed desire for such correspondence.

LISTSERVS AND USENET NEWSGROUPS   Posting topic-specific organizational and product information on listservs and Usenet Newsgroups guarantees an audience already interested in the subject. PR practitioners may have to research the thousands of available forums to choose those most likely to capture the attention of their target audience. Many listservs and Usenet groups frown upon anything that even hints of a sales message; it is good practice to contact a forum's manager for permission before posting online messages.

Electronic forums readily lend themselves to issues research. PR specialists tapping in to online dialogue keep abreast of public opinion and attitudes. Informal, spontaneous discussions are useful for uncovering shifting trends in consumerism. Casual exchanges are often substituted for conventional focus groups, and they can be more meaningful to a company than formal discussions with experts. Usenet and other talk forums are often thought of as being nonscientific and informal, with discussion centering around controversial issues. On the other hand, listservs, such as the *Public Relations Society of America* and *PRForum,* tend to attract discussants who are more serious about the subject at hand; thus the dialogue is more educationally oriented and revolves around sharing information. Topic-specific listservs are teeming with experts who are more than happy to share their knowledge with others and to steer novices to more information. Lofty in-depth conversation, scientific data, and serious inquiry and discussion are more likely to be found on listservs than on bulletin boards and chat forums.

THE WEB   Setting up a homepage is an invaluable public relations tool. A well-designed Web site subtly lures the public into the deeper recesses of the company, organization, or agency. Users have entrée to information that would otherwise take great effort and days or weeks to obtain. PR practitioners are free from having to persuade the media to print or broadcast their releases; they can simply netcast their own news. Additionally, having direct control over content is another benefit of establishing one's own online presence. Electronic press releases are not subject to outside editing, or confined to space and time restrictions. Also, saving on printing costs allows full-color graphics online, and in many instances information can be enhanced with audio and video files.

A Web site can be considered pull technology, as users have to seek out the site. All too often a Web site is nothing more than an online static brochure that gives users plenty to read but nothing to do. Pages of press releases, sales data, and annual reports can become pretty mundane. Users are more likely to pull public relations messages if they are presented in a lively interactive mode. Audio of a CEO's speech, video of a sponsored event, interactive games, and product demonstrations liven up a Web site and pique visitors' interest.

A well-designed Web site also includes a push component where users request additional information, such as catalogs, and allows visitors to customize the information they would like to receive. For instance, one reporter may request a full press kit, while another may not want the accompanying photographs. Additional information such as testimonial letters, media reviews, and newsletters can also be used as push options.

Corporations such as _Intel_ have established their own online press room where the latest company news, products, and events are posted. The page includes news and photo archives, and press kits. Media can pull whichever information they are most interested in, or they can customize the types of releases they want to receive.

The Web is rife with publicity opportunity. Video and audio of live speeches, ribbon-cutting ceremonies, guest interviews, product unveilings, and other sponsored events draw customers who cannot attend in person. Cyber-publicity is a great way for a company or organization to show itself at its best and to spread goodwill throughout the local and online communities.

Companies can take fuller advantage of the Web by using their sites to recruit clients and provide additional client services. Dedicating a section of the Web site aimed directly at prospective and current clients reflects a strong commitment to client services and concerns. Many public relations agencies are designing Web sites for their clients as part of the overall public relations strategy and package.

While the Web is widely recognized as a promotional tool, it is also looked upon as a research instrument. The Web is brimming with various types of information helpful to the practice of public relations. Although using the Web for research is often seen as an academic pursuit, it behooves public relations professionals to exploit the medium for their own research purposes. There are many public relations–oriented Web sites, such as _PRWeb_, that provide links to industry news and major firms and agencies. The _Public Relations Society of America_ (PRSA) and the _International Association of Business Communicators_ are two of many other sites important to public relations practitioners.

SUMMARY: ONLINE MARKETING AND PUBLIC RELATIONS

Marketers and public relations specialists are discovering the importance of the Internet as a new medium ideal for the practice of their professions. The Web offers new opportunities, unheard of even a few short years ago, for reaching the public. Integrating the Web into the marketing mix and public relations strategies is a new endeavor, and one that is yielding a range of public responses. While many Internet users enthusiastically embrace the Web as a purveyor of business news and as a shopping outlet, others are concerned about the lack of privacy and security and are resentful of unsolicited promotions. Weaving the Web into the existing framework of marketing and public relations takes much trial and error.

Businesses and organizations must first decide whether it is worth their efforts and resources to establish an online site. It may take years before a site becomes profitable, necessitating careful planning of resource expenditure. Also, Web site design considerations must encompass both the overall look of the site as well its effectiveness in attaining corporate goals.

The Web, along with other newer communication technologies, is changing old ways of doing business. In the marketing mix, the traditional "Four P's" (product, price, place, promotion) are giving way to the "Four C's" (consumer, cost, convenience, communication) as marketers are moving from mass marketing to niche marketing. The newer media environment is bringing consumers in closer contact with marketers and public relations specialists, and consumers' opinions and attitudes are bearing greater weight on business decisions than ever before.

Online commerce requires a new mode of thinking to satisfy techno-savvy consumers. Marketers are experimenting with new pricing models for online selling, innovative ways of establishing relationships between sellers and consumers, creative methods of providing product information and demonstrations, and new techniques of online persuasion. Market analysis is uncovering which products are selling the best online, and consumer and public relations research is examining just how much and what types of information should be "pushed" to consumers or just made available for customers to "pull" from the Web.

The Internet and its resources are fast becoming invaluable public relations tools. Public relations practitioners have an unprecedented means of connecting with their audiences. Web resources readily lend themselves to press agentry, publicity, public information, persuasion, and two-way communication. As an increasingly large number of people are flocking to the Net for information, the public relations profession is recognizing the power of this new medium and have come to depend on it as a conduit to the public. The Web gives public relations specialists an unrestricted voice in promoting their company or cause and keeps them out of the clutches of conventional media. The Web is not just a one-way road to the public; it is a multilaned highway with information flowing in both directions. Savvy public relations practitioners are keeping an electronic eye on the marketplace through e-mail, discussion-type forums, and listservs.

The Web is an ever-changing dynamic structure that defies mastery. Marketing and public relations professionals are breaking new ground and developing new models within existing frameworks in attempts to understand this new medium. Online commerce and public relations are mostly hit-and-miss propositions, as no clear-cut guidelines exist that guarantee a successful run on the Web. As the online information business matures, lessons will be learned, and new models for creating a successful Internet presence will emerge.

CHAPTER LINKS

The Abstract Funhouse—http://www.starcreations.com/gamedowner/

Amazon.com—http://www.amazon.com

American Express University—http://www.americanexpress.com/student

Ann Hemyng Candy Inc.'s Chocolate Factory—
http://mmink.com/mmink/dossiers/choco.html

Anonymizer—http://www.anonymizer.com

Auto-by-Tel—http://www.autobytel.com

Ben & Jerry's—http://www.benjerry.com/

Business Wire—http://www.businesswire.com/

Buyer's Index—http://www.buyersindex.com

The Catalog Site—http://www.catalogsite.com

CDNow—http://www.cdnow.com/

Chicago Tribune—http://www.chicago.tribune.com

College Freshman—http://www.collegefreshman.com

Computer Superstore—http://www.css.isn.com

Downtown Anywhere—http://www.awa.com

The Electronic Marketing Home Page—http://www.america.net/~scotth/mktsite.htm

First Auction—http://www.firstauction.com

FreeRide—http://www.freeride.com

Gap—http://www.gap.com

Hot Hot Hot—http://www.hothothot.com/hhh/index.shtml

Industry.Net —http://www.industry.net/

International Association of Business Communicators—
http://www.iabc.com/homepage.htm

Internet Shopping Network—http://www.isn.com/

Intel—http://www.intel.com/pressroom/

J. Crew—http://www.jcrew.com

Newstips—http://www.newstips.com/

New York Times— http://www.nytimes.com

PRForum—listserv@UTKVM1.UTK.EDU

PRNewsWire—http://www.prenewswire.com

PRWeb—http://www.prweb.com

Public Eye—http://www.thepubliceye.com

Public Relations Society of America—http://www.prsa.org

Quote.com—http://www.quote.com

Student Advantage Network—http://www.studentadvantage.com

T@p Online—http://www.taponline.com

Tennis Warehouse—http://www.tennis-warehouse.com/

Tripod—http://www.tripod.com

Total Entertainment Network—http:www.ten.net

URLWire—http://www.urlwire.com

Virtual Vineyards—http://www.virtualvin.com/

REFERENCES

The accidental superhighway. (1995, July 1). A survey of the Internet, special insert. *Economist, 336* (7921), S1–S18.

Amirrezvani, A. (1995, April). The merchants of cyberspace. *PC World, 13* (4), 155–57.

Amos, D. S. (1995, September 10). More firms get caught up in Web. *St. Louis Post Dispatch,* pp. 1E, 8E.

Armstrong A., & Hagel, J., III. (1996, May–June). The real value of on-line communities. *Harvard Business Review, 74* (3), 134–41.

Bayne, K. M. (1998, February, 16). Music business makes waves on the Internet. *Advertising Age,* 28.

Benjamin, R., & Wigand, R. (1995, Winter). Electronic markets and virtual value chains on the information superhighway. *Sloan Management Review,* 62–72.

Bernoff, J., Morrisette, S., & Clemmer, K. (1998, March). Consumer eCommerce readiness. *Forrester research.* [Online]. Available: http://www.forrester.com/reports/mar98ctr.htm [1998, April 21].

Blunt, J. (1995). Internet security: An oxymoron? *DECUS Magazine.* [Online]. Available: http://www.decus.org/decus/pubs/magazine/spring95/oxy.html

Bobbitt, R. (1995). An Internet primer for public relations. *Public Relations Quarterly, 40* (3), 27–33.

Branscum, D. (1996). The Web targets kids. *Family PC.* [Online]. Available: http://www.zdnet.com/familypc/cntent/960916/columns/savvy/current.html

Business models for Web sites—Electronic advantages and value propositions equal dollars. (1997, April). *Internet Marketing & Technology Report, 3* (4). Carlsbad, CA: Computer Economics, 1–4.

Computer hacker plants porno on Air Force. (1996, December 30). *CNN Interactive.* [Online]. Available: http://cnn.com/TECH/9612/30/air.force.porn/index.html [1998, February 28].

Croal, N. (1997, June 9). Want a job? Get online. *Newsweek,* 81.

Cross, R. (1994, October). Internet: The missing marketing medium found. *Direct Marketing, 57* (6), 20–23.

Cuneo, A. Z. (1997a, July 7). The Gap readies electronic commerce plan for Web site. *Advertising Age,* 18.

Cuneo, A. Z. (1997b, November 17). Holiday shopping could spur booming Web commerce. *Advertising Age.* [Online]. Available: http://adage.com/ns-search/interactive/daily/archives/19971117

Cutlip, S. M., Center, A. H., & Broom, G. M. (1994). *Effective public relations.* Upper Saddle River, NJ: Prentice-Hall.

Deighton, J. (1996, November/December). The future of interactive marketing. *Harvard Business Review,* 151–62

Easton, J. (1996, December). Hidden revenue hotspots. *ZD Internet Magazine,* 99–106.

Electronic commerce. (1997, May 10). *Economist,* 1–18.

Engel, E. (1997, February). Something for everyone. *Webmaster,* 21–21.

Faust, F. (1996, March 4). Net hopes high, sales low. *St. Louis Post Dispatch,* pp. B11–B12.

Feeding your head. (1998, January 12). *Newsweek,* 10.

Goldstein, A. (1995, October 11). Net gain. *St. Louis Post Dispatch,* p. 5C.

Grunig, J. (1984, April 9). What kind of PR do you practice? *PR Reporter, 44* (150).

Guglielmo, C. (1997, January 13). Services offer free ticket to ride. *Inter@ctive Week, 4* (1), 29.

Hawn, M. (1996, April). Stay on the Web. *MacWorld,* 94–98.

Henley, M., Gennarelli, D., Hon, L., & Kelleher, T. (1996). *Public relations and the World Wide Web: Designing an effective homepage.* Paper presented at the annual convention of the Association for Education in Journalism and Mass Communication, Anaheim, CA.

Hoge, C. C., Sr. (1993). *The electronic marketing manual.* New York: McGraw-Hill.

Internet helps Scottish Islanders win back their land. (1997, December). *National Geographic.*

Internet shoppers aren't spenders. (1997, June 11). *Advertising Age.* [Online]. Available: http://adage.com/ns-search/interactive/daily/archives/19970611

Internet Shopping Network. (1997). *ISN homepage.* [Online]. Available: http://www.isn.com/html/about_isn

Janal, D. S. (1995). *Online marketing*. New York: Van Nostrand Reinhold.

Kalgaard, R. (1998, April 6). Up and to the right. *Forbes,* 11.

Kotkin, J. (1998, April 6). The mother of all malls. *Forbes,* 60–65.

Levy, S. (1997, April 14). What shakeout? *Newsweek,* 82–86.

Maddox, K. (1997, October 6). Information still killer app on the Internet. *Advertising Age,* 42, 48.

Maddox, K., Wagner, M., & Wilder, C. (1997, February 2). Making money on the Web. *Internet Week.* [Online]. Available: http://techWeb.cmp.com/ia/22issue/22cover.html

Mannes, G. (1996, January). Digital dollars. *Popular Mechanics,* 53–55, 103.

Marlow, E. (1996). *Electronic public relations*. Belmont, CA: Wadsworth.

McCarthy, V. (1997, January). Web security: How much is enough? *Datamation,* 112–17.

McLaughlin, L. (1997, February). Online vendors: How can you tell the good from the bad? *PC World,* 56, 58.

Memon, F. (1996a, November 18). Keeping an eye on retail ventures on the net. *Inter@ctive Week,* 39.

Memon, F. (1996b, December 9). PGP wants to zap cookies. *Inter@ctive Week,* 5.

Memon, F. (1996c, December 9). Will cookies make the cut? *Inter@ctive Week,* 1.

Michals, D. (1997, February). www.catalog.com. *Working Woman, 22* (2), 8–10.

NCN survey: Online newspaper readers more likely to shop on Web. (1997, August 22). *Advertising Age.* [Online]. Available: http://adage.com/ns-search/interactive/daily/archives/19970822

Neuwirth R. (1997, December 29). '97 Newspaper Web losses. *Editor & Publisher Interactive.* [Online]. Available: http://www.mediainfo.com [1998, February 7].

New survey shows big rise in Internet use, but not for shopping. (1997, October 14). *CNN Interactive.* [Online]. Available: http://www.cnn.com [1997, October 16].

Noglows, P. (1995, November 27). Business on the Net: Safer than you think. *Interactive Week,* 68.

Online retail strategies. (1998, April). *Forrester Research.* [Online]. Available: www.forrester.com [1998, April 24].

Online shopping accepted. (1996, April 12). *Advertising Age.* [Online]. Available: http://adage.com/ns-search/interactive/daily/archives/19960412

Paul, P. (1996). Marketing on the Internet. *Journal of Consumer Marketing, 13* (4), 27–37.

Perry, S. (1997, December 14). Security at risk for many Web sites. *San Francisco Chronicle,* p. C1.

Privacy concerns need to be met for success on the Web. (1997, April). *Internet Marketing & Technology Report, 3* (4). Carlsbad, CA: Computer Economics, 5–7.

Pushing the envelope—Net marketers reach out through "push" media. (1997, May). *Internet Marketing & Technology Report, 3* (5). Carlsbad, CA: Computer Economics, 1–4.

Quinn, J. B. (1997, October 14). http://www.jbq.ok.com. *Newsweek,* 71.

The real numbers behind Net profits. (1997). *ActivMedia.* [Online]. Available: http://www.activmedia.com [1998, February 9].

Rebello, K., Armstong, L., & Cortese, A. (1996, September 23). Making money on the Net. *Business Week,* 104–18.

Resnick, R. (1996, May). Follow the money. *Internet World, 7* (5), 34, 36.

Rigdon, J. E. (1996, February 14). Internet users say they'd rather not share their cookies. *Wall Street Journal,* p. B6.

Rosner, H. (1996, April 15). Trapping students in the Web. *Brandweek,* 50.

Rothfeder, J. (1996, February). No privacy on the Net. *PC World, 15* (2), 223–29.

Schultz, D. E., Tannenbaum, S. I., & Lauterborn, R. F. (1993). *Integrated marketing communication.* Chicago: NTC Publishing.

Search engines most popular method. (1997, April 16). *CommerceNet,* press release. [Online]. Available: www.commerce.net/news/pres/0416.html [1997, October 27].

Shaw, R. (1996, October). Is it safe yet? *Yahoo! Internet Life,* 72–73.

Simmons on online buying. (1996, December 11). *Advertising Age.* [Online]. Available: http://adage.com/ns-search/interactive/daily/archives/19961211

Spar, D., & Bussgang, J. J. (1996, May–June). Ruling the Net. *Harvard Business Review, 74* (3), 125–33.

Sterne, J. (1995). *World Wide Web marketing.* New York: John Wiley & Sons.

Supermarket for online shopping. (1998, January 20). *Advertising Age.* [Online]. Available: http:adage.com [1998, April 21].

Tedesco, R. (1996, October 26). Site costs soar as Web weaves a spell. *Broadcasting and Cable,* 36.

Tedesco, R. (1997, June 2). That's intertainment. *Broadcasting and Cable, 127* (23), 54–62.

Tubbs, R. (1996, May). The Internet—A security proposal. *Internet marketing and advertising association.* [Online]. Available: http://www.imaa.org/security.htm

Turner, R. (1997, July 14). Selling a little Net music. *Newsweek,* 54–55.

Web sites lack privacy disclosures. (1997, June 10). *Advertising Age.* [Online]. Available: http://adage.com/ns-search/interactive/daily/archives/19970610

Wilcox, D. L., Ault, P. H., & Agee, W. K. (1995). *Public relations strategies and tactics.* New York: Harper and Row.

Wildstrom, S. H. (1996, December 16). Privacy and the "cookie monster." *Business Week,* 22.

CHAPTER
SEVEN

ADVERTISING

Is there money to be made on the Net? That is what a lot of people want to know, and several have taken the plunge to find out. Instead of advertising a product or service, these cyberbeggars are simply asking people to send them cash. Yes, that's right. These Web moochers are asking people to plunk some money in an envelope and send it directly to a post office mail box.

The Amazing Send Me a Dollar Page has yielded $298.27 as of February 6, 1998. The site does not post its origination date, but in December 1996, the page's "graph-o-meter" registered $127.00 in revenue. By July 18, 1998, the take had amounted to $428.27. The annual income is not hard to figure out. On the site's "rate-a-beggar" page, the author writes fun, snappy critiques of other Web panhandler sites, such as Cindy Lou's Get Me Rich Quick operation. Cindy Lou is seeking money from generous individuals who will help her make her dreams come true. Although Cindy Lou's hopes and aspirations are illustrated with charming graphics, she has only reaped enough money for a "good can of beer. A pretty good beer though, not one of those cheap American beers."

Jonathan Chance lays it on thick with his "depending on the kindness of strangers" shtick. This Internet freeloader seems to have more success attracting international money than American dollars. His take amounts to one rupee, twenty pounds, two dollars, and one quarter.

FIGURE 7.1 The Amazing "Send Me a Dollar" Website

ADVERTISING AND THE WORLD WIDE WEB

The Internet and World Wide Web are the catalysts that set off the explosion of online services, multimedia information, and interactive technology that is changing the way goods and services are advertised and sold to consumers. The Internet was once considered to be "above" commercial endeavors like advertising and marketing. The emergence of the World Wide Web, with its inherent advertising appeal, has changed such thinking. Today, the advertising community is racing to establish its place on the Web. The Web is an interactive medium that is the driving force behind a new kind of advertising and a new kind of consumer. The Web creates a global marketplace that presents a fresh approach to advertising and creates a competitive online environment that has plenty of room for growth and exploration.

With the increasing number of upscale Web viewers, advertisers have discovered a prosperous target market. Advertisers recognize the Web as a new realm for reaching savvy and technologically educated consumers. Ultimately, advertisers have an interactive medium on which to "netcast" their messages and to explore a new approach to advertising and promotion.

FIGURE 7.2 Red Lobster Banner Ad on *USA Today* Homepage. Copyright © 1998 USA Today.

This chapter examines various aspects of Internet advertising. The chapter begins with an explanation of online advertising and online marketing and a discussion of the benefits and challenges associated with using the Web as a promotional vehicle. Different strategies of Internet advertising are discussed, along with tools for creating online ads, pricing issues, efforts to standardize Web ratings, and overall ad revenues. The chapter closes with a look at online advertising associations, agency presence on the Web, and a summary of the effectiveness of online advertising.

Web Advertising versus Web Marketing

There is a difference between establishing a Web presence as a marketing function and using the Web for advertising. When a company establishes a Web site that presents its own products, ordering information, customer feedback options, and so on, this is considered a marketing site rather than an advertisement. Web advertising is a marketing function, but with advertising, companies or agencies pay or make some sort of financial or trade arrangement to post their logos or other company and product information on someone else's Web site. For example, if Toyota pays to place its logo on the _CNN Interactive_ site, this is considered Web advertising, whereas if Toyota creates its own Web site, it is considered Web marketing. Think of it as being similar to Toyota buying ad space in a local newspaper in contrast to printing its own brochure; the former is an ad, the latter a marketing function.

The **banner ad** is one of the earliest types of Web advertisements, and it remains the most prevalent form of online advertising. Banners are typically about 6½ inches wide by about 1 inch high (468 × 60 pixels). On the Web, image sizes are converted from inches to **pixels.** Pixels are tiny dots of color that form images. Computer monitors display 72 pixels per inch, and thus, one inch equals 72 pixels or dots per inch (dpi). Traditionally, banners have been little more than the advertiser's logo with some embellishment.

To increase consumer curiosity and interest, banners are increasingly being designed as **active links** to the advertiser's homepage. In other words, the posted logo doubles as a direct connection to the advertiser. For instance, clicking on a Pizza Hut banner ad takes consumers to one of the company's Web pages, where hungry individuals can order a large pizza with everything, including anchovies.

When banners first appeared in 1994 on HotWired's Web site, most people and industry specialists gave them little thought ("Why Internet Advertising," 1997; Williamson, 1997c). Few imagined that the Web would become the hottest advertising medium around. Mid-1996 analysis by Competitive Media Reporting shows that within fifty-five selected magazine-related Web sites, 310 different brands were promoted in close to 1,500 advertisements (Freeman, 1996; Sucov, 1996).

The Transition to Internet Advertising

Advertising executives of the 1980s developed annual media plans that included only a few budget line items. Print or broadcast ads received the majority of funding, typically 70 percent or more. Approximately 15 percent was allocated for direct mail, with 7 percent for public relations and the remainder for miscellaneous expenses (Cross, 1994).

By the 1990s, changes in media planning and budgeting were dictated by new line items, such as "place based and in-home media," "interactive direct mail," "online services," "infomercials," and "electronic public relations." Rather than shifting extra resources from the television or advertising budget, many are establishing a separate line item for the Web. Web sites and other new media initiatives that increase interaction between customers and companies are well worth the typical 5–10 percent budget allocation. With customer feedback and fine-tuned demographic data, advertising campaigns can be effectively customized to targeted audiences who are changing along with the new media. Old models of advertising based on hype and flash no longer carry as strong an impact on techno-savvy consumers as ads that are based on information and rational buying appeals do (Cross, 1994; Napoli, 1996).

Benefits of Online Advertising

ADVERTISER'S PERSPECTIVE   Advertisers are turning to the Internet to sell their goods and services for several reasons: (1) the Internet and Web serve as worldwide marketplaces that deliver a vast and diverse audience to advertisers; (2) the Internet and the Web are ideal for targeting consumers by posting ads on select Web sites and by e-mailing product announcements to interested customers; (3) online advertisements are free from the constraints of time and space, as are traditional print and broadcast ads; (4) updating and changing cyber-ads can be accomplished much more quickly than traditional media advertisements; (5) Web advertisements are generally less expensive to produce and have longer exposure and run times than ads in traditional media; and (6) Web advertising is prestigious, and its low cost allows businesses with small advertising budgets to compete with companies that have larger advertising resources (Hawkins, 1994; Hoffman & Novak, 1995; "@once!," 1995).

Global Marketplace   The Web is a worldwide network accessed by consumers who have widely varying demographics and product needs. From an advertiser's standpoint, the Web is a single medium that has the potential to reach a vast audience. An advertisement placed on a Web page has the potential circulation of perhaps hundreds or thousands of newspapers worldwide. On the Web, companies sell products to consumers who were previously unreachable or at least very difficult to reach with traditional media. For instance, a store or small company may specialize in products unique to its geographic location, such as pure maple syrup from Vermont or Inuit artifacts from Alaska. Prior to the Web, advertising these products may have been limited to local media, and sales limited to those who could physically come into the store and purchase the product, or who could order by mail. With Web ads, companies can now reach out to millions of physically distant customers. Interactive ads display products, tout product features and benefits, and allow online ordering for the convenience of both sellers and buyers.

Targeting an Audience   Advertisers are moving quickly to send their messages to the millions of consumers accessing the Net. The most effective marketing tool has been the Web's ability to carry messages to targeted groups (Executive Guide, 1996). On many sites users enter their zip codes to bring up local advertisements. The benefits of regional services are summed up by a Saatchi & Saatchi executive who claims that about 80 percent of all business transactions take place within twenty miles of a consumer's home (Hodges, 1996). Local advertising in the form of classifieds, local business sites, and customizable ads by zip code accounted for nearly 12 percent of total online ad revenues in 1997 (Hyland, 1998).

Recognizing the potential to reach a specific group of customers online, several companies have developed proprietary software that delivers targeted advertising to customers based on their demographic profiles, psychographics, IP address or domain name, type of Web browser, and other criteria. *Accipiter* and Bellcore's *Adapt/X* are just two targeting services that have emerged since the mid-1990s. Contracting with these targeters can cost advertisers over $24,000 per year (Cleland, 1996a; Damashek, 1996). Still, many businesses feel the expense is well worth it to reach an audience that is likely to purchase their products.

Web browsers' cookies tool is designed to download ads targeted at specific consumer groups. Whenever users fill out personal information on Web pages, cookies save the information to create customer profiles that companies then use to customize their pages and advertisements. For instance, a young man could see a sports car displayed on a Web site, while an older family man visiting that same site would see a four-door sedan or sport utility vehicle ad. Although cookies have not been widely implemented because of privacy issues, it has an enormous potential for target marketing.

The *New York Times* advertisers target their market by using demographic data acquired from the newspaper's online registrants. The paper charges advertisers a premium for sending ads to a targeted audience. The premium amount varies depending on the specific audience. For example, an advertiser aiming at men, regardless of their demographic profiles, would be charged less than an advertiser who is specifically targeting men who have college degrees and are over the age of fifty (Kerwin, 1997).

Time and Design   Traditional media vie for advertising dollars by promoting the advantages of their medium over others. Print media have a long shelf life. People can read newspapers and magazines at any time after publication. Commercial radio spots can run several times during the day and capture an audience's ear with catchy jingles, and television brings life to ads through video and sound. The Web has all of these advantages of traditional media and more. Web ads are visible for as long as the advertisers post them, and they can be accessed any time of day and as often as users wish. Web ads can be print-based, or they can be more dynamic with graphics, audio, and/or video presentation. Web ads can be downloaded and stored on users' computers for future reference. All of these advantages enhance the Web's allure as a viable advertising medium.

Updating and Changing Ad Copy   Non-online media strictly adhere to publication or broadcast deadlines. Buying space and commercial time, and creating, updating, and changing copy typically require long lead times. Unfortunately, rigid time

FIGURE 7.3 USA Today Sponsor Index. Copyright © 1998 USA Today.

constraints and long production schedules often lead to mistakes in broadcast commercials and print ads.

Web advertisements can generally be designed and posted within a relatively short period of time. Web sites tend to have shorter deadlines than print or broadcast media. Moreover, online ads are easy to correct and change, minimizing the chances of oversights and mistakes.

Production Costs   Ads for traditional media can be expensive to produce; full color separation, audio and video tapes, and other production costs can be very steep. Web ads generally do not require the extensive production techniques of traditional media, and they can often be designed using digital imaging software such as Photoshop, assisted by HTML codes and JavaScripting. Low production costs are instrumental in attracting a wider range of businesses that have small advertising budgets to the Web.

Competition   Web advertising is becoming a business necessity. By utilizing the Web, companies can reduce major production and distribution expenses for direct mailings as well as reduce their overall advertising expenditures. Additionally, smaller businesses are not so small on the Web. The Web closes the gap between large and small enterprises by placing them in the same competitive arena.

CONSUMER PERSPECTIVE Online advertisements hold many benefits for Web users. Convenience is presumably the most significant benefit. It is easy for consumers to use the Web for gathering product information and, in many cases, making a purchase. The Web provides a single, unified interface for shopping, information retrieval, and entertainment (Hawkins, 1994). Interested consumers can instantly click on icons for information and, in some cases, order products by simply entering a credit card number. Additionally, some sites, like *USA Today,* aid Web users seeking products by featuring a sponsor index that provides links to all of their advertisers' homepages.

ADVERTISING RATES

Although major companies such as AT&T, IBM, MasterCard, Sun Microsystems, Zima, and Tower Records are heavily investing in Internet advertising, they and smaller advertisers are concerned about Internet advertising rates. It is often difficult to measure what advertising on the Internet is worth and, thus, how much it should cost (Berniker, 1995b).

Cost per Thousand

Until recently, only flat monthly or quarterly rates were charged for Web advertising. But agencies and Web publishers are attempting to sell this medium with traditional ad rate structures based on **cost-per-thousand (CPM)** impressions. Generally, CPMs are used to sell print and broadcast media. CPMs are the most effective means of comparing the price of advertising across different media, such as comparing newspapers to television, or radio to magazines. CPM is calculated by dividing the cost of an advertisement by the number of individuals or households (in thousands) that are reached. For example, if a newspaper charges $8,000 for an advertisement and has 500,000 subscribers, the CPM is as follows:

CPM = $8,000/500 = $16 per thousand

Compare $16 per thousand to a radio station that charges $5,000 for a commercial and reaches 250,000 listeners:

CPM = $5,000/250 = $20 per thousand

In this case, although the radio station charges less money for its commercials, it is a more expensive purchase, because it reaches a smaller audience than the newspaper. However, media planners are often more interested in other factors, such as demographics, the advantages of the medium itself, and the efficiency of reaching the targeted audience. Thus, they base their buying decisions on a combination of factors and not just on the cost of reaching the total audience alone (Boveé & Arens, 1986; Head, Sterling, & Schofield, 1994). For instance, although Web CPMs tend to run about 66 percent higher than television CPMs, a direct comparison may be misleading, because the Web reaches a select target audience rather than a mass audience. Although television CPMs are lower than Web CPMs, advertisers are paying for television viewers who are not part of their target audience. Thus the cost for reaching a select group is in many cases actually higher on television than on the Web. Therefore, comparisons between Web CPMs and CPMs of other media should factor the cost of reaching one thousand *targeted* individuals against the cost of reaching just *any* thousand people in the mass audience (Boyce, 1998).

With traditional media, audience size data are generally acquired from circulation figures and the number of subscribers, or are estimated based on local market size and ratings, so that CPM calculations are easy and reliable. However, it is difficult to estimate the number of Web users who chance upon a site and are thus exposed to an advertising message, making Web CPM comparisons highly questionable.

Perhaps Web measurement should model itself after radio's "time spent listening" (TSL) or television's "time spent viewing" (TSV) models of pricing, rather than on the number of page views. People who spend greater amounts of time reading a page and traveling within a site are more valuable to advertisers than those who just land on a page for a few seconds and then move on to another site. Adapting the TSL and TSV models to the Web would provide advertisers with the amount of time viewers spend on a page as well as the number of viewers, which would give advertisers a clearer picture of who they are reaching.

Web site managers are experimenting and trying out various pricing structures for online advertising. For example, Netscape Communications Corporation started out by charging flat fees but later changed to CPMs with prices varying from $5 to $50 per thousand impressions, depending on whether ads are placed on the Netscape homepage, an internal site page, or on a Netscape newsletter page. However, since advertising pricing structures do not readily apply to the Web, flat-fee and CPM models will eventually be replaced with more precise Web-based pricing measures (Edmonston, 1995; Schwartz, 1996). Until then, advertisers, agencies, and Web site operators are struggling to price Web spots effectively.

To make it easier for media planners and others to compute CPMs, the *Web Digest for Marketers* has posted an online CPM calculator. By simply plugging in the cost of the ad and the number of exposures, the calculator figures out the CPM.

Size-Based Pricing

Some Web sites charge advertisers using **size-based pricing** that is calculated by the size of the online ad. Charges are assessed by a minimum dollar amount per pixel area. By multiplying an ad's width by its height, the number of square pixels is calculated and then a fee assessed per pixel or by the area (Snyder & Rosenbaum, 1996).

Click-Through Rates

Click-through rates for banner ads are based on the percentage of visitors who click through a banner ad. The rates are calculated by dividing the number of visitors who see the ad by the number who actually click on it. For example, if five hundred visitors land on a Web site but only fifty of them actually click on a banner ad, the ad has a click-through rate of 10 percent (Easton, 1996).

USA Today, a pioneer in click-through rates, charges advertisers slightly over $33 for every thousand people they expect to download an advertiser's logo or image during a two-month period. The charges drop to about $20 for every thousand users who click on the logo and link to the advertiser's own site. These prices are based on the anticipated number of click-throughs, so advertisers are not charged for all of the nearly 800,000 visitors who land on any of the 140,000 pages that make up *USA Today*'s site. They are charged only for those who click through to the advertiser's homepage (Schwartz, 1996; "Inside USA Today," 1998).

USA Today is about 80 percent advertising supported and 20 percent transaction supported, but future plans call for a shift to about 50 percent advertising revenue, 40 percent transaction revenue, and 10 percent third-party sales (Karpinski, 1997). Nonetheless, *USA Today* saw profits rise to $4 million in 1997, and executives are hoping that the site will finally pull a profit in 1998 (Tedesco, 1997a).

Click-through fees work better for some companies than for others. For instance, PointCast and other companies that push content to customers would be shortchanging themselves if they just report to advertisers the number of page views pulled by customers. It makes sense for push companies to charge for click-through rates. PointCast charges advertisers from $1 to $2 per click-through (Riedman, 1997). Many companies, such as _Procter & Gamble,_ will pay for online ads based on click-through rates only (Voight, 1996).

Overall, banner ads are clicked through by only between two and thirteen of every hundred individuals who notice the ad (Hutheesing, 1996; Improving Their Swing, 1998; Voight, 1996). New video banners (**V-banners),** which are simply banner ads containing video clips, significantly increase click-through percentages. Goldwin Golf posted the first V-banner on *Golf Magazine*'s Web site. The Goldwin V-banner included a three-second looping video of golfer Nick Price endorsing the

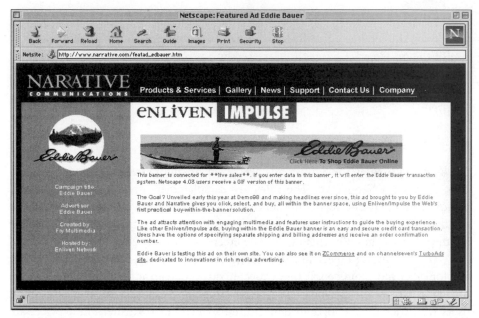

FIGURE 7.4 Eddie Bauer Banner Ad Using Enliven Technology by Narrative Communications

company's line of golf clubs. When the V-banner's click-through rates were compared to a similar Goldwin non-video banner ad, the V-banner had far more click-throughs (5.8 percent) than the static ad (1.8 percent). Even though the V-banner click-through rate represents a 250 percent increase over traditional banners, advertisers are concerned about the low rate of click-throughs in general ("Improving Their Swing," 1998).

While V-banners hold the promise of increasing click-through rates, new Enliven/Impulse technology by *Narrative Communications* connects users to product information without clicking through. Companies such as Godiva Chocolates, Eddie Bauer, Citibank, Sears, and Toshiba have used Enliven banners that are designed to reach users who are interested in obtaining product information but do not want to bother with clicking through to an advertiser's homepage. Enliven banner ads are designed with a built-in response form that can be filled in on the spot rather than obtained from a corporate site ("Online Shopping Gets Even Easier," 1998).

Click-through rates may be affected by placement of the banner ads on the page. In the early days of the Web, pages would download from top to bottom, so content at the top was visible before content at the end of the page. Advertisers used downloading to their advantage by inserting banners at the top of Web pages. The banner would then be the first image consumers would see as the page appeared on the screen. However, with the emergence of **interlacing technology,** most Web pages no longer download in an unrolling fashion, but rather the whole page comes into focus all at once. Interlacing works by first displaying a low resolution version of the entire image or page, then the resolution increases in stages until the highest possible resolution is reached and the image or page is fully focused. Banner ads can be placed anywhere on the screen. Since the advent of interlacing, the top of the page no longer holds an advantage (Holden & Webster, 1995; Waltner, 1996).

Some University of Michigan students set out to find the best position for a banner ad. They found that banner ads placed next to the right scroll bar in the lower right-hand corner of the screen had a 228 percent higher click-through rate than banners placed at the top of the page. Additionally, banners inserted about one-third of the way down the page were clicked through 77 percent more often than banners at the top of the page (Gupta, 1997).

Several companies make clicking-through a fun activity by linking users to interactive games and contests. *Riddler,* hosted by Interactive Imaginations, requires consumers to click on banner ads to participate in any of the site's activities. Target consumers are lured to advertisements through their desire to play games or enter contests. Riddler is packed with a variety of games, puzzles, scavenger hunts, contests, and other amusements. In exchange for personal information such as age, occupation, and media use, users can play for cash awards, cars, Caribbean cruises, and other fantastic prizes. In its first two years online, Riddler awarded over $300,000 in cash and prizes. Small wonder that it has emerged as one of the more popular Web sites for consumers and advertisers (Resnick, 1997).

Riddler makes everyone a winner. Users win by having fun and possibly winning prizes, advertisers win by creating awareness for their products and gathering marketing information about their audiences, and Riddler wins with a wildly popular site that brings in revenues by charging advertisers for every individual who clicks through (Hutheesing, 1996).

Result-Based Fees

Many advertisers are hoping that click-through pricing models will evolve into a **result-based fee** structure. In other words, advertisers would be assessed a minimal charge, or in some cases, no charge at all, for ad placement; actual costs would be based on the number of consumers reached (Schwartz, 1996). This fee structure is similar to per-inquiry (PI) fees charged for broadcast advertising, where stations negotiate a fee or a percentage of the advertiser's net or gross sales based on the number of inquiries that can be directly attributed to the ad. Of course, this type of fee policy for Internet advertising is not possible until new ways of measuring the number of viewers are implemented.

Advertising Exchanges

For smaller companies that cannot afford to place banner ads all over the Web, a new **cooperative exchange approach** is being initiated. Headed by Internet Link Exchange, the system works on a quid-pro-quo basis, where advertisers help direct traffic to each other's sites. Member companies exchange free advertising space on their Web sites for a free spot for their own banner on another company's site (Resnick, 1997).

Discounts

Most traditional print publications offer advertisers camera-ready discounts for advertisements that are complete and ready for page paste-up. It has been proposed that Web sites offer similar discounted rates if ads come in on disk "online-ready," fully coded in HTML and complete with all graphic, audio, or video files. Additionally, a sliding fee could be formulated depending on how much formatting the Web site manager has to do to an ad before posting it online (Snyder & Rosenbaum, 1996).

What Advertisers Want to Pay

Advertisers tend to prefer the pricing structure that best matches their needs. For instance, push services and direct marketers tend to prefer paying click-through fees, while advertisers more interested in building brand awareness may prefer CPM rates. Generally, no one pricing mechanism is preferred by online advertisers. Forrester Research interviews with fifty-two major Web advertisers found that slightly more than one quarter favor click-through rates, slightly less than one-fourth like result-based fees, 15 percent prefer CPM rates, and the remaining one-third would like to see some sort of a hybrid or combination pricing mechanism (Forrester Research, 1996).

SELLING THE MEDIUM

Sales Force

Several companies are assembling Web advertising sales teams separate from their traditional sales forces. Time, Inc., has established an autonomous group of representatives to sell ads on its Web site *Pathfinder*, which includes titles such as *Sports Illustrated, Entertainment Weekly*, and "Virtual Gardener." The cyber-sales force does more than just sell available ad space; they also assist advertisers in online ad design. Many advertisers do not know how to design Web-appropriate ads. That is where special sales teams step in to help create online ads that are engaging, interesting, and eye-catching (Huhn, 1995).

CBS considers the Web a separate medium, and employs an outside firm to handle online sales. CBS's new media director believes that sales representatives need to have a deep understanding of the Web, because online sales are different from broadcast sales. Therefore, CBS's sales reps with extensive Web backgrounds are selling Web space, and those with expertise in broadcast sales are selling radio and television time (Williamson, 1996a).

Regional ad placement programs have begun cropping up as a means of providing advertisers with area-wide Web advertising coverage. Many companies and services are interested in reaching local consumers, but they find it time consuming and difficult to negotiate for ad space with each online publisher individually. Thus, advertising sales collectives, such as the New York Regional Advertising Program (NYRAP), allow Web site representatives to sell space on member sites. Under NYRAP, sales reps for the online versions of Long Island–based *Newsday,* the *Village Voice,* several Gannett-owned regional newspapers, local radio stations, and other regional or local media peddle each medium's ad space to advertisers wishing to cover the New York/New Jersey/Connecticut region or any local tri-state area with one buy (Outing, 1997).

Online Campaign Management

As a result of poor measuring and online advertising tracking techniques, managing an online advertising campaign is much more time consuming than buying space and tracking placement in traditional media. Online campaigns average one employee for every $150,000 in billing, while traditional agencies require one employee for every $1 million billed.

Keeping track of online ad placement can be a nightmare as compared to tracking traditional ads. Television and radio stations provide advertisers and agencies with station logs verifying that commercials were inserted correctly and aired at the contracted times. Printed newspapers and magazines send copies of ads or tearsheets from the original issues as testimony of ad placement. Additionally, reliable ratings and circulation figures are calculated into the media buy for cost/reach comparisons.

Online verification of ad placement and reach and standardized tracking systems are way behind those in place for traditional media. Without adequate measurement and auditing techniques, Web site operators and advertising buyers are blindly selling and buying online space. Online campaign managers are forced to call or e-mail each Web site operator to verify that banner ads are placed as ordered, to confirm the number of times rotated ads appeared, and to check on other placement concerns. Moreover, the lack of reliable audience measurement techniques makes reach and frequency comparisons to other media and across Web sites difficult, and it makes online campaign management an even more cumbersome process (Maddox & Bruner, 1998).

Online placement services have arisen out of the need for adequate methods of selling, buying, and tracking cyber-advertisements. Media placement services such as WebConnect and Focalink Communication's *Market Match* specialize in delivering targeted consumers to their clients. Market Match locates Web sites whose users' demographics and psychographics match an advertiser's target audience. Market Match also provides advertisers with a list of best-suited sites along with pricing information. These online placement services also advise advertisers on how much they should pay for ad placement, design online campaigns, and measure advertising response.

The Web auditor I/PRO pushed for an early 1998 launch date of Dispatch, its automated online media buying service. Dispatch takes the guesswork out of online buying and placement with standardized insertion orders, tracking and reporting systems, and cost/reach comparisons across sites (Maddox & Bruner, 1998).

Other companies, such as Flycast Communications Corporation and Narrowline, have developed special software for agencies to target their audience in real time. When a targeted consumer appears at the Web site, the software brings up the appropriate ad. The system pairs clients with publishers and states the price clients are willing to pay for the space. In turn, publishers set a rate for placement, and they often unload extra ad space at discounted prices (Williamson, 1997a).

Advertising Sales and Buys

BANNER ADS   Web advertising rates vary from $30 to $100 per thousand impressions (Rebello, Armstrong, & Cortese, 1996). Prices for a banner ad in some online magazines can run about $15,000 (Hafner & Tanaka, 1996), while sites such as *H.O.T. Coupons* sells local electronic coupon spots for as little as $100 for a six-month posting (personal e-mail correspondence, 1998, April 22).

NBC reputedly offers the most expensive advertising on the Web, with prices ranging from $42,000 per month for a year-long commitment to $58,000 per month for a six-month contract. Infoseek, which offers sponsorship packages at $40,000 per month, and ESPN SportsZone, which charges $15,000–$33,000 per month, are examples of two other popular sites with high advertising fees (Mandese, 1996; ESPN SportsZone, 1998). Despite the high ad costs, ESPN SportsZone attracts over $4 million in annual advertising revenue (Tedesco, 1997a).

The New York Times on the Web makes its *Online Media Kit* available on its Web site. The media kit outlines the cost of running a Web ad, CPMs, guaranteed impressions, and maximum run times. The costs range from $20,000 per month for 500,000 impressions ($40 CPM) to $150,000 for a one-year commitment and a guaranteed seven million impressions ($22 CPM). The media kit site also displays audience demographics, traffic, production specifications, and sales contracts.

CHAT ROOMS Cyberchat, one of the most popular Web pastimes, is attracting advertisers who see chat rooms as great places to post their banner ads. Some discussion sites have hired outside companies to handle their online ad sales. For instance, advertising sales for *WebChat Broadcasting*'s more than two hundred public chat rooms is conducted by Softbank Interactive Marketing. Marketers are still somewhat hesitant to advertise in talk rooms but are enticed by the overwhelming number of online chatters. WebChat claims about 5.5 million page views per day and offers companies the chance to tap into this huge online audience by selling ad space outside the chat rooms for a cost-per-thousand price ranging from $18 to $50 and by giving free ad space within chat rooms. Many chat rooms and discussion forums are topic-centered and thus attract audiences with common interests, hobbies, and lifestyles, propelling many advertisers to vie for the opportunity to reach these targeted audiences. Chat rooms are becoming such a popular venue for posting product messages that by the year 2000 they are expected to contribute close to $1 billion of the total online advertising revenue (Cleland, 1996b, 1997).

ONLINE GAMES From an advertiser's standpoint, Web sites that feature games attract a young audience of loyal, imaginative players who are prime customers for many products. Most players of online games are males between the ages of 18 and 34 who stay on for twenty-five minutes to more than one hour per session. There are many places on the Web to play games, some in exchange for demographic information, and some for a fee. *Total Entertainment Network* (TEN) charges subscribers a flat monthly rate and places ads in the center of pages so users cannot help but see them when selecting games (McGinty, 1997).

Hewlett-Packard posts an online ad that is a playable version of the old electronic game Pong, except a player competes with the computer. While players are hitting the "ball" back and forth, they are continually exposed to the HP logo that is placed in the middle of the playing field.

Berkeley Systems has devised an online interactive ad-game based on its "You Don't Know Jack" computer game. Full-motion ads appear between the quiz show's rounds, accompanied by lively, sarcastic voice-overs. The ads are with-it and attention-getting, are an important part of the game, and add to the overall feeling of fun and excitement (Bannan, 1997).

SPONSORSHIPS Many companies are looking for new ways to entice advertisers and a steady revenue stream to their Web sites by promoting cyber-sponsorships. Similar to television in the 1950s, where one company would sponsor an entire program, such as the *Colgate Comedy Hour,* Web sites, chat rooms, and discussion forums are ripe for advertising sponsorships that give companies exclusive rights to send their messages to a targeted audience.

Rather than just selling banner ad spots, many Webmasters are offering to share their online space with an advertiser's products or service. For example, the *Washington Post*'s online book review section recently accepted a sponsorship deal from Crown Books, which sells its books directly from the site. *Epicurious,* Condé Nast's gourmet-food cybersite, offers visitors a combination of editorial and advertising content with sponsor Robert Mondavi offering tips on serving wine with food. Starbucks coffee appropriately sponsors Warner Bros.' Insomniacs Asylum page, and *CNN Interactive* offers sponsorship packages for such online features as the golf report and the skiing report (Cleland, 1996c).

Some sites are coming under fire for not clearly indentifying their sponsors. A San Francisco entertainment site emerged as a hot new online place to go for the latest Bay Area happenings. Although on the surface, *Circuit Breaker* appeared to be similar to hundreds of other sites of its ilk, it turned out to be sponsored by Brown and Williamson tobacco (makers of Lucky Strike cigarettes). This was not mentioned anywhere on the site. Before gaining access to interactive features, unsuspecting visitors were asked to share information about themselves including whether or not they were smokers. After the Center for Media Education threatened to expose the site to the Federal Trade Commission for unethical business practices, Circuit Breaker added the Brown and Williamson logo to the homepage and made it clear that the site was sponsored by the cigarette maker (Chapman, 1997). By the summer of 1998, Web users could no longer access the site without first typing in a password and user ID. Entering the URL brings up a window requesting the required information.

Many consumers are concerned about being caught off guard by sponsored pages that blur product information with sales pitches. In traditional media, most everyone knows how to differentiate between advertising and editorial content, but on the Web the distinctions may not be so clear, especially to novice users. Many new users approach the Web with trepidation. After all, it is a new medium and people may feel its content to be somewhat unreliable. Therefore, it is crucial that Webmasters maintain a Web site's integrity by clearly marking and separating advertising messages from editorial content. Sponsored Web pages should be designed so that consumers are aware of the source of information and possible content bias.

PRODUCT PLACEMENT   A lovable ET munching on Reese's Pieces in the movie *ET* sealed product placement as a viable alternative to traditional advertising. Movies do not sell advertising space, of course, but showing actors and characters using a product can be just as effective as a traditional ad. Product placement is not limited to movies; television and radio also embed products and company names within their programs. In the early radio soap opera *Oxydols' Own Ma Perkins,* references to the laundry detergent were often written into the script.

Now, products are being placed within Web "programs." Honda and K Swiss were among the first companies to pay the popular online soap opera *The Spot* about $15,000 to weave a month's worth of product mentions into the story (Grumann, 1996).

INFOMERCIALS   Even the Web cannot escape infomercials. Narrative Communications has designed an infomercial format for selling products online. The infomercials are designed to attract the attention of Web users who may gloss over traditional banner ads. Using its Enliven technology, Narrative Communications employs compelling animation, colorful graphics, and interactivity to create jazzy infomercials that disguise sales pitches as product information. Online infomercials are as poorly received online as they are on television, with many Web users reacting unfavorably to ads that resemble editorial content. Users' negative attitudes toward infomercials are causing many Webmasters to rethink and resist accepting infomercials on their sites (Wingfield, 1997).

CLASSIFIED ADVERTISING   Whether people are searching for jobs across the country, looking for a summer home in a faraway resort area, seeking a classic car, or just curious about who is selling what, online classifieds are an easy-to-access, all-in one search tool. Newspapers are hoping to reap a profit from posting their classifieds online. As one newspaper spokesman remarked, "The Internet is probably the most significant new event we've had since someone figured out what a classified ad is" (Kelly, 1996, p. S23).

Classified ads have long been a strong revenue-generating service for newspapers and a favorite section with readers. Classified ads contribute to almost 40 percent of newspapers' overall revenue, translating into about $40 billion annually. And now, newspapers are taking their classifieds online to promote themselves globally, provide an important service to readers, and generate additional revenue. Industry experts predict that 60 percent of all online newspapers will soon offer classified sections (Kelly, 1996).

Overall, online classifieds generated $16.6 billion in revenue in 1997, up from only $100 million in 1996. Further, classifieds are expected to bring in $1.5 billion by the year 2002. Newspapers need to capture a large share of those online classified dollars. They face losing almost 10 percent of their printed classified revenues to online sites, especially to sites such as employment services and others that specialize in classified ads (Fessler & Shinkle, 1997; Vadlamudi, 1997).

Some newspapers are offering classifieds on their home sites, while other papers are combining their efforts by listing their classifieds en masse on neutral Web sites. *The New York Times* and *The Chicago Tribune* offer their employment, auto, and real estate classifieds free of charge to their Web site visitors. *The Chicago Tribune* initially charged advertisers a small fee to post their ad on the Web. More recently, the newspaper has increased overall classified rates but now includes the Web as part of the print package (Kelly, 1996).

Several online ventures compile classified listings from newspapers around the country into searchable databases. *New Jersey Online* offers classifieds from three regional state papers, and *CareerPath* combines employment classifieds from over fifty-seven newspapers nationwide. *CitySearch* and Microsoft's soon to be launched CityScape are examples of Web sites especially designed as real estate classifieds with regional guides (Kelly, 1996).

A new issue in classified advertising centers around the inclusion of URLs in the ads. For example, a realty company that purchases a large amount of advertising space in the *Patriot News* in Harrisburg, Pennsylvania, was not allowed to include URLs that would direct readers to its Web site in its classified ads. Apparently the *Patriot News* and other newspapers are concerned that businesses that place their URLs within their ads are doing so to direct readers to their Web sites, where they promote their goods and services, rather than purchasing larger ad space for the same purpose. Some newspapers are charging premiums for URLs and others are allowing them in the printed ads but do make them clickable links when repurposed for the online issues. Still other papers encourage the inclusion of URLs in both the print and online issues and are aghast at the thought of restricting them. As one publisher said, "Could we imagine telling people they could not publish their address or phone number in their advertisement?" (Outing, 1998).

COUPONS Even **coupons** are online. Money Mailer recently introduced *H.O.T. Coupons,* a coupon database of local, regional, and national products and services. To localize the coupons, the site asks visitors to enter their home or work zip codes or cities. Web browsers then simply download and print the coupons for discounts at their local retailers. One quick search located downloadable discounts from Fox Photo, Sears Portrait Studios, and Breath Assure.

In competition with H.O.T. Coupons, *Val-Pack Direct Marketing Systems* has launched its own coupon site, and other coupon outlets have gone cyber with Web sites like *The Coupon-Pages, ClipNet,* and hundreds of others (Fitzgerald, 1996). Clipping coupons from online services is easier and more fruitful than rifling through the pages of a Sunday newspaper or a weekly shopper. Many sites neatly organize their coupons into headings such as automotive, entertainment, restaurants, and shopping, which in turn may be further sorted for quick online searching.

Cyber-couponing carries the same advantages as print coupons and more. Localizing cybercoupons attracts new local customers and increases return visits and repeat buys through discounting. Additionally, consumers can download and print out-of-area coupons for vacation or business travel that may not be available from their local print media. Although advertisers have been slow to post online coupons, many are beginning to include coupons as part of their Internet advertising campaigns.

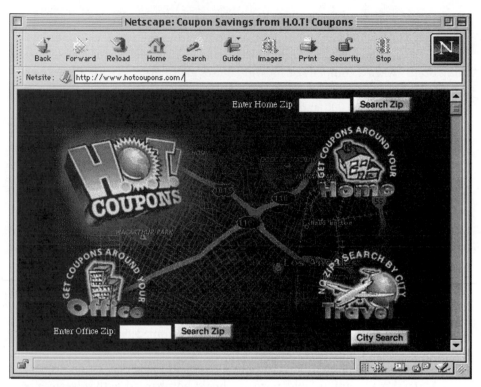

FIGURE 7.5 HOT Coupons Homepage

NEWSLETTERS Just as people subscribe to favorite magazines that are mailed to the subscribers' home addresses, many are subscribing to e-mail newsletters and information sheets that are sent to their e-mail boxes on a regular basis. E-mail newsletters are hot advertising vehicles because they deliver a targeted audience that is already interested in products relating to the newsletter's content.

TipWorld, one of the premiere online publishers of computer-related information, offers subscriptions to various online newsletters. Subscribers are regularly treated to tidbits of information concerning such topics as Web sites and software. TipWorld delivers a loyal audience of interested readers and claims it retains 83 percent of its subscribers each month. For a CPM of about $30, top advertisers, such as Microsoft, get a half-screen banner ad and several text-only mentions scattered throughout the newsletter (Resnick, 1997).

E-MAIL ADVERTISING E-mail is still the most widely used Internet service, and one that has caught the eye of advertisers. E-mail may appear to be a promising method of delivering commercial messages, but it has captured the wrath of users who are up in arms at receiving unsolicited sales pitches. E-mail advertising is widely thought of as an unacceptable use of e-mail and has earned the term **spamming.** According to Web folklore, the term *spam* comes from the popular Monty Python saying, "Spam, spam, spam," pronounced with a British accent, of course. Spamming occurs when a company or individual uses the Internet as a low-cost advertising vehicle by sending out unsolicited promotional messages. America Online alone handled between 700,000 and 4.2 million pieces of junk e-mail *per day* in 1997, about twice as much as in the previous year (Branscum, 1998). It is hard to imagine just how many spammed messages travel through the network in addition to the ones passed on through AOL.

While many people blast spamming, others feel that old-fashioned "netiquette" (polite Net behavior) should acquiesce to free enterprise. One such defender of spamming is Sanford Wallace, president of Cyber Promotions, Inc., a bulk e-mail company. Wallace's company makes its server available to its clients to send unsolicited e-mail. For a small fee, anyone can deluge the network with junk e-mail, and they can even disguise their identity. Spamming opponents have filed suit against Cyber Promotions and spamming in general. They claim that if every business were allowed to clog the network with unsolicited e-mail, the whole system could shut down. After Earthlink, an ISP, settled a $2 million suit against Cyber Promotions, Wallace retired from the spamming business (Branscum, 1998). While efforts are under way to make spamming illegal, several companies have developed software that blocks junk e-mail, although none are 100 percent foolproof (Branscum, 1997).

Many e-mail address holders resent being bombarded with advertisements through what is considered by many to be a personal electronic mailbox. Despite objections to e-mail advertising, companies such as *Hotmail, Juno Online,* and *NetCreations* have initiated advertiser-sponsored e-mail services. Companies specializing in e-mail advertising are betting that people will tolerate and even welcome advertising creeping onto their screens in exchange for free e-mail access—so far, Hotmail's 13 million customers are happy with the arrangement.

Hotmail may well be the hottest free electronic mail service available. By spring 1998, Hotmail claimed 13 million subscribers and a growth rate of 80,000 new signups per day (Gajilan, 1998). Subscribers are drawn to Hotmail's hassle-free system, which is accessible from any browser. Hotmail includes a built-in spell-checker, a thesaurus, and other writing tools for e-mail perfectionists. Hotmail sends its customers personalized news feeds and advertisements in exchange for free e-mail. Although they will not reveal how much money they bring in, Hotmail's advertising revenue is increasing between 15 and 20 percent per month, demonstrating that profits can be made on the Internet ("The Top Twenty-Five," 1997).

To use Juno Online's free service, users need to download a special software package available on the company's Web site. Users then dial a local number to retrieve and send their e-mail. The company offers two advertising options: an expanded banner ad or showcase ad. Banner ads are displayed in thirty-second rotations with a minimum of five exposures per user, and are linked to the advertiser's expansion screen, where customers can get more information. Showcase ads are four times larger than banner ads and are displayed more prominently. Showcase ads dominate the screen while customers connect to the main computer to access or send e-mail.

NetCreations asks users in advance if they would like to receive promotions and if so, what types. For example, someone interested in gardening could sign up to receive special offers for gardening tools. Companies that sign on with NetCreations have their ads sent to targeted consumers for as little as 10 to 15 cents per e-mail, a huge savings over the U.S. Postal Service. NetCreations reported revenues of $500,000 in 1996, and estimated between $1.5 million and $2 million at the end of 1997 (NetCreations, 1997).

From a marketer's standpoint, sending out promotional material via e-mail is much more effective than waiting for potential customers to stumble upon their Web page or a page that contains their ad. Most marketers figure that it takes users only a few seconds to recognize and delete a promotional e-mail message, so the addressee is spared from any real harm. In some cases, however, unsolicited e-mail could be detrimental to the advertiser. Recipients of unwanted e-mail could harbor negative feelings toward the advertiser and thus may boycott the company. Despite these objections surrounding e-mail advertising, it just may emerge as a viable delivery system for many types of commercial messages.

INTRANETS Advertising on the Web has become so big that many companies are turning to the idea of selling advertising on their own intranets. An **intranet** is simply a network using Internet software that transmits proprietary and open information among computers housed within an entity such as a corporation. The initial costs of establishing an intranet can be high, leading companies to look for ways to offset the expenditures. First Chicago NBD Corporation plans to include advertising sales as part of its intranet business plan to help defray its costs. It is highly likely that product logos and sales messages like "Nike, Just Do It" will one day crawl across the tops of employees' computer screens as they are checking their e-mail.

WEB RATINGS AND MEASUREMENT

Web Ratings

Most people are familiar with television ratings services that monitor how many households are watching a program, and how many households out of all households watching television at a given time are tuned to a specific program. Ratings also rank television and radio stations in a given market. Ratings and rankings are then used to determine how much money stations should charge for commercial time. Newspapers and news magazines use their circulation figures to determine the cost of ad space. Generally, the program, station, or newspaper that draws the largest audience charges more for its commercial time or advertising space.

Through the years, reliable and accurate means of measuring traditional media audiences have been developed. The Web is a new medium, and one in which commonly used methods of audience measurement do not apply. Earlier in this chapter, several different ways of charging for online ad space were discussed. Determining how much money to charge is largely dependent on how many customers a Web site draws.

Advertising rates based on CPMs, click-through rates, or other price policies raise questions about Web measurement. The most significant problem with establishing a reliable method for counting Web visitors is the difficulty of knowing how many people actually view a Web ad. With traditional media, audiences can be measured and gross impressions can be calculated. There is no precise way to measure the number of Web impressions. Although the number of Web visitors is monitored by number of hits, number of click-throughs, and other means, reliable and accurate measuring tools have yet to be developed. The accuracy and reliability of existing measurement methods are at issue.

Agencies, media buyers, and advertisers want to know how large an audience they are paying for with their purchase of online ad space. During the first few years of the Web's existence, the number of visitors was largely determined by the number of "hits" received on a page. Hits are typically understood as the number of times users access a page. Hits, however, are a very poor measure of the number of unduplicated site visitors. Twelve hits on one site could mean twelve visitors, one user visiting twelve times, or a small number of users visiting several times. There can be, therefore, a much larger number of hits than users, making it virtually impossible to say that the number of hits equates with the numbers of visitors (Edmonston, 1995).

New push technologies and greater reliance on robots and spiders that comb the Web looking for information may further confound estimates of the number of visitors to a site. Each time an automated agent scans through a Web page it is counted as a page view, although a human never saw any of the content. Very few sites are technologically sophisticated enough to differentiate human eye contact from computer eye contact. Robots and other automated searchers account for about 5 percent of all Web traffic. Translated into advertising dollars, a 5 percent overestimation of visitors could mean that in the year 2000, advertisers could waste $250 million on Web ads that people do not see. Conversely, deflating the number of human page views could cost advertisers and publishers millions of dollars in lower ad rates (McGarvey, 1997).

Advertisers are calling for effective methods of determining which banner ads have the farthest reach for the least amount of money and for a reliable means of comparing traffic and other activity across Web sites. Web site operators are clamoring to know who is tapping into their site, and how valuable their audience is to potential advertisers, so that they can set the maximum price for ad space that the market will bear. Besides simply measuring use, more sophisticated Web measurements are needed for understanding how customers respond to cyber-ads, advertisers' Web sites, and the Web itself.

Web Auditors

Many companies are joining the race to establish themselves as the premiere Web ratings service. Many of the companies that measure Web site traffic are referred to as *third parties* because they monitor what goes on at their clients' Web sites. These services employ various auditing techniques and audience measuring methods to go beyond simply counting the number of visitors to a site. Many auditors also monitor click-through rates, verify how many times rotating banner ads were visible, report that ads were placed according to the purchase agreement, provide information on site traffic by day, week, month, and by other variables, and monitor other Web site activity. The price of auditing services varies by firm. Some charge flat monthly fees determined by the amount of information requested. Others charge set-up costs along with monthly fees, and still others charge for each report. Prices generally range from $500 per report to thousands of dollars per month for ongoing monitoring (Maddox, 1997a).

The battle for Web measurement standards is intensifying as companies and organizations experiment with new methods and techniques for delivering reliable and accurate Web ratings. One company that has received publicity for its efforts in Web measurement is Media Metrix, formerly known as PC Meter. The company monitors Web activity by attaching metering devices to thirty thousand home computers. Media Metrix employs a metering system similar to that used by television rating systems. In addition to measuring Web use, the meters gauge what software applications are being used and for how long, and the length and time of day the computer is in use. Media Metrix plans to expand its metering to chat and e-mail usage as well as propriety services such as AOL (Shaw, 1998; Williamson, 1997b).

Mirroring television ratings methods, RelevantKnowledge places its proprietary software in about eleven thousand randomly selected Web users' homes and work computers. The ratings service prides itself on measuring the number of different people who visit a Web site rather than the total number of visits. RelevantKnowledge provides its clients with information such as Web site activity compared to total Web traffic, average page visits per user, demographics of visitors, and site activity broken out by areas within the site (Shaw, 1998; Tedesco, 1997b).

Long known as the leader in measurement of television audiences, Nielsen is entering the arena of Internet audience measurement. Nielsen's *WebAudit* package claims to take the best of television ratings systems to the Web. Subscribers to WebAudit receive user profiles by region, number of hits for all pages within the Web site, average number of user sessions per day, and amount of Web site activity by day and by hour of the day.

Nielsen Media Research partnered with Internet Profiles Corporation (I/PRO) to develop and market software that counts and analyzes Internet user activity. Together, they offer I/PRO's Internet measurement system, I/COUNT, and its site auditing service, I/AUDIT. Data from I/COUNT provides Web site operators with information on numbers of visits to sites and to sections within each site. It also yields information on users' demographics and system configurations of users (Krantz, 1995).

I/AUDIT provides more detailed site analyses than I/COUNT. Monthly or quarterly reports detail audience composition. The software also tracks user habits, including every page users access and the amount of time they spend on each page. I/AUDIT and I/COUNT both provide important customer demographic and Web use information that Web site operators use to determine the cost of ad space on their sites (Krantz, 1995).

Nielsen Media Research, together with Microsoft, has pioneered a ratings measurement system for intercast programs delivered by computers. Although computers are not yet an alternative to television, the companies are banking on the convergence happening soon. Both Nielsen and Microsoft are maintaining their reputations as leaders in their fields with the first ratings system that measures computer intercast programs (Rich, 1997; Tedesco, 1998).

Other companies, such as @plan, NetRatings, and Millward Brown, have joined other third-party monitors in the sprint for the development of the most reliable and accurate Web measurement tools (Rich, 1998). Also in the ratings race are measuring services that provide Web site operators with the software needed to monitor their own sites. Microsoft's Interse server software collects Web site data but allows managers to interpret and analyze the data based on their own business objectives and terminology rather than purchasing a report from a third-party service (Cooper & Duckart, 1997; Vonder Haar, 1997).

Web Auditing

Only about 20 percent of the approximately 1,500 advertiser-supported Web sites are being monitored. Although these sites receive about 80 percent of the Web traffic, many less-accessed sites do not have estimates of the number of visitors to give to their advertisers (Maddox, 1997c).

While many media buyers and advertisers do require site audits before purchasing advertising space, many are still not demanding audited information. Web site operators are reluctant to pay upward of $15,000 per year to have their number of visitors audited, especially when advertisers are hesitant to use the information because of the lack of auditing standards. Until more media buyers and advertisers start demanding audited accounts of Web traffic, many Web site managers will not pursue auditing (Maddox, 1997c).

Measurement Standards

Without measurement standards it is almost impossible to compare sites based on viewership, and no one knows with any certainty which sites are the most cost effective. Particularly troublesome is that Web audience ratings are often taken as absolute numbers rather than as estimates calculated by a less than perfect system. One Internet expert summed up the current state of Web measurement by asserting that ratings numbers "represent a measurement process that is in evolution, but for now has serious shortcomings" (Shaw, 1998, p. 17).

The entire industry is calling for standardized measures of the effectiveness and viewership of World Wide Web advertising. Foremost, there is a need to count total unduplicated site visitors and record the depth of consumer interactivity. Third-party monitors are vital to the accuracy of viewer numbers. Nielsen Media Research, Arbitron, and Audit Bureau of Circulation, among others, are each working on Web measurement tools (Kelly, 1995).

The Coalition for Advertising Supported Information and Entertainment (CASIE) publishes guidelines for cyberspace and interactive television. Entitled *Guiding Principles for Interactive Media Audience Measurement,* their working paper provides an important framework for Web measurement. Definitions of such terms as *hits, pages, visits,* and *users* offer the industry precedents for both acceptable measures of its opportunities and indications of its viability as compared to other media (Berniker, 1995b; CASIE, 1996; Marx, 1996).

ESPN SportsZone is a perfect illustration of the difficulties of Web measurement. Internet Profiles Corporation (I/PRO) identifies ESPN SportsZone as the most frequently accessed of seventy-five selected sites. Media Metrix, on the other hand, lists ESPN SportsZone among its top ten sites, but does not identify it as the number one site, further claiming that it has far fewer visits than previously reported. Different methods of measurement may account for these results. I/PRO measures hits, not users, and fails to distinguish between hits from the same household and hits from different households. Media Matrix samples a universe of only four thousand households, ignoring Web access from workplaces or college campuses (Tedesco, 1996a).

Despite the number of companies developing Web tracking software, no version has yet emerged as the industry standard, resulting in inconsistent measurement. However, the promise of new, consistent measurement services raises hopes that advertisers' acceptance of the Web will boost online spending.

BOX 7.1 TOP WEB SITES

*PC Meter/Media Metrix—Web Audience Reach Estimates**

Web Site	Percentage of Web Audience
1. Yahoo!	36.6%
2. Netscape	35.8
3. WebCrawler	31.9
4. Excite	21.6
5. Microsoft	21.2
6. Infoseek	16.5
7. Lycos	16.3
8. ZDNet	8.0
9. Pathfinder	6.8
10. Weather Channel	4.9
11. Disney	4.8
12. C/NET	4.5
13. AT&T	4.1
14. Sony	3.8
15. Macromedia	3.5

December 1996

*Reach is defined as the percentage of Web-active persons who visited a page within the domain during the month.
Source: Williamson, 1997b

The growing need for standardized measurement tools is matched by the growing demand for verifying third-party monitors. Companies such as the Audit Bureau of Circulation (ABC) and the Business Publishers Association (BPA) examine Web accounting data. Their job is to make sure that third-party trackers and self-monitors comply with measurement procedures and reporting standards. Auditors also check that collected data is error free and that third-party monitors and companies do not misstate or manipulate their records (Cooper & Duckart, 1997).

THE TECHNOLOGY OF WEB ADVERTISING

New interactive capabilities made possible through Java, JavaScripting, and HTML framing codes are changing the look of Web ads. With these tools, alluring interactive graphics and logos create image- and brand-building Web ads.

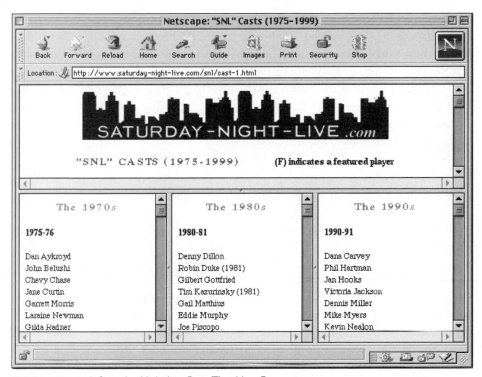

FIGURE 7.6 A *Saturday Night Live* Page That Uses Frames

JavaScripting transforms motionless ads into animated interactive logos that command consumers' attention. ESPN SportsZone uses JavaScripting to rotate ads, and *PointCast Network* creates animated ads for its Web site. The graphics on Honda's banner ad change from the company logo to a car approximately every three seconds. Animated and interactive ads are clicked on more often than motionless banner ads. C/NET contends that its Java-enhanced ads and icons draw four times as many clicks as its inactive ads (Waltner, 1996).

HTML framing codes allow the construction of pages with multiple windows that run simultaneously. In this way, users can see ads in one corner of the screen even as they browse to other Web pages. Generally, Web pages are viewed as one large screen or window display; framing divides the page into smaller, separate windows. Each frame is surrounded by its own border and may even have its own scroll bar. Framing allows Web pages to be divided into separate windows displayed on the same screen at the same time, yet each frame contains separate content and operates independently of the other. Sometimes a frame may even be a separate document with its own URL. In a way, framing operates like television's picture-in-picture, which divides the screen so that two or more programs can be viewed at once. While on many pages frames are clearly visible, on the other pages the frames may purposefully be invisible dividers. Framing technology may one day permit full-motion video commercials to appear in one frame while users surf other pages (Holden & Webster, 1995; Waltner, 1996).

Armed with improved technology, advertisers are creating captivating Web sites that draw viewers with interactive graphics, alluring premiums, and simple navigation. Such innovations inform and interest customers while promoting name and brand recognition, sales, and repeat visits.

EFFECTIVENESS OF ONLINE ADVERTISING

Just as important as the number of people who see an online advertising is the impact the ad has on viewers. From an advertiser's viewpoint, an online ad offers much more than traditional advertising. An analyst for Forrester Research asserts that a traditional ad "tells" customers that a product exists and "sells" customers on the product's benefits. But online advertising picks up where traditional ads leave off. Internet ads also link potential customers to a product Web site that gives them information to think about before purchasing the product. A traditional ad just tells and sells customers, but an online advertisement adds the "link" and "think" elements to the sales process (Schwartz, 1996).

Advertisers need to know whether online visitors are paying attention to the ads they come across while traveling around the Web. Many users claim that banner ads take too long to download. Some banners carry high-resolution pixels, slowing the process of downloading the page to the screen, especially on a computer with low memory. Others gripe that banner ads remind them of junk mail—they are boring and intrusive. This type of complaint, along with interlacing technology and the typically small size of banners, causes many to doubt the ads' effectiveness (Taylor, 1996). Yet others claim that banners yield a high number of advertising impressions, thus making them an effective means of creating brand awareness and influencing buying decisions (Elliott, 1996). Additionally, the lower ad-to-editorial ratio found on most Web pages increases the visibility of banner ads. Web pages that accept banners typically consist of 90 percent editorial content and 10 percent banner ads, whereas printed newspapers generally follow close to a 50/50 ratio of editorial to advertising content (Boyce, 1998).

Advertising rates are often based on how many people click through from a banner ad to the advertiser. New research conducted by the Internet Advertising Bureau shows that awareness largely comes from viewing the ad rather than by clicking through to the advertiser's homepage (Hall, 1997). After tracking slightly more than sixteen thousand individuals' reactions to online advertising, the Internet Advertising Bureau concluded that banner ads are effective. Researchers found that just one exposure to a banner ad increases consumer awareness. Brand perception, affinity toward the advertised product, and purchasing intention all increased after viewing a banner ad. These findings indicate that advertisers need to pay just as much attention to consumers who just look at their banner ads as they do to those who actually click through to an advertiser's site, and that hyperlinking may not be as important to overall advertising effectiveness as once believed.

Other research by DoubleClick claims that banner ads are only effective the first two times an individual views the ad. Beyond the second sighting, banners have little to no impact on the viewer. Advertisers should rotate banners on a site, and they should place banners on various sites to reach as many different individuals as possible for maximum effectiveness (Forrester Research, Inc., 1996).

Fun interactive ads are a great way to increase product recall. Consumers are more apt to remember a company name and product if they have the opportunity to interact with an ad by playing a game or engaging in some other type of activity (Bannan, 1997).

Many advertisers wonder if an online banner ad is more effective than an ad placed in a traditional newspaper or on television. Media buyers are carving up and distributing advertising dollars among many different media, and the most effective media get the largest share of advertising. Studies comparing the effectiveness of one medium against others are nothing new, and research comparing traditional media to online sources is now being conducted. One study declares that about 12 percent of online visitors remember seeing a banner ad, whereas 10 percent of television viewers can recall seeing a commercial (The Internet Index, 1997). In another study, a single exposure to a banner ad was shown to create greater awareness than one exposure to a television commercial or print ad ("Why Internet Advertising," 1997). The differences in recall and awareness may be attributed to the Web being largely an active medium that demands users' attention, whereas television is a more passive medium that require little thought. Only about two-thirds of television viewers report giving programs their fullest attention, and only about one-quarter even pay attention to commercials. Thus, it is not surprising that advertising recall levels are lower on television than on the Web, which requires more concentration and attention from its users (Boyce, 1998).

Other researchers, however, discovered that ads placed in traditional printed newspapers were remembered more often and in more depth than when they were placed online (Sundar, Narayan, Obregon, & Uppal, 1997). The memory difference between ads printed in traditional newspapers and ads placed in online newspapers could be attributed to what is known as a **novelty effect** (Sundar et al., 1997). When people first begin to use a new technology or any new gadget, they tend to use the item just because it is new, and they use it with more frequency than they do when they have owned the product for a while. When products are new, or novel, people also tend to use them differently than when they are more familiar with the products. For example, when people buy a new car, they tend to make unnecessary trips just as an excuse to get behind the wheel. They also drive more carefully, pay more attention to the car's major features, and put off playing with all the extra doodads until they are more comfortable with the car in general. The same may hold true with the Web. Because online newspapers and advertising are a novelty, users may concentrate more on accessing the stories and are less likely to notice the extras such as the advertisements on the page. Users who are unfamiliar with the Web may not yet be able to differentiate between ads and editorials.

The best of Web banner ads can be viewed on the *Microscope* site, which selects and critiques top ads of the week and the best ads of each quarter. Microscope is devoted to excellence in banner ads, and offers tips on selecting appropriate sites, setting advertising objectives and strategies, and gives other online advertising advice.

Overall, Web site advertisers share several goals. Web advertising should enhance brand image, provide product information to a target audience, spur sales, and attract loyal customers (Schwartz, 1996).

ONLINE AD SPENDING AND REVENUE

Several research firms and advertising agencies claim that Web ad spending took a tremendous jump from $55 million in 1995 to $200 million–$300 million one year later. Nineteen ninety-seven saw just over $9 million in ad revenue, with Web spending growing faster than traditional media spending ("Internet Advertising Becomes Mainstream," 1998; Maddox, 1998). Further, forecasters anticipate ad revenues to grow to between $4.3 billion and 7.5 billion by the year 2000 (Cooper & Duckart, 1997; Elsworth, 1997; Hall, 1997; Maddox, 1998; Rebello, Armstrong, & Cortese 1996; "Web Becomes a Viable," 1997). However, other claims of online advertising revenue are not so high. Forrester Research reports that online advertiser spending reached only $74 million in 1996, and Simba Information, Inc., claims revenues climbed only to $110 million. Moreover, both companies, along with several other Web analysts, forecast that by the year 2000 the Web will reap about $2 billion in advertising revenue, which is less than half of other spending projections (Blundon, 1996). The discrepancy in spending forecasts may be due to the belief that the Web's enormous advertising capacity and low demand will result in declining Web ad prices and overall spending (Curme, 1996).

Although an enormous amount of money is spent on Web advertising, it is still significantly less than the amount invested in traditional media. After the first half of 1996, Web ad expenditures were only about 10 percent of the amount spent

BOX 7.2 TOP TEN ADVERTISERS ON THE WEB (1996)

By advertising spending		By advertising revenue	
Microsoft	10.7 million	Netscape	24.3 million
AT&T	6.7	Yahoo!	16.5
Excite	5.9	Infoseek	16.3
Netscape	5.3	Lycos	10.9
IBM	4.9	Excite	10.7
Infoseek	4.6	C/Net	9.3
Nynex	3.6	ZD Net	8.7
Yahoo!	3.5	WebCrawler	6.7
Lycos	3.5	ESPNET	5.7
C/Net	2.6	Pathfinder	5.3

Source: Elsworth, 1997

on television network commercials alone, and far less than the $200 billion spent annually on U.S. advertising (Curme, 1996; Williamson 1996b). Two-thirds of Web advertising spending is done by telecommunication and computer companies, with Microsoft leading the way, followed by AT&T (Elsworth, 1997).

Although it is difficult to estimate Internet ad spending and to determine who is really making money, it is estimated that online advertising revenue distribution is skewed, with about 60 percent of it going to the ten most visited Web sites, including the search engines (Easton, 1996; Elsworth, 1997). Netscape reaped the largest Web advertising profits in 1996, followed by Yahoo! and Infoseek (Elsworth, 1997).

In many cases, dollar for dollar, Web advertising can be more expensive than television or newspapers. It costs roughly $40–$70 to reach one thousand adults through Web advertising, but only about $30 to reach the same number of adults with a television commercial aired during prime time (Hofner & Tanaka, 1996; The Internet Index, 1997).

Inconsistent pricing and imprecise Web ratings make it difficult to compare advertising costs with traditional media and to calculate the value and effectiveness of cyber-ads. Uncertainty of costs, effectiveness, and revenue have kept many companies from committing ad dollars to the Web. Coca-Cola and Procter & Gamble are just two companies that have invested very little in the Web and view their online efforts as experimental (Elsworth, 1997). Although online advertising is emerging as a profitable venture, Activmedia reports that only about 16 percent of the commercial sites bring in revenue from advertising (The Internet Index, 1997).

ZAPPING CYBER-ADS

Just as remote control devices (RCDs) are used to zap television commercials by changing channels and VCRs to zip through them by fast-forwarding, Internet Fast Forward (IFF) software also "erases" ads from the face of the screen. IFF, introduced in late 1996 by PrivNet, Inc., uses artificial intelligence and database technology to zap online advertising. Advertising avoidance, a long-time concern of the television industry, has now made its way onto the Web.

The advertising industry operates under the basic premise that intensive exposure is necessary for commercial message recall. Television commercial avoidance is clearly of concern to the media and advertising industries, as viewers are no longer a passive, captive audience, but an active one with the capability of selecting what they want to see. And now, with IFF, Web users can also be an active audience, deciding for themselves if they want to see an online advertising message.

Many studies have been conducted examining the effects of zipping and zapping on the effectiveness and recall of television commercials. The less commercial exposure a viewer chooses, the less message effectiveness, perception, and recall. With RCDs, viewers can zip or zap commercials and thus choose their own level of exposure to advertising messages. But before viewers have the time to push their RCD channel button to avoid a commercial, they usually end up seeing at least a few seconds of it—long enough to identify the product. When fast-forwarding through taped television programs, researchers have found that viewers attend to their screens and thus see and recognize commercials, albeit only in portions or in double or triple the speed. But even with a small amount of exposure the effects of zipping and zapping can in many cases be minimized, especially if the product or product name appears on the screen during most of the commercial's duration (Stout & Burda, 1989).

IFF's biggest threat to advertisers is that unlike zipping and zapping television commercials, Web users do not have to see any portion of the ads. Clearly, IFF jeopardizes Web ad recognition and recall and raises concerns about the economy of Web advertising. Web sites will have a difficult time justifying their advertising rates if consumers are blocking the ads. Just as the television industry bases its advertising rates on a guaranteed audience, so do many Web sites. With new ways of blocking cyber-ads, these audiences can no longer be guaranteed, which may eventually decrease the effectiveness of online advertising and thus lower its cost.

Online advertisers and industry experts express mixed opinions concerning any widespread use of IFF. Some claim that Web users think online ads are intrusive, and they resent having to spend the extra time waiting for them to download. Others cite online advertising response as support for their contention that users like Web ads and appreciate the ease of obtaining product information. According to one research company, 33 percent of all users have bookmarked at least one advertiser's homepage, 26 percent requested additional product information, and 10 percent have purchased a product online, leading at least one Web publisher to claim that users read its Web newspapers and magazines primarily for the advertisements (Sucov, 1996).

Advertisers have not yet expressed much concern about IFF because online advertising activity is on the rise and IFF has not been widely adopted by users. However, once consumers discover IFF, and do not mind paying the $10 fee, they may happily opt to zap commercialism from the Web (Sucov, 1996).

ONLINE ADVERTISING ASSOCIATIONS

With burgeoning Web commerce comes the need to support and promote online advertising and to establish ethical standards. The Internet marketplace attracts diverse companies and a global audience, necessitating a forum for discussion and decision making regarding business on the Web. Several associations have been organized to tackle Web advertising issues.

The formation of the Internet Advertising Bureau (IAB) is an indication of the intense need to bring a unified code of advertising to the Web. The IAB was organized in 1996 by some of the Web's biggest players, such as Microsoft, Juno Online, and Infoseek, who are putting aside their rivalries for the sake of setting advertising standards and studying ways to maximize the effectiveness of cyber-ads (Voight, 1996).

One of the IAB's first attempts at standardization came with its recommendation for establishing eight standard sizes for banner ads. Standardization is common in the advertising industry as television and radio commercials typically run 15 seconds, 30 seconds, 45 seconds, or 60 seconds long, and many print publications' advertisements are generally sized using standard column inches. Yet, there seems to be some difficulty establishing standard cyber-ad sizes. Designers are reluctant to make significant changes in their Web sites to accommodate the ads, and advertisers do not want to spend the time and money it takes to resize ads to fit each site's specifications. Additionally, organizations, such as CASIE, are proposing other standard sizes that do not necessarily coincide with the IAB's. For instance, the current most common size for banner ads, 468 × 60 pixels, was not among the six standard banner sizes recommended by CASIE, which caused the IAB to balk at CASIE's recommendations (Taylor, 1996).

The Internet Advertising Association (IAA), which boasts just over seven hundred members, was established in 1996 to develop standards for online advertising. The IAA is committed to the following activities regarding Web advertising: (1) setting ethics standards, (2) developing guidelines for self-regulation, (3) assisting members with creating effective online campaigns, (4) conducting seminars and conferences, (5) assisting individuals in removing their names from advertising distribution lists, (6) working with Congress and other governing bodies in establishing legislation, and (7) promoting the Internet as a new medium.

Another association, the Internet Local Advertising and Commerce Association (ILAC), is a nonprofit organization primarily devoted to local Internet market issues. Some of ILAC's goals include establishing standard directory search categories and developing standards and strategies to ease advertising buys across multiple, local Internet products (New Internet Association, 1997).

AGENCY PRESENCE ON THE WEB

Advertising agencies are gearing up for an interactive world. They are in the forefront of Web development and recognize the importance of moving their clients onto the Web. Agencies are operating under the premise that interactivity is in and is here to stay. Agencies are breaking new ground in Web advertising sales, development, maintenance, pricing, and medium measurement.

Online technology allows advertising agencies to sell their most important product: themselves. Thousands of advertising agencies of all different sizes have posted homepages of their own; however, only half of the top ten revenue grossing agencies have set up shop in cyberspace (Carmichael, 1998).

BBDO, DDB Needham Worldwide, TBWA/Chiat/Day/Venice, Young & Rubican, and _Ogilvy & Mather_ are a few examples of well-known agencies that are going strong online. On many agency sites, visitors can find information such as client lists, agency history, staff biographies, and even interactive games (Carmichael, 1998). Ogilvy & Mather's Web site, _BrandNet,_ includes downloadable commercials (Riedman, 1996).

A spokesperson for TBWA Chiat/Day/Venice claims that an effective Web presence must precede an agency's attempt to meet clients' online advertising needs: "We have to experiment on ourselves before we can ask our clients to get involved" (Riedman, 1996, p. 25).

The Web has prompted many agencies to update their corporate structures by creating interactive media departments. Years ahead of its time, Ogilvy & Mather established an interactive department in the early 1980s. The agency has since emerged as one of the best new media agencies today. Although Ogilvy & Mather started experimenting with interactive media a long time ago, it is the medium and small-sized agencies that have taken the lead in online advertising. Smaller agencies are generally more flexible and can more quickly add an interactive component to their organizational structures. New personnel with online skills can be quickly hired and are more easily integrated into a smaller agency's corporate culture (Gleason & Williamson, 1996).

Recognizing the need to stay ahead of the game, larger agencies such as J. Walter Thompson's San Francisco office, McCann-Erickson Worldwide, and BBDO have opened separate operating units for interactive media (Williamson, 1995). While many agencies are hiring their own Web designers and technical programmers, interviews with some of the countries' top advertising agencies found that as late as 1996, about six out of ten did not have personnel dedicated to Internet efforts (Forrester Research, Inc., 1996).

Rather than hiring their own team of online specialists, many agencies have shopped out their online work to stand-alone interactive or Web firms. Many advertisers have also contracted with Web specialists rather than with traditional agencies. Many Web design companies are launched by entrepreneurs with expertise in Web design but not necessarily in advertising and marketing. Conversely, many advertising experts lack Web design experience. Spurred by increasing competition and the need for personnel with expertise in online media, many larger agencies have purchased smaller interactive firms.

Omnicom, a leading advertising agency, spent over $10 million to purchase seven small Web design companies. This landmark purchase strengthened the Web's legitimacy as an advertising medium. Omnicom's strategy merges the best of the advertising and the Web worlds.

In contemporary agencies, Web developers work closely with advertising experts to create Web sites that are graphically appealing and yet sophisticated enough to produce brand recognition and sales. Agencies are leading their clients to the Web and showing them how to make the most of the new medium through the creation of homepages and cyber-ads.

Agencies anticipate that online advertising will be hugely profitable. Although online revenue generated by designing client Web pages and selling ad space is flowing in, many agencies have yet to realize much of a profit. The Web is still a new medium, and agencies are still determining appropriate fees for interactive work. Agencies negotiate the lowest possible price for their clients who buy Web ads, but at the same time they are getting the highest price possible for their clients who offer ad space on their sites. Designers are struggling with setting appropriate fees for Web site creation and maintenance, and for creating online campaigns and banner ads. Agencies are pouring money into new equipment and personnel, and into establishing interactive departments. Investments are in many cases exceeding revenues.

SUMMARY: A NEW MEDIUM FOR ADVERTISING

The Internet, particularly the Web, gives advertisers an unprecedented means of reaching a global marketplace. The Web has the unique capability of reaching both a mass audience of individuals from around the world and selected target audiences. With the number of Web users increasing at an explosive rate, a prosperous target market enhances the total advertising package. With online buys, advertisers can connect directly to their consumers and receive immediate feedback about their products and services.

There are many benefits to online advertising. Advertisers benefit by reaching both a worldwide market and a specific group of customers. Online ads can be posted and changed quickly and are less expensive to produce than traditional media ads. Small time advertisers who go online can easily compete head-to-head with firms that have deeper pockets. Web technology allows companies to compile demographic profiles about their customers and receive feedback on a daily basis.

Consumers benefit from interactivity and the convenience of having product information and ordering forms at their fingertips. The Web empowers consumers, inaugurating new levels of dialogue between advertisers and the public. For perhaps the first time, consumers have a direct and powerful voice in product innovation and advertising strategy.

The Web is a dynamic force that is changing basic advertising tenets. Web advertising sales teams are hitting the streets with new pitches in the hope of selling this important medium. Yet, confusion abounds as a hodgepodge of different ad sizes and imprecise audience measurement techniques addle media buyers. Additionally, new opportunities, such as Web site sponsorships, classified ads, coupons, intranets, and e-mail advertising, further confound buying strategies.

Cyber-advertising expenditures and revenue indicate that marketers and customers are flocking to the Web. Online commerce is a rapidly growing new business phenomenon, and advertising is one of its most important elements. Even with some unresolved pricing and measurement issues, the Web has become the hottest advertising and marketing medium around.

Ad agencies are creating their own Internet advertising departments as businesses are learning of the World Wide Web's marketing potential. With new Web page creation tools like Java and JavaScripting, alluring graphics and interactive logos create image- and brand-building Web pages that push the boundaries of traditional media. For the first time in history, consumers are able to interact with advertisements by clicking on banners, playing games, exploring corporate Web sites, and providing feedback.

Internet associations such as the IAB, the IAA, and the ILAC are hard at work devising new strategies and making recommendations for standardizing Web advertising. Consistency in ad sizes, audience measurement, and ethics are just a few areas of concern and are necessary if cyber-advertising is going to continue its rapid growth and be viewed as a serious and viable advertising vehicle by corporations and consumers.

Overall, the World Wide Web is a powerful tool that is changing the way goods are bought, sold, and advertised. It is also changing the face of information, technology, and communication worldwide. The Web has already revolutionized advertising and marketing. Now, advertisers and marketers must appeal to techno-savvy consumers to enhance opportunities for growth in Internet marketing. Large and potentially profitable, the medium changes relationships to technology in our techno-society. Where it goes from here, however, remains to be seen.

CHAPTER LINKS

Accipiter—http://www.accipiter.com

The Amazing Send Me a Dollar Page—http://server.tt.net/send-me-a-dollar/

(Bellcore) Adapt/X—http://www.bellcore.com/Adaptx

Berkeley Systems—http://www.berksys.com

BBDO—http://www.bbdo.com

BrandNet (Ogilvy & Mather)—http://www.ogilvy.com

The Chicago Tribune—http://www.chicago.tribune.com

C/NET Online—http://www.cnet.com

CareerPath—http://www.careerpath.com

CitySearch—http://www.citysearch.com

ClipNet—http://www.Webomatic.com/ClipNET/

CNN Interactive—http://cnn.com

The Coalition for Advertising Supported Information and Entertainment (CASIE)—http://www.commercepark.com/AAAA/casie/index.html

The Coupon-Pages—http://www.couponpages.com/index.html

DDB Needham Worldwide—http://ddbniac.com

Epicurious—http://www.epicurious.com

ESPN SportsZone—http://ESPN.SportsZone.com/

Get Me Rich Quick—http://www.supranet.com/cindylou/index.html

H.O.T. coupons—http://www.hotcoupons.com/

Hotmail—http://www.hotmail.com

Infoseek—http://www.infoseek.com/

Jonathan Chance—www.fastlane.net/~sandman/help

Juno Online—http://www.juno.com/

Market Match—http://www.marketmatch.com

Microscope—http://www.microscope.com/index.html

Narrative Communications—http://www.narrative.com

NBC—http://www.nbc.com

NetCreations—http://www.netcreations.com/

New Jersey Online—http://www.nj.com

The New York Times—http://www.nytimes.com

The New York Times, Online Media Kit—http://nytimes.com/adinfo/media-main.html

Ogilvy & Mather—http://www.ogilvy.com

Pathfinder—http://pathfinder.com

PointCast Network—http://www.pointcast.com/

Procter & Gamble—http://www.pg.com

Riddler—http://www.riddler.com

The Spot—http://www.thespot.com

TBWA Chiat/Day/Venice—http://www.chiatday.com/factory/

Total Entertainment Network—http://www.ten.net

USA Today—http://www.usatoday.com/

Val-Pak Direct Marketing Systems—http://www.valpak.com

Washington Post—http://www.washingtonpost.com

Web Digest for Marketers (WDFM)—http://wdfm.com/advertising

WebAudit—http://www.nielsen.com

WebChat Broadcasting—http://wbs.net

Young & Rubicam—http://www.yandr.com

REFERENCES

AC Nielsen launches the first independent Internet audit service. (1996, August 22). *AC Nielsen home page.* [Online]. Available: http://acnielsen.com/ [1998, February 21].

@once! Marketing and Advertising. (1995). *@Once home page.* [Online]. Available: http://aoma.com/ima.html

Bannan, K. (1997, February 4). Peppery ads flavor the Web. *PC Magazine,* 29.

Berniker, M. (1995a, October 9). CASIE challenges Nielsen for online/Internet ratings system. *Broadcasting & Cable,* 73.

Berniker, M. (1995b, September 11). Nielsen, I/Pro link to track Internet use. *Broadcasting & Cable,* 57.

Blundon, W. (1996, December). Off the charts: The Internet in 1996. *Internet World, 7* (12), 46–51.

Boveé, C. L., & Arens, W. F. (1986). *Contemporary advertising.* Homewood, IL: Irwin.

Boyce, R. (1998, February 2). Exploding the Web CPM myth. *Advertising Age,* Supplement—Online Media Strategies for Advertising, A16.

Branscum, D. (1997, May 12). King of "spam" and proud of it. *Newsweek,* 90.

Branscum, D. (1998, June 22). The big spam debate. *Newsweek,* 84–86.

Carmichael, M. (1998, March 9). Brochureware dominates in survey of agency sites. *Advertising Age,* S7.

Chapman, F. S. (1997, August). Web of Deceit. *PC World,* 145–52.

Clark, T. (1996). Will Web ad services boost online spending? *Internet Week.* [Online]. Available: http://www.zdnet.com/intweek/print/960603/Web/doc3.html

Cleland, K. (1996a, September 9). Accipiter latest entrant in race to manage ads. *Advertising Age,* 44.

Cleland, K. (1996b, August 5). Chat gives marketers something to talk about. *Advertising Age,* 22.

Cleland, K. (1996c, September 4). Web narrows gap between ads, editorial. *Advertising Age,* S3, S14.

Cleland, K. (1997, January 27). Chat backers are turning talk into action. *Advertising Age,* 32, 37.

Coalition for Advertising Supported Information and Entertainment. (1996). CASIE Guiding Principles of Interactive Media Audience Measurement. [Online]. Available: http://www.comercepark.com/AAAA/bc/casie/guide.html

Cooper, L. F., & Duckart, C. R. (1997, February 10). Zooming in on users. *Communications Week* [Online]. Available: http://tcchWeb.cmp.com/cw/Webcommerce/649Web.htm

Croal, N., & Stone, B. (1996, May 27). Cyberscope: More sites. *Newsweek,* 10.

Cross, R. (1994, October). Will new technology change the marketing rules? *Direct Marketing,* 14–40.

Curme, O. (1996, July, 15). Web commerce in transition—Today's Web advertising will be replaced by a broader business model. *Information Week,* 94.

Damashek, H. (1996, September 4). A tool belt for Web publishers and advertisers. *Advertising Age,* S32.

Donaton, S. (1995, July 10). New media digging up old tools. *Advertising Age,* 16.

Easton, J. (1996, December). Hidden revenue hotspots. *ZD Internet Magazine,* 99–106.

Edmonston, J. (1995, August). When is a Web ad simply too costly? *Business Marketing,* 18.

Elliott, S. (1996, December 3). Banner ads on Internet attract users. *CyberTimes—New York Times.* [Online]. Available: http://www.nytimes.com/Web/docsroot/library/cyber/week/1203ads.html

Elsworth, P. C. T. (1997, February, 24). Internet advertising slowly. *New York Times,* p. C5.

ESPN SportsZone. (1998, February 16). Advertising rate card, ESPN SportsZone home page. [Online]. Available: http://www.starwave.com/saleskit/sz.html

Executive guide to marketing on the new Internet (1996). *Industry.Net home page.* [Online]. Available: http://www.industry.net/guide.html

Fessler, K., & Shinkle, K. (1997, November 2). Papers go online to keep classified ad business. *The Stuart News,* p. D6.

Fitzgerald, K. (1996, March 18). A redeeming opportunity for local coupon providers. *Advertising Age,* 26.

Forrester Research, Inc. (1996). *Media & technology strategies.* [Online]. Available: http://www.forrester.com [1998, January 21].

Freeman, L. (1996, June 22). Internet visitors' traffic jam makes buyers Web wary. *Advertising Age,* S14–S15.

Gajilan, A. T. (1998, April 13). You've got mail—and it's free. *Newsweek,* 80–81.

Gleason, M., & Williamson, D. A. (1996, February 26). The new interactive agency. *Advertising Age,* S1.

Grumann, C. (1996, February 21). Soap operas invade the Internet. *St. Louis Post Dispatch,* p. 3E.

Gupta, S. (1997). Banner ad location effectiveness study. *WebReference.* [Online]. Available: http://Webreference.com/dev/banners [1998, February 1].

Hafner, K., & Tanaka, J. (1996, April 1). This Web's for you. *Newsweek,* 74–75.

Hall, L. (1997, September 29). A banner day for Web ads: Study says they do work. *Electronic Media,* 16.

Hawn, M. (1996, April). Stay on the Web: Make your Internet site pay off. *MacWorld,* 94–98.

Hawkins, D. T. (1994, March). Electronic advertising on online information systems. *Online,* 26–39.

Head, S. W., Sterling, C. H., & Schofield, L. B. (1994). *Broadcasting in America.* Boston: Houghton Mifflin.

Hodges, J. (1996, February 26). It's becoming a small World Wide Web after all. *Advertising Age, 67* (6), 26.

Hoffman, D., and Novak, T. (1995). *Marketing in hypermedia computer-mediated environments: Conceptual foundations.* [Online]. Available: http://www.2000.ogsm.vanderbilt.edu

Holden, G., & Webster, T. (1995). *Mastering Netscape 2.0.* Indianapolis: Hayden Books.

Hutheesing, N. (1996, May 20). An online gamble. *Forbes,* 288.

Huhn, M. (1995, March 20). Time taps WWW sales unit. *MediaWeek, 5* (12), 6.

Hyland, T. (1998, February 2). Web advertising: A year of growth. *Advertising Age,* Supplement—Online Media Strategies for Advertising, A20.

Improving their swing. (1998, February 2). *Advertising Age,* Supplement—Online Media Strategies for Advertising, A45.

Inside USA Today Online. (1998). *USA Today homepage.* [Online]. Available: http://www.usatoday.com/ads/online/online02.htm [1998, February 26].

Internet advertising becomes mainstream. (1998, April 14). *NUA Surveys.* [Online]. Available: http://www.nua.ie/surveys [1998, April 26].

The Internet Index. (1997, October 10). *Open Market homepage.* [Online]. Available: http://www.openmarket.com/intindex

Kaplan, B. M. (1985). Zapping—The real issue is communication. *Journal of Advertising Research, 25* (2), 9–12.

Karpinski, R. (1997, October 6). The Web delivers all the news that fits—and then some. *InternetWeek,* 31–36.

Kelly, K. J. (1995, August). MPA: Pick one standard. *Business Marketing,* (80), 18.

Kelly, K. J. (1996, November 4). Classifieds prove to be a gold mine for online outlets. *Advertising Age,* S23, S27.

Kerwin, A. M. (1997, July 14). "NY Times" Web site lets advertisers get personal. *Advertising Age,* 35.

Krantz, M. (1995, September 11). Web feat: Site auditing. *Mediaweek,* 23.

Maddox, K. (1997a, September 29). IAB study: Click-throughs not as effective as banners. *Advertising Age,* 41.

Maddox, K. (1997b, June 30). K2 unveils interactive banner forms. *Advertising Age,* 27.

Maddox, K. (1997b, September 22). Media buyers want more from Web site audits. *Advertising Age,* 29.

Maddox, K. (1998, April 6). Internet ad sales approach $1 billion. *Advertising Age,* 32, 34.

Maddox, K., & Bruner, R. E. (1998, January 26). New services automate online media planning. *Advertising Age,* 38.

Mandese, J. (1996, January 1). NBC asks $350K for six-month online deals. *Advertising Age,* 4.

Marx, W. (1996, February 26). Light years ahead but still confusing. *Advertising Age,* 18.

McGarvey, J. (1997, March 17). Agents: Artificial inflation of the Web kind. *Interactive Week,* 66–67.

McGinty, R. (1997, March 3). Marketers see Web games as perfect fit for their ads. *Advertising Age,* 26.

Napoli, L. (1996). Omnicom boutique investments mark turning point for advertising on the Web. *New York Times—CyberTimes.* [Online]. Available: http://search.nytimes.com/Web/docsroot/library/cyber/week/ 1018omnicom.html

Nash, K. (1997, January 27). Intranet builders consider ad dollars. *Computerworld, 13* (4), 1.

NetCreations. (1997, Winter). *The Silicon Alley Reporter,* 8, 22.

New Internet association to serve local advertising and commerce marketplace is holding organizational meeting. (1997, February, 20). *Business Wire.* [Online]. Available: http://www.businesswire.com/

Online shopping gets even easier. (1998, May 11). *Newsweek,* 90.

Outing, S. (1997, June 28). Regional Web ad program. *Editor & Publisher.* [Online]. Available: http://www.mediainfo.com

Outing, S. (1998, April 11). Newspapers bar URLs in ads. *Editor & Publisher,* 6.

Rebello, K., Armstrong, L., & Cortese, A. (1996, September 23). Making money on the Net. *Business Week,* 104.

Riedman, P. (1996, January/February). Netscrape. *Creativity,* (4), 24–25.

Riedman, P. (1997, July 21). PointCast direct offers per-click ad banner model. *Advertising Age,* 26.

Resnick, R. (1997, February). Marketing riddle. *Internet World.* [Online]. Available: http://pubs.iworld.com

Rich, L. (1997, August 4). On the right track? *Brandweek*, 46–48.

Sargeant-Robinson, K., & Kaye, B. K. (1997). *Determining the strength of new technology: The World Wide Web's effect on the advertising industry.* Proceedings of the 1997 conference of the American Academy of Advertising, 217–228.

Schwartz, E. I. (1996, February). Advertising Webonomics 101. *Wired*, 74–79.

Shaw, R. (1998, March 2). At least there are no Web sweeps (yet). *Electronic Media*, 17.

Snyder, H., & Rosenbaum, H. (1996). *Advertising on the World Wide Web: Issues and policies for not-for-profit organization.* Proceedings of the American Association for Information Science, 33, 186–191.

Stout, P. A., & Burda, B. L. (1989). Zipped commercials: Are they effective? *Journal of Advertising*, 18 (4), 23–32.

Sucov, J. (1996, October 15). Web-ad blockers don't scare publisers. *Folio*, 25 (15), 27–28.

Sundar, S. S., Narayan, S., Obregon, R., & Uppal, C. (1997). *Does Web advertising work?* Paper presented at the Association of Journalism and Mass Communication annual convention, Chicago, IL.

Taylor, C. (1996, October, 7). Agreeing and disagreeing: CASIE and the Internet Ad Bureau spar over advertising size. *MediaWeek*, 6 (38), 3.

Tedesco, R. (1996a, August 12). Internet spawns new ratings race. *Broadcasting & Cable*, 71–72.

Tedesco, R. (1996b, September 30). NBC makes Olympian showing in 'Net ratings. *Broadcasting & Cable*, 71–72.

Tedesco, R. (1997a, November 17). Internet profit sites elusive. *Broadcasting & Cable*, 74–84.

Tedesco, R. (1997b, September 15). RelevantKnowledge debuts 'Net ratings system. *Broadcasting & Cable*, 107.

Tedesco, R. (1998, February 9). New yardstick for a new medium. *Broadcasting & Cable*, 54.

The top twenty-five unsung heroes of the Net. (1997, December 8). *Interactive Week*. [Online]. Available: http://www.zdnet.com/intweek/ [1998, January 14].

Vadlamudi, P. (1997, October 28). For sale: Classified ads are online moneymaker. *Investor's Business Daily*, p. A9.

Voight, J. (1996, December). Beyond the banner. *Wired*, 196.

Vonder Haar, S. (1997, June 9). Online advertising tools do battle. *Interactive Week*, 23.

Waltner, C. (1996, March 4). Going beyond the banner with Web Ads. *Advertising Age*, 22.

Web becomes a viable channel. (1997, December 22). *Advertising Age*, 21.

Why Internet advertising. (1997, May 5). *MediaWeek*, 7 (18), S8–S13.

Williamson, D. A. (1995, July 17). When buyers become sellers. *Advertising Age*, 12.

Williamson, D. A. (1996a, January 9). CBS to outsource Web ad sales. *Advertising Age*, 3.

Williamson, D. A. (1996b, September 2). Web ad spending at $66.7 million in 1st half. *Advertising Age*, 10.

Williamson, D. A. (1997a, February 24). Online buying moves towards a virtual market. *Advertising Age*, 76.

Williamson, D. A. (1997b, February 24). PC Meter forms two units: Web media and technology. *Advertising Age,* 78.

Williamson, D. A. (1997c, June 16). Study shows banners increase brand awareness. *Advertising Age,* 42.

Wingfield, N. (1997, February 11). It was inevitable: Webomercials. *C/Net.* [Online]. Available: http:www.news.com/News/Item/0,4,7821,4000.html

CHAPTER EIGHT

WEB SITE DESIGN, PRODUCTION, AND AESTHETICS

DESIGNING A WEB SITE

Once a public relations or advertising agency, television or radio station, or any other company or person decides to establish an online presence, their real work of creating a Web site begins. Creating a Web site is not as simple as writing a couple of pages of HTML text and adding some jazzy-looking graphics. Site design requires a thorough understanding of the Web and of its users, and an expertise in marketing, design, and Internet technology.

Detailed planning is the key to a successful Web site. Content, graphics, video, audio, linking pages, and overall site architecture should be mapped out in as much detail as possible before the site goes online. Also, mapping gives designers an image of how each page fits in with the site's overall architecture.

Sites are generally structured as levels. Most sites open at the door, or home-menu page, which introduces the site and links visitors to the various first-level sections or areas within the site. First-level opening pages are linked to second-level material, and those in turn are linked to third-level documents, and so on, with the material on each level usually becoming more specific. For example, the *CNN Interactive* Web site opens with a colorful menu page containing the company logo and three columns of clickable indexes. The first column is a menu of clickable links to areas within the site including "world news," "weather," and "showbiz." The middle of the page is dominated by a summary of the latest news, and in the left-hand column are hypertext links to other top stories. On October 27, 1997, the sell-off of U.S. stocks was the featured late-breaking summary on the main page, which in turn linked to the full story on another page. The complete stock market article mentions that Intel had cut its Pentium chip prices, and it contains hyperlinks to a more detailed story about the price cut and to a menu of other Intel-related documents. From here, visitors can continue to delve deeper into the site and into other Intel-specific information.

Web site design should be approached from the perspectives of both the Web site provider and its users. An online site may be perfectly designed from a company's point of view, but if it does not attract users or encourage repeat visits, then the site is not worth the time and resources of upkeep. On the other hand, numerous and repeat visits mean little if users are just skimming around the site but not using it as the company intended. In the long run, the quality of the visit is just as important as the number of visitors.

Web site design begins with understanding why users access the Web, and then combining the users' needs with the provider's purpose in establishing the site. Putting it all together involves deciding on the site's purpose and goals, content, presentation, design and image, feedback mechanisms, page links, and other architectural considerations, and determining how the site will attract its target audience.

BOX 8.1 DESIGNING A WEB SITE

I. Going online
   A. Outline the primary and secondary purposes for going online
   B. Set goals and objectives
      1. Specify outcomes and measurements
   C. Research and identify target audience
   D. Determine the type of site needed
   E. Select Webmasters and hire supporting staff
      1. Complexity of site
      2. Amount of updating and maintenance

II. Content
   A. Determine content function
   B. Select products and services to feature
   C. Write new content or modify existing content
   D. Include value-added content and interactivity
   E. Encourage repeat visits
   F. Add feedback mechanisms
   G. Schedule updating and changing

III. Organizing a site
   A. Create a site map
   B. Establish category structure
   C. Develop linking pages

IV. Rating and evaluating a site
   A. Develop evaluation criteria
   B. Create a rating scheme

The Web is not a "field of dreams," where if a site is built, people will come; it requires careful, deliberate planning.

Going Online

ESTABLISHING A PURPOSE AND SETTING GOALS   The rush to the Web is in some ways similar to the California Gold Rush, when thousands of people were hoping to strike it rich on their patches of claimed land. In the modern world, many people are galloping to cyberspace and elbowing their way to a patch of claimed Web space where they hope to find handfuls of gold. Removing the dollar signs from before their eyes helps Web site providers form a clearer vision of the Web's potential and a sounder purpose for establishing a site.

It is folly to post an online site without defining clear objectives and goals. Determining the type of site needed is foremost in the planning process. While one provider might need a simple billboard-informational site, another may require an interactive storefront. The overall site architecture depends on the provider's purpose for establishing the site. Careful analysis of the provider's products or services, target audience, budget, and technological expertise should drive the site, not the other way around. Purposes for establishing a Web site include generating revenue, providing basic corporate information, building brand image, offering low-cost, convenient product information, improving customer service, enhancing consumer interest, building a community of online consumers, educating site visitors, acquiring new customers, and maintaining relationships with regular customers.

While the purpose guides a site's basic design and functions, specific goals and objectives measure its success. Goals should be set in quantifiable terms, such as the number of monthly visitors, the number of items sold, the dollar amount of monthly sales, the number of new subscribers, the amount of e-mail feedback, or the number of product inquiries. Also, a fair method of measuring goals should be put in place during the planning stage. For example, some Web sites may measure the number of visitors by counting the number of hits on the opening page, while others may record only those who travel beyond the first-level pages. While some may measure sales by the number of items purchased directly from the site, others may also include items purchased by telephone if the purchaser made a Web inquiry prior to the sale. The absence of clear guidelines that specify exactly how the goals and objectives should be measured could easily mislead executives into thinking their site is successful, when in fact it is performing well below expectations, or the other way around. Setting specific desired outcomes and a reliable system of evaluation keeps providers on top of the site's performance and alerts them to any problems so that changes can be made promptly.

UNDERSTANDING MOTIVATIONS AND TARGETING AN AUDIENCE   The Web is a new interactive medium that is undergoing many changes, and reasons for using it are shifting as it develops and evolves. People are turning to the Web to satisfy their needs for entertainment, social interaction, information and news, and self-enhancement. Individuals also look to the Web to conduct research, shop, and often just to pass the time or escape from other responsibilities (Kaye, 1998; Wilson, 1997).

At times, people may access the Web instrumentally, only when they have a clear purpose in mind, and at other times they connect ritualistically, just to give themselves something to do. Motivations can change from one Web session to another. Sometimes an individual may be linking from site to site just to pass the time, and at other times he or she may connect for the sole purpose of accessing a specific item from a favorite news site. Also, some users may be more inclined to constantly move from one site to another, while others would rather explore a small number of sites in more depth.

Web site designers need to be aware of these changing motivations and should attempt to create sites that accommodate the needs of their target audience. Identifying the target audience and researching their needs is a first step in Web site design. Next, the Web site provider's needs and goals should be woven in with their identified customers' needs and motivations. A Web site cannot possibly be all things to all people, but it should focus on meeting the needs of its most likely customers. Also, site designers may want to start out addressing one or two of the most important motivations and needs, and gradually add features that will satisfy a larger audience.

DETERMINING THE TYPE OF SITE NEEDED AND HIRING PERSONNEL Once the goals and objectives have been set and the target audience identified, Webmasters and supporting staff need to be hired. Webmasters and executives should work together to design the type of site that will best fulfill the provider's objectives. Time and budget considerations often influence the general design and complexity. If a firm is in a great hurry to get a site online, or is facing severe monetary restrictions, it may be best to begin with a billboard-type site, and gradually add interactive elements and sales components. However, a company may choose to go with a large, multilayered, in-depth site that contains many interactive elements, a security or password system, and a transaction element. Another, such as a news site, may opt for a less complex presence, but one that requires frequent or daily updates. Complexity and depth, together with the projected amount of maintenance and updating, determine the size of the supporting staff needed to keep the project online. Other personnel issues include the Webmaster's role and which staff will perform roles such as content editor, art designer, technician, purchaser of new software, online security manager, and liaison to read and respond to e-mail.

Before even one word is written in HTML script, the goals, objectives, and the budget need to be set, a target audience identified, personnel hired, and the general type of site determined and mapped out.

ONLINE CONTENT A Web site's success depends on how well the content matches the needs of the targeted audience and the provider's goals and objectives. Just because the Web is not limited by space and airtime does not mean that all possible content should be put online, or that the editorial can ramble or be disjointed. A strong editorial plan prioritizes content so the most important information is featured up front, followed by links to less important pages. Also, items of little consequence should not be put on the same page as important or frequently accessed information. There is nothing more annoying than waiting and waiting for a page to download only to discover that the delay was caused by a photo of the company mascot, which is totally irrelevant to the rest of the content.

Content needs to be planned around the general theme or purpose of the site. If generating revenue through sales is the main purpose, then the site should be designed around the featured products and services. The general tone of the site, including content, graphics, and audio or video, must be consistent with the overall objectives.

Those new to creating Web sites often erroneously think that simply posting existing content is all they need to do. Thus, Web pages are often nothing more than boring product specs, or seemingly endless lines of colored text. Using existing materials created for other media, such as print or broadcast, saves time and resources, but most must be modified and adapted for use on the Web. Often print layouts need to be adapted for on-screen viewing, which may involve deleting or adding white space, adding hyperlinks and other navigational tools, changing fonts and font sizes, condensing or editing text, and rewriting long sentences and paragraphs into shorter blocks for quick reading. Additionally, editing and cutting long video and audio components significantly reduces downloading time (Thompson, Thompson, & McLaughlin, 1996). While it may make good sense for a Web site creator to use existing material, much of the material should first be modified and adapted before posting to the Web.

Value-added content often serves to hold visitors' attention and increase time spent on the site. Inclusion of value-added content and interactivity largely depends on the overall objectives of the site and the resources available for extra bells and whistles. However, many people insist that value-added content and interactivity are essential to the success of any site, and that simply placing existing text-only documents on the Web is very short-sighted and misses the point of having an interactive medium in the first place. Interactivity and value-added content create interest, delight visitors, initiate two-way communication, and spur users to take actions that increase their involvement with the site and, hence, with the company and its products and services. Exploring the Web's potential and challenging existing sales and marketing models leads to fascinating sites that keep visitors coming back for more adventures in cyberspace.

Frequently updating and adding content keeps a site interesting and fresh. It is poor practice to keep material posted for months before making changes. Depending on its timeliness, some copy should be updated on a monthly, weekly, or even daily basis. Even copy that is not time-sensitive should be spruced up and altered after it has been online a while. The Web is unlike most other media, where the publishing or broadcast date lets users know if the information is current. Generally, most Web users do not have any way of knowing how long information has been online unless the posting date has been added to the page. Although there are no clear guidelines on how often Web material should be changed, many sites tell visitors when the material was last updated and when they can expect further updates.

Planning online editorial involves matching the content's general look and tone with overall objectives and goals, selecting which products and services to feature, deciding which types of content to provide, determining whether to write new material or adapt existing documents for the Web, determining how much value-added content and interactivity should be included in the site, and developing a schedule for updating and changing the editorial. Additionally, building feedback mechanisms and creating a cyber-environment that encourages repeat visits strengthens an online presence.

Organizing a Web Site

The overall organization of a Web site largely depends on the provider, the purpose of the site, and the type of site being developed. A site should be organized for the sake of the visitors and not for the provider. It is the designer's responsibility to create a site through which visitors can easily navigate to find whatever information they are seeking. Visitors who cannot find their way around tend to get frustrated and leave the site altogether. Visitors do not want to waste time clicking on one dead-end page after another, especially if they are connecting through a slow modem. Organizing an easy-to-navitage site is a very important part of establishing an online presence and is crucial to the site's success.

MAPPING   Web sites can be as simple as a main menu page with a few linking pages, or they can encompass hundreds of pages housed within many linking sections. Just as blueprints are used to design a house, Web blueprints are used to design a site. A blueprint is a map that shows how various sections and pages are located within the site and how they are linked together. A map presents a larger view of the overall design and is used as a guide for developing the site.

Web sites are configured in many different ways with different systems of navigation. Some sites are organized like books, where the menu page acts as a table of contents and visitors read the pages in some sort of orderly, linear fashion. Most other sites are mapped in some sort of a hierarchical manner, with a center homepage that links to each of the site's various sections, each of which is made up of a set of linking pages. Still other sites are configured as a wagon wheel, with the main page as the hub that is linked to all other pages, which are in turn linked to each other. Many sites are designed using a combination of these structures, and others use their own unique systems of organization and links.

Movement through a site is either horizontal or vertical. The homepage is usually considered the top of the site and movement from it to other sections or

Linear Design

Menu to Link Design

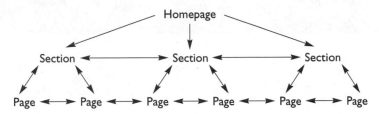

Wagon Wheel

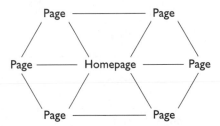

FIGURE 8.1 Examples of Three Web Site Designs

pages is a vertical move to the next layer. Linking between sections or pages on the same level are horizontal moves. Movement between pages should be as logical and easy to follow as possible. Many homepages include maps to guide users through the site.

The *United Nations* Web site follows a standard menu-to-link design. The general organization is based on an umbrella structure, in which sections link from the opening page, but not all sections and pages are linked together. In other words, visitors at any of the "About the UN" sections must return to the main menu page before they can link to another section like "UN documents."

On the other hand, *Saab*'s and *The New York Times*'s Web sites are designed as wagon wheels, where the door pages to various sections feature complete menus

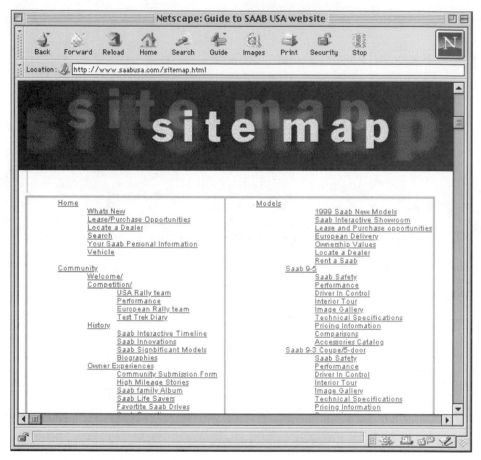

FIGURE 8.2 Saab Web Site Map

that will link to the next desired section without the user having to go back to the main menu page. Visitors who are checking out the newest Saab cars and who then decide to read about the history of Saab need only click on the "Communities" section from within the new models page and then click on the "History" link, without having to return to the main homepage.

GROUPING SUBJECTS TOGETHER Web sites can be arranged in a wide variety of ways depending on the content and the purpose. Information can be categorized by who, what, when, where, and how. For example, book titles may be organized by target audience, such as children or the elderly, information can be categorized into broad subject areas containing subtopics, current news stories are often listed in

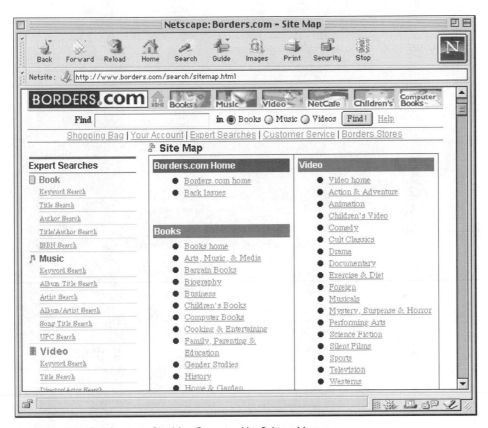

FIGURE 8.3 Borders.com Site Map Organized by Subject Matter

chronological order, international information by geographic location, and "how-to" directions usually follow some sort of step-by-step progression.

Some Web sites are made up of a variety of organizational schemes. For example, a first-level subject index of news stories may lead to a second-level news area that is chronologically ordered; a Web site of universities in the United States may be geographically organized by state, but within the state menu institutions may be listed alphabetically or ordered by size of the student body. Whichever organizational schemes are chosen, they must be easy to follow and make sense to visitors.

ESTABLISHING LINKING PAGES Linking pages on each level should be consistent with the general section or area. For instance, if a menu page links to nonfiction books, then all books within that section should be nonfiction. However, an

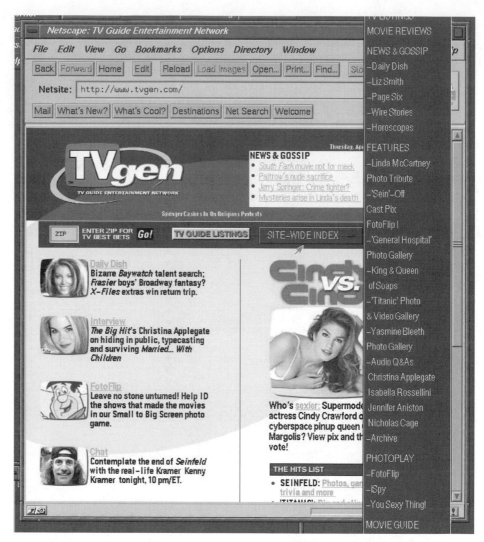

FIGURE 8.4 TVgen Pull-Down Index

additional link may be established that takes visitors directly to fiction books without their having to go back to the main page. The network of links depends on a site's overall design: whether it is linear in nature or whether it is arranged like a wagon wheel. Make sure that visitors do not have to dig deep into a site. Desired information should not be more than three to four clicks away from the menu or door page. In other words, Web sites should not be designed with more than three or four levels. *TVGEN*, the online TV Guide Entertainment Network, is a large, complex site, but they make it easy for users to get right to where they want to go with a pull-down site index on the main menu page. Visitors need only click on one of the many options such as "TV listings," "Soaps," and "Games" to travel directly to the information they are seeking.

Generally, links should connect users to material that exists within the site. All too often, homepages contain links to outside resources, which is similar to sending customers to someone else's store ("Building Profits," 1996; Hawn, 1996; Henley, Gennarelli, Hon, & Kelleher, 1996). Providers should strive to keep visitors within their sites by adding extra pages as necessary. For example, a travel agency promoting a Hawaiian vacation could post information and photographs of Hawaii within its own site, rather than linking its clients to a Hawaii page posted by someone else. In all likelihood the outside Hawaii page links to other vacation spots and agencies, and the chances that clients will eventually make their way back to the original agency are pretty slim. It is worth investing the resources to create additional pages to keep visitors within the site. On the other hand, there are instances where providers purposely link visitors to outside resources. Professors and teachers often post course materials and other information on the Web, but then direct students to other research materials outside of the course site.

GRAPHIC ISSUES

Regardless of the technical sophistication a Web site might have, such as spinning logos, animation, audio, or even video clips, the first thing that visitors to a site will see is the graphic work. Graphics that are attractive and quick-loading will keep people coming to the site and staying long enough to get the provider's desired message. Web designers must understand how graphic files work and be aware of some of the pitfalls that can cause surfers to click on their browser's stop button before a Web site even finishes loading.

Types of Graphic Files

Graphic files on the Web are generally of two types: .gif files or .jpg files. These suffixes are file extensions that indicate how a graphic file is encoded in digital form.

GIF FILES The .gif files or "GIFs" (Graphic Interchange Format) are the most common form of image on the Internet, including the Web and bulletin board services. This file format is owned by CompuServe, and users that make heavy use of this format are supposed to license its use. (This is not necessarily true for small users who do not profit from the use of GIFs.) There are two versions of the GIF format, 87a and 89a, representing the years that the format version was developed. Most images on the Web were created in the 89a format. GIFs that are 89a can display a transparent image that allows layering of images, and they also allow the use of some animation within a single GIF file. GIFs are commonly used for the banner ads that are pervasive on the Web.

GIFs are especially suited for images that contain large areas of one color and are generally very good for line art or simple logo art. GIF files are easy to compress, and allow for short loading times for Web pages. Graphics files that are in other formats can be converted to GIF with a number of software programs, for example, Alchemy Mindworks Graphic Workshop for Windows.

JPEG FILES   The .jpg or "JPEGs" (Joint Photographic Experts Group) are files that are created for high-quality, complex images on the Web. JPEGs are created by selecting from a range of compression levels. Since graphic files are large, compression is used to make them smaller. Compression is a process that reduces the amount of data in a file by eliminating redundant information. The higher the quality image desired, the lower the compression. JPEGs are criticized for being "lossy," meaning that they are not easy to compress without making large sacrifices in image quality. JPEGS are best used for images, such as photographs, that require a natural look. The natural look comes from a high resolution and a large number of colors. The higher the resolution and higher the number of colors, the larger the file. Although the size of the image can be reduced from the original using JPEGs without problems, increasing the size of a JPEG image often results in digital artifacts, like smooth lines becoming jagged lines, that appear unnatural. The JPEG file format is best for viewing on the computer screen, because the image that results from printing is often not as good as what is seen on the screen. On the other hand, GIFs seem to fare better when printed because of their simplicity and ease of compression without artifacts.

File Size

File size increases with the size of the image, the resolution of the image, and the number of colors in the image. Reducing the number of colors from 256 to 16 allows the file to require only 4 bits per pixel (picture element or dot on a computer screen) instead of 8 bits per pixel. This reduction in the number of colors will change the file to one half of its original size. However, this type of file reduction is only practical with GIFs, because the simplicity of line art graphics does little to reduce quality. Reducing colors in the JPEG format yields no advantage (Fisher, 1996).

There are some programs on the market that are used to reduce the file size of graphic images. These programs are known as "Debabelizers" and can reduce file sizes significantly by reducing the "bit depth" by simplifying the image. Generally, the best method of reduction is to cut down the number of colors.

Although there is a temptation to always use very high resolution to yield impressive-looking graphic images, this may sometimes be counterproductive. As resolution increases, so does file size and thus downloading time. Using graphics with a resolution of more than 72 dpi (dots per inch) is totally wasteful. Computer screens cannot show any resolution higher than 72 dpi, and file size is increased for no reason.

There are modified forms of GIFs and JPEGs that do not reduce the size of the image file, but still help to prevent the loss of impatient Web surfers while downloading. These modified forms are interlaced GIFs and progressive JPEGs. These files yield a fast version of progressively higher-resolution images as the file is being received. The viewer at first gets a low-resolution image that gets progressively better as a reward for viewer patience.

Downloading Graphics

Downloading graphics is a relatively easy thing to do. Conceptually it is similar to cutting and pasting in word processing. The process is accomplished with the browser. When using a Macintosh computer, simply click on the desired graphic. Hold down the mouse button. The screen will then show a pull-down menu with the option "Save image as." The image can then be saved to a folder on the hard drive. When using a Windows machine, use the mouse to point to the desired image. Right-click the mouse button. The menu, with an option to "Save image as," should appear. The image can then be saved to a location on the hard drive. The image is labeled with the appropriate file extension (.gif or .jpg) by the browser and stored.

Backgrounds, either full-screen or tiled, can also be downloaded by the same process. A full-screen background can be 40Kb to 70 Kb, which would be a large file. A tiled background is comprised of many small images that are repeated throughout the background. When this type of background is downloaded, the image received is a small version of the large background. It is more efficient to download one tile from a tiled background, because it is a small file that will load quickly. Rebuilding the full background can be accomplished easily in HTML.

Legal Considerations

Although downloading graphics is easy and quick, many legal issues must be considered. Copyright laws (discussed in Chapter 11) protect material posted on the Internet. Before using someone else's graphics, use common sense and ask for permission. This may seem like a lot of trouble, but it can avoid legal problems. Common sense dictates that taking a graphic of Mickey Mouse from a Disney site and using it without permission will create problems. Not all corporations would

BOX 8.2 MODIFYING EXISTING MATERIALS FOR THE WEB

Component	Possible Modifications
Layout, formatting	Change aspect ratio Adjust amount of white space Redefine spatial relationships between text and graphics Remove or adapt unnecessary elements (page numbers, running headers and footers, tables of contents) Add hyperlinks Add navigational components Adjust typography for on-screen viewing Add HTML tags for formatting Create PDF files Add buttons, other calls to actions, tie-ins to other sites
Text	Edit for faster reading, easier scanning Condense and/or reduce content Convert long linear text flows into shorter, hyperlinked chunks Add headers Add hyperlinks Add navigational components
Graphics	Crop and scale as appropriate Adjust bit depth, color palette Convert to GIF or JPEG Make backgrounds transparent (GIF) Decide on interlace (GIF) or progressive (JPEG)
Video	Edit Optimize for Web delivery and playback Embed in HTML or PDF file
Animation	De-compose, tag as HTML component and/or Write Java applet and/or Create run-time file (e.g., QuickTime movie or Shockwave for Director file)
Audio	Edit Optimize for Web delivery and playback Embed in HTML or PDF file, or build into QuickTime or Shockwave movie
File Structure	"Chunk" the information, build file structure, and establish file naming conventions for optimal online delivery

Source: Thompson et al., 1996, p. 39

care if material is copied from their site, but some corporations aggressively pursue individuals who use identifiable graphics without permission. Copying a simple small graphic of an envelope or some other generic object is probably safe, but copying a trademarked logo or a complex graphic created by the original owner at some expense is asking for legal problems.

When in doubt about copyright issues, simply ask permission before using any graphics created for other Web sites. The process of doing this is often relatively easy. Many Web sites give viewers the opportunity to give feedback with a "Contact us" icon or menu item. Other Web sites list the Webmaster's e-mail address as a link for the purpose of contacting the Webmaster quickly and easily. When doing this, state the reason for using graphics and how the graphics will be used. When the Webmaster responds to the request, make a copy of the response and save it. Corporate policies and Webmasters can change, so a copy of the permission to use the graphic material will provide the necessary protection against legal action.

Downloaded graphics can be changed and then reused. In such cases, permission for use of the graphics and the changes should be requested. If changes are made to downloaded graphics so that the original is not recognizable, then permission may not be necessary, but if the changes are that extensive, it may be best to start from scratch.

The best rule of thumb for downloading and reusing graphics is simply, "When in doubt, ask permission." Material posted on the Internet should be considered as having been published. Individuals and groups who publish deserve to have their materials protected.

Graphics Differences among Browsers

Until recently there were significant differences in the ways that browsers handled graphic material. Graphics designed for Netscape Navigator did not always look good on Internet Explorer and vice versa. Even in the late 1990s, simple graphic elements like underlining did not translate well from browser to browser. In the more recent versions of browsers, most of the graphic inconsistencies have been reconciled, and graphic display is now mostly standardized. Some Web sites also try to standardize the images that viewers receive by placing a line on the first page of the site with a suggestion to adjust the browser to fit that line. This minimizes differences among browser displays of the Web site.

Plug-ins that used to be browser-specific are now almost always produced for both Netscape Navigator and Internet Explorer. Authoring software has also helped make Web pages consistent among browsers. Differences among browsers are now more attributable to differences in the default settings that users set themselves than in the way browsers handle graphics. As the Web continues to develop technologically, increased standardization will help both Web users and Web developers to communicate efficiently and effectively.

Using Graphics Wisely

The saying that "Less is more" is appropriate for Web page design. Overly busy Web pages can be confusing to the viewer and aesthetically displeasing as well. Well-designed Web pages use graphics sparingly and only when there is a strong need for them. Following are some simple rules for designing a good Web site using graphics:

1. Select good looking, appropriate fonts that are readable on screen.
2. Keep graphics simple, and use only graphics that are needed.
3. Try to keep the file size as low as possible to allow short loading times for viewers.
4. Keep in mind that sites with too much happening graphically will lose viewers quickly.

Another technique for saving file space is using "thumbnail" images. Thumbnail images are small, low-resolution versions of photos or other high-resolution, many-color images. A large full-color image can take up almost 100 Kb; a thumbnail takes up about 6 to 8 Kb. Use thumbnail images as links to the full images when the viewers may not need to see the full image immediately. This can be especially helpful when there are several images on a page and the viewer can select among them. To see a good use of thumbnails, go to the *Alternative Entertainment Network* site, then click on "Programming Guide."

TIPS FOR EFFECTIVE WEB SITE DESIGN

While there are no hard and fast rules governing site design, there are guidelines for effective organization and easy navigation. Some of the basic principles of good Web site design include:

1. Start small and let the site take on a life of its own. Test and analyze a site's performance and visitors' reactions before posting more pages. Design the site to suit the customers' needs and tastes.

2. Start with an attractive and easy-to-understand home or menu page to pique visitors' interest and induce them to explore the site further. The homepage should be the entrance to the site and should be the site's menu, not the full meal. Visitors should not be overwhelmed with too much text or blinded with excessively bright and flashy graphics.

3. Homepages should post an e-mail address of a contact person, a copyright statement, and the date of last changes.

4. Keep the opening page uncluttered. Put information where visitors can quickly find what they are seeking, and make sure content is never more than three clicks away from the menu. Burying material frustrates visitors and often causes them to give up their search. Add a separate table of contents or pull-down index on complex, multilayered sites.

5. Post clickable icons and other navigation buttons where they are easy to find, and avoid those that may be hard to interpret.

6. Make it easy for users to travel through the site by linking pages back to the homepage and by posting location markers that show visitors where they are within the site. Also, frequent postings of logos or other identifiers help visitors remember which site they are traveling around in.

7. Include a search engine on complex, multilayered sites to direct visitors quickly to specific content.

8. Use a consistent look throughout a site. Colors, type font, and graphics should follow some sort of scheme, so that visitors will know that they are still within the same site. For example, a page with an orange background will seem out of place if the rest of the pages have a green and purple background.

9. Use graphics, audio, and video icons that are visually stimulating and inviting, but beware of ones that take too long to download or are irrelevant to the site. Visitors may become impatient and leave.

10. Stress interactivity through image maps and clickable icons that provide quick and direct access to the information consumers are seeking. Games, contests, and other value-added interactive content set an exciting Web site apart from a mere online brochure. Attract visitors through a creative, fun, and imaginative site.

11. Keep sales pitches indirect and benefit-based, rather than excessively commercial. Do not oversell.

12. Balance content-heavy sites with graphics, audio, and video. Write in smaller blocks of text for quick reading and scanning.

13. State privacy policies. Inform users if personal information is kept confidential.

14. Always include an e-mail address or other means of encouraging visitor feedback.

15. Provide links to other sites with caution. Create additional pages if necessary to keep customers from straying to other sites.

16. Last, give visitors a reason to return. Keep sites fresh by frequently updating and changing content. Promote upcoming products, services, and other activities, and let users know when new information will be available online. ("Building Profits," 1996; Del Prete, 1997; Hawn, 1996; Henley, Gennarelli, Hon, & Kelleher, 1996; Judson, 1996; Sargeant-Robinson & Kaye, 1997; Sweetman, 1997; Thompson et al., 1996).

More information on Web site design can be found on the Web itself. *Vincent Flanders' Web Sites That Suck* page is a great tutorial for site design. Working from the premise of "Learn good design by looking at bad design," Vincent present

BOX 8.3   GUIDELINES FOR EVALUATING A SITE

Rate the site on a scale of 1 to 5. 1 = not at all, 2 = not very much, 3 = somewhat, 4 = moderately so, 5 = very much.

Purpose and Goals

A. Does the site have a clear purpose and goals?	1 — 2 — 3 — 4 — 5
B. Does the site attract the target audience?	1 — 2 — 3 — 4 — 5
C. Is it easy to identify the site's sponsor?	1 — 2 — 3 — 4 — 5
D. Are logos and other identifiers posted throughout the site?	1 — 2 — 3 — 4 — 5
E. Is the site easy to navigate?	1 — 2 — 3 — 4 — 5
F. Is most information three clicks away from the homepage?	1 — 2 — 3 — 4 — 5
G. Is it easy to find information within the site?	1 — 2 — 3 — 4 — 5
H. Is the site's organization logical and easy to understand?	1 — 2 — 3 — 4 — 5
I. Is the design consistent from page to page?	1 — 2 — 3 — 4 — 5
J. Do links keep visitors within the site?	1 — 2 — 3 — 4 — 5

Total Score _____

45–50 = excellent, 40–44 = very good, 35–39 = average, 30–34 = below average, below 30 = poor

examples of the worst of the Web with suggestions for creating the best of the Web. Users learn about "bad, bad buttons," "pretentious front page," "free backgrounds that suck," "too much text," and many other topics of site design through fun, yet informative lessons.

Professor Pete's Insider's Guide to Business Web Design is cleverly designed to look like a college course syllabus outlining the lessons for the semester. Professor Pete's three-lesson tutorial is targeted to inexperienced users who want to learn how to conduct online business. The professor discusses the importance of the Internet, gives tips for defining business needs, and actually designs a site based on information provided by students. Clicking on the "Honor Roll" icon takes pupils to sites that "aced the final exam." Professor Pete's and Vincent Flander's sites are must bookmarks for anyone interested in learning Web design.

EVALUATING A WEB SITE

Creating a Web site is a complicated task that takes a good deal of time to complete and requires keen attention to detail. Even the smallest error can result in technical glitches or some other problems that may keep users from revisiting the site. Every page of the site must be thoroughly evaluated and tested before going online. Once

BOX 8.4 GUIDELINES FOR EVALUATING PAGES WITHIN A SITE

Rate the site on a scale of 1 to 5.
1 = not at all, 2 = not very much, 3 = somewhat, 4 = moderately so, 5 = very much.

1. **Purpose and Goals**
   A. How clear are the page's purpose and goals?   1 — 2 — 3 — 4 — 5
   B. Does the page attract the target audience?   1 — 2 — 3 — 4 — 5
   C. Does the page encourage repeat visits?   1 — 2 — 3 — 4 — 5
   D. Is the page title meaningful?   1 — 2 — 3 — 4 — 5

            Subtotal _____

2. **Accuracy and Credibility**
   A. Can posted information be easily verified through other sources?   1 — 2 — 3 — 4 — 5
   B. Are all materials properly cited and attributed to their sources?   1 — 2 — 3 — 4 — 5
   C. Is the information credible?   1 — 2 — 3 — 4 — 5
   D. Is the source reliable?   1 — 2 — 3 — 4 — 5
   E. Is the information free of grammatical errors?   1 — 2 — 3 — 4 — 5
   F. Is the information free of spelling and typographical errors?   1 — 2 — 3 — 4 — 5

            Subtotal _____

3. **Readability**
   A. Does the text stand out from background colors and patterns?   1 — 2 — 3 — 4 — 5
   B. Is the typeface consistent throughout the page?   1 — 2 — 3 — 4 — 5
   C. Is the color scheme attractive?   1 — 2 — 3 — 4 — 5
   D. Is the page uncluttered?   1 — 2 — 3 — 4 — 5
   E. Is the reading level appropriate for the target audience?   1 — 2 — 3 — 4 — 5
   F. Can the text be read quickly?   1 — 2 — 3 — 4 — 5

            Subtotal _____

4. **Content**
   A. Is the content appropriate to the overall objectives?   1 — 2 — 3 — 4 — 5
   B. Is the content appropriate for the target audience?   1 — 2 — 3 — 4 — 5
   C. Is the content meaningful?   1 — 2 — 3 — 4 — 5
   D. Is the content interesting?   1 — 2 — 3 — 4 — 5
   E. Is interactivity stressed?   1 — 2 — 3 — 4 — 5
   F. Is the provider presented in a favorable light?   1 — 2 — 3 — 4 — 5

            Subtotal _____

5. **Currency**
   A. Is the information kept current?   1 — 2 — 3 — 4 — 5
   B. Is it easy to find when the page was last updated?   1 — 2 — 3 — 4 — 5
   C. Is it clear when the next update can be expected?   1 — 2 — 3 — 4 — 5
   D. Is the document's origination date visible?   1 — 2 — 3 — 4 — 5

            Subtotal _____

   (continued)

BOX 8.4 GUIDELINES FOR EVALUATING PAGES WITHIN A SITE *(continued)*

6. **Design and Layout**
   A. Does the page download in a reasonable amount of time?   1 — 2 — 3 — 4 — 5
   B. Does the design draw readers to the text?   1 — 2 — 3 — 4 — 5
   C. Do the page elements work together?   1 — 2 — 3 — 4 — 5
   D. Is the page well-organized?   1 — 2 — 3 — 4 — 5
   E. Are the links up-to-date?   1 — 2 — 3 — 4 — 5
   F. Are feedback mechanisms in operation?   1 — 2 — 3 — 4 — 5
   G. Is the author or contact person identified?   1 — 2 — 3 — 4 — 5
   H. Are the clickable icons and other navigation buttons easy to find?   1 — 2 — 3 — 4 — 5
   I. Are the clickable icons and other navigation buttons easy to interpret?   1 — 2 — 3 — 4 — 5
   J. Are logos and other identifiers visible on the page?   1 — 2 — 3 — 4 — 5

                                                                    Subtotal _____

7. **Graphics**
   A. Are the graphics of high quality?   1 — 2 — 3 — 4 — 5
   B. Do the graphics have a consistent look?   1 — 2 — 3 — 4 — 5
   C. Do the graphics enhance the text?   1 — 2 — 3 — 4 — 5
   D. Are the graphics necessary and useful?   1 — 2 — 3 — 4 — 5
   E. Are the text and graphic elements balanced?   1 — 2 — 3 — 4 — 5

                                                                    Subtotal _____

                                                                    Grand total _____

185–205 = excellent, 165–184 = very good, 145–164 = average, 125–144 = below average,
below 124 = poor

Adapted from criteria developed by Dr. Diane Witmer, California State University, Fullerton, adapted from criteria developed by Jan Alexander and Marsha Tate, Reference Librarians, Wolfgram Memorial Library, Widener University.

a site is up and running, frequent reevaluation alerts site owners of any problems that may be occurring or any basic changes that should be made.

Having a clear, thorough, and systematic method of assessing a site speeds the evaluation process and assures providers that the site is free from error. While there are existing site evaluation guidelines, it is ultimately up to providers to set their own standards of excellence. Many providers have come up with ways of judging their sites based on a checklist of criteria unique to their goals and objectives.

The rating system presented in this chapter is not set in stone. Individual providers may wish to alter, omit, or add their own criteria to the guidelines.

SUMMARY: SITE DESIGN

It takes a strong online presence and personality for any Web site to stand out from the thousands of other existing sites. The Web demands that online information providers use imagination and creativity to reach their cyber-goals and objectives. Constructing a Web site takes more than HTML skills and a desire to be a "Webbie." Successful Web site design requires a knowledge of the network and of its audiences, and an understanding of users' motivations for going online. Additionally, incorporating marketing strategies into the overall design and promotion can attract new customers and widen the base of visitors.

A thorough online plan should be in place before one launches into cyberspace. Some early tasks include establishing a purpose; setting goals, objectives, and specific outcomes; identifying the target audience; and hiring a Webmaster and support staff. The next step in site design involves creating the general content and any value-added components. Developing feedback mechanisms, encouraging repeat visits, and scheduling content updates and changes must also be included in the plan.

Organizing a site includes mapping or blueprinting the overall structure, grouping subjects together in a logical fashion, and establishing relevant linking pages. Once online, periodic evaluation and ratings can lead to updates and changes that will keep a site and its pages fresh and contemporary.

CHAPTER LINKS

Alternative Entertainment Network—http://www.aentv.com

CNN—http://cnn.com

Graphics Wiz Making Thumbnails—http://www.photodex.com/gwthumb.html

New York Times—http://www.nytimes.com

Professor Pete's Insider's Guide to Business Web Design—
http://www.professorpete.com/

Saab—http://www.saabusa.com/sitemap.html

TV Guide Entertainment Network (TVgen)—http://www.tvgen.com/

United Nations—http://www.un.org/

Vincent Flanders' Web Sites That Suck—http://www.Webpagesthatsuck.com/

REFERENCES

Benjamin, R., & Wigand, R. (1995, Winter). Electronic markets and virtual value chains on the information superhighway. *Sloan Management Review,* 62–72.

Building profits on the Internet. (1996, September 9). *Advertising Age,* book excerpt, 42.

Del Prete, D. (1997, January 20). To catch a surfer. *Marketing News, 31,* 19.

Fisher, Y. (1996). *Spinning the Web.* New York: Springer.

Groves, D. (1996). *The Web page workbook.* Wilsonville, OR: Franklin, Beedle.

Hawn, M. (1996, April). Stay on the Web. *MacWorld,* 94–98.

Henley, M., Gennarelli, D., Hon, L., & Kelleher, T. (1996). *Public relations and the World Wide Web: Designing an effective homepage.* Paper presented at the annual convention of the Association for Education in Journalism and Mass Communication, Anaheim, CA.

Hoge, C. C., Sr. (1993). *The electronic marketing manual.* New York: McGraw-Hill.

Janal, D. S. (1995). *Online marketing.* New York: Van Nostrand Reinhold.

Judson, B. (1996). *Net marketing.* New York: Wolff New Media.

Kaye, B. K. (1998). Uses and gratifications of the World Wide Web: From couch potato to Web potato. *The New Jersey Journal of Communication, 6* (1), 20–41.

Pushing the Envelope—Net marketers reach out through "push" media. (1997, May). *Internet Marketing & Technology Report, 3* (5). Carlsbad, CA: Computer Economics, 1–4.

Sargeant-Robinson, K., & Kaye, B. K. (1997). *Determining the strength of new technology: The World Wide Web's effect on the advertising industry.* Proceedings of the 1997 conference of the American Academy of Advertising, 217–228.

Sweetman, B. (1997, March). Web site strategies. *Internet World,* 63–68.

Thompson, H., Thompson, C., & McLaughlin, J. (1996). *Thinking it through.* Cupertino, CA: Apple Computer Inc., Publishing and New Media Marketing Group.

Wilson, R. F. (1997). Why in the world should anyone come to your Web site? *Wilson Internet Services.* [Online]. Available: http://www.wilsonWeb.com/articles/why-come.htm

Households in the United States have at least one television set on for approximately seven hours per day. Some say that our nation has become a nation of couch potatoes. Television is our primary source for news, information, and entertainment. Now that the information superhighway is becoming both available and familiar to most of the population, how will our media habits change?

The World Wide Web holds the promise of news and information that will be "pushed" to us effortlessly. Radio and television entertainment is rapidly becoming available from the Web as well.

If we are now a nation of "couch potatoes," will we soon be a nation of "mouse potatoes"? Will the information superhighway become our main link to the rest of the world?

SOCIAL IMPLICATIONS

According to a poll conducted in 1997, 21 percent of all adults in the United States use the Internet, the World Wide Web, or both. This number represents about 40 million people (Cortese, 1997). In addition, the Clinton Administration has declared that Internet access for all schools is both a desirable and an attainable goal for the near future. In the early 1990s, the pervasiveness of the Internet would not have been predicted. In a short time, use of the information superhighway has become commonplace for people in this country. Its use is often required in the workplace, and it is becoming increasingly important in schools.

The Internet is changing the way society seeks information and entertainment. It is also changing the ways in which people communicate. Obviously, these changes demand that three researchers look more closely at how society is changing as a result.

INTERNET USE, ABUSE, AND ADDICTION

As use of the Internet grows, so do the questions regarding its use. Much of the discussion deals with the technology and capabilities of the Internet. Questions usually revolve around issues such as how to use it, what hardware is needed, what software or browser works best, and so on. Many people regard the Internet as merely a group of computers connected together, and thus do not give much thought to the impact the information superhighway can have upon our lives. However, researchers have been studying the social and psychological impact the media, and especially the Internet, have on society, because understanding the impact of the technology is just as important as studying the technology itself.

In the United States, about 98 percent of all households have at least one television set, which is turned on for an average of about seven hours per day. Added to the hours of television watching are the hours spent listening to the radio, cassette tapes, and CDs at home, work, or in the car. People also spend a great deal of time reading newspapers, magazines, and books. Once other activities like sleeping, eating, and work are added, it seems that there is hardly enough time for anything else, especially extra time to wile away on the Internet; yet people are spending many hours online.

There are some indications that overall media usage patterns are changing as a result of the accessibility of the information superhighway. People were asked the question, "Over the course of the last year, in terms of time spent, did you find yourself reading magazines/newspapers more, the same amount, or less (than the year before)?" The findings were that about 45 percent of the respondents spent about the same amount of time with newspapers and magazines, over one-third (34.9 percent) spent less time, and about 20 percent spent more time. When asked, "Over the same period of time what has been your pattern of Internet usage?" almost three-fourths of the respondents stated that they were spending more time with the Internet (BBDO, 1997). This is not surprising, and it does appear that the Internet is beginning to steal readers from print media.

Some people spend hours and hours with online activities like e-mail, chat rooms, and simply surfing the Web. In fact, people who seem to spend too much time on the Internet. This can certainly be an annoyance if that person has to be contacted by telephone and his or her line is tied up because of an Internet connection. Some pundits have stated sarcastically that use of the Internet (and the resulting jammed phone lines) might lead to a benefit that actually causes people to visit other people face-to-face to avoid the busy signal.

Some people have become so entrenched with the Internet that they cannot think of anything else and must have a daily fix of surfing. Internet addiction is a topic that is more openly discussed as researchers are finding that many people's behavior is changing for the worse because of their heavy Internet use. Research shows that people are flunking out of school, splitting up relationships, and even seeking treatment in hospitals as a result of compulsive Internet use. Some people who have these kinds of problems are addicted to MUDs newsgroups, e-mail, and the World Wide Web in general.

Dr. Ivan Goldberg, a professor of psychiatry at Columbia University, has coined the term *Internet Addiction Disorder* (IAD) and has created a support group for Internet addicts. Goldberg has listed a number of behaviors that are associated with this disorder: a need for markedly increased amounts of time on the Internet to achieve satisfaction, obsessive thinking about what is happening on the Internet, fantasies or dreams about the Internet, and even involuntary typing movements of the fingers (Belluck, 1997).

Internet addiction is similar to other addictions, like compulsive gambling, shopping, smoking, and alcoholism. Some common warning signals for Internet addiction are (1) compulsively checking e-mail; (2) always anticipating the next Internet session; (3) spending too much time online; and (4) spending too much money online. Based on this research, the University of Pittsburgh has founded a Center for Online Addiction.

In other research, a survey conducted about online overuse found that 22 percent of the respondents reported a cocaine-like "rush," and 12 percent said computer chat lines helped them to relax (Griffiths, 1997). Some groups have been formed to help people who have become addicted or show significant signs of overuse. Unfortunately, many of these support groups are online, which just further feeds the addiction. As the director of a hospital clinic has stated, "Online support groups for the online addicted is like having an Alcoholics Anonymous meeting in a bar" (Orzack, 1996).

MASS MEDIA USE

The phenomenon of heavy Internet use certainly has antecedents with both radio and television. Radio started out as an experimental point-to-point medium developed first for applications like ship-to-shore communication. The technology improved as people demanded voice communication rather than Morse code. Bell's invention of the telephone, which preceded radio by about twenty-five years, was the catalyst for radio. Scientists took the idea of voice communication from a one-to-one medium—telephone—and applied it to a mass medium—radio. By 1920, radio became an entertainment medium, using voice communication to send news, information, comedy, drama, action, and music to its many listeners. By the late 1920s, most of what is known as broadcast network programming was in place and available on a regular basis to listeners across the country.

Small screen black-and-white television became available in the late 1940s, after World War II. The adoption of color television was slow in the 1950s because of industry wars, expensive technology, and the small number of television programs that were shot and broadcast in color. Cable television, starting in the 1970s, changed viewing habits considerably. While many people in the 1950s and 1960s had three to five channel choices from over-the-air broadcasters, cable systems offered eight to twelve channels as basic service. By 1976, when HBO entered the mix, cable systems were commonly offering thirty or more channels. Now, in the late 1990s, people expect a huge channel selection. A remote control device, allowing effortless surfing, is now a standard feature on even the least expensive sets. For those who want more channels than their local cable companies can offer, there are several digital satellite television systems that can be purchased for less than $200 and offer over one hundred high-quality television channels and numerous audio channels as well.

This last statement begs the question: What do people do with all these channels? Research has suggested that people do not regularly view more than a small selection of the channels. The answer might lie in what our society has become accustomed to—people like having lots of choices. And perhaps, that is why the Internet, with its millions of Web sites, is embraced by the public. The Internet is not just a super cable television system. The Internet is interactive and provides the opportunity for individuals to become creators of information and entertainment as well as consumers. Most people who use the Internet were introduced to it as part of their work or school environment. Users access the Internet to gain information as well as to pass information to others. Society uses it not only for retrieving information, but also to pass information to others. Individuals can set up homepages with information about their personal lives, beliefs, and even personal information such as age, address, favorite color, height, and weight.

Another aspect of the Web is that moving from site to site is almost effortless through hypertext links. When seeking information about the rare white tigers of Asia, it is easy to find links to information about other rare animals of Asia, information about Asia itself, or other related topics. E-mail provides an easy, quick, and economical means of sending and requesting information to individuals and organizations. As Internet technology evolves, allowing for more information to be sent in shorter periods of time, the entertainment aspect of the Internet, specifically the World Wide Web, will increase significantly. In the near future, it will be possible to go to the Web site of a favorite television program, click on "Latest episode," and watch the program in its entirety. Soon, a whole season of a program's episodes will be stored for viewing at the Web site. Although this is not a reality yet, it will occur in the near future. The quality of both the video and the audio will be as high quality as standard cable television and most CD players. It is at that point that the use of the Internet may become as ubiquitous as television in households across the country.

As television and the Internet merge into one appliance known as the PCTV, on which both television programs and the Web can be "watched" simultaneously, the average hours of daily use will likely rise sharply. Serious social effects may result, as a nation of "Net potatoes and mouse potatoes" rarely stray from the front of their PCTVs.

SOCIETAL CHANGES AND TECHNOLOGY

For a better understanding of the Internet's influence on societal changes, it may be helpful to look at the nature of our society and how it has evolved over the last few hundred years. Generally, society has moved from having a community orientation with strong social bonds to an individual orientation, in which people are more isolated and community bonds are not strong.

Gemeinschaft *and* Gesellschaft

In the late 1800s, Ferdinand Tonnies suggested two different types of societal organization: Gemeinschaft and Gesellschaft. *Gemeinschaft* can be characterized as a society that is tightly bound together in many ways: blood relationships, tradition, religion, or work. In this type of society, people have close relationships because they come from similar heritages, have common beliefs, work together, and are deeply committed to one another. Tonnies proposed that this type of society was typical of those in villages and small towns before the industrialization of society, but the concept is meant to be a general one. As the Industrial Revolution changed much of Europe and the United States, Tonnies believed it also changed societal relationships (Tonnies, 1957).

The industrialization of society brought division of labor, specialization, and urban growth. These things brought a different type of social relationship, a contractual one that Tonnies labeled *Gesellschaft*. In this type of society, relationships are often formed through contracts. Two parties agree to provide goods or services to each other. Failure to fulfill the contract results in penalties set forth in the agreement. The agreements are often formal and supported by other parts of society, such as a judicial system. As Tonnies stated, "Everyone is by himself and isolated, and there exists a condition of tension against all others" (Tonnies, 1957, p. 65). Where Gemeinschaft is based upon sentiment and reciprocal commitment, Gesellschaft is based on contractual agreement and is obviously impersonal. These two concepts can be viewed as polar opposites that do not really describe all of society either now or then, but they can be very useful in understanding the general changes in society that have occurred in the last two hundred years.

Until the early 1800s, society was fairly stable and had a traditional system where people were closely tied to one another. This began changing noticeably in the 1830s, as technology became more available and society became more complex. As a result, people became more socially isolated. Telephone conversations replaced face-to-face visits. Radio and television entertainment encouraged people to stay home rather than go out to socialize. Western society experienced increases in heterogeneity and individuality, decreases in the social control of its members, increases in alienation of the individual from strong identity with the community, and a general increase in the psychological isolation of individuals (DeFleur & Ball-Rokeach, 1989). From these changes grew the concept of mass society that can be characterized as "a vast mass of segregated, isolated individuals, interdependent in all sorts of specialized ways yet lacking in any central unifying value or purpose" (Young, 1949). It is worth noting that the concept of *mass* refers more to an aggregate of people than a group that exhibits coherence. This was the society that nurtured mass media in the twentieth century.

Mass Society and Mass Communication

The effects of mass communication on society have been studied for most of the twentieth century. The interest began during World War I, when leaders in Europe and the United States realized that a total effort from the population was needed in order to win the war, but the diverse, heterogeneous, and differentiated populations of industrial societies did not exhibit the group mind-set needed. Propaganda was used as a means to achieve the motivation for a concerted war effort. Mass media was selected to disseminate propaganda that was designed to encourage citizens to hate the enemy, love their country, and make a commitment to the war effort.

After the war, former propagandists came forward to tell stories about how they used propaganda to encourage people to support the war effort. One story involved the swapping of captions beneath two pictures seized from the Germans during the war. One picture showed dead German soldiers being carried back behind their lines for burial. The other showed dead horses on the way to a soap factory. The British general who had seized the pictures released the one that showed the dead German soldiers with the caption, "German Cadavers on Their Way to the Soap Factory." This photo and caption was particularly powerful in China, where people revere the dead. Although there were many other factors, China declared war on Germany soon after the release of the photo (DeFleur and Ball-Rokeach, 1989). Obviously, manipulation of public sentiment against a common enemy could be easily accomplished with the help of the media.

It was about this time that the relationship between mass society and mass media began to be studied in a formal way. People started to question the effects of media upon society and postulate causal relationships.

EFFECTS OF MEDIA MESSAGES

Generally, the effects of mass communication on individuals and society have been categorized in three different ways: cognitive changes, emotional or attitudinal changes, and behavioral changes. A communication message can result in any or all of these changes.

Cognitive Change

Cognitive change occurs when an individual learns something from a message. This could be something in addition to what the person already knows, or this could change the person's knowledge about something they already know.

The Internet provides unlimited access to information that can create cognitive change throughout society. For example, young people who need information about a sexually transmitted disease can visit a site like the *Herpes* homepage. Instead of a sobering and dull printed brochure like the kind at a doctor's office, this site delivers information about the herpes virus in an interesting way. As with many well-designed Web sites, this site has a lengthy menu that allows visitors to seek information on related topics. In a chat room, young people can discuss the disease with others. In addition, the site can direct people to other locations for support and help.

Students who are too squeamish to dissect a real frog could avoid some of the pain by accessing the *Virtual Frog* site. This site provides a virtual high school course on the topic. It guides students through a step-by-step procedure and allows

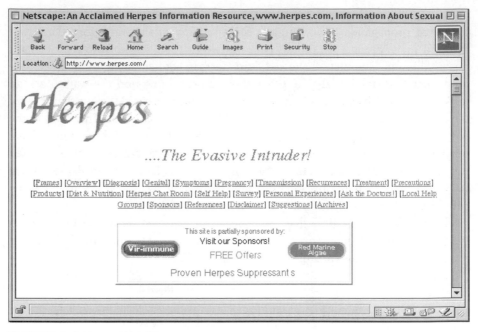

FIGURE 9.1 Herpes Web Site

them to use their mouse as a scalpel to "dissect" photos of frogs. A video can be downloaded to give a closer look at the "surgery." This course also provides quizzes and tests.

These are just two examples of cognitive changes. In both, additional or totally new information about topics is delivered while discomfort that may be associated with the topics is minimized.

Of all the changes that are discussed as a result of communication—cognitive, attitudinal, and behavioral—cognitive change is the easiest to measure in a reliable and valid way. Simple tests can be given to evaluate what people have learned from being exposed to various Web sites. Using before and after tests, the cognitive change from exposure to Web sites can be measured.

Emotional or Attitudinal Change

It is relatively easy to imagine that exposure to a message can create a change in emotions or attitudes. Viewing documentary films about the horrors of the concentration camps of World War II, the starving populations in some parts of Africa, or

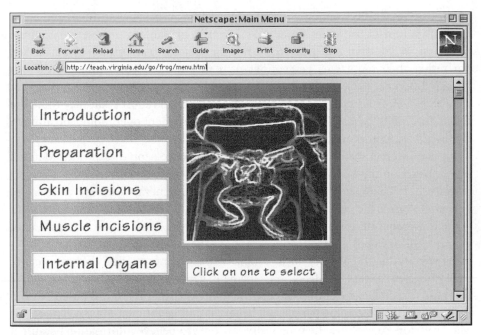

FIGURE 9.2 Virtual Frog Web Site

the human suffering inflicted by anti-personnel land mines can certainly have an emotional impact on viewers. People can be surveyed before watching documentary films like these and then surveyed again after viewing. Chances are good that if the questions are asked properly, a change in attitude or feelings about the subject of the film would become apparent after viewing. But most communications are not so dramatic. Measuring attitude or emotional change regarding affinity to a product, politician, or service is difficult, because one exposure to a message usually does not create significant changes. Often, a message must be repeated many times and attitudes or emotions be measured must be tested over time in order to find a real change in attitude.

Repeated exposure to Internet messages may also bring about emotional or attitudinal changes and the Internet's storage capabilities make it easy for users to return to archived information. Repeat visits to search engine sites and favorite sites often provide frequent exposure to Web advertising. Browsers make repeat visits easy by providing the Bookmark or Favorites feature to facilitate a quick and easy return to interesting sites. After visiting a desirable site, a user can place it on a bookmark list that allows the user to revisit the site by selecting it from a list, rather than having to type in the URL (see Chapter 1).

A survey or questionnaire is typically used for measuring attitudes and emotions. This type of test relies upon the subjects to give totally honest and accurate responses. What often gets measured is not the subjects' true emotions or attitudes, but rather their reports or perceptions of their attitudes. Unfortunately, there is often a difference between what people feel and what people say (or report) about what they feel. In addition, it is common for subjects to report what they think the researcher wants to hear. Obviously, accurate measurement of emotion and attitude is difficult and sometimes not possible.

The Internet seems to have the power to influence people's attitudes. Material that appears on the Web seems to have a status of truth conferred upon it merely because it is "published" on the Web. Web pages generated by individuals can appear alongside the venerated *New York Times* or *USA Today* Web sites. Since truth is *not* a prerequisite for publication on a Web page, the veracity of material is not guaranteed. Although many people agree with the saying, "You can't believe everything you read in the papers," most people do believe information they receive, not only from newspapers, but from mass media in general. This creates an atmosphere that lends credibility to all mass media, including the Internet. If it is published and disseminated widely, some people will believe it and be influenced by it. The recent Mars mission exemplifies the propensity for some to believe information because it is on the Internet. The famous pictures that were sent back from Mars were available for viewing on Web pages published by NASA. Some of these pictures, such as the one at the *Widgetmagic* site were downloaded by users, altered, and then published at other "Mars Mission" sites. These unauthorized sites showed pictures of the Mars landscape with some interesting things added to them. Some pictures showed buildings in the distance; others showed things like skulls. For some people, these pictures were proof that life exists on other planets.

Behavioral Change

Behavioral change caused by mass media occurs when a person acts differently than he or she normally does as a result of exposure to a mass-mediated message. From the perspective of professional communicators, desired behavioral changes are often behaviors such as buying a product that audience members have not bought before, or voting for a candidate who has been advertised heavily. At first glance it seems that behavioral change should be easier to measure than attitudinal change. The difficulty arises again in measurement. Unless subjects can be followed around all day, a researcher must rely upon the subjects' reports of behavior. In other words, researchers cannot go into the voting booth with the subjects; they must rely upon the subjects' reports of how they voted. It is easier to measure changes in larger groups, by looking at sales figures of a new product or simply by looking at the results of an election.

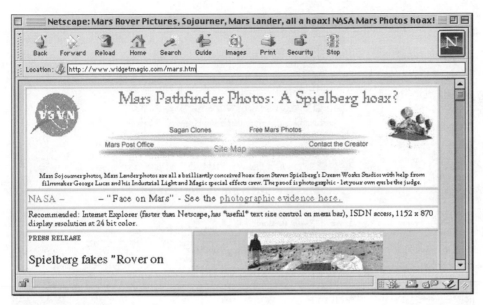

FIGURE 9.3 Widgetmagic Site

The Web is a very appealing information-distribution vehicle for nonprofit organizations that want to get out a message. In the past, nonprofit organizations that had a message to distribute to a mass audience had two choices: either find the money to buy advertising time or depend upon a broadcast station or network's policy of free airtime for public service. The Web allows these organizations to reach millions of people with their messages. The costs associated with getting the message out is much less than the cost of buying broadcast time or print space. Visits to nonprofits' Web sites can certainly have an effect if the messages are informative and attractive enough to be noticed by the audience.

Individuals can even get this kind of exposure on the Web. The *Master Anti-Smoking Page*, administered by an individual, is a site designed to help people quit smoking and to help people refrain from starting to smoke. It offers behavioral aides like software, links to other antismoking sites, a forum for antismoking, and other features, all for the purpose of helping people quit smoking.

A CHANGING SOCIETY

In addition to the general considerations mentioned above, there are a number of specific issues about the Web and the Internet that are of concern to society. Technologically, the Internet and World Wide Web offer much that can benefit society.

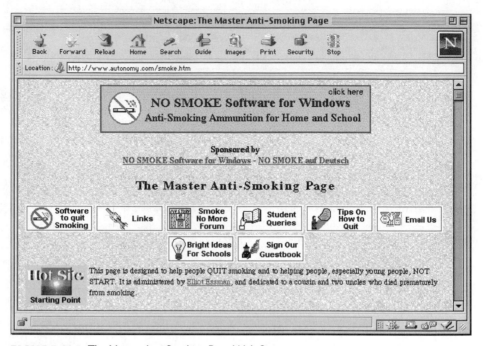

FIGURE 9.4 The Master Anti-Smoking Page Web Site

People can easily access information about almost everything useful in everyday life, like medical, investment, weather, and travel information. In addition, people can download the information and manipulate it for their own uses, connect with corporations, government, and organizations of all kinds and with other individuals who use the Internet. Web users can purchase products and services, locate people, and access entertainment. The Internet changes the way individuals go about some of their normal daily routines. Instead of traveling to a library, people travel the information superhighway. Instead of calling directory assistance to find a phone number, people can go to the *Yellow Pages* Web site. These behavioral changes are not modifications as a result of exposure to a communication, but changes because of the technology itself.

In addition to changes in individual behaviors, institutions are changing or have changed considerably because of the Internet. Corporations have changed dramatically in the way their employees access information, and the way they do their jobs. Many corporations have an internal Internet, known as an intranet, that has simplified work in many ways. For example, when employees are required to fill out a form, such as a report of travel expenses, they can access the form through the company's intranet, fill it out while it is onscreen, and then send it electronically to the appropriate destination. Push technologies go one step further to make work easier. When a deadline is approaching, employees can be warned through the company intranet or through a customized push program that sends the employee information or a simple reminder about the deadline.

Institutions in society are also changing as a result of Web technology. Holdings of libraries can be instantly accessed via Internet databases. Universities are planning and offering courses that are taught completely on the Web; students can learn at their own pace and in their own homes. Democracy is going online, with the ability to vote from home via the Internet soon to follow.

Just as orders for merchandise can be placed by giving personal information and a credit card number, online voting will be carried out by giving a social security number or some type of voter identification. Feedback to institutions is instant, as e-mail messages zip through the network from citizens' computers to government agencies. A more participatory democracy, where government services are more accessible to all, is a possible outcome of the information superhighway.

During the 1996 presidential campaign, both Bob Dole and Bill Clinton had Web sites to promote their candidacies. One study captured the effectiveness of candidate and other politically oriented Web sites on voting intention. Slightly more that one-half of the respondents reported that the Web moderately to heavily influenced their intent to vote, and the more they relied on the Web as a source of political information the greater the Web's influence on voting intention. It is conceivable that a visit to a candidate's Web site, in conjunction with other sources of information, helps voters to make a final decision and to even induce a nonvoter to cast a ballot (Johnson & Kaye, 1997).

SOCIAL CONCERNS AND THE WEB

Information Haves and Have Nots

Perhaps the most vexing social issue that concerns the information superhighway is the likelihood that it will be difficult for many people to find the "on-ramp" and get up to speed. That is, there are barriers that must be overcome by all users in order to utilize the Internet and benefit from its vast resources. First, there are technical skill considerations. Although the Internet is getting easier to use, it still requires an ability to get connected, start the browser, and enter the appropriate URL. Though the computer operating skills needed are very basic, many people still do not have the technical expertise to access the Internet adequately. These skills will remain necessary, at least for the foreseeable future and until innovations like PCTV access to the Internet becomes common.

Financial Barriers

Financial considerations can be a barrier to getting on the information superhighway. A computer with a modem or network connection to the Internet and a processor powerful enough to handle the large amount of information that must be processed for appropriate display and navigation of Internet sites costs about $1,000. Add peripherals like a color printer and larger monitor and the cost reaches over $1,500. The connection to the Internet from an Internet service provider costs at least $15 per month.

The Internet appears to be most commonly used by the affluent. As of spring 1997, 42 percent of Internet and Web users have household incomes of more than $50,000 a year, while only 18 percent take in $25,000 or less. Since the lower-income category probably includes many students, it may overstate Internet use by the country's poorest households (Cortese, 1997).

These figures, relevant to our country and perhaps much of the highly industrialized world, do not reflect the dilemma faced by developing countries where the infrastructure for many of the basic needs for sustaining life are simply not there. Many countries cannot provide running water, sewer systems, or telephone systems for their citizens. These societies cannot even think about connection with the Internet for years to come. Obviously, these people are going to be left out of cyberspace for the foreseeable future.

SUMMARY: THE WEB'S POTENTIAL IMPACT ON SOCIETY

The Internet is changing society by changing the way people obtain information and entertainment. People can visit stores, virtual museums, and libraries by clicking on a mouse. Interpersonal communication is also changing, as e-mail becomes widespread. Video technology on the World Wide Web holds the promise of a "video telephone" service, where we can see the people we speak to electronically. The ability of the World Wide Web to deliver entertainment in a form similar to broadcasting looms on the horizon and might revolutionize the way we entertain ourselves electronically. While technological change is fast, sociological change is much slower. As people adjust to the technological opportunities presented by the Internet, what changes will occur in society and in individuals?

CHAPTER LINKS

Herpes—http://www.herpes.com
The Master Anti-Smoking Page—http://www.smokefreekids.com/smoke.htm

Virtual Frog—http://teach.virginia.edu/go/frog/menu.html

Widgetmagic (Mars landing hoax)—http://www.widgetmagic.com/mars.htm

Yellow Pages—http://yp.uswest.com

REFERENCES

Belluck, P. (1997, December). Net addiction: True disorder or just a cyber-psycho-fad? *New York Times CyberTimes.* [Online]. Available: http://nytimes.com/library/cyber/week/1201addict.html

Cortese, A. (1997, April 24). A census in cyberspace. *Business Week Online.* [Online]. Available: http://businessweek.com/bwdaily/dnflash/april/nf70424a.htm

BBDO. (1997, May). BBDO Techsetter Hotline, as cited in *Internet Marketing & Technology Report.* Available: http://www.computereconomics.com/news4/pubs/imt.html.subscriptionrequired.

DeFleur, M., & Ball-Rokeach, S. (1989). *Theories of mass communication* (5th ed.). White Plains, NY: Longman.

Goldberg, I. (1997). As cited at Internet addiction. [Online]. Available: www.ifap.bepr.ethz.ch/~egger/ibq/intadd.htm

Griffiths, M. (1997). As cited at Internet addiction. Available: www.ifap.bepr.ethz.ch/~egger/ibq/intadd.htm

Johnson, T. J., & Kaye, B. K. (1998). *A vehicle for engagement or a haven for the disaffected?: Internet use, political alienation, and voter participation.* In T. J. Johnson, C. E. Hays, and S. P. Hays (Eds.). *Engaging the Public* (pp. 123–135). Lanham, M. D.: Rowman & Littlefield.

Orzack, M. (1996, December 1). As cited in Belluck, P. Net addiction: True disorder or just a cyber-psycho-fad? *New York Times CyberTimes.* [Online]. Available: http://nytimes.com/library/cyber/week/1201addict.html

Tonnies, F. (1957). *Community and society (Gemeinschaft und Gesellschaft)* (C. Loomis, Trans. and Ed.). East Lansing: Michigan State University Press.

Young, K. (1949). *Sociology* (p. 24). New York: American Book.

CHAPTER TEN

THEORETICAL
CONSIDERATIONS

When broadcasting became a medium and then a mass medium, researchers began to rethink the impact that mass media had upon society. Instead of a once-a-day newspaper or once-a-week magazine, broadcasting became an everyday, all-day influence upon the audience.

Now that the Internet is rapidly becoming ubiquitous, how must researchers reconsider the impact of mass media upon society? Is the Internet just a mass medium? Since it features not only one-to-many, but also one-to-one communication, does the Internet have more potential power than the traditional electronic media? Does the interactive nature of the Internet compel scholars to place research regarding the Internet into a theoretical perspective other than that of mass communication?

Early mass communication researchers Lazarsfeld and Merton (1974) noted a narcotizing dysfunction of the mass media. According to these researchers, the mass media lulled the viewing or listening audience into a passive state that prevented them from acting to benefit society through positive social action. Evidence is now becoming available that shows that a percentage of Internet users are becoming addicted to the Internet.

What would Lazarsfeld and Merton say about the narcotizing dysfunction of the Internet? Is the Internet addictive?

A THEORETICAL PERSPECTIVE FOR THE WORLD WIDE WEB

As more and more people find the "on ramp" to the information superhighway, researchers and communication scholars seek to understand more about how the Internet is affecting society and how it might affect society in the future. In order to get a better understanding of this recent technological phenomenon, one can attempt to place the Internet and World Wide Web into some theoretical context. After all, a good theory helps predict what will happen in the future by giving practical insights into how the phenomenon being studied works. Theoretical thinking forces the organization of large amounts of information into simple statements or relationships. Theories allow a prediction of events that have yet to occur. Theories foster a better understanding of what is happening and perhaps what might happen in the future, but theories are also often maps that attempt to describe a reality. Theories, like models, represent reality that can be used to understand and predict the future, but they are not always accurate. Theories provide a structure for us to use as we think, study, test, predict, and discuss reality.

Rather than start from "scratch" to build theories about the Internet and its impact upon society, using some existing theories and theoretical perspectives can be very helpful. Although not a perfect fit, it seems appropriate to place the Internet and World Wide Web in the context of mass media, and therefore include studies that deal with the information highway within the general framework of mainstream mass communication research.

Mass Media and the Internet

Traditional mass media have offered an ever-increasing number of choices for entertainment and information. Even though listening to radio and watching TV have long been considered by many people as passive activities, the broadcast audience selects from many choices and often switches or "surfs" among the choices. The viewing situation for broadcast has generally been one of convenience for the viewer. A person can use a remote control device to turn on a TV set (or a stereo system with a tuner for radio). Since the 1970s, audiences have become adept at "time shifting" or recording programs off the air for viewing at another time. This procedure is conceptually similar to downloading files from Web sites for later use. The Internet can provide hours of entertainment and "volumes" of news and information just like traditional broadcast and print media, but mass media do not have the interactive dimension that is a salient feature of the Internet.

Beginnings of Mass Communication Research

After revelations surfaced about the uses of media and propaganda during World War I, many people began to wonder about the power and uses of the mass media. It was widely held that the media had the power to shape public opinion. Further, people felt that those in control of the mass media could manipulate public opinion (and thus behavior, to some extent) by creating persuasive messages and distributing them in the mass media. This overall view portrays the media as powerful and the people who make media messages as even more powerful.

It is significant that this theoretical perspective came forward at a time when instinct psychology was very popular. The audience was viewed as having inherited biological mechanisms that caused people to react in specific ways to communication stimuli, especially those stimuli that contained emotional appeals. Obviously, this view portrays the audience as being at least somewhat nonrational, passive, and subject to the influence of whatever stimuli it came across. This view, which came to be known as the "magic bullet theory" or the "hypodermic needle theory," was generally congruent with theoretical views of human behavior that were popular in both sociology and psychology at the time (DeFleur & Ball-Rokeach, 1989, p. 165). This point of view was strengthened by the tremendous growth of advertising and subsequent consumerism of society.

Although the magic bullet theory was a good fit for the beliefs of the time, it simply did not account for a number of aspects of both the audience and the media exposure situation. The nature of individuals was studied extensively in the 1920s, and a preponderance of evidence was discovered that disagreed with the notion that all human behavior was dictated by biologically inherited instincts. Instead, factors like socializing and learning led researchers to describe human reaction to communication as somewhat of an individual process. In other words, people demonstrated individual and cultural differences when reacting to communication. The notion of instinct is now more useful in describing animal behavior than human behavior.

Attitudes

Instead of viewing instinct as the central motivator for reaction to communication, researchers eventually came to believe that there was another intervening variable between a communication stimulus and some type of behavioral response. That factor was the concept of attitudes. Attitudes explained the differences between human reactions to communications better than instincts, since the instincts explanation predicted that all humans would react to the same communication stimulus in the same way. Attitudes were easier to measure than instincts; attitudes could be measured with scales that generated numerical information that allowed statistical testing. In addition, attitude change could be measured by administering the same test both before and after exposure to a communication stimulus.

Social Differentiation

This change in research focus also brought a change in the way researchers considered society. If attitudes could intervene in the communication stimulus–behavioral response relationship, and attitudes of individuals were used as the explanatory mechanism for differences in responses to communication, then the early concept of society as an undifferentiated mass had to be reassessed. This reassessment led to the social categories approach to the study of society. This approach, similar to classifying people by demographic characteristics (i.e., religion, age, sex), acknowledged that people in society were differentiated, but had some ties and characteristics in common that could be described. Within a particular category, such as schoolteachers or truck drivers, there would be strong similarities in attitudes and behavior. These similarities were thought to help predict how individuals would respond to communication stimuli.

Media Selection

Up to this point, the basic assumption about audience response to communication was that the audience, when subjected to a stimulus, would then react. Studies in the 1930s that investigated media use and selection led researchers to reconsider the notion of the passive audience. Although many people today believe that exposure to the mass media is truly passive, especially when the medium studied is television, it is also generally accepted that the audience is very *active* when it comes to selection of media. People seem to seek out media that serve some type of purpose. If the medium of magazines is used as an example, it is obvious that people have a huge selection from which to choose. Why do people select one magazine over another? People often select a magazine because it gives them information that is relevant to their interests. People who enjoy antiques might be inclined to select a magazine that gives them information about which antiques are more valuable than others, how damaged antiques can be restored, the best places to find antiques, and so on. Vegetarians might select a magazine that offers articles about vegetarian meals. In addition, the magazine might have opinion articles that reinforce attitudes held about the benefits of avoiding meat and poultry. Magazines that hold political viewpoints attract people who hold similar views. In some cases, magazines serve the purpose of supporting attitudes and values held by the audience. In most situations, people select the magazines they want to read. The selection process can occur by mail, by purchase at a newsstand, or at a location like a doctor's waiting room,

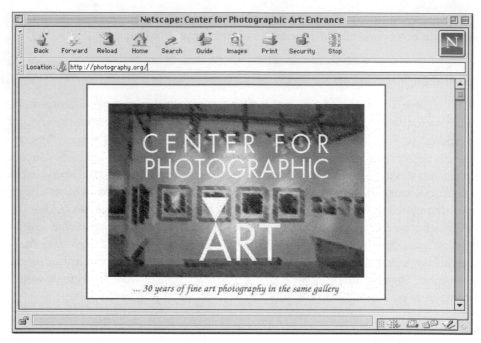

FIGURE 10.1 Center for Photographic Art Web Site

where selection is somewhat limited. In all of these situations, the audience has a choice of selecting one or more magazines or reading nothing at all. Electronic media offer many options as well. A typical cable system in the late 1990s offers thirty or more television channels from which to choose. The audience decides to watch, read, listen, select more than one medium, or avoid media altogether.

The example of magazines can be directly compared to the Internet. Internet users face a huge assortment of selections. Like magazines, the Internet offers many selections by interest area. Photography enthusiasts can go to the Web site for the *Center for Photographic Art*. This site features a juried virtual exhibit of photographs. Interested persons can become members of the Center or purchase copies of photographs. Unlike magazines that may offer only information about joining or purchasing, the Web site allows users to complete the action of buying or joining online easily and quickly.

People interested in gourmet cooking can go to a Web site that features *Italian cuisine*. The site not only gives information about Italian cuisine, but it also has classes (taught in English or other languages) for the dedicated enthusiast. For those interested specifically in gourmet cooking with caviar, a Web site called *Mr. Caviar and Gourmet Food* from LaFayette International Trading explains how caviar can be

FIGURE 10.2 Gourmet Food Web Site

served with champagne and, of course, purchased through the company. *Antique car* enthusiasts can go to a Web site that offers a classified listing of antique autos for sale.

It appears that the World Wide Web actually supplants magazines in some ways. Web sites offer quick information and the opportunity to get more information either at the site or through links. In addition, it offers something print magazines cannot: the ability for users to take action by giving feedback, joining, or even buying online.

Now that Internet use has become widespread, it becomes even more difficult to believe that the audience is passive. People seek out Web sites because the sites offer information or entertainment that they want. The process that must be followed in order to get to a specific site is often complicated and can be thought of as purposeful, motivated behavior. Getting on the Internet requires starting a computer, accessing the Internet service provider, activating the browser, and then either typing in a URL or going to a Favorites list and clicking on a favorite, or selecting from a menu offered by the browser. Once a desired Web site is found, the user can buy products, join a group or club, or communicate with the person(s) in charge of the site.

Agenda Setting

Over seventy years ago, Walter Lippmann (1922) noted that the news media had the ability to help define our world. The media were adept at bringing issues, personalities, and events to the attention of the public. In fact, society was somewhat dependent upon media to bring these things of interest to the public in a world that was becoming more complex each day. Lippmann suggested that there is an *environment* (reality) and a *pseudo-environment* (the pictures and perceptions in our head). The pseudo-environment is dependent upon the media to help sketch these pictures. This notion, that the media help us shape our perception of reality and the relative importance of people, issues, and events is referred to as *agenda setting*. The media helps us to decide what is important to know about by showing us what is "out there" and giving some opinion as to the relative importance of each piece of information. The audience can easily tell how important a news item is by where it is placed in a newscast, or how long the story about the item lasts on air.

While the audience ascribes credibility to information from traditional news sources, such as newspapers, radio, and television, the Internet does not quite enjoy the same credibility. As mentioned earlier, information disseminated on the Internet may or may not be edited or reviewed by trustworthy professionals, as it is in the major vehicles of the mass media. The screening process on the Internet has more to do with the author's access to space on the Internet rather than accuracy or importance. The process of gatekeeping in the mass media, which involves professionals deciding what information is presented and for how long, does not have a general equivalent on the information superhighway. The exception to this can be found at sites sponsored by traditional organizations that maintain credible news operations and images found in other media (e.g., *New York Times on the Web, USA Today, CNN* Web sites).

NEW THEORETICAL PERSPECTIVES

It became impossible to avoid considering the audience as essentially active, not passive, and therefore mass media researchers and theoreticians had to adapt their perspectives to accommodate that important notion. This new theoretical perspective developed in the early 1970s and became known as the uses and gratifications perspective on mass media.

Uses and Gratifications

The uses and gratifications approach to the study of mass media has three initial objectives. The first objective is to attempt to explain how people use media to serve some inner purpose. The second is to try to understand the motives for using media. The third objective is to identify functions or consequences that are a result of audience needs and behaviors. In addition, there are some underlying assumptions: that (1) audiences are goal-oriented and actively pursue communication; (2) audiences seek communication to serve needs and desires; (3) there are individual differences in the way people select and respond to communication; (4) media compete with other forms of communication for audience attention; and (5) interpersonal communication is usually more powerful than media (Rosengren, 1974; Rubin & Windahl, 1986; Palmgreen, Wenner, & Rosengren, 1985).

These objectives and underlying assumptions seem to be a good approach for the study of Internet use. People use the Internet to fulfill needs. They use the Internet to find needed information. A user might search the Internet for intellectual research purposes, such as looking for information about climatic conditions in New Zealand for a college term paper. Rather than physically going to the library, Net users can use a search engine to find what they are looking for. Entering the phrase "New Zealand weather" can produce references that would provide information on the topic. A term paper on the War of 1812 can be researched by typing "War of 1812" into a search engine. This should yield over two thousand relevant sites with subtopics such as diaries and autobiographies of people who lived through the war, payrolls and muster rolls from the army, a chronology of the war, and a listing of scholarly journal articles about the war.

Another purposeful information-gathering use of the Internet is getting travel information, like airplane departure times or fares. There are a number of sites that offer discount fares on major airlines. Making a plane reservation can also be accomplished directly at an airline Web site.

The Internet allows users to communicate with others. In some ways, the use of e-mail is supplanting use of the telephone. It is easier to pick up a phone and call people directly rather than use a computer that requires procedures like selecting a program, connecting to an Internet service provider with a modem, and then entering the appropriate e-mail address, but one advantage of using e-mail instead of the telephone is cost. ISPs commonly charge a flat fee for use, regardless of where messages are sent or how long they are. Another attractive aspect of using the Internet for communicating with others has to do with connecting with like-minded people who may be unknown to users outside of the Internet. Interest groups, listservs, and bulletin boards all go beyond telephone calls or face-to-face communication because they connect people who have common interests and want to discuss them. Fans of rock groups, hockey players, and various breeds of dogs, cats, or birds can go to Web sites to discuss these topics with other people who have similar interests and the time to discuss them. The *Antique Firearm Network* Web site offers separate listservs for rifle collectors, pistol collectors, shotgun collectors, black powder shooters, and others.

E-mail can be used at any time of the day or night. People can send or respond to messages when it is convenient. Although most people would be hesitant to call another person at two in the morning, sending e-mail at that time is quite acceptable. E-mail doesn't wake anyone up or disturb them while they are eating or working.

Internet use for entertainment continues to increase. A Web site like *Rodney Dangerfield*'s is one for a passive audience. Audience members who seek an interactive site can visit the *Comedy Central* Web site. This site encourages the audience to interact with a fictitious cartoon character, Dr. Katz, Professional Therapist.

Selective Exposure

A concept central to the study of communication is *selective exposure* (Zillmann & Bryant, 1985). Stated in simple terms, it is the process of audiences' choosing media. The concept has been studied from numerous perspectives, such as which programs audience members select to view when they are in various mood states (Zillmann, Hezel, & Medoff, 1980) or what types of comedy programs people in bad moods will select (Medoff, 1982). This process is also demonstrated when a buyer selects a magazine from a rack that carries many magazines or when a reader goes to the sports section of the daily newspaper, skipping the opinion and editorial pages. Related to this concept is *selective perception,* which is the process whereby audience members tend to focus on information that supports their interests or viewpoints. In a radio story about a local political campaign, supporters of a political candidate might "hear" how the candidate spent his or her own money running the campaign, while nonsupporters might hear that the candidate could not raise enough money from supporters.

People often remember those things from communication messages that support their viewpoints or are in keeping with their views of reality. This is referred to as *selective retention* or recall. Although some scientists claim that the human brain records everything to which it is exposed, humans rarely can recall a large portion of what they have seen or heard in the media. Humans often recall what supports their beliefs, is extremely pleasurable (e.g., a new rock song by their favorite group), or is extremely unpleasant and/or memorable, such as news about a recent airline tragedy or terrorist attack. Simply stated, selective exposure, selective perception, and selective retention refer to the way people generally approach the mass media: they look for certain types of messages, they perceive messages in keeping with their viewpoints, and they retain or remember facts that support their personal viewpoints.

The general idea of selectivity is especially appropriate for the study of the Internet, since the Internet offers almost limitless selections for the audience. No Web sites are mandatory; users voluntarily visit the sites. Another feature of the

Internet is the overwhelming amount of information it contains. Users need to demonstrate selective exposure just to manage the huge amounts of information that come to them via the Net.

Critical Mass

The notion of critical mass as it applies to the adoption of a new communication technology is helpful in understanding how the technology becomes widespread. The term comes from physics, where *critical mass* refers to the minimum amount of material needed to trigger and sustain a radioactive chain reaction. The term has been loosely applied to communication and refers to the minimum number of people needed as adopters before a new communication technology can have a permanent place in society.

Markus (1987) used this term in describing the adoption of interactive communication technologies. She suggested three propositions in the adoption process. First, the adoption and use of the technology is an all or nothing proposition. When sufficient numbers of adopters exist in the community, eventually all members will adopt the technology. The best example of this is the telephone, which has nearly ubiquitous use. Second, resources of the individual are important. The fewer resources required to adopt the technology, the greater the chances are that the technology will be adopted. Third, the early adoption by individuals who have extensive resources is needed as well as a heterogeneity of resources throughout the community. When these requirements are met, the chances that a critical mass will be reached are enhanced. Examples of the critical mass perspective on communication technology adoption in the recent past are fax machines, telephone answering machines, and e-mail. It would be useless for corporations or individuals to purchase fax machines for sending and receiving print material if their intended receivers do not have fax machines. Similarly, people who have e-mail capability would not use it often if e-mail were not widespread enough to reach most of their intended audience.

An interesting aspect of the critical mass perspective is that widespread use appears to have a snowball effect. Once a perceived critical mass is using the technology, those without it are strongly motivated to adopt it. The reasoning here is that despite the drawbacks, such as cost or difficulty in using the technology, people (and institutions) are pressured to adopt the technology because failure to do so may exclude them from existing communication networks (Williams, Strover, & Grant, 1994).

Diffusion of Innovation

Diffusion of innovation is an area of study that embraces a general theory regarding how a population adopts new processes and technologies. This area of study includes evaluating how information about the processes and technologies are communicated, evaluated, and adopted (or not adopted). This type of analysis has been applied to a variety of innovations, not just those in communication, although the method of inquiry is similar whether the innovation is a communication technology, an agricultural process or implement, or a household appliance. This approach is related to the critical mass concept in that it looks at percentage of adoption as an important outcome. In addition, it also considers the rate of adoption, or adoption of the innovation over time. This theoretical perspective offers four steps in the process of adopting an innovation: knowledge, persuasion, decision, and confirmation. Knowledge is the part of the process where an individual gets information about the innovation. This generally occurs before the individual forms attitudes about the innovation. Persuasion is the second step of the process and is the point at which the potential adopter makes an evaluative decision about the innovation. The next step is the actual behavior that results in adoption or nonadoption. The final step in the process is confirmation, where communication is used to appraise the decision. If a negative decision was made, the decision may be reversed at this point (Williams et al., 1994).

Play Theory

Social scientists have long been influenced by the notion that mass media should provide the information necessary for people in society to learn about society and take action to improve it. This notion has been a basis for criticism of mass media for many years and is based upon work published by Lazarsfeld and Merton (as restated in Lazarsfeld & Merton, 1971). Specifically, these authors state that one of the social consequences of mass media exposure can be referred to as the narcotizing dysfunction of mass media, because it serves a *dys*function to society by rendering a large part of society apathetic and inert. The authors of this notion suggest that the vast amounts of information available to society via the mass media tends to cause members of society to be complacent with a cursory understanding of societal issues and elicits only a superficial concern with actually dealing with the problems. Thus, media is good only if the result has some social value that impacts society as a whole.

Stephenson put forth a contrasting view. Rather than looking for social action, Stephenson suggested that use of media by individuals is a step in an *existential* direction, that is, a matter of subjectivity, which invites freedom where there had been little or none before (Stephenson, 1967). Essentially, Stephenson sees an important function of media use being *play*, rather than work. Citing Huizinga (1950), Stephenson states that play is important to society because it permits culture to evolve and stabilize. Play teaches loyalty, competitiveness, and patience. Using play, people can check the monotony, determinism, and brutality of nature.

The Internet and World Wide Web certainly offer fuel for both perspectives. Where the narcotizing dysfunction theory offers a view of society being bombarded with information that creates inertia, play theory seems to say that media has a beneficial effect upon society. The amount of information available on the Internet is truly mind-boggling. As mentioned in Chapter 9, people have become so involved with Internet use that they can be considered addicted to its use. Certainly this can be considered a negative effect of the information superhighway. On the other hand, the Internet offers a nearly limitless opportunity for play behavior. Various sites, such as the *Solaria Interactive* Web site, offer games to play by oneself or with others and other sites offer information and entertainment that provide pleasant stimulation for the Web surfer. Many pre-teens (mostly girls) have visited the official Web site of the *Hansons,* a pop rock group of three young brothers. Fans of the situation comedy *Seinfeld* can try to satisfy their desire for more information about the show and its stars by visiting sites like the *Seinfeld Trivia Challenge,* or *The Soup Nazi Headquarters.*

Boston University and *Online Games* offer interactive games that are engaging and easy for both children and adults to play. For a more complex game, try *To Boldly Go,* a game based on the popular Star Trek television programs.

Zarf's List of Interactive Games on the Web lists Web games, Web adventures interactive strategy games, Web MUDs, and more for surfers looking for a variety of games and diversions. Adults who feel that game playing for fun is pointless can try their luck with money at stake at a Web gambling site (also known as Net gambling or nambling) like the *Grand Dominican* or the *Casino Royale* site.

Cultivation

The cultivation perspective on mass communication research represents a slightly different approach to the study of the effects of mass media on society. Rather than looking for noticeable changes in individuals, cultivation focuses on research that shows the absorption of diverse conceptions and attitudes into a common mainstream (Gerbner, Gross, Morgan, & Signorielli, 1980). Heavy television viewers that come from diverse backgrounds tend to share similar attitudes and behaviors. Essentially, the cultivation effect of heavy television viewing is the mainstreaming of the audience. In addition, this perspective suggests a two-way effect between the media and the audience. Just as the media affects the way the audience thinks and behaves, audience behavior influences the program material that becomes successful in the media. The cultivation perspective assumes a broad and sometimes subtle influence of the media upon the audience and vice versa.

Cultivation is especially intriguing when applied to the Internet. Audiences can certainly be affected by the content of the Internet, especially those audience members who spend large amounts of time online while decreasing other media

FIGURE 10.3 Central Plaza, an Interactive Game Web Site

use. The Internet becomes a powerful source of information on a wide variety of topics and behaviors, such as medical information or shopping. As the cultivation perspective suggests that the audience influences the media, Internet audience members can also be Internet information suppliers by creating their own Web pages that can disseminate their own information or creativity. This "direct contribution" facet of the Internet lends support for viewing the effects of the Internet through the cultivation perspective.

SUMMARY: USING MASS COMMUNICATION THEORIES TO UNDERSTAND THE WEB

Rather than attempt to create a new theoretical perspective through which to view the Internet, it seems best to consider the Internet as a new medium of mass communication. Therefore, an overview of theoretical perspectives that have been developed through the study of the mass media should be helpful to facilitate a better understanding of the Internet.

Mass communication research began after World War I when society became aware of the power of propaganda. A first view of the effects of mass media on the audience was the "magic bullet theory." This theoretical perspective predicted that mass media had a very powerful direct effect on individuals.

Further study yielded evidence that an intervening variable, attitudes, influences the effect of the media on individuals. This research also influenced researchers to view the mass audience differently than before. The new view categorized the audience into groups that had ties, characteristics, and attitudes in common.

Researchers also became interested in how the audience actively sought out desirable mass communication and mass media, a notion that is appropriate for the study of Internet use. At about the same time, the importance of the agenda-setting function of mass media was beginning to be studied.

As researchers became more convinced of the active nature of the audience in media selection and use, a new theoretical perspective, the uses and gratifications approach, generated numerous studies and interest. This perspective attempts to explain how and why people use media. The study of selective exposure to the media investigates how the audience makes media selections, what part of the media the audience attends to, and what aspect or information contained in the media the audience remembers.

The concepts of critical mass and diffusion of innovation deal with the adoption of new technologies by society. Critical mass refers to a minimum number of people that must adopt a technology before that technology can have a permanent place in society. Diffusion of innovation is a general area of study that investigates how information about a new process or technology is communicated and evaluated. This approach is similar to the critical mass view because it contends that a certain minimum percentage of a population is required in order for the innovation to be accepted and have a permanent role in the development of society.

Play theory suggests that mass media provides an important role in society, that of escape. Play theory contends that society benefits from individuals who can obtain some freedom from monotony and determinism by seeking out mass media.

The cultivation perspective views the effects of mass communication on society in a very general way. Rather than look for specific cause-and-effect relationships, the cultivation perspective focuses on how the audience tends to blend into a mainstream of culture as a result of heavy mass media consumption. People in society tend to become more similar over time because they are exposed to the same set of stimuli from the mass media.

The role of theory is not merely to state how things work, but also to help researchers explain the past and the present. When theories are most useful, however, is when they can help us to predict the future. Studying the Internet is extremely difficult because it is changing so rapidly. As the technology changes, the audience changes. The usefulness of the Internet is changing daily with faster speeds, more information and Web sites and new functions, such as high-quality sound and video. The intention of placing the Internet into a theoretical framework is to help us use what we know about audiences and the media and apply that knowledge to predict how audiences will use the Internet and what effects the Internet will have on its audiences.

CHAPTER LINKS

Antique Cars—http://www.commercial.net/vault/ads/antcars.html

Antique Firearm Network—http:oldguns.com/AFNLists.htm

Boston University Interactive WWW Games—http://scv.bu.edu/games/

Casino Royale—http://www.funscape.com/makeorder.htm

Center for Photographic Art—http://www.photography.org

CNN—http://www.cnn.com/

Comedy Central—http://www.comedycentral.com

Discount airfares—http://www.best.com/~vacation/discountair/cairfares.html

Grand Dominican—http://www.granddominican.com

The Official Hanson site—http://www.hansonline.com

Italian cooking and travel links—http://www.italycookingschools.com/links.html

Mr. Caviar and Gourmet Food—http://www.wines.com/caviar/

The New York Times on the Web—http://www.nytimes.com/

Online Games—http://www.gegd.com/GAMES.html

Rodney Dangerfield—http://www.rodney.com

The Seinfeld Trivia Challenge—http://members.aol.com/SeinChal/index.html

Solaria Interactive (games)—http://www.solariagames.com/

The Soup Nazi Headquarters—http://members.aol.com/rynocub/soupnazi.htm

Stellar Crisis—http://www.televar.com/~acamp/sc.main.html

To Boldly Go—http://www.pbm.com/tbg/

USA Today—http://www.USATODAY.com/

Zarf's List of Interactive Games on the Web—http://www.leftfoot.com/games.html

REFERENCES

DeFleur, M., & Ball-Rokeach, S. (1989). *Theories of mass communication.* White Plains, NY: Longman.

Gerbner, G., Gross, L., Morgan, M., & Signorielli, N. (1980). The "mainstreaming" of America: Violence profile no. 11. *Journal of Communication, 3,* 10–29.

Huizinga, J. (1950). *Homo ludens.* Boston: Beacon Press.

Lazarsfeld, P., & Merton, R. (1974). Mass communication, popular taste, and organized social action. In W. Schramm & D. Roberts, *The process and effects of mass communication.* Urbana, IL: University of Illinois Press.

Lippmann, W. (1922). *Public opinion.* New York: MacMillan.

Markus, M. (1987). Toward a "critical mass" theory of interactive media: Universal access, interdependence and diffusion. *Communication Research, 14* (5), 491–511.

Medoff, N. J. (1982). Selective exposure to televised comedy programs. *Journal of Applied Communication Research, 10* (2), 117–32.

Palmgreen, P., Wenner, L. A., & Rosengren, K. E. (1985). Uses and gratifications research: The past ten years. In K. E. Rosengren, L. A. Wenner, & P. Palmgreen (Eds.), *Media gratifications research: Current perspectives.* Beverly Hills, CA: Sage

Rosengren, K. E. (1974). Uses and gratifications: A paradigm outlined. In J. G. Blumler & E. Katz (Eds.), *The uses of mass communications: Current perspectives on gratifications research.* Beverly Hills, CA: Sage.

Rubin, A. M., & Windahl, S. (1986). The uses and dependency model of mass communication. *Critical Studies in Mass Communication, 3,* 184–99.

Stephenson, W. (1967). *The play theory of mass communication.* Chicago: University of Chicago Press.

Williams, F., Strover, S., & Grant, A. E. (1994). Social aspects of new media technologies. In J. Bryant & D. Zillmann (Eds.), *Media effects: Advances in theory and research* (pp. 463–82). Hillsdale, NJ: Lawrence Erlbaum Associates.

Zillmann, D., & Bryant, J. (Eds.). (1985). *Selective exposure to communication.* Hillsdale, NJ: Lawrence Erlbaum Associates.

Zillmann, D., Hezel, R., & Medoff, N. (1980). The effect of affective states on selective exposure to televised entertainment fare. *Journal of Applied Social Psychology, 10,* 323–39.

CHAPTER ELEVEN

ETHICS AND LEGAL ISSUES

A nine-year-old girl was doing a simple search on the Internet for a school paper. She chose Los Angeles as her topic and did a search, listing the city name and "pictures." The response was one she did not expect. She received a direct link to a Web site that contained X-rated pictures. It has been found that entering words like animals, cheerleaders, or even school into a search engine can lead people to sexually explicit sites (Flynn, 1998).

As the Internet becomes available in schools and households throughout the country, many people are concerned that material on the Internet that is not suited for children will become easily accessible. Children are learning how to use the Internet in school and becoming adept at surfing the Net rapidly. Parents have become concerned that young children will have access to pornography on the information superhighway. Both the executive branch and the legislative branch of government shared their concern by including the Communication Decency Act in the Telecommunications Act of 1996. The Communication Decency Act has since been judged to be unconstitutional by the Supreme Court, because it interferes with the First Amendment that protects free speech for individuals and the press. Should children be protected from offensive material on the Internet? How can this be accomplished? Should the First Amendment, written when only print media existed, apply to the Internet?

"In my ignorance, I have to accept the real possibility that if we had to decide today just what the First Amendment should mean in cyberspace, we would get it fundamentally wrong."

(Supreme Court Justice David Souter, 1997)

ETHICS AND ETHICAL BEHAVIOR

Ethics is concerned with how people make decisions that lead to behaviors. It focuses on questions of right and wrong, good and bad, responsibility and irresponsibility. If behavior is viewed as a series of choices between alternative actions, people choose between "good" choices and "bad" choices. Ethics helps people to decide which choices to make; however, ethics does not always dictate or even guide behavior.

There is no rigid standard for what is ethical behavior and what is not, but most people do think about ethics when making behavioral decisions. This is the case even for small children, who often intuitively choose the right kinds of behaviors. In young children the difference between the two kinds of behaviors is often simple and clear-cut. Stealing from another child or hurting others is considered bad behavior, while sharing and being considerate of others is considered good behavior. As children mature, they learn to understand the subtleties that help them to distinguish between bad and good behavior. Sharing may not always be appropriate, and too much consideration of others can be harmful to one's self.

The ethical choices of famous people are often in the headlines; however, ethics is not confined only to newsworthy people. President Clinton received an enormous amount of press attention when word of his extramarital sexual behavior with a White House intern surfaced (on a Web gossip sheet called the Drudge Report). When the famous suicide doctor Dr. Jack Kevorkian assists a person in committing suicide, it is a legal issue in some states. In Oregon, where assisted suicide is now legal, it is an ethical issue. But ethics also applies to a student who cheats on an exam or a taxpayer who gives misleading information to the IRS on an income tax form. Ethics goes beyond issues of legality and illegality. Behaviors that are legal may be unethical. In everyday life, lying is not necessarily illegal (except in court), but can certainly be improper.

ETHICS AND THE MASS MEDIA

Since the 1980s, electronic media in this country have enjoyed a progressively deregulated environment. Following the lead of the Reagan White House, Congress repeatedly reaffirmed that the marketplace, rather than government, should decide how the electronic media in our country should operate and continue to grow. The *Telecommunications Act of 1996* was written to update the Communications Act of 1934 and bring regulation of electronic media more in line with the profound technological and social changes that have had an enormous impact upon mass media. Generally, the 1996 Act maintains a posture that encourages competition while relaxing some of the restrictions on broadcast station ownership. (For more information about the Telecommunications Act, go to the Telecommunications Act—Summary.)

It is in this deregulatory environment that the Internet has become widely accessible to a large portion of our country's population, and the World Wide Web has arguably become the newest mass medium. In general, deregulation leads to an increased need for an emphasis on ethics. For people who use the Internet users will behave appropriately—that is, to be fair to others, to make the "right" decisions—if they have to have a sense of ethics.

As this courtry's laws governing electronic mass media have become more relaxed, the need for self-regulation and ethical media behavior increases. Some key areas of broadcasting regulation have either expired or have been changed by the Telecommunications Act of 1996. Two noteworthy examples of changes in regulation are financial syndication (fin-syn) and station ownership.

Fin-Syn Rules

The Federal Communication Commission worked for years to regulate the television networks' financial control over television programming. The FCC's goal was to stimulate diversity of programming by preventing networks from selling programs that were produced by the network. Essentially the FCC wanted to keep the networks out of the syndication business. Beginning in 1965, the FCC labored continuously to achieve its goal of restricting network financial control over programs. The rulings put forth by the FCC were known as the "fin-syn" or financial syndication rules.

The rules expired in 1991, and the FCC tried to put in place a modified set of fin-syn rules. The attempt failed, and now the networks are free to own as much or as little as they choose of the programming they distribute in prime time. The major networks now have the legal ability to maintain very tight control over which programs will air on the networks, when these programs will go off the networks, and how these programs will be aired after they are off the networks. This ability to vertically control the programming market can deleteriously affect independent stations or new networks. Programs that go "off-net" such as *Seinfeld* or *Mad About You,* if owned by the network, can be restricted in the syndicated showings of the program. If the NBC network owned these sitcoms, it could have the policy that only NBC-owned and operated stations or NBC affiliate stations can show the programs after they leave the network prime time schedule. This ability to control competition presents a potential ethical problem for the networks, since control of programming is no longer a legal issue.

Station Ownership

The number of radio and television stations that can be owned by a single entity was restricted for many years. The FCC's motivation behind these rules was to diversify ownership of electronic media. Diversity in ownership, it was believed, would lead to diversity in opinion when stations editorialized and chose programs. One owner was allowed to no more than twelve television stations nationwide. The rule also stated that a group of stations could not reach more than 25 percent of the television households in the country. Other restrictions prevented an entity from owning more than one television station in one market. As a result of the Telecommunications Act of 1996, the 25 percent ruling has been raised to 35 percent, and the one station per market rule will also be relaxed, especially when UHF stations are involved.

Before the Telecommunications Act of 1996, radio restrictions had set ownership levels at twenty FM stations and twenty AM stations per entity (increased from even tighter restrictions set by the Communications Act of 1934). Currently, there is no limit on the number of stations that can be owned by an entity, but there are some local limits. One entity cannot own more than 50 percent of the stations in any one market.

Ethical Guidelines

In the absence of specific laws or regulations to govern behavior, some of the mass media engage in self-regulation. This self-regulation establishes ethical guidelines to help direct behavior in ways that are appropriate for the organization, the individuals in the organization, the people who conduct business with the organization, and the audience.

Over the past seventy-five years, professional associations have continued to attempt to lift the ethical and moral standards of media practitioners. One of the earliest attempts was in 1923, when the American Society of Newspaper Editors adopted a code of ethics known as the Canons of Journalism. Similar codes exist among advertising, public relations, and broadcast professionals. In 1929, the National Association of Broadcasters (NAB) established a code of ethics for radio. In 1952, the NAB established a code for television. The codes were amended to keep up with the times and changes in broadcasting and the audience. These codes were voluntary, and individual stations or groups of stations either subscribed to them or they did not. About 50 percent of all radio stations subscribed to them, and about 65 percent of all television stations subscribed. Obviously, management policy dictated the willingness of the individual stations to adhere to the policies put forth by the NAB Code. The codes dealt with issues like political broadcasting and programming for children. Both programming and advertising issues were covered.

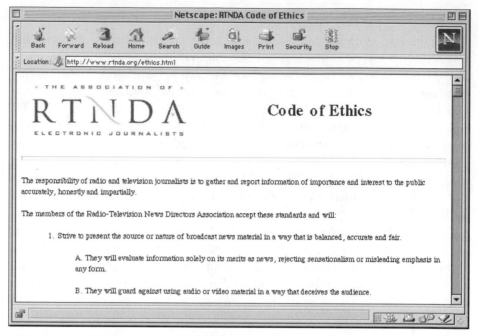

FIGURE 11.1 Web Site Featuring the RTNDA Code of Ethics for Professional Behavior in Radio and Television Reporting

Because of several factors, including an antitrust suit that found that broadcasters were forcing advertising prices to remain high by limiting the number of allowable advertising minutes per hour, the NAB revoked its Code in 1983. In broadcasting now, much of the "code of conduct" material exists within station groups and station management. Some professional associations deal with certain aspects of the media, such as news, that continue to provide codes for ethical conduct.

The Radio-Television News Directors Association (RTNDA) has drawn up one such set of guidelines. This set of guidelines, also known as the Code of Broadcast News Ethics, carries with it no force of law. The RTNDA, comprised of leaders of broadcast news organizations, hopes that the guidelines will protect both the newscasters and the audience. The Code of Broadcast News Ethics is typical in electronic media in that it "prescribes" or gives rules for acceptable behavior for practitioners. The guidelines discourage news reporting that relies on sensationalism or audience deception. News that is presented as spontaneous should not be rehearsed or staged. Opinion should be labeled as such. Errors, when they occur, should be corrected promptly. Confidential sources should be protected, and everyone's right to a fair trial should be respected. When another broadcaster's work is used, it should be given appropriate credit, or permission should be obtained for its use. Obviously, these guidelines attempt to promote truth and fairness in news reporting. There is value in the guidelines, because they can lead to audience trust and a beneficial environment for the dissemination of news and information. By gaining audience trust, news organizations can benefit financially. The guidelines help to establish credibility, which leads to a loyal audience.

ETHICAL PERSPECTIVES

Of numerous ethical perspectives used by theorists and media practitioners, two will be discussed in this chapter: the deontological and teleological perspectives.

Deontological Perspective

The deontological (from the Greek word *deon,* meaning "duty") perspective views ethics from a purely moral standpoint. It states that human behavior should be guided by moral principles, which can be obtained through religion, human conscience, reason, or society in general. This perspective believes that good behavior comes from a set (or sets) of good rules. Using this perspective, outcomes or results of actions are not considered, even if violating a rule from a deontological viewpoint leads to a benefit for the individual or society. An example of this type of thinking comes from the "categorical imperative," a principle developed by Immanuel Kant. The categorical imperative dictates that proper behavior comes from acting on principles that you would want to become universal law. Similar to the golden rule, it states that people should behave in a way that would be appropriate for all.

An example of deontological ethics at work in cyberspace would be strong anti-obscenity rules that apply to the Internet. Since obscene and pornographic material is often viewed as bad for society and especially for young people, the deontological perspective would hold that this type of material should be outlawed and either not available in general or, at least, not available to children.

Teleological Perspective

Teleological (from the Greek work *teleos,* which means "result") perspectives view the rightness or wrongness of behavior based on the results of that behavior. Behaviors that result in overall good for society are ethical and moral. Behaviors that may be right in some situations may be wrong in other situations, depending on their outcomes or consequences. A good example of this type of ethical thinking is utilitarianism. Teleological ethics suggests that ethical behavior is behavior that results in the greatest good for the largest number of people. Or, similarly, it will result in the least harm to the most people. This perspective can be simplified to a ratio or fraction: good divided by evil or good/evil. The larger the result, the more ethical the behavior (Vivian, 1997; Dominick, Sherman, & Copeland, 1996).

The example concerning obscenity and pornography discussed previously can be used here as well. From a teleological perspective, preserving the integrity of the First Amendment will lead to the greatest good for the greatest number of people in society because it guarantees the freedom of speech to all. Therefore, allowing obscenity and pornography to be accessible to all on the Internet actually preserves the First Amendment, leading to the largest beneficial result for society.

Ethical decisions are not a result of sheer calculation. Ethics are related to conscience, too. Determination of what is ethical and what is not is partly a subjective decision and partly a determination of outcomes (although not for deontological thinkers). In addition, what is considered to be ethical can depend upon which ethical perspective is chosen. In a sense, ethics and ethical decision making are something of an art. The resolution of ethical issues is not exact; it is ongoing and evolving. Any two people may have very different ideas about what is ethical in any given situation. But when there is a strong consensus about what is ethical, there is a likelihood that the ethical belief may become a law.

Such is the case with the First Amendment to the Constitution. The language, "Congress shall make no law . . . abridging the freedom of speech" gives wide freedom for people in this country to speak their minds about almost anything. Since the amendment was first written in the eighteenth century, the writers had no vision of electronic media in general and certainly no visions about the huge interconnection of networks that has become the Internet. It appears, however, that the Internet will enjoy the freedom of speech as intended by the First Amendment. This creates a situation on the Internet where there is protection from government intervention in an individual's right to "speak out," or in Internet terms, post a message or create a Web page that expresses the individual's opinions. Media often has an organizational structure that includes levels of review before publication. Newspaper articles are often corrected by experienced editors and sometimes reviewed by management and publishers. The evening news on television is usually read and/or viewed by editors or persons in a chain of responsibility that tries to ensure that the stories presented on the broadcast are accurate. This system of gatekeeping, though far from perfect, gives a media organization an opportunity to screen its information before it is disseminated. This process is assisted by professional guidelines, such as the RTNDA Code of Broadcast News Ethics, because many professionals in broadcast journalism are familiar with the practice dictated by the Code and subscribe to it.

Internet publishing is often guided by the conscience of the individual provider rather than by rules, laws, or professional ethical guidelines. When a pro-

FIGURE 11.2 Freedom Forum Web Page

fessional news organization, such as the *New York Times* or CNN, is the Internet publisher, the organization abides by professional guidelines and the material that the organization places on the Internet is reviewed for accuracy and appropriateness. Internet material published by individuals or groups that do not adopt professional ethical guidelines can be opinionated, biased, or simply inaccurate. Facts can be misrepresented or totally fabricated to suit the needs of the person or group publishing the information. The hope is that in the marketplace of ideas, human beings are capable of discovering the truth. This concept, expressed in John Milton's *Areopagitica* in 1644, is an eloquent argument against censorship. By having a wide selection of ideas from which to choose, people can apply reason to select the very best ideas. Even a bad idea or inaccurate information should be available, because it may present parts of ideas or opinions worth considering.

Whether the Internet should be protected by the First Amendment is still debated. There are public interest groups that feel the Internet should be regulated in order to protect children from being exposed to indecent material. Other groups feel that any restrictions on the content of the Internet would be inappropriate, because the restrictions would violate the right to free speech.

LEGAL ISSUES

Free Speech on the Internet

Although the question of whether the Internet is truly a mass medium is still being debated, the lack of resolution of the question has not slowed discussion of how the Internet relates to the issue of free speech. Generally, the rule-making has to do with ease of entry and availability of channel space. Print media, with its ease of entry (conceptually, at least), enjoys the full protection of the First Amendment of the Constitution. This essentially prevents any bona fide rule-making body (e.g., Congress, federal regulatory agencies, or any state legislative body) from making a rule that would prevent or discourage a free press. Electronic media, on the other hand, are treated more on a case-by-case or technology-by-technology basis. While cable and satellite television enjoy few restraints, broadcasting requires a lengthy licensing procedure with many legal constraints on operation. Most of these restraints are technical in nature, but when considering content, broadcasting only enjoys partial First Amendment protection. The restriction and general basis for regulation are justified on three principles. The first is that there are few frequencies available for use in the electromagnetic spectrum. Since the electromagnetic spectrum is a limited natural resource, Congress retains the right to protect it. The second principle is that electronic media is pervasive, making it nearly impossible to prevent it from reaching children. The third principle is that the citizens of this country own the airwaves through which the signal travels.

The notion that Congress has the right to regulate electronic media has been upheld by the Supreme Court. The Court has taken the position that "the amount of protection offered to information by the First Amendment varies according to the medium in which the information is conveyed" (*Red Lion Broadcasting Co. v. FCC*, 1969). More information about the *Red Lion* case is available at the *Media Access* site.

The idea that Congress must protect the scarce frequencies that are available for use, born in the early days of radio, does not include similar media that reach the audience through other delivery systems (e.g., coaxial cable or telephone lines). Pay cable channels such as HBO or Showtime often show frontal nudity and allow four-letter words not heard on broadcast stations. Television broadcasters do not show frontal nudity or allow spoken obscenity on their programs, because to do so may draw complaints from audience members who find it offensive or feel that children should not be exposed to it. This would result in FCC scrutiny and possible punitive action, which is something broadcasters studiously avoid. Cable channels that charge a subscription fee, such as HBO, can show material that would not be shown on broadcast television, because households that receive HBO have made an informed and conscious decision to receive the material.

The logic for treating the Internet as similar to the printing press has had much support.

> Both allow the easier, more widespread distribution of wrong information, irrelevant information, and even evil information. Yet few would argue today that the printing press did not provide an overall social benefit and few will argue in the future that the Net was not similarly a boon. (Wallace & Mangan, 1996)

Specifically addressing the comparison between broadcasting and the Net:

> . . . the Court has specifically relied on spectrum scarcity, pervasiveness of the medium, special harm to children, and potential for monopolization to justify a lower standard of First Amendment protection for telegraphy, telephony, and broadcasting. These justifications, while problematic even as applied to date, have little application to the variety of information networks spreading across the nation and around the globe. To the extent the justifications have any relevance, existing law, particularly antitrust law, is sufficient to deal effectively with any issues that may arise without offending vital First Amendment principles. (Cate, 1995)

Recent Legislation

The Telecommunications Act of 1996 was meant to revise the Communications Act of 1934 and bring legislation up to date with new technologies in communication. In the new Act was a piece of legislation called the Communications Decency Act (CDA), which attempted to sharply limit "indecent" communication. The intention of the amendment was to prevent Internet pornography from being accessible to children. Under this law, offenders who were caught posting indecent material could be punished with fines up to $250,000 or even be sentenced to prison. Although the amendment sounded like a good idea, it drew immediate criticism from civil libertarians and proponents of the Internet who felt that the amendment was a direct attack on Internet free speech. Critics also felt that the term *indecent* was too vague and would make complying with the amendment difficult and enforcing the amendment even more difficult.

In the case of *Reno* (Janet Reno, Attorney General of the United States) *v. ACLU* (American Civil Liberties Union), the Supreme Court ruled that the CDA was unconstitutional because it was overly broad in its attempt to eliminate indecent material from the Internet. In addition, the Supreme Court dealt directly with the idea of interfering with free speech on the Internet:

> As a matter of constitutional tradition, in the absence of evidence to the contrary, we presume that governmental regulation of the content of speech is more likely to interfere with the free exchange of ideas than to encourage it. The interest in encouraging freedom of expression in a democratic society outweighs

any theoretical but unproven benefit of censorship. (Supreme Court Justice J. P. Stevens, *Reno v. ACLU*, 1997)

The Court's ruling confirmed previous rulings by lower courts that concluded that regulation of content on the Internet must meet the strictest Constitutional requirements under the First Amendment and that filtering technologies provide a less restrictive means to protect children.

Groups that led the fight against the CDA strongly prefer that parents use blocking or filtering software to prevent their children from accessing pornography and that Web sites follow the example of the movie and television industries by initiating a voluntary rating system. Lori Fena, executive director of the Electronic Frontier Foundation stated, "What this [ruling] means is that the responsibility for controlling our content lies on us—the citizens and the parents—and this is a call for all of us once again to demonstrate how we can be trusted to use this medium responsibly" (Fena, 1997).

A new attempt at CDA legislation, an amendment to an appropriations bill, attempts to limit commercial distribution of material "harmful" to minors (Gunn, 1998). More information about the CDA and related issues can be found at the *ACLU* Web site or the *Electronic Frontier Foundation* Web site.

Community Standards

The question of what is indecent poses an interesting dilemma. Typically, the courts have upheld the restrictions to material that is obscene according to the standards of the local community (*Miller v. California*, 1973). This model works for local radio stations or even local community newspapers, but does it work for the Internet? The nature of the Internet is not local. A message posted on the Internet can be visited by Web surfers next door, in the next block, next county, or a continent away. Whose standards are applied to a Web site posted in New York City but read in Peoria, Illinois? This question can also be asked about a clear-channel AM radio station based in New York or Chicago but heard in Florida, or a television station like WGN in Chicago that is retransmitted by cable to homes throughout the country.

Although there is a compelling government interest in protecting children, the Supreme Court rejected the analogy that equates the Internet to broadcast radio or television. The court believes that the Internet is less invasive than broadcasting and that obscene materials on the Internet are *not* commonly encountered inadvertently.

Privacy

An ongoing concern of the American public is the right to privacy—not only the kind of privacy that people like to have behind closed doors, but also privacy regarding their personal information. For example, citizens are concerned that others may learn about how they spend money (through credit card information or online buying), how they spend their time (which sites they visit when surfing the Internet), or other personal information like their phone number, address, medical records, or mortgage payment. People have long complained that the government has too much access to this type of personal data; now people are becoming concerned that corporations and even other individuals can access this information through the Internet.

E-mail

Most people feel relatively confident that conversations over regular telephone lines (not cellular communications) are private. Many people feel (and perhaps appropriately) that e-mail conversations are *not* totally private.

Recently, some government officials have been chastised for e-mail correspondence that was believed to be private, but became public. Using colorful terms like *slimebucket* and *putrid* to describe people encountered during work for the local county government provided a lesson in the privacy of e-mail for one government official. The e-mail was somehow obtained by another government worker and leaked to the local newspaper. As the supervisor of the embarrassed employee stated, "E-mail in a government setting is really the equivalent of a government memo. You better be ready to have it show up in the newspaper" (McCloy, 1997).

Many companies can obtain an individual's e-mail address and send solicitations and advertising to that person without consent. Since e-mail addresses appear on business cards, publications, directories, and similar public communication, strangers can send e-mail messages to almost anyone. While some of these can be informative or desirable, they are often considered unwelcome and unwanted. The term *spamming* refers to unsolicited e-mail messages sent to an unsuspecting (an often unreceptive) audience.

Electronic Transactions

Electronic transactions on the Internet have been an ongoing concern for individuals, the media, and lawmakers. This issue centers on the concern that transactions conducted over the Internet may yield information to third parties. The information may reveal an individual's Internet purchases as well as information that is traditionally kept secret: charge account numbers and other information that might allow unauthorized (and therefore criminal) use of a person's credit cards. Although this concern was also expressed some years ago when the use of 800-numbers for credit-card purchases became common; people embraced the ease and relative security of placing an order in this manner, even if it did not require the signature of the cardholder. This type of telephone transaction is actually very similar to the process of using credit cards for purchasing products through the Web.

Encryption

There are groups in this country (for example, the Electronic Frontier Foundation and the American Civil Liberties Union) that believe that the issue of privacy on the Internet can be solved by allowing individuals to use software that would scramble Internet communication. This type of software, called encryption technology, could conceivably allow businesses and individuals to communicate online without the information being retrieved and understood by unrelated third parties who have no right to the information. This technology is touted as able to prevent eavesdropping on private communication or theft of information. At present there are laws that restrict the availability of powerful encryption programs. The logic here is that the government feels that it should have access to this information, but a powerful encryption program can prevent such government access. In addition, export controls discourage software companies from developing these types of products.

KEY ESCROW Congress has received several proposals that consider the notion of regulating encryption products. One feature of these proposals would force the encryption software products to include a trusted third party that would hold the key to the encryption process. This notion, also referred to as key escrow, would allow governmental officials the legal right and ability to go to the third party and get the encryption key, which would allow the government to read the data streams of suspected criminals (Machrone, 1997).

At first glance, the idea of key escrow seems to make sense. Stroryption software products can be used to prevent outsiders from accessing private information about the buying behavior of individuals, groups, or corporate entities. If, for legal reasons, the government must access this information, the law enforcement agency can go to the third party that holds the specific encryption key "in escrow." Except for bona fide law enforcement agencies, privacy for electronic commerce would be intact. However, some pundits and Internet proponents disagree.

These people have expressed the opinion that if strong encryption without key escrow is outlawed, only outlaws will have strong encryption. They believe that once key software is deposited with the trusted third party, then hackers at all levels will try to break into the escrow accounts of these third parties. If any of the hackers are successful, then the encryption of all of the depositors becomes compromised and is therefore worse than useless. The thinking here is that using encryption programs whose keys have been stolen by hackers would be worse than using no encryption at all. The users would believe that they still have security when in fact they do not. There is more here than just the fear that an individual's privacy would be invaded; some knowledgeable Internet professionals feel that key escrow could have a chilling effect on all of Internet commerce, slowing growth and generally causing people and corporations to avoid completing transactions on the Internet.

Sale of Information

Another concern that deals with privacy involves the sale of information. A computer service company can obtain information about an individual or household and sell that information to a third party. Recently there has been some regulation proposed (H.R. 98, Consumer Internet Privacy Protection Act of 1997) that would require the prior written consent of the individual before private information could be sold to a third party. The Federal Trade Commission has recently been conducting computer database studies to examine what types of personal information are being held by private companies for the purpose of locating individuals.

Two members of Congress, Representative Bob Franks of New Jersey and Senator Diane Feinstein of California, have introduced the Children's Privacy Protection and Parental Empowerment Act. This bill attempts to establish fair information practices for personal information about children and reduce abuse of this information by the direct marketing industry. More information about this Act can be found by conducting a search of the archives of the *Electronic Privacy Information Center*. Highlights of this proposed legislation point to areas of concern held by many individuals regarding the ease of obtaining information about children:

- Prohibit the sale or purchase of personal information about children without consent of their parents;
- Require list brokers and solicitors to disclose to parents, upon request, the source and content of personal information on file about their children;
- Require that brokers disclose to parents the names and entities to whom they have sold personal information about that parent's child;
- Prohibit prisoners and convicted sex criminals from processing the personal information of children;
- Generally prohibit exchange of material about children if there is a belief that doing so might harm a child;
- Establish civil remedies and criminal penalties for violations.

The issue of privacy of information is one that pervades the Internet. As information gets passed around more quickly and more frequently, the risks to personal freedom increase. As are other attempts to regulate information on the Internet (such as the Communications Decency Act), H.R.98 has the intention of protecting children. Obviously the concept of free speech and the right to privacy can come into conflict when dealing with issues that affect children. The Clinton administration has expressed its stance on privacy by stating that the Administration favors consumer education, technologies such as privacy and content filters, and self-regulation among businesses to deal with issues of security of information (Piller, 1997).

COPYRIGHT AND INTELLECTUAL PROPERTY

Intellectual property can take many forms. Essays, poems, computer programs, scientific studies, songs, paintings, and photographs are all examples of intellectual property. They are the result of creative thinking and skillful use of tools like computers, paintbrushes, and even pencil and paper. Original work that is created by individuals or groups has the protection of copyright law, even without a formal request for this protection. The work may or may not be published, but its reproduction or use by others is still greatly restricted. Limited use for educational purposes is allowed, but if other people's intellectual property is used for commercial gain, the users are almost certainly breaking the copyright law. The advent of the Internet has created an enormous opportunity for individuals to create intellectual property and make it available to a huge audience, but the ease of entry into the Internet publishing arena also brings with it a concomitant problem. Because of the digital technology involved, materials posted on the Web can be downloaded with 100 percent accuracy, altered, and then reproduced. Individuals can download just about anything from the Web, change it, and reuse it. Creative people such as musicians, authors, or artists have long used existing works to inspire them to create new works—such as a painter who listens to music and then paints images that are inspired by the music, or a musician who listens to classical music to stimulate the creativity that results in a rock and roll song. It has long been possible to photocopy printed material or make video- or audiotape copies of electronic media, but exact duplication was very difficult, expensive, or both. The copying process resulted in copies that were adequate, but not as good as the original. Copying or downloading a file digitally, whether it is text, graphics, or audio, creates an *exact* duplicate of the original.

Most Internet-capable computers can easily download materials for later alteration or reuse. In fact, all that is required to use someone else's material is to first download the material and then "paste" it into another document. Once the material is downloaded, the person who has downloaded it can easily change it. If the material is text, any word processor can be used to seamlessly edit the material. Words, phrases, sentences, paragraphs, or even chapters can be added, changed, or deleted. A downloaded photograph can be altered with computer software like Photoshop. Colors and size can be easily changed. With some additional work, the appearance of people or the geographic location in the photo can be changed. People can be removed or added to photos to make it seem as if they have been to places they never visited or know people they never actually met. Some pundits fear that this widespread capability to plagiarize will lead to a culture where nobody's material is safe from theft. Rather than stimulate creativity, cyberspace might create a subculture of people who steal intellectual property, leading to a stifling of public thought and a reluctance to publish creative work on the Internet.

Subject Matter of Copyright

The Copyright Act of 1976 is the law that determines intellectual property ownership rights in this country. The Act states that copyright protection is given to original works of authorship that are placed in any tangible medium of expression now known or "later developed." Works of authorship include literary works, musical works, dramatic works, pantomimes and choreographic works, pictorial, graphic, and sculptural works, motion pictures and other audiovisual works, sound recordings, and architectural works. Clearly, the Internet is a tangible medium that was "developed" after 1976. Therefore, copyright law would apply to material posted anywhere within the Internet. (More information about copyright law and the Internet can be found at *Copyright Law Materials* page of the Cornell Law School Web site.)

Fair Use Doctrine

Section 107 of the 1976 Copyright Act provides educators with the general right (under certain circumstances) to make copies of copyrighted material without the consent of the author. This section of the Act was designed to be a general guideline that educators could follow to use copyrighted material and still comply with copyright law. Specifically, the fair use section provides an exemption from copyright law. These guidelines do not have the force of law, but they are expected to assist educators in making sure they comply with the law.

The question of unauthorized use of protected work has never been an easy one and several principles need to be considered in the determination of fair use. These principles deal with the issues of (1) the purpose or use of the material, (2) characteristics of the original work, (3) the amount of the original work used, and (4) the possible impact that this use might have on the market for the original work (Demac, 1993).

Some Copyright Guidelines

For uses other than education, it is incumbent upon the user of other people's material to follow general copyright law. Some practical tips are listed below.

1. Material that is found on the Internet should be regarded as being copyrighted whether or not a copyright notice appears in the work. Generally, the courts consider works to be copyrighted as they are created, even if a copyright notice is not found on the work. This would apply to the scanning of graphic material that is private property or material found in a publication.

2. If other people's work is used on a Web page without permission, it violates copyright law even if no commerce is involved. This is especially true if the posting could decrease the profitability of the original work.

3. Material posted on a listserv or Usenet is not in the public domain unless specifically designated. This means information or graphics can be received, but should not be reused without permission.

4. The holder of a copyright on material need not actively pursue copyright or defend it in order to retain rights to the material. Instead, copyright holders must deliberately give the rights away before that copyright is lost.

5. Copyright violation is a crime punishable by monetary fines, and in some cases it is treated as a felony. Obviously, a felony conviction would be the result of a very serious copyright infringement.

6. Some people think that reposting commercial information or using advertising information from a product advertised on the Internet merely helps the advertiser. This is risky behavior, because without permission, people who repost may be subject to fines or criminal prosecution. In the case of using advertising information, it is far safer to ask permission first.

Piracy: Music

It is generally believed that the Internet is full of stolen music, but producers of music have paid little attention to the Internet until recently (Silverthorne, 1997). The quality of music played over the Internet has generally been low, but this has changed with the advent of a music-over-the-net technology referred to as MPEG Audio Layer 3 or MP3. This new technology compresses a song that once required 60 MB of space into about 5 MB of space. Software capable of playing music compressed in this way is available in newer versions of browsers from both Netscape and Microsoft. To translate this into what it means to listeners, MP3 will allow music on the Internet to sound similar to a CD. Student-run Web sites at some universities have been transferring their music into MP3 files and posting them for downloads. This behavior has triggered action from record companies, which fear that the high quality of these files and ease of downloading them might have adverse effects on sales. This same argument surfaced when home audio recording from CDs became prevalent. The result has been threats of legal action by the record companies. In addition, the Recording Industry Association of America has decided to distribute information regarding piracy to Internet service providers and universities with radio Web sites. New software that will provide some protection for artists and music copyright holders has become available from a company called Intersect. This software can systematically check the World Wide Web (a process referred to as *sniffing*) and can locate music and video that has been pirated (ZDNet, 1997).

Piracy: Software

The problem of software piracy has existed for some time. Computer users can devise ways to make unauthorized copies and circumvent paying for use of the software. Before the Internet, piracy was accomplished by physically copying the software onto a disk and then passing the disk or additional copies of the disk to others. Although this practice has been widespread since the 1980s, it required personal contact from the person who made the copy to the person who received the pirated disk. The Internet, with its one-to-many method of communicating, allows a software pirate to "warez," that is, make unauthorized copies available to others by posting the software on a Web site or a warez newsgroup. One clever pirate can supply hundreds or thousands of people who want copies of the software and know what Web site to visit. This type of piracy is known as direct infringement of copyright.

Direct infringement of copyright includes behaviors such as

- Downloading software;
- Uploading software;
- Making software available for downloading;
- Transmitting software files.

Another type of infringement is called indirect infringement; it involves behaviors that assist, induce, or materially contribute to infringement of copyright of protected software. This includes behaviors like:

- Posting of serial numbers of software programs;
- Posting of utilities to assist in pirating;
- Linking to sites that offer unauthorized software downloads;
- Aiding others to pirate software.

Vicarious liability for infringement by another person occurs when someone has the authority and ability to control a person who is infringing the copyright of another, but fails to do so. This might occur when an Internet service provider has sites for downloading pirated software or simply has pirates as customers, or when a system administrator for a newsgroup fails to stop pirating within the newsgroup. This vicarious liability notion applies to music as well. The Harry Fox Agency, a New York–based music licensing organization, has sued CompuServe because CompuServe users were using the service provider to exchange copyrighted songs without permission (Blankenhorn, 1995).

INTERNET TAXATION

The Internet and World Wide Web hold the promise of enormous commerce in the future. In 1997, Internet sales totals have been estimated at $2.4 to $13 billion.

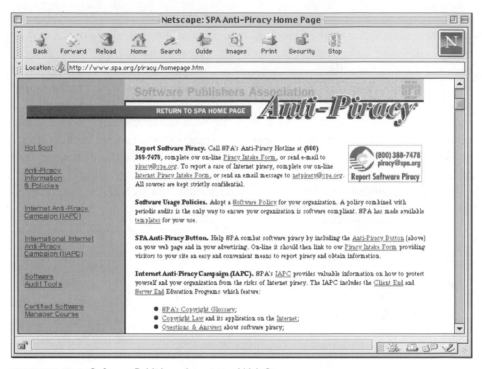

FIGURE 11.3 Software Publishers Association Web Site

Projections of electronic commerce on the Internet have suggested figures in the tens of billions of dollars in sales by the year 2000.

There are over thirty thousand entities capable of some type of tax jurisdiction that are eyeing Internet commerce transactions and that envision possible tax revenue generation. This raises the issue not only of the taxation of Net commerce, but also the possibility of multiple taxation on the same transaction.

Someone in Arizona can use Virginia-based America Online to buy a South Dakota company's computer, which is then shipped to the buyer's daughter, who is attending college in California. Could all of the states involved tax the transaction? At present the answer is no, but there has been and will continue to be pressure to change tax laws that govern online transactions.

One issue here is that Net commerce is just beginning, and change is ongoing. A system of taxation devised in 1998 may be obsolete by 2000. Another issue is that many "pro-growth" proponents feel that multiple taxation would impede the growth of commerce on the Net. On the other side of this issue are many legislators and politicians who believe that it is the right of the local jurisdiction (such as state, county, or city) to impose taxes as they see fit. Among these people, the thinking is that the federal government should not impede local taxation because the federal government repeatedly stated a commitment to giving greater power and authority to state and local governments. The mayor of Scottsdale, Arizona, stated that her city could lose over $10 million a year in tax revenues by the year 2002. For cities like Scottsdale, which depend heavily on sales tax rather than real estate tax, loss of sales tax revenue could have serious implications for conducting important city business. Mayor Harry Smith of Greenville, Mississippi, stated that a loss of 2 percent of sales tax revenue would translate into taking 7 percent of the town's police officers off the street (Haussler, 1997).

The federal government's stance on the issue of taxation is based upon the inclination to favor Internet growth. In addition, the Clinton Administration seems to be resistant to the idea of creating more bureaucracy to watch over the Internet. This reflects the viewpoint that existing federal agencies like the Federal Communication Commission and the Federal Trade Commission can adequately protect individuals who use the Internet without the creation of another agency to oversee commerce and taxes (Charski, 1997; Piller, 1997).

The favored approach at the federal level seems to be one of allowing the market to dictate policy. A senior adviser to President Clinton, stated, "Buyers and sellers should be able to come together freely and do business on the Internet" (Piller, 1997).

In late 1997 a bill called the Internet Tax Freedom Act of 1997 was introduced in the House of Representatives. As introduced, the bill would:

- Prohibit state or local governments from imposing taxes on Internet access and on-line services;
- Direct the Administration (Secretaries of the Treasury, Commerce, or State in consultation with Congress) to study U.S. and international taxation of Internet commerce and make recommendations to Congress on how to apply the principles of interstate commerce to Internet commerce;
- Amend the Communications Act of 1934 to bar federal or state regulation of the prices subscribers pay for Internet and computer services;
- Express the sense of the Congress that the President should seek bilateral and multilateral agreements through various international forums to establish that activity on the Internet be free from tariff and taxation.

More information on the Internet Tax Freedom Act can be found at the *U.S. Internet Council* Web site.

For the foreseeable future, it seems apparent that there is strong sentiment both from the organizations that use the Internet and from the government to maintain a "hands-off" approach toward regulating and taxing Internet commerce. This sentiment supports a market-driven approach to regulating the Internet. In other words, two things seem certain at least for the time being: first, the marketplace, not the government, will determine prices for Internet access service; and, second, commerce conducted on the Internet will not receive special taxation from numerous jurisdictions.

SUMMARY: ETHICS AND LAW AS BEHAVIORAL GUIDELINES

Ethics is a system of beliefs that guide behavior. Ethics functions as a conscience and helps people to decide about bad behavior and good behavior. Media professionals have adopted ethical guidelines to help them carry out their media-related tasks in ways that benefit society. Ethical guidelines in media also have helped to reduce the need for outside regulation by governmental agencies. Ethics can be viewed as being deontological or teleological: deontological ethics are derived from morals or other sets of rules for behavior as determined by religion, conscience, or human reasoning; teleological ethics view ethical behavior based upon the outcome of that behavior. Teleological ethics judges behavior as good when the behavior yields the greatest possible benefits to society. When ethical issues are uniformly agreed upon by society, such as the belief that murder or lying under oath is wrong, these issues become laws.

Legal issues are more clear-cut than ethical issues, because violations of legal issues lead to punishment from government. What can and cannot be posted on the Internet is currently a legal issue. If the Internet is treated similarly to the print media, it would receive full protection for freedom of speech by virtue of the First Amendment. If the Internet is treated as other electronic media, it would receive only partial First Amendment protection, similar to the broadcast media. Recent court cases indicate that the Internet will receive full First Amendment protection.

Privacy has long been a concern in this country. When people use the Internet they should understand that not all of the personal information that may be used in a communication will necessarily remain private. E-mail can be read by others, and some people think that others who may have no right to do so may monitor electronic commerce that is conducted using the Internet. Encryption is a method of maintaining privacy for Internet communication and commerce, but currently the government prevents individuals from using powerful encryption programs. The government has suggested that people may use encryption, but the key to the encryption code should be held by a trusted third party. This issue will be debated for some time.

Internet users are also concerned that information about them might be sold to companies who have no right to obtain this information. Legislation is pending to restrict access to certain kinds of personal information and prevent abuse of personal information about Internet users.

The digital nature of the Internet creates an environment where material that is posted on it can be easily duplicated for later use. Not only can the material be taken and reused, but the material can be taken, altered, and reused. Both situations raise serious copyright questions.

As the Internet is being used more for commerce, entities that generate tax laws—such as federal, state, county, and city governments—are becoming interested in creating taxes to benefit their jurisdictions. At present, the federal government seems inclined to protect Internet growth and has discouraged taxation of Internet commerce. Obviously, part of the federal inclination to prohibit taxation of Internet commerce is based upon the perplexing question of which jurisdictions have the right to set taxes. If this trend continues, it will be the marketplace rather than the government that guides Internet growth.

CHAPTER LINKS

Copyright Law Materials—http://www.law.cornell.edu/topics/copyright.html

Electronic Frontier Foundation—http://www. EFF.org

Electronic Privacy Information Center—http://www.epic.org

Red Lion v. FCC—http://www.mediaaccess.org/definitions/redlion.html

Reno v. ACLU—http://www. ACLU.org

Telecommunications Act of 1996—http:www.fcc.gov/telecom.html

Telecommunications Act—Summary—http://www.technologylaw.com/techlaw/act_summary.html

Overview of the Telecommunications Act of 1996—http://www.technologylaw.com/techlaw/act_summary.html

U.S. Internet Council—http://usic.org/asummary.htm

REFERENCES

Blankenhorn, D. (1995). CompuServe settlement could set price for music on Web. [Online]. Available: http://technoculture.mira.net.au/hypermail/0028.html

Cate, F. (1995). The First Amendment and the national information infrastructure. *Wake Forest Law Review 1*, 1, 4.

Charski, M. (1997, May 22). Senate subcommittee holds hearing on Net taxation. *PC World*. [Online]. Available: http://www.pcworld.com/cgi-bin/database/body.pl ID=970522173009

Demac, D. (1993). Is any use "fair" in a digital world? New York: Media Studies Center, Freedom Forum. [Online]. Available: www.mediastudies.org/CTR/Publications/demac/dd.html

Dominick, J., Sherman, B., & Copeland, G. (1996). *Broadcasting/cable and beyond.* New York: McGraw-Hill.

Fena, L. (1997). Legal cases—EFF, ACLU, et al. v. Dept. of Justice. Electronic Frontier Foundation Archive. [Online]. Available http://www.eff.org/pub/Legal/Cases/ACLU_v_Reno/19970626_eff_cda.announce

Flynn, A. (1998, January 28). Senate panel fights kids' easy access to sex on Internet. *Arizona Republic,* p. E1.

Gunn, A. (1998). Another "indecent" proposal. Yahoo! Internet Life, October 1998, p. 94.

Haussler, A. (1998, January 11). Shopping a Net loss for sales tax. *Arizona Republic,* p. A1.

Machrone, B. (1997, January 20). Key escrow: Bad idea, bad law. *PC Magazine,* p. 85.

McCloy, M. (1997, January 19). Official's e-mail is leaked: She apologizes for hurtful tone. *Arizona Republic,* p. 8.

Piller, C. (1997, May). Net regulation: How much is enough? *PC World,* 60.

Red Lion Broadcasting Co. v. FCC, 395 US 367 (1969).

Silverthorne, S. (1997, June 2). Music industry fights back against cyber piracy. ZDNet. [Online]. Available: http://www.ZDNet.com/ZDNN/content/ZDNN/0602/ZDNN0006.html

Souter, David. (1997). *First Amendment Calendar,* January 6, 1998. Arlington, VA: Freedom Forum.

Stevens, J. (Reno v. ACLU, 1997). [Online]. Available: http://www.aclu.org/renovacludec.html

Wallace, J., & Mangan, M. (1996). *Sex, laws, and cyberspace.* New York: Henry Holt.

U.S. Internet Council. (1997). A summary of the Internet Tax Freedom Act. [Online]. Available: http://www.Usic.org/asummary.htm

Vivian, J. (1997). *The media of mass communication.* Boston: Allyn and Bacon.

After being laid off as an auditor in February 1995, Tom Wilson started looking for a new position. Tom really wanted to move out of California, but didn't know how to go about finding a job out of state. For four months he scanned local newspaper want ads for openings and used other traditional job search techniques. Tom's job search was getting him nowhere fast until he discovered the Web. As Tom puts it, "Suddenly I had access to jobs all over the world." A short time later, Tom accepted an auditing job with a firm in North Carolina. Tom swears by the Web as a job searching tool. "The Internet absolutely decreased the time I was on unemployment. . . . I never would have gotten out of California without it."

(Markels, 1996)

CHAPTER TWELVE

CAREER OPPORTUNITIES AND FUTURE DIRECTIONS

CAREER OPPORTUNITIES

The World Wide Web has emerged both as a generator of new jobs itself and as a place to find employment in many other fields. The Web has created many new employment opportunities that did not even exist before the early 1990s, and it has become an excellent resource for job hunters.

Finding that first job out of college, or finding any job for that matter, can be difficult and frustrating. In today's competitive world, job seekers cannot afford to overlook any opportunity. Conducting out-of-state employment searches is even tougher than looking around one's home town.

Prior to the advent of electronic searching techniques, job seekers subscribed to out-of-area newspapers that would often arrive days after publication. Applicants would frequently hear of openings through friends or relatives and would rely on their word about the suitability of the job. Many times, headhunters or employment agencies offered the only avenues to career opportunities, but most unemployed people could not afford the steep search fees, nor could they afford to travel to distant cities in search of work.

The old job seeking techniques of pounding the pavement, knocking on agency doors, or asking friends and relatives for jobs have been replaced with new electronic searching tools. The Web is a worldwide resource for jobs. On many sites, such as *CareerPath*, employment searches can be conducted by geographic area, by field, by company, or by other specific criteria. Many employers are posting openings online as a way of broadening their applicant pools. The Web connects job seekers to career opportunities that might otherwise be out of reach. Best of all, most online job site services are free to applicants.

Searching for Employees

For an employer, finding just the right person to fill a position is often a time-consuming and expensive proposition. Employers typically advertise in newspapers and trade magazines, recruit from college campuses, and often list openings with employment agencies and headhunters. While it can take days and even weeks to place an employment ad in a newspaper classified section and sometimes even longer in a trade magazine, an online posting can be up within a day. Employers are claiming that online hiring takes less time and is less costly than traditional recruitment methods (Markels, 1996).

The high cost of traditional classifieds keeps the ads short, with brief descriptions. On most online job posting services, the size of ads is not as restricted, so announcements can be more detailed and employers more clear on who they want to hire. Running a twenty-line employment ad in the *New York Times* classified section costs about $1,700 per week, whereas a similar ad posted on an online job

FIGURE 12.1 CareerPath Web Site

site runs $100–$150 for one month (Willmott, Kwon, Levin, & Rupley, 1997). Many companies are happily contracting with online job sites for annual job postings at costs of 5–10 times less than what they would pay for one year's worth of ads in large metropolitan newspapers (Cafasso, 1996). For example, a recruiter for Kaiser Permanente hospital services in Oakland, California, claims that a quarter-page employment ad in a San Francisco newspaper costs about $10,000, whereas by signing up with an online job site, the firm can run an unlimited number of ads for just less than $4,000 per year (Alexander, 1997). Companies committed to online recruiting to the tune of $30 million in 1997, and that figure is expected to rise to $218 million by the year 2000 (Croal, 1997). Low costs and access to a wide range of job seekers are leading more companies to intensify online recruitment. According to one survey of two hundred companies, 93 percent of companies surveyed plan to focus their recruitment efforts on the Web and rely less heavily on traditional means (Jobs.Search@Internet, 1998).

In addition to posting job openings online, recruiters seek out applicants who post their résumés online. Scanning the résumé boards for qualified job candidates is a hassle-free process on most online job sites. Additionally, employers get to select from among a broader pool of applicants than they would be able to access through traditional recruitment outlets.

Searching for Employment

When using the Web for any purpose, knowing where to look can save countless hours of fruitless searching. Web sites list a countless number of job openings from numerous companies and businesses in many fields from many cities across the country and sometimes from around the world. Although many new job titles and functions have sprung from Internet technologies, they are not the only ones posted on the Web. Online job searching yields information about all types of jobs from accountants to zoologists, and many employers direct their online searches to college graduates new to the job market. About 94 percent of all college students have access to the Web, and slightly more than half have used online job placement services (Croal, 1997).

There are two basic strategies for online job searching: placing a résumé on a job-oriented site and looking through posted job openings. Many job seekers start by putting their skills on résumé pages with the hope that an employer will come looking for them, but once their qualifications are online, job seekers need to employ more aggressive searching strategies. While it may seem like a good idea to bombard a potential employer with self-promoting e-mail, job seekers should resist that temptation at all costs. Pestering a recruiter with phone calls and voicemail messages is widely acknowledged as a bad idea, and the same applies to e-mail. Online job searching calls for slightly different tactics than traditional searching. Tailoring résumés for electronic display and narrowing one's searches increases the possibility of finding the perfect job.

POSTING RÉSUMÉS ONLINE   Posting a résumé on the Net is a passive way of looking for work, and by itself is unlikely to meet with much success. Although many people have landed positions using this method, it takes electronic expertise coupled with a carefully crafted résumé. Constructing a résumé for online display is different from simply typing one up on an $8\frac{1}{2} \times 11$ sheet of gray or off-white paper. Screen size, key word searching, and other technical considerations are all part of the new cyber-résumé. Properly formatting and designing a résumé for online presentation increases the chances of catching an employer's eye. All too often candidates are passed over for jobs only because their résumés were poorly prepared (King, 1996).

Before computers and networks became such a large part of the business world, résumés were generally organized into one of three basic formats: chronological, functional, or a combination of the two formats. A chronological résumé lists work experiences in order by date, and is most appropriate for those whose background and projects build on one another within the same field. A functional

BOX 12.1 JOB AND CAREER SITES ON THE WEB

General

America's Job Bank—http://www.ajb.dni.us
CareerCast—http://www.careercast.com
CareerMagazine—http://www.careermag.com
CareerMosaic—http://www.careermosaic.com
CareerPath—http://www.careerpath.com
Career Resource Center—http://www.careers.org
CareerWeb—http://www.cWeb.com
Cruise Line Jobs—http://cruiselinejobs.com
Cybercareers—http://www.cybercareers.com
Espan—http://www.espan.com
Help Wanted USA—http://iccWeb.com
HotJobs—http://www.hotjobs.com
JobHunt—http://www.job-hunt.org/
JobSat—http://www.jobsat.com/
JobTrak—http://www.jobtrak.com
NationJob Network—http://www.nationjob.com
Online Career Center—http://www.occ.com
The Internet Job Source—http://www.statejobs.com
The Monster Board—http://www.monster.com
The World Wide Web Employment Office—http://www.harbornet.com/biz/office/annex.html
Work Avenue—http://www.WorkAvenue.com
Yahoo! Classifieds—http://classifieds.yahoo.com

Communication/New Media/Computer Jobs

Advertising Age Job Bank—http://www.adage.com/job_bank/index.html
Advertising & Media Jobs—http://www.nationjob.com/media
Cable Online—http://www.aescon.com/cableonline/
Copy Editor Jobs (Editor & Publisher)—http://www.copyeditor.com/jobs.overview.html
Creative Freelancers' Registry—http://www.ghgcorp.com/cfr
Editor & Publisher Classifieds—http://epclassifieds.com
Find Network—http://findnetwork.com
Insurance Marketing and Communication Jobs—http://www.insurancerecruiters.com/insjobs/market.htm
JobLink for Journalists—http://www.newslink.org/joblink.html
NetComTalk—http://com.bu.edu/getajob/
SelectJobs—http://www.selectjobs.com
TV Jobline—http://www.ultimatetv.com/jobs/
University of Iowa Journalism Job Resouces—http://bailiwick.lib.uiowa.edu/journalism/jobs.html

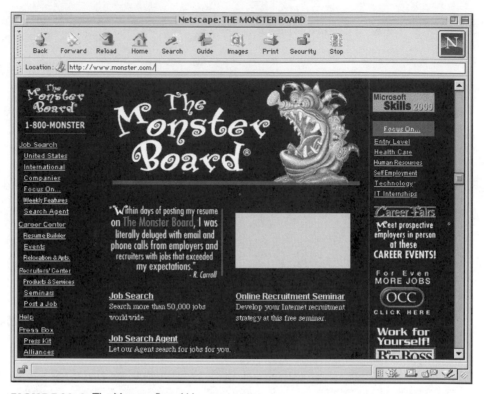

FIGURE 12.2 The Monster Board Homepage

résumé emphasizes work experiences, training, and skills, and is best used for those with little experience or those who are switching careers. Many job seekers prefer to combine the two formats, depending on their experience and the type of job they are seeking. Résumés generally open with a statement of career objectives or a summary of experience, and are written in the active voice, emphasizing verbs (Krannich, 1996).

While the three basic résumé formats are still appropriate for paper distribution, they must be modified for electronic posting. There are several adaptations that should be made before putting a résumé online:

■ Many companies scan online résumés looking for key words that match their requirements. Many tracking systems look for specific terms by scanning through a set number of words or lines rather than through the entire résumé (Puetz, 1997). Thus, the career objectives or summary statement becomes more of a key word preface laced with industry lexicon.

- Describe qualifications and experience using industry-specific nouns and verbs rather than generic ones. Online résumés that describe skills, actions, and qualifications using the names of software programs, computers, equipment, job titles, and other key words are more likely to be flagged by scanners than ones containing more generic terms.

- Abbreviations should generally be avoided. Common ones such as B.A. are acceptable, but others may not be picked up in key word searches.

- Many online job sites require that résumés be formatted with flush-left margins, lots of white space, and other site-specific requirements. Fancy graphics, shaded boxes, and horizontal rules should be saved for the non-online versions.

- Like traditional résumés, online ones should be kept short. Optimally, the length of an electronic résumé should equal a little over one printed page, and should not exceed the equivalent of three printed pages. Many cyber-job sites limit the overall length of résumés and sections within résumés.

- Disclose with discretion. Do not post personal information on the Web beyond what is minimally required by the job site.

On most cyber-job sites, résumé information is entered using a standard form. Typically, a job seeker is first asked to enter his or her name, e-mail address, and other such information. The user is then prompted to enter in career objectives, technical skills, prior experience, education, and other work-related information in the appropriate boxes. Résumés are then formatted to the specifications of the job Web site. On some online sites, such as *The Monster Board,* users select either a standard résumé layout, or they can paste in their own format. Passwords are issued to job seekers so that they may view, update, or delete their résumés.

Rather than relying on official Web placement services, many job seekers are putting up their own homepages, where they are free to display their best work and market themselves to potential employers. For example, an advertising student, frustrated with the old-fashioned way of looking for employment, showcased his designs on the Web and registered his site with Yahoo! Within a short time, a Web-design company executive spotted the student's work and eventually offered him a job (Croal, 1997). Unemployed marketing and management executive *Bob Wilson* of Evanston, Illinois, has deployed an impressive site touting his abilities and qualifications. Even Bob's wife, Jody, lists her own "Ten Good Reasons to Hire Bob." Bob's serious bid for employment presents a nice touch of humor and displays strong marketing and Web design skills.

Another option combines posting a résumé on a job site along with creating a personal homepage. For example, adding a personal homepage URL to a résumé could direct a recruiter to the applicant's site where he or she could feature creative

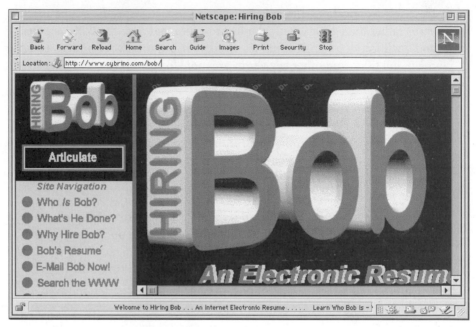

FIGURE 12.3 Bob Wilson's Homepage

work, Web design skills, or other special qualifications that were not included on the résumé.

Because the Web is truly a global enterprise, and anyone can access a Web site, one should exercise caution before posting an online résumé or homepage that contains personal information such as a home address or telephone number. An e-mail address is a sufficient means of contact for most recruiters.

USING ONLINE EMPLOYMENT SERVICES   The Web contains a wealth of job openings, and knowing where and how to look is the key to a successful search. By 1996, the top fifteen online job sites were collectively posting about 500,000 openings, compared to only 15,000 postings in 1994 (King, 1996). There are many sites that list jobs across many categories and companies, and there are other sites that are more industry-specific. Most sites include an on-site search tool so users can look for jobs by company, geographic location, job title, and other categories.

Many sites, such as *IntelliMatch,* connect employers to employees. Job seekers specify their skills and qualifications, and personnel seekers provide detailed information about job-related duties and requirements. The service then matches qualified candidates with openings and provides employers with leads. The service is free to those looking for work, but charges those looking for workers. IntelliMatch's database contains about fifty thousand résumés and job listings from about one hundred major employers (King, 1996). Most online job sites operate in a fashion similar to IntelliMatch. It is up to job seekers and employers to check out the various online employment opportunities to discover the ones that best fit their needs.

Jobs in a Cyberworld

When many students think about working in an Internet-related job, they all too often think that they have to possess highly technical computer skills to get a foot in the door. Although there are many jobs that call for computer programming and related experience, there are many jobs that do not require such expertise. Many mass communication, journalism, advertising, marketing, and radio/television majors have made a smooth transition from a traditional media environment to the world of the Web.

New job opportunities exist in multimedia and CD-ROM companies, Internet technology firms, advertising and public relations agencies, media outlets, and many other companies and corporations. One industry expert estimates that one out of seven television stations has an Internet specialist on board. It is difficult to know just how many new jobs have been created nationwide as a result of new communication technologies; however, some regional estimates are available. In the New York metropolitan area, the Internet, multimedia software, and other applications generated jobs for just over 71,000 workers in 4,200 companies. Further, from 1993 to 1996, the number of communication technology jobs doubled. The job prospects are just as good on the West Coast, where Internet and multimedia technology created 62,000 jobs at 2,200 companies in the San Francisco nine-county area (Mermigas, 1996).

Jobs associated with the Internet vary according to company. Many employers are looking for people with Web site design skills who can oversee the construction and maintenance of complex multilevel sites. People with graphic design, HTML, and Java programming experience are always in demand. Knowledge of audio and video streaming and networking skills will make almost anyone an invaluable employee at firms that conduct online business. Radio and television stations, advertising and public relations agencies, marketing firms, media companies, and newspapers are just some of the many communication enterprises that need employees with up-to-date knowledge and skills in newer communication technologies.

WEBMASTER Webmaster is probably the most talked about cyberposition. *U.S. News & World Report* ranks Webmaster as one of the hottest and better paying jobs in the marketplace. Webmasters are commanding salaries ranging anywhere from $50,000 to $100,000 per year, and the demand still outstrips the supply (Master of the Cyperspace Universe: Webmaster, 1998). However, entry-level Webmaster positions may earn as little as $10 per hour.

Webmaster is an elusive term, however, because what a Webmaster does at one company may not be remotely related to the job duties of a Webmaster at another company. However, Webmasters generally manage some aspect of a Web site, while Webtaskers work under a Webmaster.

Some Webmasters oversee the technical components of a Web site, while others manage the nontechnical elements. In the Internet world, Webmasters come from a variety of backgrounds. Webmasters with computer skills may design a site's interactive elements and the security and privacy components. Those with art and computer graphics backgrounds may guide the site from a creative perspective. Employees with marketing, advertising, and business degrees may be in charge of Webmastering a site for promotional and sales purposes. There are Webmasters with English and writing degrees who drive a site's design from a content standpoint (Master of the Cyperspace Universe: Webmaster, 1998).

Webmaster and other Web positions are not limited just to those people with computer science degrees, but are open to people with a wide variety of skills and educational backgrounds. Adapting traditional sales and marketing techniques to online commerce and Web design, writing for the Web, and modifying content for online sites are examples of nontechnical Web-related jobs that are in high demand. Well-rounded employees are qualified to work in non-online, media-related jobs, and they can also apply their skills to the Web. The only requirement is an interest in the Web and an understanding of the Web as a new medium.

OTHER INTERNET JOBS   *Cybercareers,* authored by M. Morris and P. Massie, is an excellent printed resource, with chapters devoted to trends in cyberjobs, preparing for careers in an online environment, the types of jobs available, the background skills required for Web-related jobs, and other helpful information.

There are far too many Web-related jobs in many industries to describe them all here, so the following list presents just a few examples of cyberjob titles and descriptions. Again, these titles and descriptions vary from company to company.

- Media Integration Specialist: Integrates HTML, Java, audio, video, and other components on a Web site;
- Software Specialist: Writes and integrates Java, CGI, PERL, or other scripts for the Web site;
- Database Expert: Develops and maintains online databases;
- Internet Sales Engineer: Sells and evaluates new Internet technologies;
- Electronic Commerce Specialist: Develops and implements security and privacy tools for online sales;

- Web Server Administrator: Oversees the thousands of Web documents and software applications housed on a server;
- Web Designer: Builds and creates a Web site, usually from a business perspective. This person determines the purpose of the site, decides how pages should link together, and basically oversees the structure of the site;
- Gatekeeper/Editor: Decides which content should be put online and may edit repurposed and original content;
- Artist: Creates the graphics and visual components including colors and fonts;
- Content Provider/Writer: Writes materials such as news stories, press releases, and technical information;
- Interface Tester: Assesses Web sites based on certain criteria, such as if they are easy to navigate, if interactivity is working properly, and if all links are active. With many sites containing hundreds of documents, quality assurance is often a full-time job;
- Online Customer Service Representative: Interacts with consumers via e-mail, and replies to e-mail messages concerning products, services, and complaints;
- Online Sales Representative: Sells ad space on Web sites;
- Online Advertising Space Buyer: Purchases ad space for clients on many different Web sites;
- Advertising Agency Account Representative: Creates online advertising campaigns in conjunction with non-online campaigns;
- Video/Audio Expert: Records and digitizes video images and audio selections for the Web;
- Online Project Manager: Oversees personnel issues for the staff working on online projects. (Morris & Massie, 1998; Goff, 1997)

Getting Experience

Many colleges and universities are beginning to offer Web-related classes and are integrating the Web into existing coursework. Stand-alone Web classes can involve an overview of the Internet and a Web site design component, and Web marketing classes are becoming popular on many campuses. Other courses tie in an analysis of the Web with the course's general subject matter. For example, marketing, advertising, and PR classes may discuss the Web as a promotional medium. Art and computer graphics classes may include Web site design, online graphics, and advertising design strategies. Business and commerce courses are bringing the Web into their discussions of sales transactions. In research methods courses, students are learning how to use the Web as a research tool. High school teachers and university professors are bringing the Web into their classrooms in many creative ways to give students the knowledge and experience they need to seek new Web-related jobs.

In addition to educational institutions, there are other places to learn about the Web. Many young people just starting their careers and more seasoned workers striving to change careers often lament that "the job requires experience, but how can I get experience if I can't get the job?" *Cybercareers* lists several solutions to this dilemma:

- Entry-level jobs in school computer labs and offices often team students with professors and other specialists.

- Internships, paid or unpaid, are excellent opportunities to work in a field of choice while earning class credits, and many interns are offered full time jobs.

- Volunteer to work at nonprofit organizations that cannot afford to hire full-time professionals. Volunteering is a great way to get experience performing many different tasks.

AS THE WORLD WIDE WEB TURNS

Predicting what the future will hold for the Internet and related technologies is possibly one of the most difficult tasks in the study of mass communication. The Internet provides access to a huge body of individual and corporate users. Many of

---

BOX 12.2 PREDICTING THE FUTURE

Vinton Cerf, one of the founding fathers of the Internet, has mixed feelings about what the future will hold for the Internet. His optimistic statement is, "The Internet will exceed the scale and capacity of the telephone network sometime in the latter half of the next decade. Ultimately there will be more devices on the Internet than there are people in the world."

His pessimistic statement is, "We won't figure out how to handle the growth in demand for capacity on the Net, the vendors won't be able to supply us with routers and switches that will go at gigabit speeds, and the whole shootin' match runs out of gas sometime in the next two years."

Which perspective is most plausible? Will Internet-related hardware and software vendors be able to keep up with the projected growth?

these people have the skills to direct the future of the Internet. Individuals and companies are continually writing programs that attempt to make the Web more interesting and more accessible while it becomes faster and technically more sophisticated. Since the number of people who use the Internet is growing rapidly, manufacturers of computer hardware and related equipment are focusing enormous time and energy on developing products to improve Internet use. The overall result of this attention is that technological and software developments are occurring rapidly and on many fronts. Changes in the Internet and related software and technologies occur almost daily; therefore an attempt to list all areas that will change noticeably in the future is impossible.

In Chapter 11, it was stated that the general position of the government is to allow the market to dictate how the Internet will develop. This attitude certainly allows development to proceed at a more vigorous pace than it would if the government wanted to be a part of every change that involved the Internet. All users, manufacturers, software designers, and Web page developers can have meaningful input into the growth process without the impediment of big government meddling in the changes. Because the government has, to some extent, stepped aside to see what happens with this developing technology, it is best for the public to do likewise. Many changes are occurring that involve almost all aspects of the Internet and the World Wide Web. The rest of Chapter 12 will touch on just some of these interesting areas and innovations. What follows is more a selection of issues and topics than an all-inclusive list.

Trends

The Internet has changed how today's society regards mass media. The Internet has provided an alternative to the traditional media that supply the audience with news, information, and entertainment. The Internet is, for most people who use it regularly, a source of information and a supplement to traditional entertainment media. The use of the Internet for up-to-the-minute financial news or late-breaking stories is now commonplace. As streaming technology improves and becomes standardized, more and more people will go to the Internet for radio-type and television-type entertainment. The future may bring changes, both technological and sociological, that allow the Internet to supplant the entertainment media to a greater extent. The Internet has altered the relationship between the audience and traditional providers of information and entertainment. Some of these changes concern issues like the directionality of information flow, the qualifications of the communicators, the cost of reaching an audience, generality of information, format, and standards.

The directionality of information flow is changing as a result of the Internet. Traditionally, news and information came to the audience from large, highly structured news organizations like CBS or the *New York Times*. Audience members tended to watch or listen to the information in a passive way. If individuals had questions, doubts, or criticisms about the method of delivery or about the information itself, their only recourse was to write letters to the network or to the editor. The response to such letters is generally slow and the impact negligible. Using the Internet as a source of information and news, however, allows audience members to give immediate feedback to the source of the information and news. The CNN Web site offers the opportunity to give direct feedback, post opinions on a message board, or even join a discussion group about the topics or CNN's coverage of topics.

The dissemination of news and information to a mass audience has been in the hands of professional communicators. News organizations with trained journalists have been the only people with direct access to the outlets and vehicles that disseminate news and information. The Internet is changing this "monopoly" by providing a forum, in the form of a Web site, to anyone with basic typing and computer skills and access to a server that can provide some space for Web pages. Cost of access also becomes an issue. Traditional mass media organizations take millions of dollars to operate and provide their services, but the cost of supporting a Web page that is accessible to a worldwide audience could be much less. Even though a properly maintained and sophisticated site can be expensive, access to a worldwide audience is no longer limited to a privileged set of professionals.

Because individual information providers now can easily access mass audiences, questions of news values and journalistic standards must be considered. Traditional news organizations have systems of content filters and gatekeepers that check the outgoing information carefully. Individuals who decide to publish Web pages will almost certainly not have such filters or gatekeepers. The audience will be somewhat at risk if they accept anything and everything they see on the Internet without checking facts. Organizations like CNN, NBC, and the *New York Times* have established credibility through years of delivering reliable information, but Web sites published by individuals or unknown groups may or may not be trustworthy.

The format of news and information delivery is changing. Traditional newscasts in broadcasting follow a rigid format for time and content. The national evening news broadcasts, like the *CBS Evening News with Dan Rather,* occur at a fixed time each day, last thirty minutes and have about twenty-two minutes of news content. News stories each last only several minutes. Programs on the Web can be any length, with news stories as long as is needed to tell the story. While traditional newspapers are linear in content and organization, Web pages can feature numerous hypertext links that allow audience members to navigate by their own time constraints and interest. In-depth information can be found easily through links, and materials can be stored and retrieved for later use.

The Internet is changing the model for mass media. Formats, styles, and perceptions of credibility are changing. As more changes in technology are adopted, the model may change even more (Kawamoto, 1997).

Speed

The Internet is a network of interconnected networks that enables information to move from point to point. The sources of information are almost endless. Individuals are creating homepages about themselves, their families, their hobbies, or their favorite causes. Museums are going online with sophisticated graphic images. News sources are constantly generating current information. There are online radio stations, and soon there will be online television as well.

The limiting factor on the development of the transfer of information from server to client is generally bandwidth. This technology allows vast amounts of information to move through wires from place to place. In the early 1990s, clients were using modems that could move data at a speed of 1200 bytes per second. In 1998, modems of 28.8, 33.6, or even 56 kilobytes per second are common. ISDN (Integrated Services Digital Network) connections are capable of 64 to 128 Kbps. Digital satellite carriers (DirecPC) are capable of 400 Kbps. Large companies that have direct connection to an Internet service provider (ISP) can get a T-1 or T-2 connection that can deliver 1.5 megabytes per second (Mbps) or 6.3 Mbps, respectively. Cable modem connections, which use coaxial cable to deliver information, are capable of a range from 512 Kbps to as much as 10 Mbps to an individual user. Ethernet users in large businesses and institutions like universities and users who have coaxial cable can get speeds up to 10 Mbps. It is expected that in the future speeds will increase dramatically, but only if the physical medium (wire) is changed from either the telephone wire (also referred to as twisted pair) or coaxial cable to optical fiber. Optical fiber is capable of carrying far more information than the other wires. Delivery methods using fiber optic cable range from 50 Mbps to over 10 gigabytes per second (Gbps). Of course, most existing computers can accept no more than 10 Mbps (Bates & Gregory, 1996; Newton, 1997).

There is a constant push to move information faster as Web sites include more multimedia displays that contain vast amounts of information. In addition to raising the rate of data transfer by increasing the capacity of the connection, technologies (like streaming) are being developed that allow faster representation and use, thereby reducing or eliminating lengthy download times.

Realism

A noticeable trend in Web development are Web sites that are remarkably accurate in their representations of reality. Art museums strive to show the beauty of their holdings using the Web and constantly work to make these representations as true to the originals as possible. High-resolution graphic files do a good job on two-dimensional work, but showing a three-dimensional sculpture within a two-dimensional representation leaves much to be desired. It is the third dimension—depth—that adds the realism that enhances appreciation. But creating the third dimension on a two-dimensional Web page is difficult, because it requires much more data. This huge increase in the amount of data needed to represent objects realistically in space causes larger files and longer file downloading times. One method of achieving the third dimension is by using a language called VRML or Virtual Reality Modeling Language.

VRML

Virtual Reality Modeling Language, or VRML, is a programming language that was developed in late 1994 as a response to the complaint that the Internet was "flat" and navigation through it was difficult. Most of the Internet is comprised of two-dimensional pages and gives the viewer the impression of being similar to a magazine or newspaper. VRML is a language designed to create a third dimension from two-dimensional data, giving the Web a more realistic appearance. VRML can be used to create a space that viewers can navigate through as though they are navigating through real space.

Locating particular places on the Internet is generally nonintuitive; users must type in long URLs that are only vaguely related to anything tangible. For example, basic information about VRML can be found at www.ZDnet.com/products/vrmluser/intro.html. Although there is some relevant information in the URL, the chances of getting to a desired site without going through several links are probably not very great. Going back another time is easy and direct if the site is bookmarked or listed as a favorite through the browser. VRML is one attempt to make finding things on the Web more intuitive by creating a three-dimensional space resembling the space it represents.

VRML allows the Internet virtually to bring stores and products into homes everywhere. Other business applications could be internal to a company. If an employee could check the inventory for certain supplies visually and in real time, it would probably be easier and quicker than interpreting two-dimensional data. In other words, the easiest way to accomplish a task online would be similar to what one does in real life. And that is what VRML tries to accomplish by creating a navigable, three-dimensional, visual representation of reality. VRML could make finding specific information or product as easy as walking through a familiar store.

VRML is, at present, the only available tool that can be used to create a three-dimensional view of the Internet. Other tools that can do the same thing may appear in the near future. The drawback at present is that the vast majority of companies that could use 3-D on their Web sites do not. They may be waiting for the technology to become more accessible, or they simply may not have the time and money to invest in a technology unfamiliar to most Internet users. But looking back at the vast growth of the Internet and World Wide Web since 1993 shows that significant growth occurred when the technology made using it easier and more logical.

Ease of Use

The use of computers and computer interconnection has long been the domain of the technically proficient. Computer programmers, scientists, and others who have been educated to use computers and software applications have always been among those most capable of using the Internet. The real growth of the Internet will come not from the technically proficient, or the "digerati" as they have been called, but rather from the average citizen. Growth will be determined not only by school and corporate use, but also by home use. People became comfortable in the 1980s and 1990s making purchases from catalogs by giving their credit card numbers to unseen salespeople who were reached by dialing an 800-number. People will soon become comfortable using their credit cards to purchase goods and services by visiting a commercial Web site and selecting from offerings shown at the site. This practice will become widespread when people are assured that their credit card numbers will be secure despite their sending them to a commercial Web site.

The Web has to become as easy as picking up a telephone or using other media before people will use it routinely. Internet technology has a long way to go before it can match traditional media in ease of use. The device that interfaces with the Internet needs to be less of a complicated, expensive computer and more of a dependable household appliance like a telephone or television set. Perhaps the future holds much promise for some type of "smart TV" like PCTV or WebTV that would be familiar to all segments of society and easy to use. As of late 1998, the devices of this type that are on the market have not created a noticeable increase in Web access by noncomputer households.

Other Useful Applications

The Internet will grow as its usefulness to society grows. Applications like voting, taking the written part of a driver's exam, taking college classes, getting medical advice or even a diagnosis, filling out income tax forms, shopping for groceries, paying utility bills, balancing a checkbook, and speaking to a relative or friend in another city are just some of the daily activities in society that could be made easier, faster, or less expensive by using the Internet. In some cases, the technologies already exist for these applications, but they are too slow or too complicated to be adopted

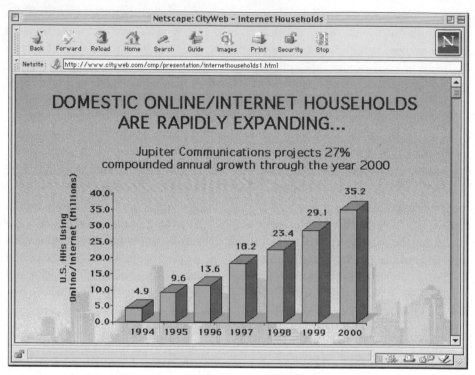

FIGURE 12.4 Projected Internet Use Through the Year 2000

widely. In the future, more and more of the routine activities that are conducted as part of everyday life will be accomplished by using the Internet, as cyber technologies and techniques improve.

Problems

The ever-increasing use of the Internet has caused many knowledgeable people who use the Internet regularly to predict that trouble looms ahead. Specifically, many have predicted that the Internet will crash or simply black out. Although this has not happened yet, many users can say that at times, the Internet is slow, and the Web can even be slower when large files from multimedia sites have to be downloaded. Some have even said that "WWW" really stands for the World Wide Wait rather than the World Wide Web. This may be annoying to recreational Web surfers and scary to those who conduct commerce, but for scientists and others, who need to use the Internet for vital information, long wait times on the Internet can be disastrous. As a result, a group of universities has joined together to develop Internet2. The problems mentioned previously were foreseen in 1995, and work on Internet2 began when leaders from universities, industry networks, and government met to plan a strategy to overcome these difficulties. Since that time, this group has grown considerably to over one hundred universities and other entities that conduct research. A new company called UCAID (University Corporation for Advanced Internet Development) was formed. The goal of this group is to connect participants to the Internet at a rate of up to a gigabyte per second, a speed that is over twenty times faster than existing connections. In addition to this increase in speed, this new connectivity will feature bandwidth reservation and multiple levels of network service. This would allow an experimental surgical procedure to be put online live, since the bandwidth required for transmission would be reserved before the actual operation, thus preventing transmission problems due to heavy Internet traffic at the time of surgery. There are arts applications as well. Theater classes could have actors performing in empty rooms or sets, with the scenery to be added later. Users who do not require large bandwidth reservations can reserve smaller bandwidths that are appropriate for their data transmission needs. This initiative has been greeted warmly by the Clinton Administration, which has its own project, Next Generation Internet, to solve traffic problems on the Internet.

HTML and DHTML

HTML is the computer language that allows Web designers to create Web pages. The problem is that HTML is a page markup language and not a page layout language, which means that control over the elements on the page is not nearly as precise as it would be with page layout software like PageMaker or Quark, which are designed for graphic designers. HTML limits the creator's control over elements on the page, while download times and technical limitations (such as not having the appropriate plug-in to show a desired effect) have hampered the creativity of multimedia designers. A new development that will help solve some of these problems is on the horizon. DHTML, or Dynamic HTML, is an extension to HTML that will allow Web page creators to control each element on a Web page much more precisely than before. This extension of HTML allows the browser to control animation with the scripting language (e.g., JavaScript), which will also result in smaller files.

Another disadvantage of HTML has been that the fonts inserted by the designer may not be the ones seen by the Web surfer. If the surfer has the font that was designed into the Web page, then the font will be seen. Otherwise, the font becomes the default designated by the browser. DHTML will have downloadable fonts, which will enable viewing of the fonts originally selected by the designer.

DHTML holds the promise for better control over all objects on a Web page for designers, more accurate representation, and quicker downloads for viewers. The end result should be better interactivity and more creativity on the Web (Coffee, 1997).

Collaborative Filtering

Collaborative filtering is a method of sending information to an individual based on the similarities of that individual's interests to those of other like-minded people. Collaborative filtering is the next step up from automatic push technology. Push technology allows consumers to select information that they want to be sent to them. Information is often customized, based on data that individuals give to the company sponsoring the push technology. Regular push technology sites (such as *My Excite Channel*) allow users to make some selections, and then the engine that powers the service sends back information based on those few selections. The result is often less than satisfying, because the amount of information that is received is either staggering or is simply not screened carefully enough to suit the recipient's needs. Collaborative filtering correlates an individual's preferences based on a system of ratings with the interests of people with similar preferences. Some companies are just beginning to change their search engines to accommodate these types of interests, which include stated preferences, buying behavior, and online behavior (types and number of sites visited) (Grunin, 1997). This type of filtering, another step in tailoring the Internet to the needs and tastes of the individual, assumes that humans are better at screening some kinds of information than computers and software. Collaborative filtering would allow selection among documents based on dimensions like "most often used by others" or "easiest to follow."

SUMMARY: BE PART OF THE ONLINE FUTURE

The Web is a fabulous place for college students to look for their first jobs. Many students attend college far from their home towns or from the cities where they would like to live. Finding a job often consumes the entire senior year and takes up time that students would rather use for studying and leisure activities. The Web is changing the way students look for jobs and careers, and it is a treasure chest full of opportunities that were previously unattainable.

Online career sites are excellent places to start searching for job openings. Many of these sites are overflowing with job postings from a wide variety of companies. Corporate Web sites often dedicate an area for job postings. For example, Progressive Networks, makers of RealAudio, frequently hire candidates who apply through their job listings page (Croal, 1997). In addition to Web placement and corporate sites, many academic associations, industry organizations, universities, trade magazines, and college placement services post general and industry-specific openings and provide other types of online career assistance.

New cyber-related jobs are available in many fields, including electronic media, print media, marketing, advertising, public relations, journalism, health and medicine, education, and electronic commerce. Although many jobs require technical skills, many others are nontechnical and call for a merging of industry-related expertise with a general understanding of the Web.

The Internet is changing how society acquires information and pursues entertainment. As the technology of the Internet becomes more sophisticated and more available to a larger part of society, more people use the Internet more often and for more purposes. In addition, the Internet provides individuals who choose to post information on Web sites access to a global audience.

One of the limiting factors for Internet growth is currently the speed at which information can travel from servers to client computers. As the uses of the Internet involve more graphic information and media like audio and video, the demand for faster data transfer increases dramatically. New delivery systems that will greatly enhance the speed of the transfer of information from server to client are now being developed.

There is a trend toward Web sites that feature information represented in a very realistic way. Virtual Reality Modeling Language (VRML) can enhance the realism of Web sites. Another trend is efforts to make the Internet and World Wide Web easier and more intuitive to navigate and use for information retrieval.

Some knowledgeable people who use the Internet feel that serious technical problems may occur in the near future. The abundance of users and large amounts of data being transferred have caused the Internet to be slower and less functional than it could be. The government has initiated an attempt to create a newer and faster Internet. Another initiative, which is supported by many universities and some Internet-related companies, has proposed (and has begun to build) Internet 2, which is many times faster than the current one.

HTML, the computer language that is used for Web page design, is not as precise as other programs that were created for page layout. Since this imprecision hampers Web developers, a new language is being developed to solve the problems of long download times and other technical limitations. This new language, DHTML, allows Web developers to have more precise control over page elements, eliminates the need for plug-ins, and permits more accurate representation of the Web site as it was originally created.

Collaborative filtering is a new method of customizing information for retrieval by an Internet user. This system is based on the notion that humans are better at screening some kinds of information than computers. Collaborative filtering will select documents based on dimensions that are user-friendly like "often used by others" or "easiest to understand."

VRML was created to make images on the Web appear more realistic by creating a third dimension in what is essentially a two-dimensional medium. Video screens are essentially flat and tend to yield flat images. A three-dimensional language like VRML will create the illusion of a third dimension. The result will be to create an Internet environment that is easier to navigate through and gives a truer representation of three-dimensional objects.

CHAPTER LINKS

Bob Wilson—http://www.cybrinc.com/bob

CareerPath—http://www.careerpath.com

IntelliMatch—http://intellimatch.com

The Monster Board—http://www.monster.com

My Excite Channel—http://my.excite.com

REFERENCES

Alexander, S. (1997, June 30). Companies fill IS jobs online. *InfoWorld, 18* (26), 99.

Bates, B., & Gregory, D. (1996). *Voice and data communication.* New York: McGraw-Hill.

Cafasso, R. (1996, October 21). Cybercruiting. *Computer World, 30* (43), 114–15.

Croal, N. (1997, June 9). Want a job? Get online. *Newsweek,* 81–82.

Getting pushed in cyberspace. [Online]. Available: http://www.adp.com/emergingbiz/tool/business/tslg.html

Goff, L. (1997, December 8). The new Web jobs. *ComputerWorld,* 73–74.

HTML User: DHTML 101. [Online]. Available: http://www.zdnet.com/products/htmluser/dhtmlintro.html

Jobs.search@Internet. (1998). *Planning job choices: 1998.* National Association of Colleges and Employers, pp. E34–E35.

Kawamoto, K. (1997). *Ten things you should know about new media.* San Francisco: The Freedom Forum.

King, J. (1996, September 30). 'Net recruiting shortens search. *ComputerWorld, 30* (40), 65–66.

Krannich, R. L. (1996, October). The new résumé for the new millennium: How to write an electronic résumé. *Black Collegian, 27* (1), 48–54.

Markels, A. (1996, September 20). Job hunting takes off in Cyberspace. *Wall Street Journal,* p. B1.

Master of the cyperspace universe: Webmaster. (1998). *Planning job choices: 1998.* National Association of Colleges and Employers, pp. E34–E35.

Mermigas, D. (1996, May 13). New media flourishing in New York. *Electronic Media,* 20.

Morris, M. E. S., & Massie, P. (1998). *Cybercareers.* Mountain View, CA: Sun Microsystems Press.

Newton, H. (1997). *Newton's Telecom Dictionary* (p. 20). Boulder, CO: Flatiron Publishing.

Puetz, B. (1997, February). Résumé writing in a wired age. *RN, 60* (2), 28–32.

Willmott, D., Kwon, R., Levin, C., & Rupley, S. (1997, February 4). Netting a job. *PC Magazine, 16* (3), 10.

APPENDIX

URLs

This Appendix contains all URLs listed within the book, plus some additional addresses that readers may find useful. Chapter numbers in which the URLs appear as Chapter Links are enclosed in parentheses ( ) after the site names. Addresses listed are current as of October 1998.

ADVERTISING

Advertising Agencies

Bates USA (7)—http://www.batesusa.com
BBDO (7)—http://www.bbdo.com
Brandnet (Ogilvy & Mather) (7)—http://www.ogilvy.com
DDB Needham Worldwide (7)—http://ddbniac.com
Fallon McElligott (7)—http://www.fallon.com
J. Walter Thompson (7)—http://www.jwtworld.com
Martin Advertising Agency (7)—http://www.martinagency.com
TBWA Chiat/Day/Venice (7)—http://www.chiatday.com/factory/
Young & Rubicam (7)—http://www.yandr.com

Advertising Pricing, Ratings, Auditing, Placement Services

Accipiter (7)—http://www.accipiter.com
(Bellcore) Adapt/X (7)—www.bellcore.com/
Intervox—Ad Tracking—http://www.intervox.com/adtrack.htm
Market Match (7)—http://www.marketmatch.com
The New York Times, Online Media Kit (7)—http://nytimes.com/adinfo/media-main.html
WebAudit (7)—http://www.nielsen.com

Advertising: Internet Organizations

The Coalition for Advertiser-Supported Information and Entertainment (CASIE) (7)—
    http://www.commercepark.com/AAAA/casie/index.html
Internet Advertising Bureau—http://www.iab.net

Advertising: Miscellaneous

Advertising Media Internet Center—http://www.amic.com/
Antique Cars (10)—http://www.commercial.net/vault/ads/antcars.html

Antique Firearms (10)—http://www.*oldguns*.com/AFNLists.htm
Electronic marketing with links to advertisers—http://www.america.net/~scotth/mktsite.htm
Epicurious (7)—http://www.epicurious.com
Internet Advertising Resource Guide—http://www.admedia.org/
Italian Cooking and Travel Links (10)—http://www.italycookingschool.com/links/html
Microscope (7)—http://www.microscope.com/
Mr. Caviar and Gourmet Food (10)—http://www.wines.com/caviar/
Narrative Communications (7)—http://www.narrative.com
Riddler (7)—http://www.riddler.com
WebChat Broadcasting (7)—http://wbs.net
Web Digest For Marketing (WDFM) (7)—http://wdfm.com/advertising

Advertising: Coupons and Classifieds

ClipNet (7)—http://www.Webomatic.com/ClipNET/
CouponNet (7)—http://www.coupon.com/coupon.html
The Coupon Pages (7)—http://www.couponpages.com
H.O.T. Coupons (7)—http://www.hotcoupons.com/
New Jersey Online (7)—http://www.nj.com
Val-Pak Direct Marketing Systems (7)—http://www.valpak.com

BROWSERS AND COMMERICAL INTERNET SERVICES

America Online (1)—http://www.aol.com
Compuserve—(1) http://world.compuserve.com/
Netscape Navigator (1)—http://home.netscape.com/
Microsoft Network (1)—http://www.msn.com
Prodigy (1)—http://www.prodigy.com/

CLUBS AND ORGANIZATIONS

Center for Photographic Art (10)—http://www.photography.org
Electronic Frontier Foundation (11)—http://www.EFF.org
Electronic Privacy Information Center (11)—http://www.epic.org
The Official Hanson site (10)—http://www.hansonline.com
Red Lion v. FCC (11)—http://www.mediaaccess.org/definitions/redlion/html
Reno v. ACLU (11)—http://www.ACLU.org
Overview of Telecommunications Act of 1996 (11)—
        http://www.technologylaw.com/techlaw/act_summary.html
Telecommunications Act (11)—http://www.fee.gov/telecom.html
U.S. Internet Council (11)—http://www.usic.org/asummary.htm

COLLEGE-ORIENTED SITES

American Express University (6)—http://www6.americanexpress.com/student/
Boston University (10)—http://scv.bu.edu.games/
Christina DeMello's College and University Home Pages—
        http://www.mit.edu:8001/people/cdemello/univ.html

Chronicle of Higher Education—http://chronicle.merit.edu/
College Board Online—http://www.collegeboard.org
College Freshman (6)—http://www.collegefreshman.com
College Guides and Aids pages—http://www.collegeguides.com
CollegeNet—http://www.collegenet.com/cnmain.html
Kaplan's College Admissions—http://www.kaplan.com/precoll
The Main Quad—http://develop.mainquad.com
Mapping Your Future (12)—http://mapping-your-future.org
Peterson's Education Center—http://www.petersons.com
The Princeton Review—http://www.review.com
Student Advantage Network (6)—http://www.studentadvantage.com
Study Abroad Program—http://www.studyabroad.com
T@p Online (6)—http://www.taponline.com
Tripod (6)—http://www.tripod.com
The World Lecture Hall—http://www.utexas.edu/world/lecture/index.html

COMMUNICATION ASSOCIATIONS

American Academy of Advertising—http://advertising.utexas.edu/AAA
American Communication Association (2)—http://www.americancomm.org/
Asian American Journalists Association (2)—http://www.aaja.org
Association for Education in Journalism and Mass Communication (2)—
        http://www.aejmc.sc.edu/
Broadcast Education Association (2)—http://www.beaweb.org/
International Association of Business Communications (6)—
        http://www.iabc.com/homepage.htm
International Communication Association (2)—http://www.icahdq.org/
National Association of Black Journalists (2)—http://www.nabj.org
National Association of Broadcasters (2)—http://www.nab.org
National Association of College Broadcasters (2)—http://www.hofstra.edu/~nacb/
National Association of Hispanic Journalists (2)—http://www.nahj.org
National Communication Association (2)—http://www.natcom.org/
Native American Journalists Association (2)—http://www.medill.nwu.edu/naja
Public Relations Society of America (6)—http://www.prsa.org
Southern States Communication Association (2)—http://ssca.net

COMMUNICATION RESEARCH RESOURCES

Academic and Communication Sites from Around the World—
        http://www.jou.ufl.edu/commres/jouwww.htm
ActivMedia—http://activmedia.com
American Association of Public Opinion Research—http://www.aapor.org
American Communication Journal (2)—http://www.americancomm.org/~aca/acj/acj.html
American Journalism Review (2)—http://www.newslink.org/
APA Study (2)—http://www.uvm.edu/~xli/reference/apa.html
CIOS (2)—http://www.cios.org

Communication Studies and Journalism Resources (2)—
    http://www.ntu.ac.sg/ntu/lib/commun.html
Electronic Journal of Communication (2)—http://www.cios.org/www/ejcmain.htm
Electronic Styles: A Handbook for Citing Electronic Information (2)—
    http://www.uvm.edu/~xli/reference/espub.html
Film and TV Studies—http://eng.hss.cmu.edu/filmtv
Forrester Research (6)—http://www.forrester.com
The Internet Index—http://www.openmarket.com/intindex
Journal of Computer Mediated Communication—http://www.ascusc.org/jcmc
The Journal of Electronic Publishing (2)—http://www.press.umich.edu/jep
Jupiter Communications—http://jup.com
Media and Communication Studies—http://www.aber.ac.uk/dgc/medmenu.html
Merriam-Webster Online (2)—http://www.m-w.com/
Modern Language Association (2)—http://www.mla.org
Museum of Broadcasting Communications—http://www.neog.com/mbc
National Weather Service (2)—http://www.nws.noaa.gov
Nielsen Media Research—http://www.nielsenmedia.com
OneLook Dictionaries (2)—http://www.onelook.com
Online! A Reference Guide to Using Internet Sources (2)—
    http://www.smpcollege.com/online-4styles~help
Radio and TV News Directors Foundation—http://www.rtndf.org
RhetNet, Cyberjournal of Rhetoric and Writing (2)—http://www.missouri.edu/rhetnet/
The Scholarly Electronic Publishing Directory (2)—http://info.lib.uh.edu/sepb/sepb.html
Scholarly Societies (Electronic Guide)—http://www.lib.uwaterloo.ca/society/overview.html
Simba Information—http://simbanet.com
Society of Professional Journalists—http://spj.org/spjhome.htm

E-MAIL AND INTERNET SERVICE PROVIDERS

My Excite Channel (12)—http://www.my.excite.com
FreeRide (6)—http://www.freeride.com
Hotmail (7)—http://www.hotmail.com
Juno Online (7)—http://www.juno.com
NetCreations (7)—http://www.netcreations.com/

EMPLOYMENT

Employment—General

America's Job Bank (12)—http://www.ajb.dni.us
Bob Wilson (12)—http://www.cybrinc.com/bob
CareerCast (12)—http://www.careercast.com
CareerMagazine (12)—http://www.careermag.com
CareerMosaic (12)—http://www.careermosaic.com
CareerPath (7, 12)—http://www.careerpath.com
Career Resource Center (12)—http://www.careers.org
CareerWeb (12)—http://www.cweb.com

Cruise Line Jobs (12)—http://cruiselinejobs.com
Cybercareers—http://www.cybercareers.com
Espan (12)—http://www.espan.com
Help Wanted USA (12)—http://iccweb.com
HotJobs (12)—http://www.hotjobs.com
IntelliMatch (12)—http://intellimatch.com
JobHunt (12)—http://www.job-hunt.org/
JobSat (12)—http://www.jobsat.com/
JobTrak (12)—http://www.jobtrak.com
NationJob Network (12)—http://www.nationjob.com
Online Career Center (12)—http://www.occ.com
The Internet Job Source (12)—http://www.statejobs.com
The Monster Board (12)—http://www.monster.com
The World Wide Web Employment Office (12)—
        http://www.harbornet.com/biz/office/annex.html
Work Avenue (12)—http://www.WorkAvenue.com
Yahoo! Classifieds (12)—http://classifieds.yahoo.com

Employment—Communication/New Media/Computer Jobs

Advertising Age Job Bank (12)—http://www.adage.com/job_bank/index.html
Advertising & Media Jobs (12)—http://www.nationjob.com/media
Cable Online—http://www.aescon.com/cableonline/
Copy Editor Jobs (Editor & Publisher) (12)—
        http://www.copyeditor.com/jobs.Overview.html
Creative Freelancers' Registry (12)—http://www.ghgcorp.com/cfr
Editor & Publisher Classifieds (12)—http://www.epclassifieds.com
Find Network (12)—http://findnetwork.com
Insurance Marketing and Communication Jobs (12)—
        http://www.insurancerecruiters.com/insjobs/market.htm
JobLink for Journalists (12)—http://www.newslink.org/joblink.html
NetComTalk (12)—http://com.bu.edu/getajob/
SelectJobs (12)—http://www.selectjobs.com
TV Jobline (12)—http://www.ultimatetv.com/jobs/
University of Iowa Journalism Job Resources (12)—
        http://www.bailiwick.lib.viowa.edu/

ENTERTAINMENT

Entertainment and Games

Casino Royale (10)—http://www.funscape.com/makeorder.htm
Grand Dominican (10)—http://www.granddominican.com
Rodney Dangerfield (10)—http://www.rodney.com
Solaria Interactive (10)—http://www.solariagames.com/
To Boldly Go (10)—http://www.pbm.com/tbg/
Zarf's List of Interactive Games on the Web (10)—
        http://www.leftfoot.com/games.html

Entertainment Companies and Sites

Alternative Entertainment Network (8)—http://www.aentv.net
C/NET Online (4, 7)—http://www.cnet.com
CPEQ, Media Co.—http://www.cpeq.com
Disney—http://www.disney.com/
MGM—http://www.mgmua.com
MCA—http://www.mca.com
Sony Pictures Entertainment (4)—http://www.spe.sony.com/
Pathfinder (Time Warner) (7)—http://pathfinder.com
Total Entertainment Network (6, 7)—http://www.ten.net/
The Ultimate Television Network (4)—http://www.ultimatetv.com/
Viacom/Paramount—http://www.paramount.com
Warner Bros.—http://warnerbrothers.com

GOVERNMENT

Bureau of Census (2)—http://www.census.gov
Federal Communications Commission (2)—http://www.fcc.gov
Federal Register (2)—http://www.access.gpo.gov/su_docs/aces/aces140.html
Federal Trade Commission (2)—http://www.ftc.gov
Telecommunications Act of 1996 (11)—http:ftp.fcc.gov/telecom.html
United Nations (8)—http://www.un.org/

INFORMATION AND MISCELLANEOUS

Copyright Law Materials (9)—http://www.law.cornell.edu/topics/copyright.html
Herpes (9)—http://www.herpes.com
The Master Anti-Smoking Page (9)—http://www.autonomy.com/smoke.com
Virtual Frog (9)—http://www.teach.virginia.edu/go/frog/menu.html
WidgetMagic (9)—http://www.widgetmagic.com
Yellow Pages (9)—http://www.yp.uswest.com

INTERNET AND WEB TECHNOLOGY AND COMPUTER COMPANIES

Berkeley Systems (7)—http://www.berksys.com
Sun Microsystems (1)—http://www.sun.com
VocalTec (3)—http://www.vocaltec.com/

MARKETING AND SHOPPING

The Abstract Funhouse (6)—http://www.starcreations.com/gamedowner/
The Amazing Send Me a Dollar Page (7)—server.tt.net/send-me-a-dollar/
Amazon.com (6)—http://www.amazon.com
Amused (4)—http://www.amused.com
Ann Hemyngs Candy, Inc.'s Chocolate Factory (6)—
    http://mmink.com/mmink/dossiers/choco.html

Anonymizer (6)—http://www.anonymizer.com
Auto-by-Tel (6)—http://www.autobytel.com
Ben & Jerry's (6)—http://www.benjerry.com/
Black Enterprise—http://www.blackenterprise.com
Buyers Index (6)—http://www.buyersindex.com
The Catalog Site (6)—http://www.catalogsite.com
CDNow (6)—http://www.cdnow.com/
Computer Superstore (6)—http://www.css.isn.com
Discount Airfares (10)—http://www.best.com/~vacation/discountair/cairfares.html
Downtown Anywhere (6)—http://www.awa.com
Eatnet—http://www.eatnet.com/
Eigg (Scottish Island) (6)—
        http://ourworld.compuserve.com/homepages/RJWinters/small-is.htm
The Electronic Marketing Home Page (6)—http://www.america.net/~scotth/mktsite.htm
First Auction (6)—www.firstauction.com
GameZone (7)—http://www.gamezone.net
Gap (6)—http://www.gap.com/
Get Me Rich Quick (7)—http://www.supranet.com/cindylou/index.html
Hot Hot Hot (6)—http://www.hothothot.com/hhh/index.shtml
Industry.Net (6)—http://www.industry.net/
Internet Shopping Network (6)—http://www.isn.com/
J. Crew (6)—http://www.jcrew.com
Jonathan Chance (7)—www.fastlane.net/~sandman/help
Onsale Computer Auction House—http://www.onsale.com/homepage.htm
Procter & Gamble (7)—http://www.pg.com/
The Public Eye (6)—http://www.thepubliceye.com
Random House, Del Rey books—http://www.randomhouse.com/delrey/index.html
Quote.com Inc. (6)—http://www.quote.com
Saab (8)—http://saabusa.com/sitemap.html
Tennis Warehouse (6)—http://www.tennis-warehouse.com/
Toyota—http://www.toyota.com
Virtual Vineyards (6)—http://www.virtualvin.com

MUSIC INDUSTRY

Atlantic Records (3)—http://atlantic-records.com
Audible Audio (3)—http://www.audible.com
BUGjuice (4)—http://www.bugjuice.com
Elektra Entertainment Group—http://www.elektra.com
imusic (3)—http://www.imusic.com
L.A. Live (3)—http://www.lalive.com
Loud Radio (3)—http://www.loud.com
Megadeth Arizona (3)—http://hollywoodandvine.com
SonicNet (3)—http://www.sonicnet.com
Swine Interactive Network (3)—http://www.generationswine.com
Warner Bros. Records (3)—http://www.wbr.com

NEWS

News Magazines

Business Week (4)—http://www.businessweek.com/
Newsweek (5)—http://newsweek.com/
The New Republic—http://magazines.enews.com/magazines/tnr/
Time (3, 5)—http://pathfinder.com/time
US News & World Report (5)—http://www.usnews.com/

News Programs

ABC News (5)—http://www.abcnews.com
CBS Eye on the Net (4, 5)—http://www.cbs.com
CBS Up to the Minute (5)—http://www.uttm.com
CBSnow (5)—http://www.CBSnow.com/
CNN Custom News (5)—http://customnews.cnn.com
CNNfn (5)—http://www.cnnfn.com
Fox News (5)—http://www.foxnews.com/

News Services/Sources

Associated Press (5)—http://wire.ap.org/
Information Express (2)—http://www.express.com
Dow Jones Investor Network (3)—http://www.dowjones.com/
Electronic Newsstand (5)—http://www.enews.com
Infobeat (2)—http://www.infobeat.com
Lawyers Weekly (5)—http://www.lawyersweekly.com/
MSNBC (5)—http://www.msnbc.com
NandoTimes (5)—http://www.nando.net
New Century Network (5)—http://www.newsworks.com
Television News Archive—http://tvnews.vanderbilt.edu/
News Link (5)—http://www.newslink.org
Newshub (5)—http://www.newshub.com
Newslinx (5)—http://www.newslinx.com
PointCast Network (1, 2, 7)—http://www.pointcast.com/
Reuters (5)—http://www.reuters.com/
TotalNews (5)—http://www.totalnews.com
Yahoo! Newspage (5)—http://www.yahoo.com

Newspapers

Boston Globe (5)—http://www.globe.com
Chicago Sun Times (5)—http://www.suntimes.com/
Chicago Tribune (5, 6, 7)—http://www.chicago.tribune.com
Los Angeles Times (5)—http://www.latimes.com/
New York Times (5, 6, 7, 8, 10)—http://www.nytimes.com
Philadelphia Inquirer—http://www.phillynews.com
Press Democrat (5)—http://www.pressdemo.com
Raleigh News and Observer—http://www.nando.net/

San Francisco Chronicle (5)—http://www.sfgate.com
San Jose Mercury News (5)—http://www.sjmercury.com
Standard Times (5)—http://www.s-t.com/
Tampa Bay Tribune—(5)—http://www.tampatrib.com
USA Today (5, 7, 10)—http://www.usatoday.com/
Wall Street Journal (5)—http://www.wsj.com
Washington Post (5, 7)—http://www.washingtonpost.com

Sports News

CBS SportsLine (5)—http://www.sportsline.com
ESPN SportsZone (5, 7)—http://www.ESPN.SportsZone.com/
Major League Baseball(5)—www.majorleaguebaseball.com
MSNBCSports (5)—http://www.msnbcsports.com
NBA (5)—http://www.nba.com

PUBLIC RELATIONS

Business Wire (6)—http://www.businesswire.com/
Intel (6)—http://www.intel.com/pressroom/
Newstips (6)—http://www.newstips.com/
PR Newswire (6)—http://www.prnewswire.com
PRWeb (6)—http://www.prweb.com/
PRwire—http://www.asiapac.net/bernama/prwire/
URLWire (6)—http://www.urlwire.com/

PR Listservs

PR Forum (6)—listserv@indycms.iupui.edu
PRSA—listserv@UTKVM1.UTK.EDU

RADIO

Radio Networks

ABC RadioNet (3)—http://www.abcradio.com
Broadcast.com (formerly AudioNet) (3, 5)—http://www.audionet.com
Bloomberg Information Radio (3)—http://www.bloomberg.com
Canadian Broadcast Corporation (3)—http://www.radio.cbc.ca/
CBS Radio Networks Online (3)—http://www.cbsradio.com
C/Net Radio (3)—http://www.news.com/radio/index.html
National Public Radio (1, 3)—http://www.npr.org
NetRadio Network (3)—http://www.netradio.Net/
Taylor Satellite Talk Radio (3)—http://www.tstradio.com

Radio Programs

ABC News Reports—http://www.realaudio.com/contentp/abc.html
All Things Considered (3)—http://www.npr.org/programs/atc

Ann Online (3)—http://www.annonline.com
C-SPAN—http://www.c-span.org/
C/Net Radio—http://www.news.com/radio/index.html
Child's Touch (3)—http://www.w2.com/
KinderNet (3)—http://www.kindernet.com/
L.A. Live (3)—http://www.lalive.com
LiveConcerts.com (3)—http://www.liveconcerts.com
MediaCast (3)—http://www.mediacast.com
Morning Edition (3)—http://www.npr.org/programs/morning/
PC WORLD Online Radio (3)—http://www.pcworld.com/news/newsradio/
RadioNet Internet Talk Radio—http://www.radionet.com/index.phtml
Rave Radio (3)—http://www.rave-network.com
SonicNet (3)—http://www.sonicnet.com
TimeCast (3)—http://www.timecast.com
WCBS—http://www.newsradio88.com

Radio Stations

KHMX-FM (3)—http://khmx.com/
KIIS-FM (3)—http://www.kiisfm.com/
KISW-FM (3)—http://www.kisw.com
KJHK-FM Kansas State University (3)—
    http://www.cc.ukans.edu/~kjhknet/index.html
KLIF-AM (3)—http://www.570klif.com/
Star 100.7 (3)—http://www.histar.com/home.html
WBAL-AM (3)—http://www.wbal.com/
WPSL-AM (3)—http://www.wpsl.com/

Radio Resources and Directories

Airwaves Radio Station Page (3)—http://www.airwaves.com
BRS Webcasters Directory—http://www.web-radio.com/
Free Radio Press—http://www.hear.com/rw/feature/rrb.html
MediaCast (3)—http://www.mediacast.com
MIT—Radio Stations on the Internet (2, 3)—http://wmbr.mit.edu/stations/list.html
Radio Advertising/Marketing—http://www.rab.com
Radio Online (3)—http://www.radio-online.com
Radionet—http://www.radionet.com/
Radiospace—http://www.radiospace.com/
Sarajevo Online (1)—www.worldmedia.fr//sarajevo/forum.html

Real-Time Audio Players

Internet Wave Selections (3)—http://www.vocaltec.com/
RealAudio (Progressive Networks) (3)—http://www.RealAudio.com
Streamworks (3)—http://www.xingtech.com
TrueSpeech (3)—http://www.dspg.com/

SEARCHING

Search Services: General

Alta Vista (2)—http://www.altavista.digital.com/
BizWiz (2)—http://www.bizwiz.com/bizwiz/
C/NET Search (2)—http://www.search.com
Einet Galaxy (2)—http://galaxy.einet.net/galaxy.html
Excite (2)—http://www.excite.com
GoTo (2)—http://www.goto.com/
HotBot (2)—http://www.HotBot.com/
Infoseek (2, 7)—http://guide.infoseek.com/
Lycos (2)—http://www.lycos.com
Magellan (2)—http://www.mckinley.com/
Open Text—http://search.opentext.com/
WebCrawler (2)—http://Webcrawler.com/
Yahoo! (2, 4, 5)—http://www.yahoo.com/

Searching Services: People, Places, Homes

Ameritech's Internet Yellow Pages (2)—http://yp.ameritech.net/
Big Yellow (2)—http://bigyellow.com/
CitySearch—http://www.citysearch.com
Four-11 (2)—http://www.four11.com
RentNet (2)—http://www.rentnet.com
WorldPages (2)—http://www.worldpages.com/
World Wide Yellow Pages (2)—http://www.mcp.com/newriders/wwwyp/index.html
YelloWWWeb Pages (2)—http://yellowwWeb.com/index.htm

Search Services: Usenet Newsgroups

Deja News (2)—http://www.dejanews.com/
Inktomi (2)—http://inktomi.berkeley.edu
Open Text—http://search.opentext.com/
Starting Point (2)—http://www.stpt.com/

Search Services: CUSI, SUSI, Meta

All-In-One Search Page (2)—http://www.albany.net/
Dogpile (2)—http://www.dogpile.com/
Find-It! (2)—http://www.iTools.com/find-it/
MetaCrawler (2)—www.metacrawler.com
SavvySearch (2)—http://www.cs.colostate.edu/~dreiling/smartform.html
W3 Search Engines (2)—http://cuiwww.unige.ch/meta-index.html

Search Services: Submitting Pages to Search Services

Submit It! (2)—http://www.submit-it.com/

TELEVISION

Television Networks: Broadcast

ABC (1, 4)—http://www.abc.com
CBS (3, 4, 5)—http://www.cbs.com
Fox (4)—http://foxnetwork.com
NBC (1, 4, 7)—http://www.nbc.com

Television Networks: Cable

American Movie Classics—http://www.amctv.com
CNBC—http://www.CNBC.com
CNN Interactive (1, 2, 5, 7, 8, 10)—http://cnn.com
Comedy Central (4, 10)—http://www.comcentral.com
Discovery Channel (4)—http://www.discovery.com
E! Online (4)—http://www.eonline.com
ESPN Sportszone (4, 5, 7)—http://ESPN.SportsZone.com/
Family Channel—http://www.familychannel.com
HBO (4)—http://hbo.com
Learning Channel (4)—http://www.discovery.com/diginets/learning/learning.html
Lifetime (4)—www.lifetimetv.com
MSNBC—http://www.msnbc.com
MTV Online (4)—http://www.mtv.com
Nick-at-Nite (4)—http://www.nick-at-nite.com/
Public Broadcasting Service (PBS) (4)—www.pbs.org
Sci-Fi channel Dominion (4)—http://www.scifi.com
The Travel Channel—http://www.travelchannel.com/
USA—http://www.usanetwork.com

Television Programs

Dharma and Greg (1)—http://www.abc.com/primetime/dharma_greg/index.html
Good Morning America (4)—http://www.abcnews.com/onair/gma/html_files/index.html
Jeopardy (4)—http://www.spe.sony.com/tv/shows/jeopardy/index/html
Late Show with David Letterman (4)—http://marketing.cbs.com/latenight/lateshow/
The Magic School Bus—http://www.scholastic.com/magicschoolbus
Melrose Place (4)—http://www.foxnetwork.com/melrose/index.html
The Outer Limits (4)—http://www.showtimeonline.com/spotlight/serover.tin?series=-16
The People's Court (4)—http://www.peoplescourt.com/
Rock & Roll Jeopardy (4)—http://www.rockjeopardy.com
Saturday Night Live (7)—http://www.saturday-night-live.com/snl/cast~1.html
The Seinfeld Trivia Challenge (10)—http://members.aol.com/SeinChal/index.html
The Simpsons (4)—http://www.foxworld.com/simpindx.htm
Soap City—http://www.spe.sony.com/soapcity
The Soup Nazi Headquarters (10)—http://members.aol.com/rynocub/soupnazi.htm
Wheel of Fortune (4)—http://www.spe.sony.com/tv/shows/wheel/thanks.html
The X-files (4)—http://www.thex-files.com/index.htm

Television and Web Program Guides

The Gist (4)—http://www.thegist.com
NetGuide Live (4)—http://www.netguide.com
TV Guide Entertainment Network (TVGEN) (1, 4, 8)—http://www.tvgen.com/

Television Stations

KCPQ-TV (4)—http://www.kcpq.com
KEYE-TV (5)—http://www.keye.com/
KGTV-TV (4)—http://www.kgtv.com
KLAS-TV8 (4)—http://www.klas-tv.com/
KPIX-TV (4)—http://www.kpix.com
WAND-TV (5)—http://www.wandtv.com
WBOC-TV (4)—http://www.wboc.com
WFLA-TV (4)—http://www.wfla.com

WEB AUTHORING AND DESIGN

Alternative Entertainment Network (8)—http://www.aentv.com
A Beginners Guide to HTML (1)—
    http://www.ncsa.uiuc.edu/General/Internet/WWW/HTMLPrimer.html, or
    http://www.w3.org/hypertext/WWW/Markup/MarkUp.html
Graphics Wiz Making Thumbnails (8)—http://www.photodex.com/givthumb.html
Introduction to JavaScripting (1)—http://www.siu.edu/~siu.edu/javascript/
Professor Pete's Insider's Guide to Business Web Design (8)—
    http://www.professorpete.com/
Vincent Flanders' Web Sites That Suck (8)—http://www.webpagesthatsuck.com/

WEB-ONLY PROGRAMS

HBO-IIIam (4)—http://www.hbo.com/IIIam
Child's Touch (3)—http://www.w2.com/
CyberKitchen (4)—http://www.foodtv.com
Encarta on the Record (4)—http://encarta.msn.com
Epicurious (7)—http://www.epicurious.com
GrapeJam (4)—http://www.crlight.com
Homicide (4)—http://www.nbc.com/homicide
KinderNet (3)—http://www.kindernet.com/
Lake Shore Drive (4)—http://www.chiWeb.com/chicago/lsd
Nye Labs (4)—http://nyelabs.kcts.org
The Spot (4, 7)—http://www.thespot.com
TV.com (C/NET) (4)—http://www.tv.com
Virtual Dorm (4)—http://www.vdorm.com/thedorm/index.html
WhirlGirl (4)—http://www.whirlgirl.com
Yack Live (4)—http://www.yack.com

GLOSSARY

active link: Highlighted text on a Web page that connects the user to another Web page

Advanced Research Project Agency (ARPAnet): Agency established to build an advanced system to interconnect computers

advertising exchanges: A *quid pro quo* online ad pricing structure in which an advertiser exchanges free advertising space on its Web site for a free posting of its own banner ad on another company's site

applet: Application associated with Java that animates Web graphics

aspect ratio: Width-to-height ratio of a television screen: four units wide to three units high on a standard TV, sixteen units wide to nine units high for HDTV

Audible Audio: Software application used for storing Web radio programs for playback

audio on demand: Radio programs and newscasts stored on servers so that users can play them back anytime they wish

auditor: Third-party Web ratings service that measures Web site traffic and other user information for Web site operators

authoring: The process of writing and producing an online document

bandwidth: The amount of data that can be electronically transmitted all at once through a communication path, such as a telephone line

banner ad: The earliest and most prevalent form of online advertising. Banners are typically about 6½ inches wide by about 1 inch high (468 × 60 pixels).

bookmarking: A method of saving the URLs of frequently visited sites so addresses do not have to be entered each time before accessing the sites

billboard Web site: A text-heavy, online brochure providing basic corporate information

bits per second: The speed at which data flow through the Internet

Boolean operators: Terms that narrow and customize searches by defining the relationship between the search words and terms using operators such as AND, OR, NOT, NEAR

browser: A program such as Netscape Navigator or Mosaic that allows a person to browse the World Wide Web by navigating from site to site using hypertext protocols

buttom: Highlighted area on a Web screen that doubles as a hypertext link to another site or document within the same site. On screen, a button may take the form of an arrow or push button.

cable modem: An alternative to a telephone modem; a device that delivers the Internet to a computer or to a television set at speeds up to 80–100 times faster than by a telephone line

cable specific programming: Original television programming produced specifically for airing on cable channels and networks

chat forums: Online discussions groups used for exchanging live, real-time messages

channel repertoire: A subset of the total number of available television channels that a viewer watches on a regular basis

click-through rates: A pricing structure for banner ads based on the number of visitors who click through from an ad to the advertiser's homepage

client computer: The computer from which original messages or requests for information are sent

compression: The squeezing of data files into a smaller size for faster transmission through the Internet

convergence: The coming together of many forms of media, such as television programming on the Web, or Internet delivery by cable television companies

cookies: A device that tracks a user's Web travels and saves online visitor information—sometimes without the user's knowledge or permission—to create personal files that companies use to customize their Web pages to target individuals

cooperative exchange: An agreement by which member companies exchange free banner ad space on their Web sites

cost-per-thousand (CPMs): A pricing structure used to sell print and broadcast media and compare the costs of different media; calculated by dividing the cost of an advertisement by the number of individuals or households (in thousands) that are reached

coupons: Product and service discounts appearing on the Web that are customized by zip codes and can be printed out for in-store redemption

critical mass: A percentage or number of users that need to adopt a new product or technology before it is considered part of the mainstream commerce or culture. A new communication technology, such as the Internet, needs to be used by about 50 million individuals before it can be considered a mass medium.

cybercast: The delivery of radio or television programs over the Web

cyberprogram: Television-type program delivered over the Web

DHTML (Dynamic HyperText Markup Language): A combination of tags and options in HTML that allows for the creation of Web pages that are more animated and responsive than regular HTML pages

Domain Name System (DNS): Rules for structuring Internet addresses in the following way: User name@host.subdomain

Direct Broadcast Satellite (DBS): Satellite transmission of non-broadcast network programming directly into homes

e-mail (electronic mail): An Internet tool for electronically transmitting messages or documents

encryption: Software that scrambles online data into codes that can be deciphered only by authorized receivers with the proper translation mechanisms

first-level domain extender: Three-letter code at the end of an Internet address that categorizes the host by type of organization or business

firewall: Online security system that keeps confidential data from unauthorized individuals by separating it from public information

Four C's of Marketing: Consumers, convenience, communication, and cost; alternatives to the **Four P's of Marketing** and frequently used in a new communication environment

Four P's of Marketing: Elements that make up the marketing mix: product, place, promotion, and price

FTP (File Transfer Protocol): The standard Internet protocol for copying files between comptuers

funhouse Web sites: Free or pay-to-play sites that contain games, contests, and other interactive amusements

gatekeepers: Newsroom executives or any person or group who decide which news items or information should be presented to the public

GIF converter: Software that converts image files to the .gif format for display on the Web. Also gives an **interlacing** option, so that instead of graphics loading from top to bottom, the full-sized graphic is displayed on the screen and loads by improving its resolution

Gopher: An early Internet tool; text-only menu-based interface for accessing Internet documents

High Definition Television (HDTV): High-resolution television system that displays crisp clear pictures using 1125 lines per screen rather than the 525 lines used on standard television sets

hot link: Highlighted area on a Web page that doubles as a hypertext link to another site or document within the same site

HTML (HyperText Markup Language): A computer language made up of a set of symbols or codes that tells the Web browser how to display a Web page's words and images, and how to link between pages and documents

HTTP (HyperText Transfer Protocol): Set of rules for transferring hypertext (World Wide Web) documents. All Web addresses begin with http://

hybrid system: An all-in-one system that combines a television with a computer. Hybrids function like full-blown computers but they also delivery the Web and television programming.

hypertext: A method of electronically linking Web pages and documents

interactivity: A term used to describe interactions between parties where both are sources and receivers of information via a communication medium such as telephone or the Internet

intercasting: A combination of the *Internet* and *broadcasting*, the reception of television signals and the Web over both a television set and through a computer via the vertical blanking interval

interlacing technology: Technology that focuses all the elements of a Web page at the same time by first displaying a low-resolution version of the entire image or page, then increasing the resolution in stages until the highest possible resolution is reached and the image or page is fully focused

Internet: Global network comprised of as many as 45,000 interconnected sub-networks worldwide with no single owner

Internet Fast Forward: Software that "erases" ads from Web page screens

Internet Protocol (IP): A set of rules that tell routers how to reassemble and address electronic data packets for transmission to the proper server and then on to the client computer

Internet Relay Chat (IRC): A type of chat software that must be installed to access a chat forum. The software is usually downloadable free of charge.

Internet Service Provider (ISP): Company that provides Internet access for a fee

InterNIC: The main registry of Internet addresses and domain names

intranet: A network using Internet software that transmits proprietary and open information among computers housed within an entity such as a corporation. Intranets are mainly used to share company information and computing resources among employees.

instrumental viewing: The practice of turning on the television for the sole purpose of watching a particular program, and turning off the television at the show's conclusion

IP Multicast: Signal repetition technique that makes replication servers unnecessary

Java: A computer programming language based on FORTRAN C++ that allows animated gifs and other movement on Web pages. Java also makes it possible for Web pages to contain programming algorithms that manipulate and manage data.

JavaScripting: A fairly easy-to-use scripting language used for animating gifs and other elements of a Web page

library/directory Web sites: Information storage areas that can be accessed by online users

listserv: An electronic mail box/discussion forum for subscribed users

MOOs (Multi-User Domain—Object Oriented): Topic-specific **MUDs**

Mosaic: First Web browser that connected Web pages through hyperlinks

MPEG (Motion Pictures Experts Group): Group that developed the compression scheme used by StreamWorks to transmit sound files

MUDs (Multi-User Domain or Multi-Uses Dungeons): Very popular interactions and on-line games where participants are involved in fantasy adventures that they help create

multicasting: A system for sending an audio file to multiple receivers simultaneously

Multichannel, Multipoint Distribution Service (MMDS): Also known as wireless cable, a microwave system used for transmitting cable service into urban areas

Multitasking: The practice of surfing the Web at the same time while performing other computer tasks

MUSHes (Multi-User Shared Hallucinations): See **MOOs; MUDs**

narrowcasting: Cable television delivery of topic-specific shows that appeal to small but loyal audiences

navigation: The process of moving from one site to another through the Web. This is normally done by following links. Various features of a browser also make navigating possible by keeping a history of where the user has been.

Net Computers (NC): Also known as Internet PCs. Low-cost computers that lack hard drive storage space and are made for the primary prupose of accessing the Internet

Netcast: See **cybercast**

niche audience: A group of people who share an interest in a specific and narrow area, such as Hawaiian music

niche marketing: Directing marketing efforts toward a **niche audience**

novelty effect: The use of a new technology or any new product more frequently and differently when it is first new, or novel, than when the product has been owned for a while

packet-switched network: The basic framework of the Internet that takes bundles of data and breaks them up into small packets or chunks that travel through the network independently

PCTV: The transmission of television signals on to a computer

Penny Press: Newspapers published in the mid-1800s that sold for one penny. Collectively known for big, bold headlines, sensational stories, and high drama

pixels: Tiny dots of color that form the images on a Web page. Computer monitors display 72 pixels per inch, so one inch equals 72 pixels or dots per inch (dpi).

press agentry: The effort of promoting a company's products or services using image-building techniques and hyperbole, rather than objective, factual information

product placement: Advertisers pay to have their products woven into the story lines of movies, television shows, and Web programs

protection: The prevention of unauthorized users from reading or writing a particular piece of data. Also known as "authentication."

public information: The dissemination of accurate, truthful, and unbiased information in a straightforward manner

public persuasion: One-way communication that attempts to influence public opinion, attitudes, or behavior

publicity: See **press agentry**

push technology: Special online software that delivers Web information, initiated by an information provider rather than by a user

radio networks: Stations that are linked on the Web and may share similar Web site properties

ratings: Measurement of the number of visitors who land on a Web site compared to other sites. Other measurements include the length of time visitors spend on pages, the number of unduplicated users, and other site use criteria. Most ratings are based on estimates.

RealAudio: Application that transmits audio on demand over the Web

RealAudio Encoder: Software that digitizes audio files for transmission over the Web

RealAudio Player: Software that plays Web audio files

relationship marketing: Marketing strategy based on building a relationship between a business and its customers

real-time streaming protocol: A proposed standard that will shorten the amount of time it takes to download data from the Web

result-based fees: An online advertising pricing framework in which advertisers are assessed a minimal charge, or in some cases, no charge at all, for ad placement. Actual costs are based on sales criteria, such as the number of consumers who buy a product as a result of the Web ad.

relevancy ranking: Criteria used to rank Web sites that most closely match a search term

replication server: A server dedicated to providing multiple audio feeds to numerous listeners

ritualistic viewing: The practice of watching television out of habit and for the sake of watching, even if there is not a program of interest being aired

robot: A software program that automatically finds, identifies, and indexes information for online databases

routers: Powerful computers that link networks together on the Internet

search engines: Searching tools that find and retrieve information from the Web

search services: Sites that contain search engines that comb the Web for information

servers: Powerful computers that provide continuous access to the Internet

set-top boxes: Systems, such as WebTV, that transmit the Web over standard television sets

size-based pricing: An online advertising pricing structure in which costs are calculated based on the size of the ad: a fixed dollar amount per pixel

spamming: The unauthorized e-mail transmission of advertising messages

spiders: See **robots**

sponsorships: A form of advertising in which a company pays to sponsor Web pages that are closely related to the company's goods and services, so that the company can add more content about their product than will fit on a Web banner ad

storefront Web site: A multilayered, product-oriented site posted for the primary purpose of generating sales

streaming: Technology that sends data through the Internet in a continuous flow so that information is displayed on a user's computer before the entire file has finished downloading

T-1 line: A telephone line commonly used by ISPs to connect servers to the Internet

tags: HTML labels that tell the Web browser how to display the text. Each tag consists of a left angle bracket (<), followed by the name of the tag and closed by a corresponding right angle bracket (>). Tags are usually paired and the ending tag is the same as the starting tag except a slash (/) precedes the text within the brackets. For example, to center the word *title*, the HTML tags would be used as follow: <center>title</center>.

target market: A group of customers with similar characteristics, who are most likely to purchase a product or service

target marketing: A sales plan directed at a specific **target market**

TELNET: A terminal emulation protocol used when logging into other computer systems on the Internet

top-level domain: See **first-level domain extender**

trading post Web site: A marketplace where customers purchase items through a middleman who charges for services or earns a commission from each sale

transaction community: A Web site that goes beyond satisfying consumers' commercial needs by providing additional information and links to other pages that gratify social needs

Transmission Control Protocols (TCP): Rules that define how computers made by different manufacturers and running different software communicate with each other on the Internet

two-way communication: Means of communication that reach an understanding between an organization and its public through feedback and interaction

Uniform Resource Locator (URL): Set of codes that specifies the location of files on Web servers. A URL includes the type of resource being accessed, the address of the server, and the location of the file. The syntax is scheme://host.domain/path/filename, where scheme is one of:

file: a file on your local system or a file on an anonymous FTP server
http: a file on a World Wide Web server
gopher: a file on a Gopher server
WAIS: a file on a WAIS server
news: a Usenet Newsgroup
telnet: a connection to a TELNET-based service

Usenet Newsgroup: A conferencing bulletin board system that serves as a discussion and information exchange forum on specific topics

User Diagram Protocol (UDP): A method of moving data through the Internet

value-added Web content: Content, such as games and contests, used to attract visitors and keep them interested and connected to a site for longer periods of time

V-banner (video banner ad): A banner ad that contains a short video clip

VRML (Virtual Reality Modeling Language): A computer language used to describe three-dimensional images; it allows a user to interact with an image by viewing, moving, or rotating it

Web site repertoire: A subset of the total number of available Web sites that a user accesses on a regular basis

Wide Area Information Service (WAIS): Text-only index and retrieval tool for Internet databases and documents

World Wide Web: An Internet resource that presents information in text, graphic, video, and audio formats

worms: See **robots**

CREDITS

Netscape Browser Frames: Copyright © 1998 Netscape Communications Corp. Used with permission. All Rights Reserved. This electronic file or page may not be reprinted or copied without the express written permission of Netscape. Netscape Communications Corporation has not authorized, sponsored, or endorsed, or approved this publication and is not responsible for its content. Netscape and the Netscape Communications Corporate Logos, are trademarks and trade names of Netscape Communications Corporation. All other product names and/or logos are trademarks of their respective owners. **CHAPTER 1 Fig. 1.1** Reprinted with permission from KWOM. **Fig. 1.2** Reprinted with permission from Academic and Distributed Computing Services, University of Minnesota. **Figs. 1.4, 1.7** Copyright © 1998 Netscape Communications Corp. Used with permission. All Rights Reserved. This electronic file or page may not be reprinted or copied without the express written permission of Netscape. **Fig. 1.5** Reprinted with permission from Southern Illinois University, Carbondale. **Fig. 1.6** Reprinted with permission from ATA. **CHAPTER 2 Figs. 2.1, 2.2** Text and artwork copyright © 1998 Yahoo! Inc. All rights reserved. YAHOO! and the YAHOO! logo are trademarks of YAHOO! Inc. **Fig. 2.2** Digital, AltaVista and the AltaVista logo are trademarks or service marks of Digital Equipment Corporation. Used with permission; Reprinted by permission. Infoseek, Ultrasmart, Ultraseek, Ultraseek Server, Infoseek Desktop, Infoseek Ultra, iSeek, Quickseek, Imageseek, Ultrashop, the Infoseek logos and the tagline "One you know, you know." are trademarks of Infoseek Corporation which may be registered in certain jurisdictions. Other trademarks shown are trademarks of their respective owners. Copyright © 1994–1998 Infoseek Corporation. All rights reserved; Copyright © 1998 Lycos, Inc. Lycos® is a registered trademark of Carnegie Mellon University. All rights reserved. **Figs. 2.2, 2.3** Excite, WebCrawler, Excite Search, the Excite Logo and the WebCrawler Logo are trademarks of Excite, Inc. and may be registered in various jurisdictions. Magellan Internet Guide and the Magellan logo are trademarks of The McKinley Group, Inc., a subsidiary of Excite, Inc., and may be registered in various jurisdictions. Excite screen display copyright © 1995–1998 Excite, Inc. Magellan screen display copyright © 1998 by The McKinley Group, Inc., a subsidiary of Excite, Inc. **Fig. 2.4** Reprinted with permission from WorldPages. **Fig. 2.5** Digital, AltaVista and the Altavista logo are trademarks or service marks of Digital Equipment Corporation. Used with permission. **Fig. 2.6** Reprinted with permission from DejaNews. **CHAPTER 3 Fig. 3.1** Reprinted with permission from KJHK 90.7 FM. **Fig. 3.2** Reprinted with permission from ABC Radio Networks. **Fig. 3.3** Copyright © 1995–1997 RealNetworks, Inc., 1111 Third Avenue, Suite 2900, Seattle, WA 98101 USA. All rights reserved. RealNetworks, RealAudio, RealVideo, Real Media, RealPlayer, and other names or logos are trademarks or registered trademarks of RealNetworks, Inc. **Fig. 3.4** Reprinted with permission from WPSL Digital AM 1590. **Fig. 3.5** Reprinted with permission from WMBR. **Fig. 3.6** Reprinted with permission from AudioNet. **CHAPTER 4 Fig. 4.1** Reprinted courtesy of ABC Multimedia, Inc. **Fig. 4.2** Reprinted with permission from Nick at Nite. **Fig. 4.4** Reprinted with permission from WBOC-TV. **Fig. 4.5** Reprinted with permission from KPIX. **Figs. 4.6, 4.8** Copyright © 1998 Columbia TriStar Interactive. All Rights Reserved. Visit the Sony Pictures Entertainment Web site at www.spe.sony.com. **Fig. 4.7** Reprinted with permission from Visionary Media, LLC. Fig. 4.9 TVGEN™, TV Guide Entertainment Network™ and the related logos are trademarks of TV Guide Financial, Inc. under license to News

INDEX